The Gift of Theology

The Gift of Theology

The Contribution of Kathryn Tanner

Rosemary P. Carbine and Hilda P. Koster, editors

Fortress Press
Minneapolis

THE GIFT OF THEOLOGY

The Contribution of Kathryn Tanner

Library of Congress Cataloging-in-Publication Data

Print ISBN: 978-1-4514-8206-5

eBook ISBN: 978-1-5064-0285-7

Manufactured in the U.S.A.

This book was produced using Pressbooks.com, and PDF rendering was done by PrinceXML.

Contents

Notes on Contributors

Rosemary P. Carbine holds master's and doctoral degrees in Theology from the University of Chicago Divinity School, and is currently Associate Professor of Religious Studies at Whittier College. She specializes in historical and constructive Christian theologies, with a focus on comparative feminist, womanist, and Latina/*mujerista* theologies, theological anthropology, public/political theologies, and teaching and learning in theology and religion. She has published widely on these topics in major reference works, scholarly journals, and books, including *Questioning the Human: Toward a Theological Anthropology for the 21st Century* (2014), *Frontiers in Catholic Feminist Theology: Shoulder to Shoulder* (2009), *Prophetic Witness: Catholic Women's Strategies of Reform* (2009), and *Cross-Examinations: Readings on the Meaning of the Cross Today* (2006). More recently, she co-edited and contributed to two books, namely *Theological Perspectives for Life, Liberty, and the Pursuit of Happiness: Public Intellectuals for the Twenty-First Century* (2013), and *Women, Wisdom, and Witness: Engaging Contexts in Conversation* (2012). Dr. Carbine has served as co-chair of the Feminist Theory and Religious Reflection Group within the American Academy of Religion, and as co-convener of the Women's Consultation on Constructive Theology in the Catholic Theological Society of America.

Paul DeHart studied at Yale and the University of Chicago, and is currently Professor of Theology at Vanderbilt University, where he also chairs the Graduate Department of Religion. His book publications include *Beyond the Necessary God: Trinitarian Faith and Philosophy in the Thought of Eberhard Jüngel* (1999), *The Trial of the Witnesses: The Rise and Decline of Postliberal Theology* (2006), and *Aquinas and Radical Orthodoxy: A Critical Inquiry* (2011). Recent shorter publications include journal articles on Thomas Aquinas and on Søren Kierkegaard. His current project is a book on Schleiermacher, German Idealism, and the fate of the Nicene Trinity in modern theology.

Mary McClintock Fulkerson is Professor of Theology at Duke University Divinity School. Her book *Changing the Subject: Women's Discourses and Feminist Theology* (2001) examines academic feminism and non-feminist church women. *Places of Redemption: Theology for a Worldly Church* (2010) is on ecclesial practices that resist racism and other forms of social brokenness. Co-edited volumes include *The Oxford Handbook of Feminist Theology*, with Sheila Briggs (2014); and *Theological Perspectives for Life, Liberty and the Pursuit of Happiness: Public Intellectuals for the Twenty-First Century*, with Ada Maria Isasi-Diaz and Rosemary Carbine (2013). A forthcoming book written with Marcia Mount Shoop is on colorblind racism in Protestant churches. Professor Fulkerson is an ordained minister in the Presbyterian Church, USA.

George Hunsinger is the McCord Professor of Systematic Theology at Princeton Theological Seminary. He has been a delegate to the official Reformed/Roman Catholic International Dialogue (2011-2015). In 2006 he founded the National Religious Campaign against Torture. He is president of the Karl Barth Society of North America. Among his most recent books is *Conversational Theology: Essays on Ecumenical, Postliberal, and Political Themes, with Special Reference to Karl Barth* (2015). He has led a verse-by-verse adult Bible study at the Nassau Presbyterian Church in Princeton for the last 20 years.

Serene Jones is the 16th President of the historic Union Theological Seminary in the City of New York and the President-elect of the American Academy of Religion. The first woman to head the 178-year-old interdenominational seminary, Jones occupies the Johnston Family Chair for Religion and Democracy and has formed Union's Institute for Women, Religion, and Globalization as well as the Institute for Art, Religion, and Social Justice. Jones came to Union after seventeen years at Yale University, where she was the Titus Street Professor of Theology at the Divinity School, and chair of Women, Gender, and Sexuality Studies in the Graduate School of Arts and Sciences. Dr. Jones is ordained in the Christian Church (Disciples of Christ) and the United Church of Christ. She is a leading theologian and the author of several books, including *Calvin and the Rhetoric of Piety* (1995); *Feminist Theory and Christian Theology* (2000); and *Trauma and Grace:Theology in a Ruptured World* (2009).

Hilda P. Koster is Associate Professor of Religion and Co-Chair of the Environmental Studies Program at Concordia College in Moorhead, Minnesota. A native of the Netherlands, she holds masters degrees in Theology from the University of Groningen (the Netherlands) and Princeton Theological Seminary, and earned her doctorate from the Divinity School of the University of Chicago. Her publications on eco-feminist theology and ethics have appeared in *Theology Today, The Journal of Religion, Anglican Theological Review, Scriptura*, and the edited collection *Christian Doctrines for Global Gender Justice* (2015). Currently, she is working on a monograph on Creation and Salvation in Ecological Theology and an edited book (with Grace Ji-Sun Kim) on *Global Women's Voices on Christian Doctrine and Climate Justice* (forthcoming, 2017). Dr. Koster is the recipient of the 2012 Omicron Delta Kappa excellence in undergraduate teaching award at Concordia College.

Charles Mathewes is the Carolyn M. Barbour Professor of Religious Studies at the University of Virginia. He is the author of *Understanding Religious Ethics* (2010); *Evil and the Augustinian Tradition* (2007); *A Theology of Public Life* (2008); and *The Republic of Grace* (2010). From 2006 to 2010, he was Editor of *The Journal of the American Academy of Religion*, and he currently serves on the House of Bishops Theology Committee of the Episcopal Church. He spent much of his childhood in Saudi Arabia, and was educated at Georgetown University and the University of Chicago.

Joy Ann McDougall is Associate Professor of Systematic Theology at Candler School of Theology and Associated Faculty in the Department of Women's, Gender, and Sexuality Studies at Emory University. The author of *The Pilgrimage of Love: Moltmann on the Trinity and Christian Life* (2005), she has published numerous essays on Trinitarian theology, doctrinal issues in feminist theology and method, gender and vocation in theological education, and feminist intercultural theologies in U.S. and Korean contexts. She recently edited a special issue of *Theology Today* on World Christianity. McDougall's current book project focuses on a feminist re-envisioning of sin, grace, and redemption. She received the

2010-2011 Mentoring for Leadership Award from the President's Commission on the Status of Women at Emory University.

Ian A. McFarland is the Regius Professor of Divinity at Cambridge University, having previously taught at the Candler School of Theology and the University of Aberdeen. He is the author of several books, including *From Nothing: A Theology of Creation* (2014) and *In Adam's Fall: A Meditation on the Christian Doctrine of Original Sin* (2010). He is also co-editor of *The Cambridge Dictionary of Christian Theology* (2014).

Hugh Nicholson is Associate Professor of Theology at Loyola University Chicago. He is the author of *Comparative Theology and the Problem of Religious Rivalry* (2011) and *The Spirit of Contradiction in Christianity and Buddhism* (forthcoming 2016).

Amy Plantinga Pauw is the Henry P. Mobley Professor of Doctrinal Theology at Louisville Presbyterian Seminary. She is the general editor for Westminster John Knox Press' theological commentary series *Belief*, and serves on the board of the Louisville Institute. Her most recent book is a theological commentary on Proverbs and Ecclesiastes (2015). Other publications include *The Supreme Harmony of All: Jonathan Edwards' Trinitarian Theology* (2002); *Making Time for God: Daily Devotions for Children and Families to Share* (with Susan Garrett) (2002); and *Essays in Reformed Feminist and Womanist Dogmatics* (with Serene Jones) (2011). Dr. Pauw is currently writing a book on Wisdom ecclesiology, for which she received a Henry Luce III Fellowship in Theology (2012-2013).

Jan H. Pranger is Associate Professor of World Christianity at Concordia College, Moorhead. He studied at Princeton Theological Seminary and the University of Chicago Divinity School, and received his Ph.D. from the University of Groningen, the Netherlands. He has published on issues related to interreligious dialogue, ecumenism, contextualization, and postcolonialism, including *Dialogue in Discussion* (1994) and *Redeeming Tradition: Inculturation, Contextualization, and Tradition in Postcolonial Perspective* (2003). He is currently working on a manuscript on postcolonialism and theology of religions.

Eugene F. Rogers, Jr. was educated at Princeton, Tübingen, Rome, and Yale, where he studied under Kathryn Tanner from 1985-1992. He taught from 1993 to 2005 at the University of Virginia, where he chaired the Program in Theology, Ethics, and Culture. In 2005 he joined his husband Derek Krueger at the University of North Carolina at Greensboro, where he is professor of Religious Studies and program faculty in Women's and Gender Studies. In 2002-2003 Rogers was the Eli Lilly Visiting Associate Professor of Christian Thought and Practice in the Religion Department at Princeton University. He has authored four monographs and some 40 articles and translations, and edited two anthologies. In 2010 *Christian Century* named his book *Sexuality and the Christian Body* (1999) "essential reading" among books published in the past 25 years. His most recent book is *Aquinas and the Supreme Court: Race, Gender, and the Failure of Natural Law in Thomas's Biblical Commentaries* (2014). This year he serves as an external member of the Board of Electors for the Regius Professorship of Divinity at Cambridge, founded in 1540 by Henry VIII. His current project, *The Analogy of Blood*, considers Christian uses of blood texts, images, and rituals.

John E. Thiel is Professor of Religious Studies and Director of the University Honors Program at Fairfield University, where he has taught for 38 years. He is the author of six books, including *Senses of Tradition: Continuity and Development in Catholic Faith* (2000) and *God, Evil, and Innocent Suffering* (2002). His most recent book, *Icons of Hope: The "Last Things" in Catholic Imagination* (2013), was awarded the 2014 Alpha Sigma Nu Book Prize for the best book on Theology published by faculty members in Jesuit colleges and universities in the past three years. His articles have appeared in *Theological Studies*, *Modern Theology*, *The Heythrop Journal*, *New Theology Review*, *Horizons*, *Philosophy and Theology*, *The Month*, and *Commonweal*. Twice a recipient of fellowships from the National Endowment for the Humanities, he is a member of the American Theological Society and served as President of the Catholic Theological Society of America in 2011-2012.

Courtney Wilder earned a Ph.D. in Systematic Theology at the University of Chicago in 2008, and is Associate Professor of Religion at Midland University in Fremont, Nebraska. In addition to her work in Christianity and popular culture, she writes on disability, and has a forthcoming book entitled *Disability, Faith, and the Church: Inclusion and Accommodation in Contemporary Congregations* (2016). Dr. Wilder is a past president of the North American Paul Tillich Society and remains active in Tillich scholarship. She lives in Omaha, Nebraska, with her two children.

William A. Wright is pastor and theologian in residence, The Church of Christ Congregational, Granby, MA. He received his Ph.D. in Theology from the University of Chicago Divinity School, under the guidance of Kathryn Tanner. His publications include "Negative Experience in Calvin's *Institutes* and its Systematic

Consequences" (2013); "The Trinity of Non-univocal Persons: Towards a Model of Doctrinal Writing" (2011); and *Calvin's Salvation in Writing: A Confessional Academic Theology* (2015).

Acknowledgements

Rosemary P. Carbine and Hilda P. Koster

The idea for this book emerged at the annual convention of the Catholic Theological Society of America where we met by chance waiting for the elevator. We reminisced about the many ways Kathryn Tanner has touched our professional and theological lives and hoped there would be a way to honor her work. We observed that there is no book yet that brings together essays on key aspects of Kathy's work, in spite of the fact that her work is widely used and that Kathy arguably is one of the most innovative and important North American theologians. Would not such a book honor and celebrate the gift of Kathy's theology, while also in itself be a true gift to scholars in the field, seminarians, and graduate as well as college students? By the time we got off the elevator, the idea for this book was born.

Our gratitude above all goes to Kathy who advised both our doctoral dissertations and served as our teacher and mentor throughout the years. Kathy taught us to appreciate theology as a discipline that matters not only, or primarily, to the academy or to the church but to society at large. As feminist and ecological theologians, we are especially attentive to the ways her theological scholarship has opened up new possibilities for us to engage church doctrines for liberative work on behalf of women and the earth.

We are particularly thankful to the contributors to this volume, who enthusiastically embraced this book's vision and who are all leading theological scholars. Indeed, it truly has been an honor and great pleasure to work with such a distinguished group. Their thought-provoking and creative essays discuss key aspects of Kathy's work while also reflecting their own distinctive theological voices. This has resulted in rich and stimulating essays that together weave Kathy's work into the tapestry of today's North American theological landscape. As editors, we have further benefitted from the willingness of contributors to respond to our comments and suggestions. Working collaboratively in this way has been a most enriching experience.

We especially thank John Thiel who wrote the foreword for this book; he not only eloquently captured the intention of its project, but also eruditely indicates the significance of Kathy's contributions for contemporary theology. Serene Jones generously agreed to write the afterword to this book, and there attends to Kathy's knack for intertextual and interdisciplinary commerce whether in the classroom, at a conference, or during a dinner party, an observation rooted in more than three decades as Kathy's friend and colleague.

We are deeply obliged to our editor, Michael Gibson, who welcomed the idea for this book and shepherded us through the process. Without Michael's energy and vision we would not have been able to launch this book project. We are also grateful to Esther Diley, who, as editorial assistant at Fortress, clarified the many details and tasks associated with this sort of book project.

Finally, we are thankful to our family, friends, and colleagues for their continuous support of our writing projects. Editing and writing for a book in the midst of other academic duties are no easy tasks, and we are grateful for the understanding and support we have received.

Hilda is grateful to her colleagues in the Religion Department at Concordia College, who have allowed her time to write and supported her in so many ways. Their passion for their own research projects and their collegiality in creating a vibrant department for and with our students continues to be an inspiration. Hilda is deeply thankful to her husband, Jan Hendrik Pranger, who, while contributing a chapter of his own, has also taken on more of the parenting role so that this book could get finished. Hilda further thanks her daughter, Emma Rachel Pranger, who endures her Mom's absentmindedness with much grace and whose imagination and love for life are a continuous source of joy.

Rosemary expresses her deep gratitude to her colleagues in Religious Studies at Whittier College, who stand as exemplary teacher-scholars of Christianity, Buddhism, and Islam. They constitute a dynamic community of collegial conversation and support which inspires and encourages Rosemary's scholarly research and writing amid pedagogical (and administrative) joys and challenges. Rosemary particularly thanks Becky Overmyer-Velazquez, her colleague in Sociology at Whittier, for their joint innovative and interdisciplinary explorations of race, religion, and U.S. society during the past four years. Finally, Rosemary delights in the innumerable ways that her spouse, Jason Carbine, walks beside her on their journey in and beyond academia. This unfailing support from colleagues and families made it possible for us to bring this book to fruition—a gift indeed!

Foreword

John E. Thiel

It is a fine thing that a volume of essays appears on the theology of Kathryn Tanner, and that its editors have solicited contributions from superb scholars who know Tanner's work so well. Currently the Frederick Marquand Professor of Systematic Theology at Yale Divinity School, Kathryn Tanner is, quite simply, the most accomplished theologian of her generation. Her dedication to and love for theology has served as an inspiring example to her colleagues and students, and her prolific scholarship has done much to shape the theological agenda of the past twenty-five years.

Postmodern sensibilities have brought a remarkable and welcome pluralism to the discipline of theology. Few theologians, though, have embraced this pluralism in their work as generously as Tanner. Her writings advance their arguments with a compelling logic that is engagingly interdisciplinary, enlisting cultural, philosophical, feminist, scientific, and economic theory to stir creative insights from the ancient riches of the Christian heritage. The range of theological and ethical concerns addressed in her published work is extraordinary—from her abiding respect in theological discourse for God's utter transcendence while yet appreciating God's gracious immanence, to her attention to the political and social implications of the message of Jesus and its expression in Christian doctrine and action, to her efforts to portray the struggle for Christian identity in a tradition that knows itself to be ever shaped by the diverse voices and perspectives of all believers, to her nuanced accounts of the ways the insidious power of sin takes shape in our prejudices, our politics, our economies, and our theologies. From her writings on creation to her writings on eschatology, and in her treatment of a host of theological *loci* in between, Tanner has made a mark on the practice of theology that may prove to be indelible.

All these themes, and too many more to mention here, find their center in Tanner's influential theology of grace. In *Christ the Key* (2010), her sixth book, based on her Warfield lectures at Princeton Theological Seminary in 2007, and in her "brief" systematic theology, *Jesus, Humanity and the Trinity* (2001), Tanner recovers a classical Cappadocian Christology for the profound truth it tells about the mystery of the incarnation—in the person of Christ, God joins the limitations of creatureliness to God's own self, humanity's nature to the divine nature. For Tanner, this divine self-giving, which reveals the very being of God's trinitarian life, is the grace that transforms human persons into the person of Christ, the true image of God. As sheer gift, this grace does not enter into the exchange of created goods that we often idolatrously valorize in our tragically commodified world. God's grace, Tanner insists, is non-competitive, a free and unconditional giving that stands at odds with the sinful forms of reciprocity ventured at the cost of so much human suffering in our competitive economies. Even though God's gift of grace cannot be earned or repaid, since no return is possible to God, Christian responsibility calls on believers to return the gift of grace to the benefit of others, a claim that Tanner develops with attention to social-ethical consequences in ways that enliven the challenge of Christian discipleship. There is a classically Protestant resonance to Tanner's insights on the non-competitive nature of grace that is yet capaciously ecumenical.

The essays in this volume offer detailed analysis of and creative engagements with these broad contours of Tanner's work, and allow us to pause and take thoughtful stock of the theological contributions of one of our very best Christian thinkers. This pause, however, will only be brief, as we turn to tomorrow and await all the ways that Kathryn Tanner will continue in her future work to make a return to us of God's gift of her theological talent that we, no doubt, will gratefully receive.

Introduction: The Gift of Kathryn Tanner's Theological Imagination

Rosemary P. Carbine and Hilda P. Koster

This book acknowledges and celebrates the salient contributions to contemporary constructive Christian theology by Kathryn Tanner, and engages a wide range of topics reflective of the scope of Tanner's theology. Tanner's work is invaluable for theology today due to its unique combination of gifts: logically clear-headed argumentation, commanding grasp of the depth and possibilities of Christian thought and practice, and a transformative incorporation of contemporary interdisciplinary insights springing from ethics, theories of culture, social and political sciences, economics, and gender studies. The aim of the book is to articulate these multiple gifts. To this end, we bring together essays by Tanner's former students and colleagues, who themselves have become leaders in the field of theological and religious studies. Among the many reasons to honor and celebrate Tanner's work, the immediate occasion for our book is that Tanner is named the 2015-2016 Gifford lecturer. The essays in this book, thus, seek to acknowledge this important moment by articulating the significance of Tanner's theological work for contemporary theology in anticipation of what is yet to come. The book therefore is very much a celebration of Tanner *in medias res.*

Tanner's impressive career has spanned three decades and started at Yale University, led to the University of Chicago Divinity School where she became the Dorothy Grant Maclear Professor of Theology (2006-2010), and most recently has brought her back to Yale Divinity School where she is the Frederick Marquand Professor of Systematic Theology. Moving back and forth between Yale and Chicago signals more than the twists and turns in Tanner's own professional appointments; it indicates the myriad ways in which her work has bridged these two, in previous eras considered opposite, schools of theology. While initially shaped by the so-called Yale school of postliberal theology and its cultural-linguistic understanding of Christianity—which originated in part with her teachers Hans Frei and George Lindbeck—Tanner exemplified a "next generation" of theologians who are more deeply influenced by postmodernism, feminism, and liberation theologies. Perhaps most characteristic of this generation is that they pressed theology to make "constructive claims of a substantive sort through the critical reworking of Christian ideas and symbols to address the challenges of today's world."[1] Rather than consider and respond to methodological and epistemological questions about Christianity's legitimacy in modern universities and societies, these now called "constructive theologians" queried "whether theology has anything important to say about the world and our place in it. How might a contemporary Christian theology promote (or not) a more adequate understanding of the world and a more just way of living? ... How would the

---

1. Kathryn Tanner, "How My Mind Has Changed: Christian Claims," *Christian Century* 127, no. 4 (2010): 40.

Christian symbol system need to be creatively and critically recast in the process?"[2]

Tanner's first two books illustrate this turn toward constructive theology in her work. Her book *God and Creation in Christian Theology* (1988) brilliantly sets out the fundamental theological principles of God's divine transcendence and non-competitive relation to the world that guide her later work. *God and Creation* then is a "wide-ranging analysis of the patterns of discourse about God and creation in Christian thought," and covers the way such patterns modify "habits of speech in the wider society in order to show (rather than explain) the coherence of various claims about God and the world."[3] Yet, *The Politics of God* (1992) reflects her growing disenchantment with that theological method and pushes toward a new method grounded in sociopolitical theory that "asks about the various ways Christian beliefs and symbols can function in the particulars of people's lives so as to direct and provide support for the shape of social life and the course of social action."[4] Rather than focusing on the coherence of Christian discourse, *The Politics of God* is preoccupied with the *normative* implications of Christian claims about God and world. The question is "how beliefs about God and creation *should* shape Christian lives—in self-conscious opposition to the way those beliefs have commonly functioned to ill effect in the past and present."[5]

---

2. Ibid., 41.

3. Ibid., 42.

4. Ibid., 41. At the same time, feminist, womanist, and *mujerista* theologies analyzed Christian Godtalk and other Christian beliefs, symbols, and practices for their critical and practical effects. See, for example, Elizabeth Johnson, *She Who Is: The Mystery of God in Feminist Theological Discourse* (New York: Crossroad, 1992); Delores Williams, *Sisters in the Wilderness: The Challenge of Womanist God-talk* (Maryknoll, NY: Orbis, 1995); Ada María Isasi-Díaz, *En La Lucha/In the Struggle: A Hispanic Women's Liberation Theology* (Minneapolis: Fortress Press, 1993); and Ada María Isasi-Díaz, *Mujerista Theology: A Theology for the Twenty-First Century* (Maryknoll, NY: Orbis, 1996).

5. Tanner, "How My Mind Has Changed," 42.

Tanner's method, then, does not insulate a Christian perspective from external criticism or ignore diversity and conflict within Christianity. Her book *Theories of Culture: A New Agenda for Theology* (1997) criticizes a definition of Christian culture as a self-contained social entity that provides norms for sustaining social stability. Tanner argues that such a monolithic notion of culture overlooks the cracks and conflicts within a culture that open up possibilities for resistance and change, hence highlighting human agency. Tanner employs critical theories of culture to further demonstrate the hybridity and internal diversity of Christian discourse. Christianity, like other cultures, has always adopted and reworked elements and ideas, most notably Jewish and Greco-Roman, that are not in and of themselves uniquely Christian. Departing from a postliberal approach that looks for static, stable, or unique rules that constitute and safeguard Christian identity, *Theories of Cultures* proposes that theologians ask themselves what Christians *do* with ideas and beliefs that they adopt from other cultures.[6] As Tanner phrases it, "it is what Christians do with these cultural influences that matters, as they grow into an understanding of their Christian commitments by way of complex processes of revision, appropriation, and resistance to them, taken one by one."[7]

What distinguishes Tanner's method is her emphasis on the need for historical analysis of Christian ideas and symbols. Indeed, Tanner's systematic theology sifts through historical debates to offer new and often unexpected perspectives on these at times worn-out dilemmas,

---

6. Kathryn Tanner, "Is God in Charge?," in *Essentials of Christian Theology*, ed. William C. Placher (Louisville: Westminster John Knox Press, 2003), 118.

7. Tanner, "How My Mind Has Changed," 45. The emphasis on the possibility of critical resistance to as well as critical appropriation and revision of theological ideas moved Tanner's work closer to the revised method of critical correlation forwarded by David Tracy, which also recognizes the fluidity between Christian claims and non-Christian resources and the importance of reworking Christian doctrine in light of today's challenges. See David Tracy, *Blessed Rage for Order: The New Pluralism in Theology* (New York: Seabury, 1975), 43–71.

such as sin and grace, creation *ex nihilo*, or the *imago Dei*. Tanner's insistence on the need for historical study is motivated also by her commitment to the *apophatic* nature of theology. Because theology's ultimate reference, God, can never be fully encapsulated or captured, and, thus always escapes the usual canons of our meaning-making, theological discourse must seek "what lies beyond a contemporary outlook and beyond the immediate context of one's own work."[8] Highlighting historical study does not imply that theologians need to imitate past solutions, or emphasize the correspondence between *the* biblical tradition and *the* Christian tradition as the litmus test for theological work. On the contrary, like Karl Rahner, who has also influenced her work, Tanner "pursues a joint venture of *ressourcement*, a critical retrieval of Christianity's historical traditions, and of *aggiornamento*, an opening up of the theological discipline to the pressing challenges of the day."[9]

In her *Jesus, Humanity and the Trinity* (2001) and her more recent *Christ the Key* (2010), Tanner spells out her constructive systematic agenda for theology rooted in the idea of God as the giver of all good gifts. *Jesus, Humanity and the Trinity* offers an overarching theological vision that affirms the world as the product of God's gratuitous gift-giving and articulates the social principles of unconditional, mutual, and universally inclusive benefit that in turn shape and sustain Christian responsibility in the world. *Christ the Key* shares this same theological vision, yet takes up an incarnational Christology to "throw fresh light on otherwise tired theological topics, opening up new avenues for approaching them by breaking through current impasses in theological literature."[10] God's gift-giving in Christ in

---

8. Tanner, "How My Mind Has Changed," 43.
9. Joy Ann McDougall, "Introduction," *Theology Today* 68, no. 3 (2011): 318.
10. Kathryn Tanner, *Christ the Key*, Current Issues in Theology (Cambridge: Cambridge University Press, 2010), vii.

the incarnation is here the key to unlock closed doors in classical doctrinal debates, and thus imagines new possibilities for contemporary theological and ethical debates.

Throughout her work, Tanner maintains that the aim of theology is to imagine ways of being in the world that serve the flourishing of all of God's creation, especially the poor and disenfranchised. This purpose has led her into a reimagining of our economic practices. Her book *Economy of Grace* (2005), written between the publications of her two systematic theologies, addresses the inequities of global capitalism and explores the implications of God's gracious gift-giving in contrast to a debt-ridden economy. Through this book, as through the gift of all her theological works, Tanner repeatedly reminds us that Christianity ultimately is an ongoing debate about how to best live the Christian life in today's world riddled with all of its inequities and injustices. Or, in her own succinct yet eloquent words: "What Christianity has going for it is its substantive proposal of a way of life—a way of life over which Christians argue in an effort to witness to and be disciples of Christ, and with which they enter into argument with others."[11]

As a testament to Tanner's method as constructive and public theologian, in what follows the contributors to this book also combine the historical analysis of Christian beliefs, symbols, and practices with specific socio-cultural perspectives in order to expand the possibilities of the Christian imaginary and lifeworld in ways that critically and constructively address our society's harmful and unjust practices. In the 1980s and 1990s, Tanner was startled and disappointed by theologians who interpreted the popularity and power of the Christian Right in the U.S. as a sign of Christianity's legitimacy in the U.S. public square, but paid little attention to

11. Kathryn Tanner, *Theories of Culture: A New Agenda for Theology*, Guides to Theological Inquiry (Minneapolis: Fortress Press, 1997), 149.

the Christian Right's theological agenda which "targeted gays and lesbians at the height of the AIDS crisis ... and maligned [to further its own political interests] welfare mothers, sexual minorities, and the urban poor."[12] So, too, these contributors—whether addressing selected theological dimensions of Tanner's work or creatively engaging with that work for the betterment of current U.S. social life and action, which is plagued most recently by religious liberty laws that disguise discriminatory practices—seek to enter into and embody a new theological imagination: "a theology that starts from, and uses as its toolbox for creative ends, materials gathered from the widest possible purview is, in my opinion, a theology with that imaginative expansiveness ... it moves beyond the narrow denominational confines to the broadest possible ecumenical vision and sees beyond elite forms of theological expression, in written texts primarily, to the popular theologies of everyday life."[13] In good Christian eschatological fashion, we live in hope that this book enacts and extends Tanner's generous gift of this method to us.

Overview of the Book

The essays in Part I, *Doing Theology: Gift and Task*, situate Tanner's theological contribution on the contemporary theological scene and recognize the many ways her theology has shaped this scene by (re)defining the place and task of theology in the academy and today's world, more broadly. In chapter 1, Charles Mathewes paints a rich picture of the geniality of her theological work, then examines Tanner's contribution to the task of doing theology and to the vocation of the theologian, comparing her theology with contemporaries such as Rowan Williams, Sarah Coakley, and Jean-Yves Lacoste. More specifically, Mathewes demonstrates the

12. Tanner, "How My Mind Has Changed," 44, 45.
13. Ibid., 43.

relation between Tanner's first-order claims about God's sovereignty and the way she conceives of the theological task as pointing "beyond" itself, which is shown for example in Tanner's affirmation of multiple legitimate theological approaches. For Mathewes, Tanner's theology is theology-logy, focusing on the different logics of theology and their ultimate strengths and weaknesses.

In chapter 2, Paul DeHart reflects on the implications of Tanner's understanding of the God-world relationship for her theology of the Trinity. Engaging her systematic theology outlined in *Jesus, Humanity and the Trinity* and *Christ the Key*, DeHart explores a fundamental Trinitarian pattern in Tanner's work, and demonstrates how Tanner's concept of the Trinity closely coordinates with key soteriological and christological themes (with accompanying anthropological assumptions). Utilizing a Catholic Thomistic view, DeHart questions the way Tanner's account of the God-world relationship ignores the "the internal topography of the subject," which seemingly leads to a strangely hollowed-out account of the human person.

Part II, *The Fullness of God's Gift-Giving*, showcases essays that reflect on the overarching vision of Tanner's systematic theology: God's everlasting and boundless gift-giving nature amid the suffering, strife, and fragility of creation. As Tanner states, "in all God's dealing with the world, God is trying to give creatures the good of God's own life by increasingly intimate relationships with them that culminate in Christ."[14] Reflecting on this central theme of Tanner's theology, in chapter 3 Ian McFarland maps the universal reach of God's gift-giving in the incarnation. Whereas many contemporary theologies downplay the uniqueness of God's gift-giving in Christ in order to maximize God's salvific presence in the

---

14. Kathryn Tanner, "Author Response," *Theology Today* 68, no. 3 (2011): 342.

world, McFarland agrees with Tanner that God's saving presence to the whole of creation is secured only by highlighting the unique character of Jesus' assumption by the Word. To this end, he reads Tanner's Christology within the context of her early work on creation in *God and Creation in Christian Theology* and *The Politics of God*. While at face value these early and later works seem only loosely connected, McFarland argues that they can be drawn together by deploying Tanner's theme of a non-competitive relationship between God and creatures with her reworking of Chalcedonian Christology, using seventh-century theologian Maximus the Confessor to build that bridge.

In chapter 4, Amy Pauw articulates the ways Christ, as the incarnated Word, is not only the giver of gifts, but also the *receiver* of gifts. She skillfully and persuasively utilizes biblical Wisdom traditions in relation to the gospel stories to affirm Jesus' dependence on the life-giving and life-orienting relations with the physical world and various human communities. The result is an evocative creation-centered account of the incarnation which traces Christ's divinity in and through his human interdependence: "Jesus is *for* others as Savior only as he is *with* others, and dependent on them." Taking her cue from the feeding stories in the Gospels, Pauw spells out a task-oriented Christology and an ecclesial practice emulating both Jesus' own dependency on others throughout his creaturely life, as well as his care for and commitment to fragile, hungry bodies in need.

George Hunsinger, in chapter 5, proposes that the saving significance of Christ's cross is not fully developed in Tanner's theology; although she engages with the early Greek Fathers in depth, Hunsinger aims to more fully flesh out a central point in Tanner's Christology about the relationship between the incarnation and the cross. Indeed, Hunsinger identifies and takes on the recurring christological dilemma of whether to affirm a disjunctive or an integrative relationship between the incarnation and the cross, utilizing selected Greek fathers from the early Christian tradition as conversation partners to sort through the attending soteriological issues of this dilemma. By elaborating on key works from Irenaeus of Lyons, Athanasius of Alexandria, Gregory of Nazianzus, and Cyril of Alexandria, Hunsinger shows that the cross is central not only to Christ's accomplishment of salvation but also to the form taken by the Christian life. For these Greek patristic theologians, there is no cross without the incarnation, and no incarnation without the cross. The cross is the divinely ordained fulfillment of the incarnation while the incarnation is the necessary premise of the cross. And vice versa—the incarnation has no saving significance that can be separated from what took place in Christ's death, while the cross plays a fundamental role in the achievement of salvation.

William Wright's carefully wrought essay, in chapter 6, ponders the absence of dialectics in Tanner's theology, more specifically in her Christology. Wright argues that retrieving a dialectical approach may lead Tanner to a different view of the theological task, namely not as primarily concerned with establishing theological principles that can somehow solve the classical *aporia* of theology, but more as collecting and ordering "the pluralism that results as Christian language through the ages falls out into conceptual conflicts." Wright's essay then puts this dialectical approach to work by demonstrating how Tanner's Christology solves the longstanding Antiochene-Alexandrian conflict, but fails to accommodate the suffering of the divine Son in Christ. Pondering this oddity while fully affirming its soteriological motive, Wright's essay raises poignant questions about the coherence of Tanner's fundamental theological principles of divine transcendence and non-competiveness.

From a rather different vantage point, namely ritual theory and evolutionary science of religion, Eugene F. Rogers, in chapter 7, constructively utilizes Tanner's non-competitive Christology to illuminate how the blood of Christ is the blood of God. Observing that "blood" is succeeding "the body" as a central theme of the humanities, Rogers's essay investigates ways in which "Christian blood-signaling," most notably in the Eucharist, can be put towards subversive social ends, to cease oppression and violence. Having established that the blood of Christ in Eucharistic ritual emulates "costly signaling" and thus allows Christians to foster virtue, cooperation, and gratitude, Rogers then emphasizes the untapped theological potential of Tanner's non-competitive account for Eucharistic theology, using Aquinas to articulate the efficacy of the Eucharistic elements.

Part III, *Christianity as Culture: A Gift to Theology*, gathers essays that reflect on Tanner's pathbreaking work in *Theories of Culture*. In chapter 8, Mary McClintock Fulkerson creatively relates Tanner's theology of God's abundant gift-giving to ministering to and with people with disabilities. Whereas DeHart in Part I challenges Tanner's lack of attention to the interiority of the subject from a Catholic perspective, Fulkerson utilizes a more radical Protestant perspective and praises Tanner's refusal to highlight cognitive abilities as a prerequisite of faith, which opens up theological pathways to honor the living faith of an interracial community that includes people with disabilities. The grace of a God who is beyond kinds does not depend on any condition in the finite world, and, hence, is radically inclusive, thereby offering rich resources for different ecclesiological, especially worship, practices.

In chapter 9, Jan Pranger explores the potential of Tanner's theology of culture for missiological discussions about inculturation—that is, for the articulation of Christian theology in intercultural situations or amidst social and cultural change—along the twin lines of theology as cultural construction and non-essentialist negotiation of Christian identity in relation to culture. Understanding inculturation via Tanner's proposal for constructing Christian identity through the creative use of existing cultural forms, Pranger discusses how missiological models of inculturation and contextualization, and ecumenical discussions about syncretism, diversity, and identity, may be advanced. He contends that postcolonial inculturation seeks to overcome the cultural trauma that was inflicted by the arbitrary creation of cultural and religious boundaries in the elite theological production by Eurocentric Christian missions while also acknowledging the simultaneous popular production of local forms of Christian theology. Thus, Pranger argues that Tanner's postmodern understanding of culture bridges the divide between inculturation and contextualization, between theological concerns with cultural identity and with issues of social justice. Exploring the ecumenical significance of Tanner's proposals for Christian identity as an open, inclusive commitment to figure out the meaning of discipleship, he suggests that such a commitment begins with practices of resistance and solidarity as a first step in learning about Christian discipleship as part of God's healing of the world.

Finally, in chapter 10 Hugh Nicholson explores Tanner's understanding of Christian identity for relations with other religions. Nicholson recaps Tanner's move away from a postliberal stance, which regards the engagement with culture as a risk to a self-contained, self-generated Christian identity, toward a postmodern understanding of Christian identity as generated relationally in the interaction with cultures, fueled by subaltern uses of elite cultural productions. Nicholson concludes that engagement with other religions, or comparative theology, is integral to the theological task, but at the same time observes a tension between Christian identity formation through creative use of other religions *pace* Tanner's theology of culture and respect for the alterity of other religions *pace* Tanner's social ethics in *The Politics of God*. This tension, Nicholson maintains, also leads Tanner to occasional lapses into notions of intrinsic identity, for instance by distinguishing between matters of internal importance to Christians and situational needs to mark Christian distinctiveness. While recognizing that Tanner's consistent insistence on openness to the freedom of the Word in theological articulations sets her apart from a postliberal approach to culture, he suspects that her appeal to style as a situationally enacted practical sense preserves a trace of intrinsic identity not entirely unlike postliberalism.

Part IV, titled *The Gift of Theology to Praxis*, elaborates on the socio-political and economic implications of Tanner's theology, especially for pressing contemporary issues such as feminist theologies of sin, ecofeminist theological concerns about global ecological crises, economic theologies of alternatives to capitalist, consumerist cultures, and feminist public theologies of antiracist activism. In chapter 11, Joy McDougall plumbs the depths of Tanner's theological insights for clues into how elements of the Christian tradition can move feminist agendas forward. In particular, McDougall highlights the potential of Tanner's notion of sin as either closing our eyes to or blocking our vision of God's gracious and abundant gift-giving for a Reformed feminist theology of sin and grace. While McDougall shows that Tanner's concept of sin overcomes unhelpful binaries in sin-talk (personal and structural sin, sinner and sinned-against), she argues that Tanner's theology of sin requires further en-gendering in order to address particular facets of gender oppression that afflict women's and men's lives. She proposes re-visioning the Reformed notion of "the bondage of the will" as "the bondage of the Eye/I," in which blindness or "blocked vision" to God's gracious gifts ensnares persons in oppressive gender roles, cultural scripts, and systemic structures not always of their choosing. This feminist conceptualization of sin ultimately seeks to re-imagine the workings of grace that free men and women from this gendered "bondage of the Eye/I."

In her essay in chapter 12, Hilda P. Koster demonstrates how key themes in Tanner's theology offer an attractive model for ecological theology, in part because they help solve some recurrent problems in eco-theological panentheisms. Specifically, Koster points out the promise of Tanner's account of divine transcendence for a non-anthropocentric, non-hierarchical, non-dualistic theology of creation and salvation that envisions God as the fecund provider and redeemer of all that is. In spite of the rich promise of Tanner's model for a green theology, its soteriology, which is characterized by the cosmic-theological scheme of God's ongoing gift-giving, tends to cast finitude *itself* as the problem addressed by the incarnation. From an evolutionary, ecological perspective, however, death and disease—while tragic—guarantee the vitality and resilience of healthy biotic communities. Koster, thus, envisions a soteriology that overcomes the suffering and death that result from human sin, while fully embracing the finite conditions of our lives as members of the earth-community. To this end, Koster utilizes the perspectives of Catholic eco-theologian Denis Edwards and eco-feminist theologian Elizabeth Johnson, especially their retrieval of "the wisdom of the cross" via the idea of "deep incarnation."

Courtney Wilder's essay in chapter 13 creatively engages Tanner's *Economy of Grace* in relation to contemporary subversive economic practices, such as Zero Waste Living, that disrupt hegemonic consumerist values. Capitalizing on Tanner's claims that a theology of God's gift-giving may open up our economic imagination in a time of economic dead ends, Wilder identifies these popular practices as allowing for an alternate economic system that reflects both a primary allegiance to God and an abiding reliance upon God's grace. Wilder thus broadens the scope of non-capitalist economic possibilities in relation to Tanner's analysis, and asks whether distinctive popular phenomena, which she sees reflected in the blog "Zero Waste Home" and the song "Thrift Shop" by the rapper Macklemore, may offer fresh resources for Christian theological reflection on economics.

Finally, in chapter 14 Rosemary P. Carbine seeks to illuminate the conversations and protests sparked by police killings of black men in America since 2014 in the light of feminist public theology, with particular reference to Tanner's reflections on Christian tradition and public theology. Stepping away from some social Trinitarian theologies which take immanent Trinitarian relations as a direct religio-political model for human social relations, Tanner instead proposes public theology as a communicative process of religio-political discourse, which parallels her understanding of the Christian tradition as a task of continued conversation. Carbine addresses and presses beyond discursive public theology in Tanner by exploring rhetorical, symbolic, and prophetic practices of public engagement by nonreligious and interreligious groups in the aftermath of Ferguson, practices which denounce racism and proclaim black religio-political subjectivity and community on theological grounds.

The book concludes with an *Afterword* by Serene Jones, in which she eloquently and personally reflects on the multiple ways in which Tanner—through the gift of her theological imagination as well as her mentoring, collegiality, and friendship—enriches the lives of all of us who enjoy the great fortune to learn from her, work with her, and collaborate with her.

PART I

Doing Theology: Gift and Task

1

Tanner's Theology-logy

Charles Mathewes

Genius is probably a category best avoided in theology.[1] Speaking genealogically, it is a Romantic idea that comes with a fair amount of complicated conceptual baggage, and that probably needs a good demythologizing fumigation before we use it.[2] It suggests a density of individuality, a self-possession in an author, which is more ideologically seductive than phenomenologically real. Certainly, we all have our heroes. Undoubtedly, we all seek our idols. This is as true of our attitude towards our contemporaries as it is towards the past. We are all, more or less, groupies. Typically, our admiration is most powerful when its object is least known to us; indeed our admiration may itself serve as impediment to our becoming genuinely

1. Many thanks to Paul Griffiths, Paul Jones, Joy McDougall, and Eugene Rogers for years, in some cases decades, of conversation on Tanner's work; to Christina McRorie, for reading this essay and offering very helpful critiques of it; and of course to Kathryn Tanner, for her generous teaching, and her more generous friendship.
2. Darrin McMahon, *Divine Fury: A History of Genius* (New York: Basic Books, 2013); David Galenson, *Old Masters and Young Geniuses: The Two Life-Cycles of Artistic Creativity* (Princeton: Princeton University Press, 2006); and Michael J. A. Howe, *Genius Explained* (Cambridge: Cambridge University Press, 1999).

acquainted with the actual human whose books we read and whose voice we hear. To call someone a "genius" is, in this way, to distance them from us, and protect ourselves from them.

There is also another, specifically theological, hazard latent in the idea of genius. In Christian thought, seeking for theological genius is a category mistake. It misleads both hearer and speaker as much about the purpose of theological reflection as about the nature of our fellow humans. Theological insight is not a matter of subjective wisdom wrested from the cosmos by a soul wrestling with God; the individual thinker and author serves more as an antenna for the various theological transmissions surging through the atmosphere of their communities. A strong case can be made that the best theology is more often some peculiar condensation of a whole climate of opinion than it is some one person's theologically disciplined barbaric yawp across the roofs of the world. If there are any theological geniuses out there, they're likely at most one step away from being heretics.[3]

There is no contemporary thinker who serves as a better counterargument to the sentiments expressed in the above paragraphs than Kathryn Tanner. For whatever our complaints about and suspicions of "genius," the category does pick out a set of phenomena that bear some organic coherence, and we know that quite well from the evidence of Tanner. *Ingenium* originally meant a natural capacity or power, an innate capacity, a kind of graced capability not given to all; Tanner certainly has something like that. It is not a matter of effort that allows her to be so clever. None of this is to dispute her many years of labor; no one could be as productive as she has been, or as reliably acute as she is, without strenuous, painstaking effort. But the sheer gift is there as well, which she has then assiduously

---

3. I am informed here by Rowan Williams, *Arius: Heresy and Tradition*, 2nd ed. (Grand Rapids: Eerdmans, 2002).

cultivated by her efforts. She is an alarmingly talented, indeed gifted, theologian. Is she not, then, a genius?

Here is where things get really complicated. If the term applies to her, her "genius" does not lie in some especially dense subjectivity on her part. It is not that her work bears, like a watermark, the indelible stamp of her metaphysically utterly distinct, haecceitatious quiddity; in terms of personality, she is more like what we know of Thomas Aquinas than she is like Martin Luther. However, it is the case that there is something deeply exceptional about the quality of her work, and of the mind that produces it. Her work strikes me as deeply, curiously, essentially undetermined by her teachers—while influenced by her teachers at Yale, her work is uniquely her own—and its impress is not clearly visible in her students. There is no "trajectory of thought" in which her work is fundamentally one moment. In this way she has no disciples, and no ancestors. There is no recognizable, reasonably textured narrative of inheritance and transmission, no picture of a theological "school" in which she plays a structural role. She is genuinely *sui generis*.

Yet, if she is truly unique, genuinely idiosyncratic, how can her work communicate so well? After all, she is recognized as a major figure in our field, not just brilliant but deeply relevant: trend setting, field defining, a person with whose views everyone must reckon, whose work everyone should read, who raises deep questions for all of us. Tanner's reputation as a "theologian's theologian" is unparalleled in this hemisphere; she is perhaps the most intelligent and far-seeing American theologian since Jonathan Edwards. Her only present-day rivals for global preeminence would be Rowan Williams, Sarah Coakley, and Jean-Yves Lacoste, with Robert Jenson, John Milbank, Eberhard Jüngel, and Jean-Luc Marion being borderline cases.[4] We admire her, and many of us stand in awe of her, but, can we learn from her? Not from her books, I mean; those are full of lessons, and every one of us has access to them. I mean from her as an exemplary theological mind, as representing one way of doing theology and of being a theologian. What can we learn in *that* register?

I believe that her example does have lessons for us, despite her remarkable independence of mind, and that a crucial clue to finding them lies in the style of her reflections. One of the most curious facts about her uniqueness is her style, or rather her anti-style, the way her work seems intentionally designed not to call attention to itself. This is so in two senses. First, her prose style is remarkably transparent. It is unparalleled in its lucidity: plain and simple, low church, almost Shaker. She rarely uses esoteric technical terms (like *epekstasis* or *parousia* or *theologoumenon* or *askesis*, all terms I confess to having used and rather promiscuously); she rarely has multi-clausal sentences, or hypotactical constructions; in general, she eschews the complicated Technicolor grammatical pyrotechnics and showboating of which the rest of us are frequently guilty. I know of no other member of the guild of professional theologians and religious thinkers whose language is more straightforward or direct; her work is the best evidence I know that theological power and linguistic complexity (let alone difficulty) are two different things. There are hardly any sentences, in any of her books, that a good ninth grader could not read and understand; and there is no paragraph in her books that any high school graduate could not comprehend. Somehow, she has managed to write remarkably incisive and fecund works without succumbing to the siren-song of flashy academic fashion, hyper-

---

4. It is worth noting that her criticisms of Marion (in her "Theology at the Limits of Phenomenology," in *Counter Experience: Reading Jean-Luc Marion*, ed. Kevin Hart [University of Notre Dame Press, 2007], 201-31) and Milbank (in her *Theories of Culture: A New Agenda for Theology*, Guides to Theological Inquiry [Minneapolis: Fortress Press, 1997]) are grounded in the two thinkers' being paradoxically too captive to modern categories, even as (particularly as) they react against them. As we will see in the rest of this essay, that is an especially significant kind of critique for Tanner.

technical esoteric jargon, or rebarbative prose that reliably courts incoherence, the confusion of linguistic difficulty and grammatical obscurity with insightful profundity. I do not know anyone else who communicates the achievement of direct effortlessness so frankly or straightforwardly. Across the past several generations, she must be the most impressive theologian with the least abstruse language.

Second, the names I associated with hers above, especially Lacoste, Williams, and Coakley, give a clue to another dimension of her work that is remarkably, for want of a better term, transparent. These three theologians share with Tanner a capacity to move freely, quickly, and smoothly across centuries and regions—talking about Teresa of Avila one moment, Basil of Caesarea the next, and Simone Weil soon after. They have no homeland, no province of theology's larger story in which they are locals and whose provinciality tints their vision of every other era and tradition. They belong, in the best way, to the whole church, and the whole church belongs to them, as their heritage. (That the figures which we provincialists are so busy single-mindedly boosting would agree with them, and flee from us, is a quiet lesson that we devotees never seem to digest.) Tanner is like them, insofar as her work is not identified with some notable historical figure of a particular epoch. Indeed, she is *more* like this than they are, for all of them were initially associated with some thinker or set of thinkers (Williams with Russian Orthodoxy, Coakley with Troeltsch, Lacoste, a good French Catholic, with Heidegger), before they each moved beyond their origins over their careers. From the beginning, Tanner's work was never so identified; she has always floated free, hovering above the various powers and principalities of the theological kingdom of this world. She seemed to emerge onto the scene with a conspective apprehension of the totality of the Christian tradition (and beyond), and has been using it effortlessly since then. Even today, I would argue that of the four of them,

Tanner's work is the least *individual*, the least imbued with the distinctive tint of her own personality, and the most likely to construct an argument by corralling a disparate hodgepodge of voices into a surprisingly harmonious chorus. Again, a comparison with Aquinas is instructive: like the "Dumb Ox," she is not prone to occupy all the space in a public setting, but lets her work speak for itself, so that even her distinctive insights into the tradition, and her innovations beyond it, are not blustery or noisy.

Now, no one is going to confuse Tanner with Aquinas, but they do share a steady, easy dialectical calm, and a panoptic appreciation of the entire theological horizon and full theological tradition that few others can manage. Both are profoundly aware of the manifold ways that an argument can have implications for a wide spectrum of theological *topoi*, so that each moment in the argument is made after full and careful consideration of its implications for the theological project as a whole. Both exhibit command of the whole tradition, and convey the feeling that, in speaking on any point, the whole tradition is standing there, silently listening in, so that the statement is subtly if silently inflected by being made in their presence. And finally, both affirm the interrelation between conservation of the tradition and creativity and innovation with(in) it. Indeed, as Tanner has suggested, the acts of conservation and innovation may not be inversely related, even though most theologians, in the United States and beyond, regularly assume that is so. Thus, like Aquinas, Tanner has achieved such a mastery of the tradition that she has gained a deep freedom beyond any of its particular formulations, thinkers, or schools, a freedom so deep that she almost becomes free of the need to be partial, in several senses, to any particular location or locution within it.

In this sense, there is a tension between the manifest distinctive intelligence and power of Tanner's work, and the equally undeniable transparency of her prose, position, and purpose. This it seems to me is where Tanner is most distinctive, and where we may have the most to learn from her. Her theological work is among the most materially rich and profound available to us today, but also oddly self-effacing; she often frankly acknowledges the availability of multiple legitimate theological approaches, and sketches how any of those logics could work, so long as they recognize a core series of affirmations they must confirm, and a set of dangers they must avoid. That is to say, her work does not call attention to itself, but points "beyond" itself to something else, something larger. I know of no one who has reflected upon this curious fact about her work—curious, at least, for a theologian writing in our deeply self-conscious age. Here I want to suggest that we can learn a great deal from this, both in *what* she is trying to do and *how* she is trying to do it.

These features of Tanner's work reveal something significant about how she conceives the theological task. For her, the professional theological task is a matter of finding resources to help us in our theological interpretations of and responses to life. Academic theology is an ancillary intellectual discipline, a service industry. This is not because she devalues theology; far from it. To the contrary, it is precisely because she thinks it is *fundamentally* important, for *every* believer. As she puts it, "[i]n order to witness to and be a disciple of Jesus, every Christian has to figure out for him or herself what Christianity is all about, what Christianity stands for in the world." This is "an essential demand of everyday Christian living."[5] This is very true: theology is not, nor should it be, essentially the province of virtuosi. It is a fundamental task of all Christians. This view reflects the rather high cognitive expectations that are put on Christians by some fundamental dynamics of the tradition, and that are then

---

5. Tanner, *Jesus, Humanity and the Trinity: A Brief Systematic Theology* (Minneapolis: Fortress Press, 2001), xiii.

redoubled in conditions of modernity. The role of the academic theologian in this setting is to generate creative resources for ordinary theological use, and to show how to test all such contributions, including his or her own, for doctrinal coherence and theological fruitfulness. What Tanner is doing, and what she imagines academic theology properly to be, is not theology but what we might call *theology-logy*; it is about the different logics of theology, their strengths and weaknesses.

This may sound strangely abstract, reflexive, and formalist, but it derives from profound first-order material theological convictions. Her method is, it seems to me, deeply connected to her vision of God's sovereignty, and flows from two fundamental convictions: *first*, that God is *absolutely free* and unconstrained by the logic of creation; and *second*, that God has *freely committed* Godself to creation as fundamentally manifest in the incarnation of Christ. These convictions, as they play out for Tanner in the shape of human participation in God's plan, first in Christ and then in the Christian community on earth, have profound implications for understanding the theologian's vocation. In fact, all of her work explores the vocation of academic theological reflection, especially as that presents a problem of theological method. In particular, it explores how to understand the work of academic theology in the service of the ongoing life of the church. The latter hangs on her understanding of the work of the church as the special mark of the ongoing presence of God in the world, *and* speaks to some basic convictions she has about the relationship between God and creation, a relationship that realizes some kind of climactic realization in the figure of Christ.

This chapter makes this argument in several steps. First, I try to put before us a brief sketch of the shape of her work as a whole, noting the way it is radically innovative across fields, then wondering whence that innovation comes. Here I want to have the reader wonder, how are these works the work of *one* theological mind? Then, in the second half, I sketch three thematic threads that span and stabilize the multiple kinds of difference in Tanner's writing: 1) a deep and abiding attention to the breadth of resources available in the history of Christian thought; 2) a fundamental methodological commitment to what I call "theology-logy," that is, conceiving of academic or professional theology as *not* first-order discourse into God (like a steamship of inquiry captained by some theologian, which will carry ordinary Christians like boat passengers), but instead as a second-order analysis of first-order theological discourse; and 3), underlying the other two, a positive vision of God's relation to the world as funding this construal of the theological task, and ensuring its vitality despite—or, more accurately, precisely because of—its remarkable self-effacing qualities.

Tanner's Path

To bring my theme more fully into view, I want to show that there is in fact a curiosity in her work to be explored, an *explanandum* in need of explanation. I will do that here through a quick summative tour of her major works. This will showcase both her repeatedly ground-breaking innovations in quite diverse areas of theological inquiry, and hopefully also raise the question of the coherence of her various works—whether, that is, they gel into something larger than the sum of their parts.

I think they do, but by way of a "something" that is quite unlike the usual contributions that thinkers make. There is no ultimately "Tannerian" stance on any of these issues—there is only the repeated mobilization of diverse thinkers' insights, from multiple historical and institutional and subtraditional perspectives, to show how theological discourse and practice can be rendered new, diversified and liberated from the idolatrous ossifications in which we sinfully indulge. In what is this approach rooted? It clearly has different anchors across her career. Different theorists appear and disappear across the pages of her books—Wittgenstein and Geertz early on, then cultural and political theorists, always theologians and philosophers, and so on. But behind these different thinkers always lie some basic convictions about God's freedom as manifest in Christ—claims about God, about creation, and the relation between them.

God and Creation in Christian Theology

Her first book, *God and Creation in Christian Theology: Tyranny or Empowerment?* (1988), explored some basic metaphysical presuppositions of philosophical theology, insisting that our conception of the categories we employed were insufficiently informed by the tradition, and confined within certain bourgeois mid-twentieth century understandings. If we only appreciated those traditional accounts, she argued, we would see that understandings of God and creation need not be constrained within the narrow framework we had been presuming. Most famously, she set forth the basic idea that the tradition repeatedly affirmed the divine's causal "non-contrastative transcendence" vis-à-vis the causal structures of the created order, and explained that it was only because modern assumptions made that vision increasingly difficult to comprehend that we did not realize that multiple theological voices had affirmed this vision throughout history and in the present. This is perhaps a surprisingly apologetic project (especially coming from someone trained at Yale at that time) that primarily "defends" the tradition by showing that no defense of real Christian discourse is needed. Along with the material positions she advanced in this book, it is also crucial for its exposition of the claim that academic theology should be concerned with articulating the "ruled structures of theological talk and their function."[6] As it offers such formal and regulative guidelines, specialized theological language is "called forth by Christian practice."[7] Furthermore, this stance requires a deep acquaintance with the historical traditions of Christian thought; as she puts it, "[t]he theologian who is to avoid the modern subversion of our rules for discourse must know the theological tradition of which he or she is a part: how traditional theological claims have been used within their discourse contexts."[8]

All of this is part of a larger rehabilitation of classical metaphysical claims of God's transcendence, in which effort Tanner had fellow-laborers in thinkers such as Robert Sokolowski and David Burrell. Furthermore, this recovery was begun at the same time that analytic philosophy was slowly recovering robust metaphysical argument, and in particular just as the field of "Christian philosophy"—informed by figures such as Alvin Plantinga, Nicholas Wolterstorff, and Peter van Inwagen—was revving up. Even in this first book, Tanner's point was not that there was *one* particular view of human and divine agency that was right—Thomist, or Augustinian, or another—but rather that several diverse languages were available in which the important distinctions and contrasts between kinds of agency could be drawn. What matters is that the chosen language must help us affirm that the experience of God is fundamentally rooted in *empowerment*, in enabling and not constraining or disabling human agency and activity.

6. Tanner, *God and Creation in Christian Theology: Tyranny or Empowerment?* (Oxford: Blackwell, 1988), 10.
7. Ibid., 13.
8. Ibid., 168.

The Politics of God

She followed her first book with a second, topically an apparently quite different one, namely, *The Politics of God* (1992). This book turned to political theology and effectively sketched *in nuce* the lineaments of a post-Schmittian theological view, in which political categories are shown to be always already theologically charged, and theological categories are able to disrupt the political status quo in ways that are profoundly liberatory. This view has more recently gathered support from figures as diverse as Oliver O'Donovan, Catherine Keller, Ted Smith, Luke Bretherton, and myself, though I suspect few of us realized that we were following trails that she had played so large a role in blazing.

Discontinuities abound between the books, but deeper continuities lurk as well. For example, *The Politics of God* looks at the same historical legacy she mined in *God and Creation*, though it uncovers in it a far more complicated legacy. She notes how these practices, which she had previously discovered to be more healthy than much modern discourse, had historically often been used to support "conservative adherence to established political and social relations, willing complicity in social injustice, quiescence before conditions that cry out for change."[9] We cannot help but hear a hint of a confession in her subsequent claim that "[i]f one is a Christian, the abhorrent character of that history will either force one to drop Christianity altogether, or incline one to start afresh as a Christian by tearing down and rebuilding from the bottom up an account of God and the world with different sociopolitical associations."[10] In response, Tanner shows how these doctrines can be mobilized—clearly, *have* been—both to reinforce human hierarchies

9. Kathryn Tanner, *The Politics of God: Christian Theologies and Social Justice* (Minneapolis: Fortress Press, 1992), 2.
10. Ibid., 3.

and to undermine them, to cast the mighty from their thrones. She clearly favors the latter, showing how our construals of God can empower humans to become more fully engaged in liberatory political action, disrupting our complacencies and puncturing our pretentions. Once again, God enables agency and power for humans—in this case, precisely by smashing the political idols we have constructed to trap us in certain political formations and formulations.

Theories of Culture

The troubles with the tradition that she acknowledged in *The Politics of God* returned yet again as a major goad for her third book, *Theories of Culture: A New Agenda for Theology* (1997). There, she showed how a great deal of contemporary theological discourse is misled by a flawed understanding of the nature of human cultural realities, based on a too-simple understanding of the category of "culture" itself. On the surface, this analysis of the contemporary theological scene was accomplished by the articulation and development of a post-modern conception of culture—or rather, the articulation and exposition of postmodern culturalist critiques of the too-coherent, too-systematic modern conception of culture. That modern conception was rooted in a Romantic understanding of organic localism, which is itself a salutary defense against over-confident universalisms in 18th and 19th century Europe and in the 20th century postcolonial world as well. This understanding of culture, Tanner helped the theological guild understand, is not a natural kind, a structural reality in nature; rather, it is a human interpretation of human phenomena and as such is susceptible to reinterpretation and contestation.

Negatively, she used this analysis to argue, surprisingly, that the postliberal theology with which she had heretofore been identified was problematically confining, trapping the kerygmatic message in a hardened shell that needed to be, if not quite shattered, at least moved beyond.[11] Positively, by recognizing this, she showed us how to see Christian practices as "always the practices of others made odd," and the impurity and borrowed character of Christian practices and language entails, she argued, that apologetics and engagement with other cultures is *internal* to Christian practices, not a contingent accident that happens to it.[12] There is no kerygmatic kernel coated in various cultural husks; the whole nature of the Christian church is exhaustively, kenotically worked out in the fleshly, contingent materialities of the everyday history of actual human lives.

The effect of this thoroughgoing worldly saturation of Christian practices is dramatic, and pedagogically powerful: "The recognition of God's free and uncontrollable Word, which respect for Christian diversity spreads, desocializes Christians, so to speak; it breaks the habit of the normal, and thereby frees them for renewed attention to the Word."[13] The churches are able to disjoint themselves from the way of the world, but not in a way that causes them to flee the world. Perhaps we can almost hear her saying that it is precisely the deep desire to escape the world, to become like God, that most decisively marks the fallen world as "fallen," but also that allows them to seek the Word *in* the world, in creation, as properly formed by the Word and thus the chosen home of the Word.

The last several sentences are not merely my theological gloss on a methodological argument. Importantly for my purposes, she surprisingly makes this argument in a frankly first-order theological manner, arguing that it is a reflection on the doctrine of the incarnation. She quotes Barth on the Prodigal to this effect.[14] I take

---

11. Tanner, *Theories of Culture*, 104-19.
12. Ibid., 113.
13. Ibid., 175.
14. Ibid., 113-14.

her to mean here that if there is some sort of *core* theological message "spun" or manifest in creation, then that "core" sets up some kind of fundamentally Docetist (or Donatist) dualism that secures a determinate theological message only at the cost of rendering it completely incommensurable with the world. (Her more recent worries about modern kenotic Christologies operate on similar grounds.) Beneath the affirmation of the postmodern critiques of modern understandings of culture, then, lies a powerful theological vision of the relationship between God and the world, and of the nature of the coherence and integrity, such as it is, of the redeemed people of God within the world.

I think it is fair to say that only now are theologians beginning to understand Tanner's book, and its potential impact on the field. She turned to anthropological accounts of culture almost a decade before anthropological theorists of culture turned to theology and Christianity. Even now, fellow theologians, and many anthropologists, are only beginning to catch on to the importance of this scholarly crossroads for both theology and anthropology.[15]

Economy of Grace and the Gifford Lectures

Since *Theories of Culture*, she has moved on to the economy, thinking about economics as the new politics—the new "final vocabulary" in which most of us will increasingly live and move, and from which we will have our being. Here her point seems to be something like this: Christianity emerged in a heavily politicized context, where the basic metaphors of divine supremacy and human agency as well as community were fundamentally political metaphors—God as *Lord*

---

15. For more of what I mean, see Michael Banner, *The Ethics of Everyday Life* (Oxford: Oxford University Press, 2014) and two recent journal issues: the *South Atlantic Quarterly* issue on "Global Christianity, Global Critique," 109, no. 4 (2010), and the *Current Anthropology* special issue on *The Anthropology of Christianity* 55, Supplement 10 (2015).

and *sovereign*, *ruling* the cosmos, ushering in a *kingdom*, with humans caught between two rival *lordships*, *citizens* of one or the other. But, we can imagine a different cultural context—say, a heavily commercial one—in which Christianity could have come to self-awareness. In such a context, the basic metaphors of Christian life would not be fundamentally *political* ones, but *economic* ones—God as *giver* of *goods*, the people of God engaged in *exchange*, grace as a *benefit* traded *for free*, and so on. What would such a different set of metaphors, Tanner wonders, have done for our understanding of Christianity? What capacities would have been enabled or disabled by this framework? Now, perhaps, such a world—a world more basically marked by economic rather than political metaphors and thinking—is coming towards us.

In *Economy of Grace* (2005), she begins to explore the basic value logic of a capitalist market system, and to present a better way in the form of a theological economy of grace. She offers this in serious—and at times quite critical—conversation with theorists of "the gift." Developing an interpretation of God in economic terms, she then uses that to reread our current system, asking where it falls short, and creatively imagining where points of contact might exist. This critique then permits her to exposit a morally motivating vision of a rival economic model to the "free market" we currently inhabit, in which zero-sum and exchange understandings of possession, responsibility, and just desert are transcended in favor of "non-competitive" relations of abundance and fullness.[16] Escaping our imaginative captivity to absolute scarcity and inevitable zero-sum competition, Tanner explains that the idea of Christ's two natures helps us see that two can exist as one; we are ourselves and each other, and we are also not our own—we are God's.

16. Kathryn Tanner, *Economy of Grace* (Minneapolis: Fortress Press, 2005), 75-80.

She is further exploring this logic in her Gifford Lectures, wherein she will explore these challenges more fully, but this time not in terms of the grasping and Pelagian logic of market capitalism *tout court*, but rather focusing on the quasi-theological (and often quite palpably apocalyptic in its effects) character of finance capitalism, especially as that theurgical system has emerged in the past several decades to make us all its sorcerer's apprentices. We anticipate much more elaboration of these issues to come, but still moving in the same direction: how might we rearticulate the Christian message in properly economic terms, and what might such a rearticulation allow us to say and do that we cannot as easily—or yet—say and do today?

In this brief survey, I have left out several of her books, in particular *Jesus, Humanity and the Trinity* (2001) and *Christ the Key* (2010), to which I will turn in the next part below. The books we have looked at do, I hope, raise in a pointed way the question of the coherence of Tanner's project. After all, what do we see in these various books? Tanner's work seems brilliant but jumpy. What is the narrative thread that joins each into a coherent whole, the spinal structure that locks in a certain logic? It may not appear at first as if her central driving convictions are properly theological. They may seem—and to students I have sometimes found that they *do* seem—"merely" political or ethical. Such readers seize on her frequent expressions of a broadly liberatory aim, and assume that it must be her final vocabulary, as it were, so that liberation is good simply because it is liberation. This would be fine, but it would not give her a very broad vocabulary within which to engage interlocutors who do not share that view; against, for example, other theological accounts that emphasize authority, such an account would have little leverage. The same could be said of efforts to engage secular libertarian accounts that prioritize private property and non-interference. If straightforward "liberation" really were the bedrock on which her spade were turned, I doubt she would have had the impact she has had.

In my view, this is not her aim. Her aim is to express something deeper and wider, about the nature of God and God's relationship to the world. Her emphasis on destabilization and liberation is part of a rich theological critique of idolatry, and also an evangel of new life, a new life not found elsewhere but in the flesh and blood of human history as lived here and now. As Tanner reads the tradition, there is a theological energy that perpetually escapes complete representation, and ceaselessly fuels the perichoretic dynamism that continually overturns our expectations. That core is found in the figure of Jesus Christ, the human being who is also the Son of God.

Stabilities across Difference

Tanner's work thus presents the reader with a puzzle. She is extremely well-regarded, she enjoys immense influence, but the nature of her impact is obscure because of the diversity of her topics and the elusiveness of some singular "position." When you read her work, it is almost always about something else, pointing beyond itself, suggesting other resources. There is no clearly "Tannerian" view or stance on any particular doctrinal loci or attitude. She has no philosophical axe to grind, no theological shtick or gimmick. Nonetheless her work is, to my mind, immediately recognizable. What is it about her books that is so distinctive? What, exactly, is her center of gravity?

I think the secret here lies in the way all of her works are manifestations of a single theological method rooted in some basic theological convictions. This is surprising in several ways; for her to be a terrific theorist of theological method is perhaps especially disorienting to us, given her training at and deep association with "Yale." Few have recognized her continued reflections on theological method, but it is a perpetual fact about her work: the main focus of academic theology is not *theology*, in the sense of language about God, but rather *theology-logy*, concerned with the various languages in which we formulate language about God. The core of her theological method rests in her explorations of the various logics in which theological claims may be formulated, in order to assess the strengths and evaluate the weaknesses of each, all in the service of enlivening the community's theological practice and speech as ways to inhabit this fundamental dynamic of a radically free God entering fully and completely into relationship with the creation whom God has made. I will talk about this in terms of three dimensions of Tanner's works or facets of her approach that, whatever else she does, remain if not stable at least durably present in different formulations across her books.

Deep Acquaintance with Tradition

The first thing to note is the regularly manifest intimate acquaintance with what is effectively the entire theological tradition in Western (and a fair amount of Eastern—at least Nicene Eastern) Christian thought. In her work, we see figures from every century, not just mentioned or discussed but regularly engaged—contemporary figures, Protestant and Catholic thinkers from the 20th century, Hegel, Kierkegaard and Schleiermacher from the 19th century, Kant, Edwards, Pascal, Luther and Calvin, Aquinas, Bernard of Clairvaux, Anselm, all the way back to Irenaeus. (On one randomly selected page in *Jesus, Humanity and the Trinity*, she references, in sequence, Athanasius, D.M. Baillie, Robert Sokolowski, Karl Rahner, and Thomas Aquinas.[17]) Indeed, she seems to have a special regard for the Patristics. Her appropriation of the tradition, she allows, may

---

17. Tanner, *Jesus, Humanity and the Trinity*, 5.

seem "eclectic."[18] Yet, she is not, she insists, an "eclectic compiler," confabulating a "syncretistic concoction;" instead, her use of the tradition means to "show the fruitfulness of a kind of internalizing of the history of Christ[ian] thought for its creative redeployment."[19] This strikes me as central to her use of tradition: the ease and creativity with which she puts the past to use in her work speaks not only to a deep familiarity with all these thinkers' works and worldviews, but also to a sense of their availability to her thinking. Her thinking presents itself not as emanating from her own mind as Romantic expression (let alone as Fordist mass-production), but rather as mobilizing the distilled insight of a great cloud of witnesses, at least 20 centuries old and counting. It means to effect a liberation of our imagination from the tyranny of the present. In this way, her work stands as a quite radical critique of contemporary academic theology, which, as she says,

> seems blinkered by current common sense and the specifics of a particular location; without availing oneself of a knowledge of what Christians have said and done elsewhere and at other times, what Christianity could be all about thins out and hardens, unresourceful and brittle. Knowledge of Christianity in other times and places is a way, then, of expanding the range of imaginative possibilities for theological construction.[20]

This has several effects. First of all, it means that in reading her work we sometimes have the impression of having cut into the main circuit cable of the tradition, with all the electrical charges that that entails. The possibilities casually mentioned and the range of voices deployed can seem bewildering and more than a little intimidating. Second, it can also seem hard to discern just where Tanner herself is in all this

18. Kathryn Tanner, *Christ the Key*, Current Issues in Theology (Cambridge: Cambridge University Press, 2010), viii.
19. Ibid., ix.
20. Tanner, *Jesus, Humanity and the Trinity*, xviii.

pandemonium. Does she endorse these various views? Which ones? The very vociferousness of the presentation can lead to uncertainty as to her own location amidst the cacophony. In sum, her work exhibits enormous creativity, but it regularly presents itself essentially as mere recovery or uncovering of earlier expressed views. Why?

Second Order Theology-logy

The second thing to note about Tanner's work is her understanding of what it is that academic theology does. Again, academic theology is not really directly a matter of first-order inquiry into God; it rather makes an indirect contribution, an aid to the development, cultivation, deployment, and use of Christian discourse and Christian practice in the first-order business of Christian living. It means to aid ordinary Christian discourse and practice, to enable people to see new possibilities for hearing and inhabiting the Word, and for showing it forth, not only with their lips but in their lives.

Tanner thus feels that there is not (nor need there be) any "norm of conformity" across the whole tradition, some simple canon against which all must be judged; rather, "knowledge of the diversity of Christian self-understandings highlights the ambiguities of theological achievements, their often limited relevance to particular times and places, and their tendencies towards obsolescence."[21] Theology is thereby a creative activity, the fashioning of new things, new languages and practices, always in contestation and conversation with the multiple cultural forms of which it is a part, some of them putatively Christian, others less so, still others not at all.

Still, is there no standard, no norm against which academic theological proposals can be judged better or worse? Initially, in *God and Creation in Christian Theology*, academic theology plays a

---

21. Tanner, *Jesus, Humanity and the Trinity*, xvii-xviii.

stable, "regulative" role in her work. But soon that view passes; academic theology is no longer simply an abstract, distantiated form of theory, but becomes one more bit of created dynamism, actively an innovative praxis. Still, on a deeper level, continuities remain between that first work and her later ones. All of them highlight the academic or specialist theologians' "secondariness" to the first-order Christian believer. She clearly thinks that academic theology, *qua* academic theology, functions more as a *resource* for theological talk and practice than as an immediate contributor to or creator of it. Yet, part of how it resources such talk is by creating new forms of talk that people can "try on," as it were, to see how fruitful they are. In this way, theology is a matter of *poiesis*, of making, and as such a contribution to the theological conversation of humanity. Nonetheless, it does not exhaustively constitute that conversation. Far from it; it always exists as secondary to the creative word and deed of the people of God, even in those moments where it stands in correction to some formulation or action of that people. To borrow from Barth, the theologian's task is to guide or inform the church's talk, so theology equally *follows*, *guides*, and *accompanies* the talk of the church.[22]

Still, this focus on theology's role cannot obscure the fact that that role is *not* the core energy of Christianity. In fact, academic theology makes sense only as a way to contest and disrupt the concepts of Christendom, in order to open up new possibilities within Christian communities. This account therefore rejects a vision of theology as a matter essentially of speculative rationality in favor of a vision that does not exclude speculation, but locates it within the larger frame of growing in the practical understanding of Christian truth as

22. Karl Barth, *Church Dogmatics, Volume 1.1, Sections 1-7: The Doctrine of the Word of God* (Study Edition), ed. G.W. Bromiley and T.F. Torrance (London: T&T Clark, 2010), 2.

learned by living. This insistence on the secondary-ness of academic theology is a distinctive note in Tanner's work.

Theological Convictions: God as Freely Present

There is a further, and I would say deeper, note apprehensible in Tanner's work. It appears throughout her work, but is perhaps most comprehensively and succinctly stated in *Jesus, Humanity and the Trinity*:

> God, who is already abundant fullness, freely wishes to replicate to every degree possible this fullness of life, light, and love outward in what is not God; this is possible in its fullness only to the extent the world is united by God to Godself over the course of the world's time. Met by human refusal to receive from God's hands in God's own time, by the creature's efforts to separate itself and others from the life-giving fount of divine beneficence, met by the human refusal to minister God's gift-giving to others, this history or process of God's giving to creatures becomes a struggle, a fight to bring the graced kingdom of God into an arena marked by sin and death.[23]

The world as we find it, with Christians and non-Christians, is a world already engaged in a life-or-death struggle with God—the world seeking death, its own death, and God seeking its life; and God will win. The struggle is graciously, mysteriously real, even if God has already triumphed. God has triumphed in two ways. First, in God's aseity, God has always been fully and satisfactorily complete and perfect—has always, as it were, already won in Godself; so, there has never been a "competition" at all. Second, because God cannot but win, because God is fully, supra-completely Lord, and thus Creator and Sustainer and (because God chooses to be) Redeemer, what God wants to be will be in God's good time (which the world mistakenly assumes is its time) what happens.

23. Tanner, *Jesus, Humanity and the Trinity*, 2.

It is this combination of the absolute transcendence of God, utterly above and apart from the created order, and the absolute commitment of God to the world, utterly *for* the created order, that for Tanner underlies her understanding of the nature of true human life, the nature of divine love, and the radical union of those two in the person and work of Jesus Christ. So understood, Christ is not found centrally at the stable (and perhaps sterile) center of the social order, but at the turbulent but fertile margins; and similarly, Christ must engage society's belief system not at its center, but from its edges, always destabilizing the cultural givens with his radical call to a faithfulness radically other than faithfulness that the social order itself solicits. If the people of God are to be disciples of Christ, they too must undertake always to be seeking the marginal location, or to hear the Word from outside their expectations, from altogether elsewhere than the satisfied center. Poor and rich alike, weak and strong alike, are to learn that these divisions are *wrong*, that they are not created nor natural but factitious, that we are larger, richer, more joyfully powerful and powerfully joyous than these distinctions let us be. The task of the church always is to try to bear the gracious generosity of God, as God seeks to inspire and instigate the living body into true life, while that body does its damnedest to refuse or evade such inspiration and instigation.

This theological conviction also has bearing on the vocation of the specialized theological task. On Tanner's account, God uses the particularity of the world in its changing relations and configurations to repeatedly, indeed perpetually, destabilize the community of believers and the theological claims that they make—to confront believers with God's always surprising action in the world. In this way theology is continually renewed and called to judgment, forgiveness, and the renewal of its true potential to speak a new word, a liberating word.

In all these ways, the life of theological creativity aims to imagine and then manifest ever-new routes of discipleship through the "theopoetics" of Christian community, simultaneously discursive and practical, word and deed. Furthermore, this is always done in the service of participating in God's gracious and utterly free love for the world that God has created, and is sustaining and redeeming, even in the here and now. It is this theological vision—this understanding of God, of the human response to God, and of the place of specialized theology in that response—that, I think, finally drives the work of Tanner forward.

Conclusion

Christians are supposed to be "well known, and yet unknown" (2 Cor. 6:9), and Kathryn Tanner may be a case study of that condition. She is certainly well known as a brilliant systematic theologian, but she is also seriously unknown for the radical challenge she presents to received understandings of what it is to "do" theology. In light of this, hers is a far richer, and more interesting, project than one that could adequately be designated by the phrase "systematic theology."

We live in an age that is radically egalitarian and meritocratic—that tells itself that all differences are, or should be, a matter of earned merit, and the merit is earned simply by hard work. There is little explicit space in our world for the idea of the seer, the genius, the inspired person who simply and right away appears to us, springing fully grown, it seems, out of nowhere. And yet at the same time, our egalitarian age hosts a continual cultural turbulence where we regularly throw up messiahs, celebrities, flashy actors. For all our avowed egalitarianism, we are avaricious for glory.

In this context, Tanner's material teaching and formal approach are equally deeply countercultural. After all, she grasps that the task of the theologian is not to call attention to her or his *own* views, but to call the church's attention to the views that the *churches* ought to hold. Again, this has less to do with some immediate doctrinal formulation than it does with 1) a perception of the vocation of the church as the site where God's judgment, forgiveness, and sanctification is most profoundly, explicitly, and self-consciously received, *and* 2) a perception of God as judging, forgiving, and redeeming out of an utterly free—and precisely because of that utter freedom, unsurpassably absolute and complete—love and care for creation. The difference between this vision of theology and our existing standard may appear superficial or trivial; but it is massive, and has substantial ramifications for our conception of what the theologian should do, and how present and visible in the work she or he needs to be—or perhaps *not* be—for it to be successful. It redefines what counts as "successful" theology altogether: away from productivity and towards a conception built first and foremost upon disciplines of listening and discernment.

I suppose that is what I—and perhaps others as well—have learned from Kathy all along. While there is certainly some solitude and individuality in this work, the aim should always be communication. Theology is not a work of solitary artistry, but a matter of sharing and sense-making with others in community. As such, it partakes in the same self- and other-forming dynamics as do all forms of human community; as Tanner herself once put it, "one perfects oneself in imitation of the self-diffusing goodness of God by perfecting others."[24] Thus, I should modify my earlier claim about her: while none of her students are easily recognized as stamped by her uniformly determinate impress, each one of us nonetheless stands as eloquently diverse testimony to Tanner's embodiment of that task.

24. Tanner, *Economy of Grace*, 27.

2

f (S) I/*s*: The Instance of Pattern, or Kathryn Tanner's Trinitarianism

Paul DeHart

Isskustvo kak priem (Art as Device)

– Shklovsky[1]

Kathryn Tanner's reflections on the Trinity have a self-effacing character. She operates within a rhetorical register that prizes quiet and careful exploration of her chosen themes rather than grandiose claims or noisy polemics. Although closely attuned to a variety of contemporary problems, she maintains throughout her doctrinally-oriented work a resolute and deeply appreciative conversation with formative pre-modern figures. This combination of stylistic restraint and fealty to classic traditions, a mark of her unique presence on

---

1. Viktor Shklovsky, "Art as Device," in *Theory of Prose,* trans. by Benjamin Sher (London: Dalkey Archive Press, 1990), 1-14.

the current scene, tends to lull the reader and to conceal the more innovative and even subversive elements of her Trinitarian thinking. In exploring those elements, I will continue to speak of her "Trinitarian thinking" or her "Trinitarianism" rather than of her theology of the Trinity because, as she reminds us, she has not yet attempted a full theological treatment of this subject.[2] In her doctrinally-focused constructive work (found in *Jesus, Humanity and the Trinity* and *Christ the Key*), that terminology is also apt because it signals the way her developing positions are shaped by a certain motif extracted from pre-modern discussions of the Trinity. Tanner makes use in a highly original way of the notion that the Trinity is to be understood as a pattern of differentiated but mutually interlocking relationships; this idea of divine constitution through a relational pattern is consciously drawn upon as a structuring element at several crucial points of her nascent systematic theology. Thus, her work is often "Trinitarian" even when she is not talking about the Trinity.

I will attempt in this essay to honor this creative aspect of Tanner's work, not only by trying to locate and describe it, but also by taking it seriously enough to raise some questions about it from a Catholic and Thomist view. The first section will identify the basic motif at work, showing how the Trinitarian pattern of divine constitution through mutual other-relation is connected with Tanner's reflections on creation and Christology. The three following sections will turn to the ways in which this pattern works itself out in different aspects of her soteriology, resulting in rather startling consequences from a more traditional view. The final section will indicate some potentially disquieting features of the resulting soteriology, tempered by a sense

---

2. Kathryn Tanner, *Jesus, Humanity and the Trinity: A Brief Systematic Theology* (Minneapolis: Fortress Press, 2001), xviii-xix. See also Kathryn Tanner, *Christ the Key*, Current Issues in Theology (Cambridge: Cambridge University Press, 2010).

of appreciation for the uniqueness and promise of her overall achievement.

Mutual Other-Relation as a Replicating Pattern

The structural role played by the dominant relational pattern in Tanner's thinking is most clearly displayed in the "brief systematic theology" which laid out the basics of her vision. Speaking of a reigning Trinitarian motif in her work might seem surprising at first, since she has repeatedly drawn attention to the centrality of Christology for her entire approach. The incarnation of God in Jesus Christ is indeed pivotal for her, and I can only admire the architectonic imaginativeness with which she ingeniously applies and unfolds a range of illuminating consequences for several theological topics, consistently beginning from and returning to this close attention to Christ. However, in context, this incarnational emphasis on the union of divine and human in Christ not only links her theological appraisal of Jesus to her broader position on God's relation to the created order, but it also refers both incarnation and creation to the Trinity itself as the founding instance.

Ever since her first book, *God and Creation*, Tanner's work has rightly been associated with an acute sensitivity to the conceptually unique causal complexity involved whenever divine activity is brought into relation with creaturely events.[3] Her often-invoked "non-competitive" account of relationality refers to her justified (and quite traditional) strictures against allowing divine causality to parallel created causality, as if they were different instances of shared agency. Less discussed has been the christological application of this principle. She regards God's providential agency in the world as providing a vital context for understanding the particular

3. Kathryn Tanner, *God and Creation in Christian Theology: Tyranny or Empowerment?* (Oxford: Blackwell, 1988).

incarnational appropriation of the humanity of Jesus, joining the company of other theologians like Athanasius, D.M. Baillie, Robert Sokolowski, and Karl Rahner.[4]

The incarnation is best understood as the unique and total creative impact of the divine reality upon the constitution of Jesus' humanity. At this one site within the created order, the creative result of the divine activity is one with, a kind of direct transcription of, that activity itself. Tanner puts it well: "[H]ere the effect of divine agency is not external to divinity."[5] Thus, Jesus can be the subject of actions that are describable, literally, as acts simultaneously of a human being and of God. Yet, this unprecedented divine-human alliance in Jesus would be a mere spectacle without inherent relation to others, were it not that Tanner stresses the implications for humanity *in toto* of this divine-human conjunction. She insists that in this union Jesus' human nature itself is already gifted; the very meaning of humanity has been constituted anew, and when other individuals take up in their attitudes and acts the human path opened by that man, they "already" come to share (though imperfectly) his intimacy with the creator.[6]

How is this intimacy to be understood? Here, Trinitarian discourse plays a central role for Tanner. The event whereby Jesus' humanity undergoes the total shaping force of divinity must be understood in terms of relations, a vocabulary evolved in early Christian centuries to describe the interplay of three persons within one God. His human career is a perfect reception and reflection of that divine sourcing called the Father, initiated and energized at every point by that dynamic impulsion called the Spirit, and hence becomes the created presence of that eternal image of the Father called the Son. So,

4. Tanner, *Jesus, Humanity and the Trinity*, xviii-xix. See also Tanner, *Christ the Key*.
5. Ibid., 21.
6. Ibid., 51.

the divinity of the humanity of Jesus Christ is solely a function of its entering into this relational pattern that defines God. Although this entry, because it necessarily unfolds within human temporality, can be described as a process coinciding with the human history of Jesus, Tanner strongly reminds readers that this is in no way a cooperative divine-human effort. Jesus' humanity is always the recipient of this unfathomable grace.[7] And what holds for him holds even more emphatically for humans who participate in the grace he incarnates. That grace must always be fundamentally "alien" to the rest of us; it arrives too late, having to compete with our own already sinfully constructed subjectivity rather than constituting us from the beginning as in Jesus' case. This, too, is inevitably a process, extending itself beyond the present created order. In keeping with Gregory of Nyssa's conception (developed from Phil. 3:13), she envisions an endless approximation toward perfect reception of divinity on our part, a stretching and straining toward the goal (*epektasis*).[8] Though our fate differs from Christ's, the basic description of salvation or union with God always involves, for Tanner, the entering of the human into the network of Trinitarian relations.[9]

Christ is "the key" for Tanner because in his life, death, and resurrection the paradigm of God's saving intent becomes visible, but that intent itself can only be understood according to a Trinitarian logic. Indeed, the way in which Tanner works out her entire theological project in terms of a single trajectory of divine initiative is one of its most impressive aspects. She writes, "God is doing [in the incarnation] what God is always doing, attempting to give all that God is to what is not God."[10] In Christ there appears to the

---

7. Ibid., 50.
8. Ibid., 43.
9. Ibid., 47.
10. Ibid., 15.

eye of faith the perfect self-bestowal of God upon creature; this gift then empowers all other receptions of God's gracious presence which shape the lives of other human beings, while it in turn is itself a natural extension of the divine life in itself, which consists in the perfect communion of God's own self-giving in the Trinity.[11] Thus the eternal pattern of divine self-giving enlarges itself through a single, majestic movement, penetrating into and transforming the created cosmos. This is the agency, the authority of the pattern (to use a German word, *die Instanz*), both in the world and in Tanner's theology.

The Algebra of Redemption

Tanner's skill is unmatched in weaving together these themes, but they do not represent innovations. They stand for the most part in the best tradition of pre-modern theology, both patristic and medieval. When she applies these themes in more particular ways to human salvation, the result is in several cases far more surprising. I will start in this section with theological anthropology, and then turn in the next sections to theological ethics and eschatology. Some soteriological instincts or conscious biases play a strong role in all three cases, and suggest a dominance of the Trinitarian pattern in a different register.

With regard to theological anthropology, the best place to begin exploring Tanner's unique conclusions is with the classic Protestant suspicion of Catholic notions of created grace. Tanner at several points claims her adherence to the Protestant view of grace, because she sees as an ever-present danger the temptation for Christians to assume "possession" of the divine gifts, as if they could be detached in some way from the continual and necessary presence of their

11. Ibid., 35-36.

divine giver.[12] To avoid this overriding danger, she proposes a drastic solution. Unlike other human acts, which must arise and take their character from the particular powers of human agency, the acts which mark redeemed human living are themselves properly divine, and always remain so. They cannot be traced back to a divine transformation of the immanent capacities of the human agent, as understood in the Catholic tradition. Tanner prefers to abandon the idea that part of the gift of grace itself lies in such an augmentation of human knowledge and will which could make the reception and exercise of this gift an act authentically attributable to the human being; perhaps the threat of becoming entangled in the rhetoric of "merit" is judged too great. Thus, she insists that there are no "created versions" of divine powers.[13]

Human reception of the gracious presence of God in union with Christ is not, according to Tanner, mediated by a supernatural but fully human "habitus." The Catholic tradition speaks of faith and charity as theological "virtues" precisely because they represent the elevation and disposition of already naturally given human capacities for knowing and willing. Although this elevation is not merited or effected in any way by the human being, once initiated by God it allows a new range and efficaciousness to human action, which is related to excellence in cognition, affection, and self-direction. In other words, in the Catholic tradition, the theological virtues which orient us to friendship and communion with God do not contradict but rather augment and extend the traces of human goodness which remain even in the unredeemed state in spite of sin, bearing witness to the peculiar gifts of human nature itself. Because human beings are made for communion with God, these peculiar gifts are dim reflections of the wisdom and love of the divine being itself. Indeed,

12. Ibid., 91; see also, Tanner, *Christ the Key*, 98.
13. Tanner, *Jesus, Humanity and the Trinity*, 50, 91; see also Tanner, *Christ the Key*, 82-83.

at this point Tanner takes a more radical step. Not satisfied with denying that faith and love are created analogues to divine powers, she denies that, in comparison with other qualities, faith and love have any inherently superior qualities as human dispositions. In other words, the propriety of faith and love as human counterparts to the reception of divine grace has nothing to do with any relative superiority they display simply as human dispositions, in "natural" terms. Only their purely "passive" or "open" quality toward the divine marks them; any pretensions they may have in strictly human terms are illusory.[14] But if faith and love defined in a Christian way thus inhabit a quite distinct moral universe, which is scarcely recognizable from within the horizon defined by our innate human capacities, then they are not virtues except in a purely equivocal sense.

The upshot of Tanner's approach can be put this way: what might be called the "psychological" character of faith and love—their particular range, modes, and interconnections within the human subject—become matters of relative indifference to her work. Indeed, her account of the human self is oddly truncated when discussing human capacities. For example, when she speaks of the results of the fall, she argues that human operations are totally corrupted, though human nature remains completely intact.[15] Only an anthropology which detached nature and act to an extraordinary degree could allow what looks like a paradox. On a more traditional reading, human acts arise from human powers, and the array of human powers with their inbuilt orientations and limitations is itself a function of the particular nature of the human being. Tanner suppresses any attention to "potencies" as inherent structures which mediate between a shared general nature and the particular activities of the individual, because only in this way can she sustain such a stark

14. Tanner, *Christ the Key*, 17, 93-95.
15. Ibid., 67.

separation of nature and operation. Since they are not tied to human nature via potencies, human operations are conceived in more abstract, functional terms.[16] Once again a Protestant worry is at work, since in another context she warns that the human orientation to God (that is, that which determines God as the proper end of any given human existence) should not be understood in terms of "internally self-generated" inclinations; the gratuity of grace would somehow be compromised if it linked up or worked with a set of already given capacities.[17]

Tanner's striking refusal to grant a theological role to human subjective components is signaled, finally, by her deep ambivalence about the rhetoric of "human nature." The counterpart of what might seem a positive insistence on the postlapsarian integrity of our nature is a resolute tendency to downgrade the traditional pretensions of that nature. For example, she implies that there must be some connection between the peculiarities of human nature and the fact that God, in becoming incarnate, assumed a human being;[18] but in those passages where a reader might look for some clue as to the "aptness" of human nature for this dignity, the reader looks in vain.[19] Only human nature, as fallen, required this saving condescension; but could we equally well conceive of the divine assumption of, say, a tree or a lobster? Indeed, when expounding on human nature, Tanner prefers to stress its limitations, its finitude, its lack of fitness to express the divine Word. Our nature seems intimately connected to what is wrong with us. Her unwillingness to discuss a positive role for natural human endowments within the salvific economy, and its link to the incarnation, is also exemplified in her description of redemptive social

16. Ibid., 108.
17. Ibid., 125.
18. Tanner, *Jesus, Humanity and the Trinity*, 111.
19. For example, see ibid., 48–49.

existence as an "unnatural community," comparable to the "naturally disparate" union of divine and human in Jesus![20]

The classically Protestant sensibility at work here is clear. Going against the grain of Aquinas's notion of grace as perfecting nature, Tanner prefers a reading in which grace corrects nature without building upon it.[21] In the final analysis, a deeper motif may also be at work. The Trinitarian persons in their mutual distinction are described by the pattern of relations in which they originate or co-originate each other. In the previous section, I explored how the humanity of Christ is distinguished by its subsumption within this relational pattern; human redemption, consequently, can equally be rendered as our being defined by these relations. In Tanner's hands, this fairly standard theological claim receives a more creative and radical reading. In the Trinity, in Jesus Christ, and in redeemed humanity, the same mechanism is at work: the constitution of persons through mutual relation. This relational pattern takes on a kind of ontological priority; little attention need be directed to individual contribution to or agency within those relationships, or indeed to the internal structures or capacities which enable such relations. This move is allied with Tanner's reading of the "stretching" image used by Gregory of Nyssa, and she boldly reimagines it to include not just a stretching forward, but also a stretching wider, such that the increasing capacity to receive God on the part of the human is the direct result of the increased "flow" of divine self-giving.[22] Hence, there is no need to analyze the graced augmentations of particular human powers, since the divine giving is all.

What role is played in the ongoing redemptive process by human intelligence and freedom in their created integrity? Tanner finds little

20. Tanner, *Christ the Key*, 242.
21. Ibid., 61–62.
22. Tanner, *Jesus, Humanity and the Trinity*, 43.

to say other than to read both in terms of radical receptivity. The ancient understanding of both the intellect as the capacity to formally "become" anything knowable and human freedom as a detachment from pre-programmed patterns of behavior become simply two more ways for Tanner to stress human beings as radically malleable. Hence her relative lack of interest in human nature, which is by definition the realm of the relatively "fixed." The end result is that the anthropological side of Tanner's soteriology has an "algebraic" feel, with the human being playing the role of an "x" whose redeemed status is predominantly rendered as "slotted" into the triune relational network. In algebra, the variable in itself is nothing; its value is only defined by the operational relations specified for it. Similarly, in Tanner's account the human individual remains rather intentionally empty; all initiative is granted to the Trinitarian relationships which, in conjunction with Christ, determine that individual anew, and to all appearances in a manner radically tangential to any discernibly given human structure (nature, potencies, virtues). The new human only "appears" at the prompting or request (the instance) of the Trinitarian pattern. As we will see in the next two sections, such a picture underlies the ethical and eschatological dimensions of her soteriology as well.

From the Social Trinity to a Trinitarian Economics

The same priority of relationships over things related plays itself out in a different way in Tanner's forays into theological ethics. This ethics emerges as a byproduct of Tanner's urgent critique of social Trinitarianism, or the theological tradition in which the doctrine of the Trinity is proffered as a divinely authorized model for human social relations. Trinitarian characteristics such as mutual conditioning of identity, utter receptiveness or openness to others, radical equality, individual dispossession in favor of communal sharing of goods, and so on are made programmatic for a Christian critique and reformulation of social arrangements; the ecclesial community in an idealized mode is sometimes held to represent in imperfect and local form this perfected realm of human relations which will hold universally in the eschatological Kingdom. Tanner has argued repeatedly that this approach misunderstands or ignores key elements of classical Trinitarian teaching, and it is unable to provide any kind of effective social prescription because the analogy between finite fallen human beings and the infinite divine "persons" is so terribly remote. The recommendations for the common life and flourishing of humanity which are derived from social Trinitarianism, she argues, end up too vague to have much political purchase.[23] Aside from the doctrinal and other details of her critique, for Tanner social Trinitarianism fails to issue in a set of strong ethical commitments that can challenge current social ills from the standpoint of an alternative communal vision. She is acutely aware of the connection between the understanding of doctrines and the shape of actual Christian living, just as she is wary of the manner in which that connection is sometimes (as in social Trinitarianism) rendered in ways that are too direct, unnuanced, and simplistic. In other words, her critique of the social Trinity is not in the interest of purifying Christian doctrine of its political or ethical implications, but rather in rendering those implications more effective.

So the structure of human action should reflect our relation to God,[24] but instead of a direct "modelling" of human relations on Trinitarian ones, Tanner insists that the human analogue must be located with reference to the general pattern of divine self-giving which takes on different forms in God's being, in Christ's being, and in the being of the redeemed. Social Trinitarianism tries to short-

23. Ibid., 77–83; see also Tanner, *Christ the Key*, 233–43.
24. Tanner, *Jesus, Humanity and the Trinity*, 79.

circuit this necessary attention to the different levels of instantiation of the divine giving relations, ignoring the appropriate mode of application to the fallen human condition.[25] However, in pushing for this new method of linking the redemptive relation to God with theological ethics, she arguably remains, in a curious way, under the hidden sway of the social Trinitarianism she opposes. In seeking to recover the social relevance of Trinitarian doctrine without joining the "social Trinitarians," she nonetheless keeps one foot in their camp. In outlining her vision of ethical transformation, she attends almost exclusively to the level of social or communal relations rather than persons.

The result is an intriguing and original set of theological "principles of sociability or relationality."[26] What is notably absent from her considerations is an account of what redemptive transformation looks like for individuals, as opposed to groups. Her approach here stands, presumably deliberately, at the opposite extreme from the individualism which has lamentably dominated so many traditionalist understandings of salvation. Tanner can hardly be faulted for making clear in this way that every Christian account of redemption must be articulable as a politics. Nonetheless, this emphasis on the communal dimension of sanctification follows naturally from the characteristic bias of her redemptive vision which has already been noted in her anthropology. In her description of the way the new life of grace changes us, the priority rests exclusively within the pattern of relationships; communal renewal is not a function of new gracious endowments on the level of particular persons, but rather persons are assumed to be reshaped in and through the renewed force of community.

Focusing on the systemic character of redemption mirrors Tanner's

25. Ibid., 81–82.
26. Ibid., 83ff.

talk about sin: human entanglement in a "body" of exploitive and corrosive structures corresponds to what is meant classically by "original sin." Yet, there is hardly any discussion of its traditional counterpart, "actual sin," the sin which is the willing, daily contribution, in a million large or small ways, of individuals (in fact, of all of us) to the system of death. Thus, our own souls further deform themselves. Though Tanner knows that our sinful persons "are constituted" as sinful,[27] she chooses to leave the agency here undifferentiated, because our own individual complicity in our corruption seems a marginal concern. How can we describe this tendency? If we imagine the ethical problematic as always involving a spectrum of agency that ranges from the individual to the group, then "politics" might be the mediating term between the extremes, since it seeks to integrate the choice of and struggle for just social arrangements with the virtues demanded of the individuals who must "operate" those negotiations and arrangements. Toward one end of the spectrum, where the individual is the exclusive focus, we speak more of "morality" and of "virtue"; toward the other end, where prime agency rests with the "block" behavior of groups and the concentration, dispersal, and circuits of material and symbolic capital, we might speak of "economy." When Tanner speaks of "a debt economy in conflict with God's own economy of grace"[28] she reveals the leitmotif of her entire ethics of redemption. The new humans are not turned and transformed from within; they are summoned into being by "relations of production" of which Marx knew nothing, an economy of grace that replicates the triune self-giving: the instance of pattern.

27. Ibid., 57.
28. Ibid., 88.

Enjoyment without Desire

A final example of Tanner's highly innovative appropriation of traditional dogma is provided by her eschatology. Her recommendation is that the new conditions of creaturely existence marking the advent of God's reign are not to be thought of as a crude interruption of the temporal course of the natural order, a miraculous suspension of the world's physical decay so that a new, better time-series can be tacked-on, as it were, picking up where the old one left off. Cosmic senescence is no more a threat to eschatology than that of individual human beings; in either case, it is the entire temporal career of humans and their common world which will be taken up and transfigured. The mere passage of worldly time in itself brings the Kingdom not a bit closer; each moment of the life of creation is equally close to the new creation because each moment will be redeemed.[29] Tanner's detailed reflections on this point are highly suggestive, though there is one aspect of this eschatology that is sharply stamped by the idiosyncratic anthropology which I have tried to identify, and that extrapolates it into eternity. Posing some classic eschatological questions might render this more visible. How should we envision the elevated state of communion with God that is the human face of the new creation? In particular, in what way can that communion be understood as the perfection or consummation of the human being?

In the Western tradition, a fairly sharp distinction is drawn between the status of redeemed humans in this life (*in via*) and their state in heaven (*in patria*). The difference between the light of grace experienced now and the light of glory that is expected demands an entirely distinct category of anthropological description: the beatific vision. The first hint of Tanner's unique approach in this

29. Ibid., 97–124.

area is her reluctance to employ this category. A dominant structural element in her theology is the suggestion that God's triune being, the incarnation in Jesus, and the entry of grace into the human sphere are linked moments in a single arc. In each case God intends to bestow the divine being-Jesus' reception of God approximates as closely as possible the perfect self-giving of Father to Son, and the redeemed approximate that gift in even less perfect ways than Jesus. As a result, Tanner construes human redemption as a sort of deficient version of the hypostatic union; as discussed above, our human nature, by sharing in the humanity of Jesus, assumes the same structural position with regard to the triune relations that constitutes Jesus' own personhood. This understanding of redemption, quite unexpectedly, allows both our existence in grace now as well as our eschatological attainment of communion with God in the future to be described in exactly the same terms. Our existence in the new creation will be a heightened participation in the triune relational pattern, closer to that of Jesus himself; "glory" is just more "grace," more intense but structurally identical.

In a way this follows from her prior anthropological moves. Tanner, as I have argued, regularly directs attention away from the anthropological dimension of redemption, that is, the way in which grace meets up with and alters already given structures of human personhood. Even in the case of Jesus, just as humanity in general has no "aptness" for being the vehicle of incarnation, so too Jesus himself is pure receptivity, an empty vessel shaped totally by the bestowal of the eternal Word. Because this union of God and humanity is "unnatural," in Tanner's view the language of grace as a "supernatural" gift enhancing our natural powers is not strong enough. Grace is always something "alien" to the redeemed.[30] The

---

30. Ibid., 51; see also Tanner, *Christ the Key*, 12.

seriousness with which she intends this claim is shown by the way she resolves the longstanding dispute about how best to affirm the intrinsic human fittingness of grace while safeguarding its sheer gratuity. She canvasses the various positions in this argument only to conclude that it is insoluble on traditional terms; the only way to escape the dilemma is to deny that human beings have a natural desire for union with God.[31]

More precisely, her bold move at this point is to claim that any desire we have for God is not "internally self-generated," but is itself a product of the proximate offer of the Holy Spirit which constitutes humanity from its origin.[32] Aside from the Barthian overtones of this decision, all of this affects Tanner's picture of human fulfillment in the eschaton. The very notion of a desire that is not somehow rooted in human appetition as human has something paradoxical about it. Moreover, as something like a "new" desire created *ex nihilo*, it seems to lack a specifiable relation to the natural range of human affections. As Tanner notes, "Humans, it is true, are determined to God.... But that is just *not* to be determined in any particular direction as other things are, since God is the absolute God and not a limited one."[33] The more traditional approach on this issue is to see an inherent connection and orientation between our desires for finite goods and our desire for God; our affective orientation to the divine is accomplished by ordering our many finite acts of will in such a way that they do not obstruct but rather serve the infinite quest as so many partial incarnations of it. By contrast, Tanner's language here is more disjunctive; our determination to God must be conceived as alternative to limited determinations to our fellow creatures.

As already noted, Tanner creatively reconfigures human intellect

---

31. Tanner, *Christ the Key*, 106-39.
32. Ibid., 125.
33. Ibid., 49.

and will as our lack of firm definition, our constitutive openness to the "alien," our ability to be "stretched" without limit in order to take in God's self-gift. To secure the radicality of grace as she understands it, Tanner is willing to pay a high price: abandoning the attempt to discern how the myriad finite acts of grasping truth and loving things which form the texture of human life are all, in spite of their confusion and corruption, aligned toward the one goal which is God, like filings in a magnetic field. The divine gift meets in us no already existing desire, since, she argues, none is necessary: it is not attractive to us because of the sort of desiring creatures we are, but rather "in and of itself," as "superior" and "source of our own good."[34] The holiness which makes us fit to dwell with God is not the completion of our natural but frustrated tendency. It is, she insists, foreign to us, even when we are translated beyond the current created realm. It is never "within" us,[35] it "adheres" to us "externally."[36] Since Christ's righteousness is ours in the sense that it stands in place of ours, salvation at his hands is better described as our cooptation than our completion.[37]

It is surely more in accord with the Western tradition to see, with a thinker like Maurice Blondel, all the dispersed acts and partial yearnings that make us who we are as so many expressions of a foundational desire for God that defines the space of the human within the natural cosmos, just as all our fragmentary intellectual achievements of finite truth inherently grasp creatures as genuine signs of the Creator. In this sense, a final loving vision of God "face to face" is not only an incomprehensible gift, but it is also the proper reward of humanity's persistent faithfulness to its own truest desire. By contrast, for Tanner our intellect and will are precisely our

34. Ibid., 127.
35. Ibid., 90.
36. Ibid., 65.
37. Ibid., 97.

lack of definition, and our final enjoyment of God can be called a consummation of our very humanity only in the most oblique way. In keeping with her intuition that grace finds no proper point of insertion within our given nature, Tanner's descriptions of our final reconciliation with God render it more as a structural arrangement, a perfected juxtaposition "cleanly separating" God's giving from the immanent workings of its human receptor.[38] God's offer of communion meets in us no merely human desire for it; it rather creates a desire that, in its way, is therefore just as little "ours" as the gift itself is. Our final enjoyment of God is the triumphant outworking of an inexorable pattern of divine giving, not a fullness whose shape matches the mysterious lack at the heart of human freedom; divine giving is not there because we want it, it is instead wanted because it is there.

L'Automatisme de Répétition and the Effacement of Interiority

Following the path of Tanner's theory of salvation through three different theological spheres (anthropology, ethics, eschatology) has brought us to the same result. The individual human person as present in Tanner's work presents a strangely "hollowed out" appearance. There is a resolute lack of interest in what we might call "interiority": the deep structures and dynamics of selfhood in their own right, logically distinct from (even if always imbricated with) the "economy" of bodied and cultural transactions. The role played in the story of redemption by the internal topography of the subject is ignored in what seems a systematic, not an incidental, way. Instead, her various descriptions of the salvific process are almost always rooted in relational patterns, grounded ultimately in christological

---

38. Ibid., 96.

and Trinitarian dogma. Can any clues to the possible reasons for this lack be drawn from Tanner's work more broadly?

A number of possibilities tentatively come to light. Theologically, there is the standard Barthian allergy to granting systematic status in the theology of divine acts to any anthropological "point of connection." In regard to non-theological resources, the sensitivity to cultural anthropology which springs from her Yale formation also probably plays a role, perhaps involving a suspicion against any appeal to supposedly universal subjective structures unmediated by particular communal linguistic formations. Ethically, it is possible to wonder whether there is a wariness, drawn from feminist and queer theory, of the rhetoric of the "normal" and "natural," which often operates oppressively to police human diversity. Methodologically, finally, there is a tendency defining Tanner's work since *God and Creation* (and especially connected with George Lindbeck), namely, tackling theological problems primarily by discerning quasi-grammatical "rules" supposedly embedded within faithful Christian discourse. Hence some issues like the nature of divine acts in the created order, or the role of human beings in the redemptive process, present conundrums which are not susceptible to a solution through translation into speculative or introspective languages, but which the theologian should formally situate within the space defined by protocol assertions deeply encoded within the Christian tradition.

More importantly, how should we respond to this tendency? I hope that any answer I provide in closing will be taken not as a final verdict on the issue, but as a sort of query to Tanner's ongoing project that registers qualms coming from my own personal theological position. At this stage, my query is not so much an attempt at refutation as a protest springing from a different theological sensibility. I hope, too, that my hesitations on this point will be read against the background of my great admiration for her work overall. That work is quite invaluable for theology today due to its unique combination of gifts: logically clear-headed argumentation, commanding grasp of the depth and possibilities of traditional Christian thought, and a delicate but transformative incorporation of contemporary insights springing from ethics and from gender theory. I am deeply honored to have been asked to engage her work in a public way; if I do so critically, I hope I am in turn honoring Tanner, one of my teachers, by attempting the sort of hard thinking she so marvelously modelled for me and tried to instill in me. In the end, what I have sought to uncover and name in this essay is only one aspect of her work; it remains to be seen how her work will further unfold, and my portrayal may be too extreme, springing from a one-sided reading. For now, I can at least attempt to signal the difficulties her work raises for me.[39]

Some of these difficulties spring from arguments or assumptions specific to only one or another of the theological topics touched on above. On the anthropological side, Tanner attempts to render human intellect and volition in negative terms, as a kind of omnideterminability marking human nature as uniquely lacking in essential inner-worldly definition for its cognitive modes and affective drives. Closely related to this, Tanner disallows any normative status to human being in purely creaturely terms; neither being human nor being redeemed have a properly natural dimension on her understanding. Eschewing a theory of the supernatural, this denatured anthropology leaves the human as such shuttling between

---

39. Apart from the theme discussed here, there are other critical remarks that could be elaborated in another context in response to aspects of her treatment of traditional themes. Her heavy investment in the Greek Fathers sometimes obscures how very selective her readings are, resulting especially in a convenient suppression of their sharp mind/body dualism. Her rooting of Trinitarian thought in a reading of the gospel narratives is salutary, but incorrectly underplays the role of the monotheistic problem. Her account of the nature/grace disputes questionably frames them in just such a way as to make them appear futile, thus helping make her own rejection of the terms of the debate seem inevitable.

"unnatural" states *and* ungraspable outside the sphere of revelation. For all the oppressive possibilities which lie within attempts to determine the normatively human, the refusal to discern the natural contours of human belonging can have its sinister side as well. With regard to her structural and communal bias in ethics, it can be argued that reflection on the full range of human goodness cannot succeed where the focus on ideal interpersonal and collective relations occludes attention to the virtuous habituating of inherent capacities needed for individuals to actualize such relations. As for eschatology, Tanner's unwillingness to connect our consummation in God solidly to a dynamic subjective orientation inherent to the creature as such ends up with a sadly attenuated theology of human desire, prohibiting a more robust development of the affective and sensual psychology of spiritual life.

In all these cases, the impoverished stock of concepts with which Tanner attempts to analyze human nature leaves her theological account of individual personhood distressingly shapeless. But this is a subsidiary set of concerns. They are preliminary contributors to what seems to me the larger issue, namely, the way in which Tanner's theological turn away from what I am calling "interiority" leads to an inability to specify in a convincing way how grace, or holiness, or God, are really and truly "in" me, a transformative ingredient to my very selfhood. Her scheme, it seems to me, cannot finally stave off the accusation that God's saving arrangement is ultimately arbitrary in human terms. From my own Catholic perspective, her Protestant fear of even the slightest claim to "ownership" of Christ's merit, intensified by certain Barthian reflexes, results in a sort of "scorched earth" policy to the created, properly human dimension of grace. Is this necessary? She has not sufficiently shown that any reference to salvation as truly befitting and perfecting the human as such harbors a covert and illicit claim on the divine favor. Besides, it seems a desperate measure that, in spite of her best efforts, threatens her scheme with a massive extrinsicism and formalism of grace, the very thing she is seeking to avoid.

On the note of formalism, let us return to the Yale heritage of a "regulative" approach to doctrine. Referring to her master image of the mysteries of faith as a series of events of God's self-bestowal, repeated in different modalities but always occurring along a single line of divine intention grounded in God's triune eternity, Tanner offers a brilliant and revealing commentary on her own method of elucidating doctrine.

> Situated within this theological structure of many different parallel or analogous relations of gift-giving unity, human life ... gains a greater intelligibility, as each aspect becomes a kind of commentary on the others. Intelligibility here is like that of myth according to Claude Lévi-Strauss, where conundrums are naturalized, rather than resolved, by repeating them across a variety of domains. Or it is like the intelligibility provided by a Freudian recounting of the compulsive repetition of traumatic events in a person's life . . . meaning is enhanced as a similar structure variously permutated becomes visible.[40]

So then: repetition rather than resolution? In some situations perhaps, but where the intelligibility of the faith is concerned I think more hard hermeneutical work is required to squeeze some human *meaning* from the incarnational and Trinitarian formulae. The attempt to illuminate our condition can only get so far with purely structural juxtapositions. "Colorless green ideas sleep furiously." Chomsky's famous sentence provides an unforgettable reminder that flawless syntactical arrangements can still coincide with semantic gibberish.[41] Tanner's bet that Trinitarian theory and the nature of human redemption in Christ can and should cast a reciprocal light on one

---

40. Tanner, *Jesus, Humanity and the Trinity*, 38.
41. Noam Chomsky, *Syntactic Structures* (The Hague: Mouton, 1957), 15.

another is a good one. But I do not see how this will happen without a much richer theology of selfhood than she has developed so far; the danger is that fuller accounts of the Trinity and of redemption will be hampered by an approach that is too formalistic and insufficiently humanistic. Classically, of course, the concept of the human being as *imago Dei* helped to mediate between the austerities of Trinitarian grammar and the richness of human self-experience. Yet, the entire approach outlined in the sections above signals a shift in the use of "image" talk: the second person of the Trinity as eternal image of the Father ends up, via the paradigmatic role of the hypostatic union, usurping human nature's positive imaging role as accessible in the rest of us. Only our inherent plasticity is left, a kind of negative image identical with our ability to be stamped by the primary image that is Christ.[42] This way of theorizing the image does indeed "turn attention initially away from the human altogether."[43] I am concerned that adequate theologizing of the human image never recovers from this "initial" neglect. The resulting danger is of a severe formalism in depicting the human dimension of redemption.

A tiny aside Tanner tucks away in a footnote on the Trinity might offer a little parable on this humane deficit. Searching for analogies to the eternal generation of the Son, she offers a model of utterance used by Gregory of Nyssa and John Damascene.[44] But the imagery is purely concerned with the physical mechanics of vocalization: the Spirit is the "breath" that "sustains and empowers the Word" as it leaves the Father's mouth. In a note, Tanner quietly affirms that this failure to attend to the classic Trinitarian model of mental process, where the Son as Word is the intelligible emanation, the perfect "concept" or "judgment" issuing from God's self-knowledge, is no

42. Tanner, *Christ the Key*, 4.
43. Ibid., 1.
44. Ibid., 177–78.

accident: "This analogy of an exterior word stands in contrast to an Augustinian focus on an interior word." We could hardly have failed to take the hint, for we cannot be surprised at this point that Tanner would resist an analogy that thematizes human psychology. The worry I am seeking to express here is that such decisions signal a characteristic void in her theology. The function of the Augustinian analogy was never to map human psychodynamics directly onto the divine being. Rather, its vital role is to invite prayer into the intelligibility of the Trinitarian mystery, pivoting on the splendid natural privileges we exercise daily, even though sinfully, in living our humanity. Our intellective grasp and our desiring are genuine natural perfections, and truly present in God their prime instance, though in a way opening out our notions of them toward their infinite depth. Only granting this positive sense to the human image allows the further precious increment of light upon the divine mystery which the psychological analogy provides: the eternal utterance of the Word is no mechanism but rather the production of an unlimited meaning. The Son doesn't just "come from" or "exit" the Father but *expresses* the Divine: God is her own symbol, her own icon. From the analogy of our mind the eternally uttered Word takes on properly living, organic, even intelligent and creative associations, beyond the mere mechanics of audible production; it is art beyond device.

The restriction of Trinitarian analogy to sub-human models is of a piece with the larger issue here, namely, applying the Trinitarian relational pattern to the understanding of redemption in a way that remains "external" to redeemed subjectivity. The rather "algorithmic" feel of such an application could tempt the adventurous to discover in the mathematical symbolism of my title a sort of formal grammar of the Trinity: (*f*)ather, (S)on, (*s*)pirit, perhaps? Tantalizing as that might be,[45] that is neither the origin of the formula, nor its relevance to my point. I only reference Tanner's evasion of a mental analogy for the Word as an indirect reflection in her God-talk of the formalist risk involved in the reduction of human interiority to pattern, a reduction that has more serious consequences in its enfeeblement of theology's attempt to speculatively imagine union with God as a truly *human* good. The title of this essay has merely taken a cue from Tanner's own reference to Lévi-Strauss and Freud, following the inevitable associational trajectory of structuralism and psychoanalysis to playfully evoke a bit of Lacanian psychological mathematics. Tanner's initial stroke of insight was structurally to align the theological loci of "Jesus, humanity, and the Trinity" by making them replications of a single motif: divine self-donation to the other. Yet, this fertile decision can become simply the reverse side of an anti-humanist evacuation of selfhood as such. According to the Lacanian formula, the delusory integrity of the human Subject is a function of signifying processes more or less opaque to it, whereby the unconscious (*le Inconscient*) endlessly works to master the signified meaning forever "barred" from direct access.[46] Here, too, subject is reduced to pattern, slipping along the unending chain of signifiers. The Christian can welcome the insight that we are constitutively "unfinished," but will do well to stipulate that this lack represents the unlimitedness of a concrete desire for the infinite it images, not the deceptive quest to cover over an unfillable void of meaning. I am not sure that Tanner's theology can so readily support this affirmation of the positive dignity of humanity as divine image. The vacated humanity that appears, in my view, at the heart of her systematic account lacks the sort of ontological solidity that would

---

45. This is in the spirit of Tanner's own coding; ibid., 195.

46. Jacques Lacan, "L'instance de la letter dans l'inconscient ou la raison depuis Freud," in *Écrits* (Paris: Editions du Seuil, 1966), 493-528. The formula is found on page 515.

make it something other than a mere by-product of putatively more fundamental impersonal transactions.

Repetition in itself is never resolution; it could simply be pathology. Neither the cyclic reassembling of mythemes nor the forced iteration of psychic gestures signifies anything in itself but a problem. If such patterns give way to light it is only as they are hooked back into the deeper region of undeformed personhood from which they have been temporarily expelled. Their significance is derivative of larger reservoirs of human meaning; only when reintegrated, through the irreplaceably human labor of interpretation, do the mechanics of blind reproduction cease. It is this "deeper region" of selfhood that appears insufficiently explored (at least up to this point) by Tanner; her rendering of soteriology as a formal reproduction of her Trinitarian and christological relational schemes looks sterile if intended as a substitute. Here the "instance" of the pattern, understood as its summoning persons into being as a result of its logical and ontological priority (the mirror image of the posteriority and poverty of individual selves in Tanner's scheme), passes into Lacan's notion of a compulsory repetition, the relentless insistence (*l'instance*) of a pattern that tyrannizes over the subject. For all its undeniable wealth of insight, barely sketched in our discussion, Tanner's Trinitarian soteriology leaves a disturbing blank space where theological attention directs us to the intricacies of human selfhood. Her automatism, which claims to be a substitute for that resolution, seems more a symptom. Of what? I am compelled to repeat: Kathryn Tanner's reflections on the Trinity have a self-effacing character.

PART II

The Fullness of God's Gift-Giving

3

"Always and Everywhere:" Divine Presence and the Incarnation

Ian A. McFarland

In her first two books, *God and Creation in Christian Theology* and *The Politics of God*, Kathryn Tanner focused on the doctrine of creation. In *Jesus, Humanity and the Trinity* and *Christ the Key*, her attention turned to Christology, though she certainly did not leave the doctrine of creation behind. Many of the key dogmatic moves in *Economy of Grace*—published halfway between her two more christologically focused books—are rooted in the non-competitive model of God's relationship to creatures initially developed in *God and Creation*. For that matter, so is the Chalcedonian framework that shapes her Christology: it is just because God, as Creator, is the sole condition of—and thus never a possible threat to—created being and action that God's taking flesh in Jesus need not entail any diminishment of his humanity. On these grounds, Tanner has characterized the incarnation as "the paradigm in a remarkably extreme form of what the Christian doctrine of creation is saying about the immediacy of God's relation to the world" as Creator.[1]

For Tanner, Chalcedonian Christology reflects a fundamental consistency between the doctrines of incarnation and creation, such that God's taking flesh in Jesus does not entail any fundamental shift in or disruption of God's way of relating to creatures generally. At the same time, the incarnation does represent a new (and, from a creaturely perspective, unforeseeable) development in the divine economy that transforms the way in which creatures experience God. Although Tanner does not put it in these terms, one way to express this novelty is as follows: if creatures are by definition always *present to God*, who is the direct and immediate cause of their existence, only in taking flesh does God, too, become *present to creatures* by living among them *as* a creature.

At first blush, this claim may seem exaggerated. The Old Testament contains no shortage of references to God's presence, not least in the promise, "I will be with you," addressed to Jacob (Gen. 26:3; 31:3), Moses (Exod. 3:12; 4:12, 15), Joshua (Josh. 1:5; 3:7), Gideon (Judg. 6:16), Solomon (1 Kgs. 11:38), and the whole people of Israel (Isa. 43:2). And yet the very terms in which this assurance is given imply that the presence that is promised must be accepted in faith rather than seen with eyes (Exod. 33:20). For while in the Old Testament God appears through such tangible forms as a burning bush, a cloudy pillar, "a blazing fire, and darkness, and gloom, and a tempest, and the sound of a trumpet" (Heb. 12:18-19), God is not to be identified with any of those things (Deut. 4:12, 15; cf. 1 Kgs. 9:11-12). Similarly, though God sets the divine name in Jerusalem and the temple (2 Kgs. 21:7; cf. 2 Chron. 6:6; 7:16), God's own dwelling remains in heaven (1Kgs. 8:39, 43, 49). By contrast, in Jesus

---

1. Kathryn Tanner, "Is God in Charge?," in *Essentials of Christian Theology*, ed. William C. Placher (Louisville: Westminster John Knox, 2010), 122.

God dwells among us as one who may be both seen and touched, the first fruits of a divine presence to (as well as in) creation that finds its climax in the vision of Revelation:

> See, the home of God is among mortals. He will dwell with them; they will be his peoples, and God himself will be with them; He will wipe every tear from their eyes. Death will be no more; mourning and crying and pain will be no more, for the first things have passed away (Rev. 21:3-4).

Importantly, this consummation of the Christian hope does not entail any blurring of the distinction between God and the world. Even in the vision of Revelation, God alone is Creator. We remain creatures. Indeed, this is arguably the heart of the good news: that it is precisely *in* our creatureliness, our finitude, our absolute and ineradicable difference from God that we are named children of God and called to life with God. And yet it is not immediately clear how God's taking flesh in Jesus brings us to that eschatological goal. Even if it is conceded that "all the fullness of God was pleased to dwell" in Jesus (Col. 1:19), he remains just one human being among many and so does not seem able to mediate God's presence to all people, let alone to the whole creation in a way that would fulfill the promise of universal communion with God. For this reason, a number of contemporary theologians have argued that Christians should reject the Chalcedonian interpretation of the incarnation as a unique and unforeseeable modification of God's manner of relating to creatures in favor of the idea that incarnation describes God's normal way of being in the world.[2] When incarnation is viewed in this way as repeatable or continuous, the spatio-temporal limitations of Jesus

---

2. See, for example, Catherine Keller, *On the Mystery: Discerning Divinity in Process* (Minneapolis: Fortress Press, 2008); Paul F. Knitter, *No Other Name? A Critical Survey of Christian Attitudes toward the World Religions* (Maryknoll, NY: Orbis Books, 1985); and Sallie McFague, *The Body of God: An Ecological Theology* (Minneapolis: Fortress Press, 1993).

constitute no barrier to God's universal presence to creatures, since God's presence in Jesus is not qualitatively different from the way in which God is present elsewhere in creation.

Although these alternatives may at first glance seem to do a better job than Tanner's Chalcedonian approach of securing God's saving presence to the whole of creation, understanding incarnation as a normative or generalizable mode of divine relating to creatures actually undermines the promise of salvation. For in such theologies either the distinction between God and creatures is blurred, so that God is insufficiently different from the world to be able to effect its salvation (since God's agency and destiny are no longer clearly separable from that of the creatures that need saving); or God's relation to creation falls short of full personal presence (so that we are back with the Old Testament model of God speaking *through* creatures but not *as* a creature).[3] In what follows, I will argue for the uniqueness of the incarnation by analyzing a text from the seventh-century theologian Maximus the Confessor that at first glance may seem to support the very opposite position: "For the Word of God, who is God, wishes always and everywhere to effect the mystery of his embodiment."[4]

The Point of the Incarnation: God Made Visible

In order to make this argument, it is first necessary to be clear about what the Chalcedonian understanding of incarnation that informs Maximus's as well as Tanner's thinking both does and does not teach. First of all (and as already noted), from a Chalcedonian perspective the incarnation does not entail any attenuation of divine

3. Tanner makes a similar point regarding Hegelian-influenced soteriologies (e.g., that of Jürgen Moltmann) that also seek to integrate God's life with the history of creation. See Tanner, *Jesus, Humanity and the Trinity* (Minneapolis: Fortress Press, 2001), 10-11.

4. *Bouletai gar aei kai en pasin ho tou Theou Logos kai Theos tês autou ensômatôseôs energeisthai to mystêrion.* Maximus the Confessor, *Ambiguum* 7 (PG 91:1084c-d).

transcendence, as though God needed to surrender any features of divinity as the price of drawing closer to the world. Indeed, already in the Old Testament God's radical transcendence of the world, far from standing in tension with divine immanence, is understood to be the condition of its possibility: "'Who can hide in secret places so that I cannot see them?,' says the Lord. 'Do I not fill heaven and earth?,' says the Lord" (Jer. 23:24; cf. Ps. 139:7). Nor, secondly, do the Old Testament writers view divine immanence as a threat to creaturely well-being, as though prior to Jesus, human experience of God gave rise to a state of fear and apprehension that required the incarnation in order to be experienced as a blessing. On the contrary, the conviction that God's presence is fundamentally gracious is no more foreign to the Old Testament than fear of divine judgment is to the New.[5]

In short, precisely because the one who takes flesh in Jesus is none other than the God of Israel, the incarnation does not cause any sort of reversal in the Old Testament's understanding of God's relation to creation, as though a heretofore distant God had now drawn near, or a fearsome God were now shown to be loving. Instead, the incarnation is best understood (following Tanner) as an unexpected intensification of human experience of God's immanence *and* transcendence, grace *and* judgment, that comes with God being present not only *in* the world, but also *to* it. In other words, although it had never been possible to flee from God's presence, only with Jesus is it possible to *identify* that presence with a particular created reality—to be able to point to a creature and say truly, "This is God."

At the same time, this confession that the Word took flesh does not involve any blurring of the distinction between Creator and creature.

---

5. In this context, see R. Kendall Soulen's convincing demonstration that in the earliest church the confession of God's saving presence in Jesus was seamlessly combined with established Jewish practices of reverence for the Tetragrammaton. R. Kendall Soulen, *The Divine Name(s) and the Holy Trinity: Distinguishing the Voices* (Louisville: Westminster John Knox, 2011), especially chs. 2 and 12.

Again, where salvation is understood as life with God, then the confession that God is with us is a necessary condition of our being saved, but that immanence does not entail any qualification of divine transcendence. After all, it is only to the extent that God is understood to be radically different from us that we can have confidence that those powers, whether of flesh or spirit, that block our capacity to flourish have no purchase on God. When God takes flesh, therefore, the ontological "space" between God and the world does not collapse; it is rather confirmed as a space of grace—the condition of creation's fulfillment rather than a threat to it.[6]

For these reasons the Chalcedonian tradition has sought to affirm *both* God's entire and unqualified presence in Jesus (cf. Col. 1:19) *and* Jesus' complete and undiluted humanity (cf. Heb. 2:17). This double affirmation is secured through the claim that Jesus has two complete natures, one divine and one human, combined (in the words of the Chalcedonian definition) "without confusion or change, without division or separation."[7] Although talk of two natures might seem to suggest that Jesus' (human) body somehow "contains" divinity along with humanity, Chalcedon in no way intended to imply that anything happened to the divine nature by virtue of the incarnation (that is the point of the insistence that the natures were united "without confusion or change"). For while Chalcedon affirms that it is none other than God who is seen and touched in Jesus, that claim is not meant to imply that the incarnation renders the divine nature in any way finite or perceptible. But if that is true, how can it be that in Jesus God is seen and touched?

---

6. For the idea of ontological (versus physical) "distance" as an appropriate way of conceiving divine transcendence, see John of Damascus, *On the Orthodox Faith* 1.13 (PG 94:853c): "all things are distant from God not by place, but by nature."

7. Heinrich Denzinger, Peter Hünermann, et al., eds., *Compendium of Creeds, Definitions, and Declarations on Matters of Faith and Morals*, 43rd ed., (San Francisco: Ignatius, 2012), §302 [hereafter DH].

In order to answer this question it is necessary to shift theological focus from the language of two natures (orthodox though it is) to a distinction that was fully developed only in the decades after Chalcedon: between nature and hypostasis. To be sure, this distinction is already present in the Chalcedonian definition and can be traced back to the Cappadocian theologians of the fourth century, who in their formulation of the doctrine of the Trinity taught that God, though one in nature or substance (*ousia*), nevertheless subsisted as three co-eternal, equally divine hypostases: Father, Son, and Holy Spirit. Yet, while sufficient to secure the Nicene principle that the Son or Word was distinct from and yet "of the same substance" (*homoousios*) with the Father, for the Cappadocians the relation between nature and hypostasis was more or less equivalent to that between the universal and the particular.[8] This usage did not mesh with the conventions of orthodox Christology that began to emerge in the early fifth century, for which "hypostasis" was correlated with personal identity and served primarily to affirm Jesus' status as a single subject.[9] This convention is reflected in the language of Chalcedon, which affirms that in Christ "each of the two natures ... came together in ... one hypostasis [*hypostasin*]."[10] At the time those words (which would come to be known as the doctrine of the "hypostatic union") were penned, however, their meaning was far from clear. Only in subsequent decades did a consensus emerge among Chalcedonian theologians that speaking of the incarnation in this

8. See, for example, Gregory of Nyssa's, *Answer to Ablabius* (of which an English translation may be found in *Christology of the Later Fathers*, ed. Edward R. Hardy [Philadelphia: Westminster, 1954], 256-67).

9. In this context, Aloys Grillmeier has argued that Nestorius's insistence that Christ possessed two hypostases as well as two natures reflects his fidelity to the Cappadocian understanding of hypostasis as a particular instance of a nature. From this perspective, to deny that Christ had a human hypostasis would mean denying the concrete particularity—and thus the reality—of his humanity. See Aloys Grillmeier, *Christ in Christian Tradition*, vol. 1, trans. John Bowden (Louisville: Westminster John Knox, 1995), 457-63.

10. DH §302.

way meant that "hypostasis" was not to be interpreted substantially as referring to some*thing* (whether universal or particular) in Jesus, but rather as identifying the some*one* Jesus is—namely, the Second Person of the Trinity. In other words, according to the view that gradually triumphed in Chalcedonian circles, the "one hypostasis" of the conciliar definition was not a product that resulted from the two natures coming together, but rather the agent and cause of their union. As a single subject (the "one and the same Lord" of the conciliar definition), Jesus is identical with the eternal Word, who, having from all eternity lived a divine life with the Father and the Holy Spirit, in these last days assumed a human nature, too, and so now lives a human life as well.

In other words, what emerged in the aftermath of Chalcedon was the clarification that hypostasis is related to nature, not as particular to universal or as concrete to abstract, but rather as *who* to *what*. This clarification is crucial for avoiding the idea that the divine *nature* is somehow more present in Jesus than anywhere else in the universe. Again following Tanner's understanding of the doctrine of creation, God alone sustains every creature in existence in every aspect of its existence at every moment of its existence. It follows that God is already fully present at every point in creation, since otherwise nothing created could exist. Because God, as the transcendent Creator, is by nature invisible (Rom. 1:20; 1 Tim. 1:17; Heb. 11:27; cf. Deut. 4:12, 15), this presence is not a possible object of creaturely perception (1 Tim. 6:16). Yet its pervasiveness means that it makes no sense to conceive of the incarnation in terms of any sort of quantitative augmentation of divine presence, since the latter is already at an absolute maximum. The difference between God's presence in Jesus and in every other creature must therefore be qualitative: the divine *nature* is present with Jesus' humanity as it is with every other created reality, but it remains invisible; what differs is that in this creature the divine *hypostasis*—the only-begotten Son of God—is revealed. In short, although *what* we see in Jesus is simply and exhaustively human flesh and blood, the one *whom* we see and hear and touch is no less than the eternal Word, the Second Person of the Trinity. Only so is Jesus rightly confessed as the visible image of a God whose nature remains inherently invisible (Col. 1:15).

Chalcedonian Christology thus teaches that Jesus of Nazareth, at once the human son of Mary and the eternal Word, the only-begotten Son of the Father, are one and the same hypostasis—a single someone. It is therefore an implication of Chalcedonian thought that when we look at or listen to Jesus, we see and hear no one other than God. This does not mean that we at any point see or hear the divine nature, which remains utterly transcendent and thus incapable of creaturely perception. And since all creaturely being and doing is in its entirety both sustained and empowered by God, God is no more present or active in Jesus than in any other creature. Once again, the incarnation involves no "quantitative" increase in divine presence. Rather, to become incarnate is for God to identify the being and doing of this creature as God's own. This is the upshot of the claim that in Jesus "the Word became flesh" (John 1:14): that one of the divine hypostases, while continuing to be divine (for the Son does not cease to live in uninterrupted communion with the Father and the Holy Spirit by virtue of taking flesh), lived a fully human life. This event is decisive because it renders God *visible*. Again, this does not happen because of any alteration in the divine nature, which remains inherently and unalterably invisible after Christmas no less than before. Indeed, it is because the divine nature is invisible that the Word must assume a nature that can be seen in order to become visible. This is what Christians claim happened when the Word became flesh. In sum, although God has always been fully present in and with creation, only in the incarnation is this *seen* to be so, because only in taking flesh is the Creator revealed as a creature and thus in a form that *can* be seen.[11]

In becoming present to us (as well as with us) by taking flesh, God shows that, while we are incapable of encountering God in created nature as such (since there is an absolute ontological divide between Creator and creature), creation is not a barrier that prevents God from encountering us. We encounter God directly in Jesus, because it is not by looking through or past Jesus' humanity that we see the divine Word, but precisely in and as this human being—"what we have looked at and touched with our hands" (1 John 1:1)—in just the same way that we see any other person in and not behind her flesh. In Christ we are confronted with God not as a "being" whose existence may be inferred (as designer, first cause, standard of perfection, or whatever) on the basis of our experience as creatures, but rather as the One who meets us directly in and as a creaturely life. The fact that God in Christ claims (or, in the technical language of later Christology, "enhypostatizes") this instance of human nature as God's own does not make that nature or its properties in any respect divine (again, the Chalcedonian "without confusion or change" holds). Rather, because Jesus *is* the Word, his human nature is immediately revelatory of God, such that—whether the viewer acknowledges it or not—to see Jesus is to see God.

But unlike Peter or Mary or John, those of us now living have not seen, heard, or touched Jesus. In what sense, then, does his incarnation matter for us? It is in the effort to give a plausible answer to this question that Maximus the Confessor's claim that "the Word

---

11. "Everywhere there has been forgiveness of sins, the miraculous outpouring upon men of the wealth of the divine mercy, signs of the forbearance and longsuffering of God. Everywhere men are being healed of the divine wounds. But it is through Jesus that we have been enabled to see that this is so." Karl Barth, *The Epistle to the Romans*, trans. Edwin C. Hoskyns (Oxford: Oxford University Press, 1968), 106.

of God, who is God, wishes always and everywhere to effect the mystery of his embodiment" is significant.

Maximus's Contribution: The Logos and the *logoi*

The claim appears in the midst of Maximus's attempt to explain a passage from Gregory of Nazianzus in which the Cappadocian refers to human beings as a "part" or "portion" of God.[12] Maximus's primary aim in his exposition of the passage is to defend Gregory's language against pantheistic interpretation, as though it implied an erasure of the distinction between Creator and creature. At the same time, he also wants to affirm in the strongest possible terms that the Christian hope of life with God includes genuine participation in the divine nature. The statement that the divine Word "wishes always and everywhere to effect the mystery of his embodiment" emerges out of his desire to defend both these convictions as equally fundamental to Christian faith.

Given his commitment to defend Gregory against the charge of conflating Creator and creature, it should come as no surprise that Maximus takes pains to stress the absolute, permanent, and unbridgeable ontological difference between God and creatures:

> For it belongs to God alone to be the end, and the completion, and the impassible.... It belongs to creatures, on the other hand, to be moved toward that end which has no beginning, and to cease from their activity in that perfect end which is devoid of all quantity, and

---

12. The complete text of the passage, taken from Gregory's *Oration* 14 (*On Love of the Poor*, in PG 35:865c) is: "What is this wisdom that concerns me: And what is this great mystery? Or is it God's will that we, who are a portion of God [*moira tou theou*] that has flowed down from above, not become exalted and lifted up on account of this dignity, and so despise our Creator? Or is it not rather that, in our struggle and battle with the body, we should always look to Him, so that this very weakness that has been yoked to us might be an education concerning our dignity." Cited in Maximus the Confessor, *Ambiguum* 7, in *On Difficulties in the Church Fathers: The Ambigua*, 2 vols., ed. and trans. Nicholas Constas (Cambridge, MA: Harvard University Press, 2014), 1:75.

to experience—but not to be or to become according to essence—the Unqualified [viz., God].[13]

With respect to human beings in particular, Maximus teaches that although the saints always remain creatures, they nevertheless participate in divine glory by virtue of the conformation of their wills to God's. According to Maximus, this conformity is possible because all created natures are characterized by a distinct principle or *logos* that defines them as the particular kinds of creature they are.[14] Moreover, the form of each created *logos* is grounded in (and thus naturally conformed to) the one divine Logos through whom they were made.[15] It is in this context, Maximus argues, that Gregory's description of creatures as "portions of God" should be understood: because the *logoi* are created reflections (or, perhaps better, projections) of the divine Logos, they can rightly be described as "portions" of the uncreated God.[16] By virtue of this rootedness in the divine Logos, each created *logos* participates in God in accordance with its own particular way of being.[17]

In short, the relationship between the one divine Logos and the

13. Maximus, *Ambiguum* 7, 1.87 (PG 91:1073b); translation altered. Cf. *Ambiguum* 7, 1.101 (PG 91:1081b): "It is impossible for the infinite and the finite to exist simultaneously on the same level of being. Indeed, no argument will ever be constructed to show that being and what transcends being are able to coincide, or that the measureless can be coordinated with what is subject to measure, or that the absolute can be ranked with the relative, or that something of which no specific category can positively be predicated can be placed in the same class as what is constituted by all the categories" (translation modified).

14. Maximus, *Ambiguum* 22, 1.449 (PG 91:1256d): "If created things are many, then they must certainly be different, precisely because they are many…. And if the many are different, it must be understood that their *logoi*, according to which they essentially exist, are also different, since it is in these, or rather because of these *logoi*, that different things differ."

15. See Maximus, *Ambiguum* 7, 1.95 (PG 91:1077c): "… the many *logoi* are one Logos, seeing that all things are related to Him without being confused with Him."

16. "We are … and are called 'portions of God' because of the *logoi* of our being that exist eternally in God." Maximus, *Ambiguum* 7, 1.103 (PG 91:1081c).

17. "For by virtue of the fact that all things have their being from God, they participate in God in a manner appropriate and proportionate to each, whether by intellect, by reason, by sensation, by vital motion, or by some essential faculty or habitual fitness." Maximus, *Ambiguum* 7, 1.97 (PG 91:1080b).

many created *logoi* means that the convergence of creature and Creator is rooted in the ontology of creation itself. The *logoi* of creatures exist in God prior to their creation and are therefore the ground and prior condition of the possibility of the being of the creatures whose differentiated particularity they define.[18] Thus, for a creature to achieve perfection (viz., the fulfillment of its existence as the particular kind of creature it is) is for it to conform as fully as possible to its distinctive *logos*, which pre-exists in the one, eternal Logos.[19] It is a crucial feature of Maximus's thought, however, that the perfection of creatures is a *process*, which although grounded in the work of creation is not identical with it. No being is created perfect. Indeed, because perfection is a natural attribute of the one divine Creator, as a matter of definition it cannot be an intrinsic property of that which is created.[20] Since creatures' createdness means that they stand at an ontological distance from the uncreated Logos who is their source and goal, their perfection can only come about through a process of movement toward that goal that follows their being created.

Each creature has its own form of movement, which corresponds to its specific form of participation in the divine established by its distinctive *logos*.[21] Insofar as human beings are rational creatures, their natural movement is characterized by freedom: whereas inanimate objects simply respond to the push and pull of physical forces and lower animals act by instinct, human beings (along with angels) are

---

18. "For we believe that … a *logos* preceded the creation of everything that has received its being from God." Maximus, *Ambiguum* 7, 1.97 (PG 91:1080a; translation altered).

19. In this context, Maximus (citing Dionysius the Areopagite) calls the *logoi* "divine wills" (*theia thelēmata*) and thus explains the possibility that God should say to a creature, "I do not know you" (Matt. 25:12) as referring to their not conforming to their *logos*—that is, to God's will for their being. See Maximus, *Ambiguum* 7, 1.109 (PG 91:1085a–c).

20. "Nothing created is its own proper end, insofar as it is not self-caused, for if it were, it would be uncreated [i.e., God], without beginning, and without motion, having no way of being moved toward something else." Maximus, *Ambiguum* 7, 1.83 (PG 91:1072b–c; translation altered).

21. See note 16 above.

agents, so that their movement is a matter of will. This means that the process whereby human beings achieve their perfection as creatures involves their agency: each of us finds perfection when our will has "surrendered voluntarily and wholly to God, and perfectly subjected itself to His rule, by eliminating any wish that might contravene His will."[22] This understanding of perfection follows from the ontology of creation: to deviate from God's will is to fail to be the creature God willed us to be in creating us, and thus to undermine the very conditions of our existence as creatures

While Maximus acknowledges the possibility that creatures might indeed fail to move toward God, that possibility cuts against God's aim in creating, which is precisely that creatures should receive and enjoy their (created) being to the fullest, which, in turn, means to exist by ongoing participation in (and thus in active orientation toward) the divine Logos. As a creature endowed with free will, a human being achieves her distinctive form of participation in God's life by freely moving in accord with her own *logos* and with the *logoi* of the other creatures that constitute her environment. Maximus describes the end of this process (known as deification or *theosis*) as follows: "The whole of God will be participated by human beings in their entirety, so that God will be to the soul, as it were, what the soul is to the body, and through the soul God will likewise be present to the body."[23] While this description may seem to weaken the distinction between Creator and creature, Maximus guards against this inference by arguing that, although the deified saint "is and is called God by *grace*" (since she will have become "wholly God in soul and body owing to the grace and splendor of the blessed glory of God"), she "will remain wholly human in soul and body with respect to *nature*."[24] In other words, we remain creatures with respect to our

---

22. Maximus, *Ambiguum* 7, 1.83 (PG 91:1076b).
23. Maximus, *Ambiguum* 7, 1.113 (PG 91:1088c; translation altered).

essential being, even though the movements of our wills so fully correspond to God's that we are able by grace to participate in the life that God enjoys by nature.[25]

It is in this context that one should understand Maximus's claim that the Word seeks "always and everywhere to effect the mystery of his embodiment." The mystery of Jesus' embodiment is that the Creator God assumed a creaturely life, to the end that we who are creatures may share in the life of God. Through this mystery we share in the same fellowship with the Father and the Spirit that Jesus shares; even though Jesus lives a human life, the way in which other humans participate in God's life is crucially different from the way Jesus does. The Word may seek to effect the mystery of embodiment (that is, the goal of creaturely communion with God) everywhere, but the mode of that embodiment in Jesus is unique. For while we are called to conform our created *logos* to the Creator Logos, Jesus *is* that Logos, having "united our [human] nature to Himself according to hypostasis."[26] Jesus therefore shares with us the common *logos* of human nature. However, whereas all other human persons stand at a distance from the divine Logos that renders their perception of the ultimate good fallible and their wills liable to turn from God to lesser goods, Jesus suffers no such incapacity: because he is the Logos, he is able infallibly to conform his created human life to its archetype in God. Moreover, as he aligns his humanity with its proper *logos*, he brings the rest of human nature with him, so that "they mystery accomplished in Christ at the end of the age is nothing other than the

---

24. Maximus, *Ambiguum* 7, 1.105 (PG 91:1084c; translation altered) and 1.113 (PG 91:1088c; translation altered). Cf. *Ambiguum* 41, 2.109 (PG 91:1308b): "the whole man wholly pervading the whole God, and becoming everything that God is, without, however, identity of essence."
25. See Maximus, *Ambiguum* 7, 1.104-105 (PG 91:1084a).
26. Maximus, *Ambiguum* 7, 1.131 (PG 91:1097b); cf. *Ambiguum* 2, 1.13 (PG 91:1037a): "He truly and without change became whole man, being Himself the hypostasis of two natures, uncreated and created, impassible and passible, for He accepted without exception all the attributes [*logous*] of human nature, of which, as we have said, He is the hypostasis."

proof and fulfillment of the mystery that our forefather failed to attain at its beginning."[27]

Importantly, for Maximus the fulfillment of this mystery is not limited to humankind. Although he clearly limits genuine participation in the "spiritual pleasure and joy" of the Trinity to human beings and angels (since they alone possess the rational *logos* that allows for participation in God at the level of the intellect),[28] it is not the case that only rational creatures participate in God. Rather (and as already noted), the fact that every creature has a peculiar *logos* of its own that is grounded in the one divine Logos means that all creatures are made to participate in God.[29] The uniqueness of human beings, therefore, does not lie in their being the only creatures of genuine concern to God, but in the fact that they, as creatures who are both body and soul, unite the sensible and intelligible realms and thus serve as the means by which all creatures come to be united to God, "so that the many, though separated from each other in nature, might be drawn together into a unity as they converge around the one human nature."[30] But humanity's unique role in this process indicates that the means by which God seeks to effect the mystery of divine embodiment "always and everywhere" has nothing to do with multiple or continuous incarnation. All creatures come to God through humanity, and all humanity comes to God through Christ.

27. Maximus, *Ambiguum* 7, 1.133 (PG 91:1097d; translation altered). Cf. *Ambiguum* 41, 2.113 (PG 91:1309c), where Maximus describes how in the ascension Christ "having passed with His soul and body, that is, with the whole of our nature, through all the divine and intelligible orders of heaven ... united sensible things with intelligible things, displaying in Himself the fact that the convergence of the entire creation toward unity was absolutely indivisible and unshakeable, in accordance with its most primal and universal logos" (translation altered).

28. Maximus, *Ambiguum* 7, 1.111 (PG 91:1088b).

29. See note 16 above.

30. Maximus, *Ambiguum* 7, 1.121 (PG 91:1092c). Cf. *Ambiguum* 41, 2.105 (PG 91:1305a, c), where humanity is described as "like a most capacious workshop [*ergastêrion*] containing all things ... mediating between the universal extremes through his parts, and unifying through himself things that by nature are separated from each other by a great distance."

But if the incarnation is a unique event in this way, how is it effected "always and everywhere"?

Conclusion: The Content of the Mystery

I have taken pains to stress that the point of the incarnation is not that a God who had been distant from creatures should now draw close to them, or that a God who had been nowhere in the world should now be everywhere. Neither claim makes sense, since God's status as Creator means that the divine presence is already maximal with respect to both intensity and extent, already everywhere upholding both the world as a whole and every creature within it quite apart from being physically embodied, whether in Jesus or anywhere else. The point of the incarnation is rather that God should be present to creation in a new, visible mode, distinctively different from the primordial relationship of Creator to creature whereby the world is sustained in being.[31]

God cannot be present visibly as divine, because the divine nature is inherently invisible by virtue of its transcendence. But God is not just a nature. God is a Trinity of persons and is able to take on a created nature without ceasing to be divine. God, who enables all creatures' being, claims the being of one creature, Jesus, as God's own. Thus, *what* we see in Jesus is flesh and blood—created substance—but the one *whom* we see is no less than God, the eternal Word.

Maximus's vision of the Word accomplishing the mystery of the incarnation "always and everywhere" thus has nothing to do with an increase in God's presence in creation, as though there had been

---

31. As Maximus puts it, God's purpose for us was not fulfilled "in any way whatsoever through humanity's proper *logos*, but rather was realized through the introduction of another, wholly new mode" of being human through the incarnation. Maximus, *Ambiguum* 7, 1.131-33 (PG 91:1097c; translation altered).

any lack. In fact, it constitutes a stark rejection of the temptation to treat divinity as a substance or principle, and incarnation as the process by which it comes to be spread throughout creation. On the contrary, for Maximus the point of the incarnation is the revelation of God as *person*. Although by nature (that is, considered as substance) God is absolutely, unalterably, and infinitely different from creatures, as person God can and does relate to them in love. This does not happen through God becoming embodied multiple times in multiple places. On the contrary, God's personal presence is a function of the uniqueness of the incarnation: because this one human being, Jesus of Nazareth, is God, to live with God is finally to live with this one. In short, the point of the incarnation is not the revelation that God is everywhere (although it does serve as confirmation of that fact), but precisely that God can be identified with a particular individual living at a specific time and place.

The incarnation does not therefore mean that God draws near to us physically in Jesus, because the divine nature is not a physical quantity for which the concept of spatial distance or proximity has any meaning. God draws near to us in Jesus in that God becomes a creature, encountering us personally by living and breathing as a flesh-and-blood human being. That God should be able to be fully present—fully identifiable as God—in this way and yet remain utterly transcendent in divinity is the mystery of the Word's embodiment. For though we are always present to God, it is only by assuming flesh—taking on a creature life that can be heard, seen, looked at, and touched (1 John 1:1)—that God is present to us. And that presence does not come to pervade creation by God becoming incarnate again and again. That would only serve to dilute God's identification with a particular creaturely life by presenting God as a power diffused through and yet finally standing behind creation.[32] By contrast, to say that God is this one—Jesus of Nazareth—highlights the particularity of the divine identity. God's presence comes to fill creation personally, as the circle of communion established by Jesus expands through time and space through the power of Jesus' Spirit active through the witness of other human beings (1 John 1:3; cf. John 15:26-27).

What is the mystery of the Word's embodiment? It is the revelation of the Logos in a *logos*, of the infinite in the finite, of the Creator as creature, such that it becomes both necessary and possible to say, "This creature is God." And yet God, as the One who alone holds all creatures in being in every aspect of their existence at every moment of their existence, is in a basic sense no more intimate to creation in Jesus than anywhere else. Moreover, every created *logos* reflects some aspect—and thereby provides an occasion for the display of the glory—of the eternal Logos. For this reason it is possible confess with Gregory of Nazianzus that every creature is a "portion of God," reflecting the presence of God as the source and goal of all created being. So, too, the incarnation of the Word is, as Tanner argues, a "paradigm in a remarkably extreme form" of the immediacy of God's relation to all creatures. And yet it remains distinct, because in all other creatures God's presence is hidden: God is there, but we do not see God, only a creature. And even in Jesus *what* our eyes behold is only created human substance no different in kind from that found in you or me—and yet the one *whom* we see is God. Because I am a creature, it is true to say that in everything I do God is active: it is God who got me out of bed this morning, who brought me to my place of work, and who enables me to type these words. But it is I and not God who got up, rode the bus, and sits at my desk. God also roused Jesus each morning of his life and set him on his way, but for

---

32. This is not to say that God could not have become incarnate multiple times, just that there is a certain appropriateness to the uniqueness of the incarnation, insofar as it is God's way of being personally present to creation. See Thomas Aquinas, *Summa Theologiae*, 3.4.5.

him alone is it also true that in this act God is the one who got up and lived the day. I am not God, and you are not God, and neither is Gandhi or Stalin or the woman outside my window. But Jesus is.

And yet because in Jesus God has become present to us as a creature, through him God's relationship to creation is revealed in a way that makes the rest of creation disclosive of God as was not the case before. As Maximus argues, there is no way for us to ascend on our own from the myriad creaturely *logoi* to the one divine Logos; the whole exceeds the fragments by too much to be deduced or extrapolated from them. Yet in the incarnation we have been shown the whole. And we are thereby enabled to see each *logos* in light of the Logos, such that the many *logoi*, though in their finitude falling infinitely short of the infinite, nevertheless do illuminate for us the unendingly gracious power and presence of God. As the Word made flesh through whom all things were created and in whom all things hold together (Col. 1:16-17), Jesus is the whole, the overarching context who enables the parts to be interpreted properly, in a way analogous to that in which knowledge of the whole novel allows proper interpretation of the various characters who come and go across its chapters.

God is present everywhere in creation quite apart from the incarnation. But in the incarnation—and only there—this presence becomes visible: we behold a creature, and yet we see God. Creation is not thereby revealed to be divine, nor is it divinized (in the sense of becoming in any way ontologically continuous with the divine nature), but it is now revealed not only as a theater of divine glory but also as a place of communion between Creator and creature. If creation has always been present to God, through the incarnation God now becomes present to the creature, through Christ calling that which is not God to life with God. Only Jesus is God's Son, but God's communion with the creature does not stop with him. For he calls all other human beings, whose flesh he took, to be God's children, too, as his sisters and brothers. Insofar as his human life is inseparable from the matrix of matter and energy from which it emerged and on which it continues to draw, it is the case that through human beings the whole creation is summoned to "the freedom of the glory of the children of God" (Rom. 8:21). So it is that the Word seeks to effect the mystery of divine embodiment—always and everywhere.

4

Christ, the Receiver of Gifts

Amy Plantinga Pauw

The giver is greater: but the receiver is not less, for to him it is given to be one with the giver.

–Hilary of Poitiers[1]

Attempts to connect Jesus and the biblical figure of Wisdom have often come at the cost of affirming Jesus' fully human life. Contemporary wisdom Christologies have taken a bewildering variety of forms—Christ as laconic sage, avatar of universal divine wisdom, eternal ordering principle of the universe, to name only a few—and remain a subject of sharp disagreements among biblical scholars and theologians. However it is fair to say that, from the early church onwards, wisdom Christologies have often yielded portraits of Jesus Christ quite removed from the ordinary processes and conflicts of human life. My aim in this essay is to explore Christ's connection with biblical wisdom traditions in a way that affirms both the acute

---

1. Hilary of Poitiers, *On the Trinity* 9.54, quoted in Kathryn Tanner, *Christ the Key*, Current Issues in Theology (Cambridge: Cambridge University Press, 2010), 183.

dependence of his creaturely life and the centrality of the gospel narratives for rendering his identity. These narratives portray Christ, in Kathryn Tanner's words, as "ever recognizing his need as a human being, grateful for what he has received and willing in prayer to call upon the Father's help as the source of all good for his own sake and that of others."[2] By raising up the dependence and mutuality that is at the heart of both creaturely existence and the triune life, I intend to complement Tanner's dominant emphasis in *Christ the Key* on Christ as the giver of gifts.

Early Patterns in Wisdom Christology

The conviction that the Word of God incarnate in Jesus Christ has been at work throughout all creation from the beginning has been at the center of a long tradition of wisdom Christologies. Links between the figure of personified Wisdom and Jesus Christ have been used to show that the particular historical revelation of God in Christ has a cosmic, creative dimension: "Creation is always already christological."[3] Over the centuries, the beautiful paeans to Woman Wisdom in canonical and deuterocanonical writings have proved irresistible to seekers of christological imagery. For example, the Wisdom of Solomon declares:

> For she is a breath of the power of God,
> and a pure emanation of the glory of the Almighty;
> therefore nothing defiled gains entrance into her.
> For she is a reflection of eternal light,
> a spotless mirror of the working of God, and an image of his goodness.
> Although she is but one, she can do all things,
> and while remaining in herself, she renews all things;

---

2. Kathryn Tanner, *Jesus, Humanity and the Trinity: A Brief Systematic Theology* (Minneapolis: Fortress Press, 2001), 75.

3. Janet Soskice, "Creation and Participation," *Theology Today* 68, no. 3 (2011): 313.

in every generation she passes into holy souls and makes them friends of God and prophets (Wisd. of Sol., 7:25-27; NRSV).

Christological appropriations of personified Wisdom start already in the New Testament writings, and represent perhaps the earliest way Christians attempted to understand the relationship between Jesus and the one he called "Father."[4] As Ben Witherington notes, "The importance of the personification of Wisdom cannot be overemphasized. It is an idea that, once introduced into the biblical Wisdom tradition, took on a life of its own and grew in importance, in complexity, and in depth as time went on."[5] The deuterocanonical texts Baruch and Sirach use the figure of Wisdom as a way of talking about Torah, which becomes a central focus of Jewish faith. But Wisdom also serves as a vehicle for talking about the center of Christian faith, Jesus. According to Witherington, when early Jewish Christians, steeped in Jewish wisdom traditions, "were looking for exalted language from their heritage that gave adequate expression to their new found faith in Jesus Christ, they found no language better suited for such praise than the paeans about personified or hypostatized Wisdom" in books like Proverbs and the Wisdom of Solomon.[6] King Solomon had great wisdom, but in Jesus Christ "something greater than Solomon is here" (Matt. 12:42).

These connections between Jesus Christ and personified Wisdom are then carried into early church patterns of reading Scripture, where the identity of the incarnate Word and Woman Wisdom is simply assumed. As Augustine put it, "she is sent in one way that she may be with human beings; she has been sent in another way that she herself might be a human being."[7] The fourth-century

---

4. See James Dunn, *Christology in the Making* (Grand Rapids: Eerdmans, 1996), 212: "The origin of the doctrine of the incarnation is in a Wisdom Christology."

5. Ben Witherington, *Jesus the Sage: The Pilgrimage of Wisdom* (Minneapolis: Fortress Press, 1994), 50.

6. Ibid., 289.

Arian controversy was a central theological context for attempts to understand the connection between Christ and personified Wisdom in the early church. In this controversy over the identity of Jesus Christ, Wisdom's self-declaration in Prov. 8:22-31 played a surprisingly large role. In Prov. 8:22, Woman Wisdom declares, "The Lord created me at the beginning of his work, the first of his acts of long ago," and goes on to claim that "before the mountains had been shaped, before the hills, I was brought forth." She describes herself as present with God at the creation of the world, "rejoicing before God always," and "delighting in the human race." Both Arius's and Athanasius's contrasting appeals to Proverbs are continuous with established Christian exegetical traditions that identify the incarnate Word with Woman Wisdom.

Debates about meaning occur within communities that share assumptions about interpretation. Athanasius and Arius confronted the tensions and ambiguities of their shared Alexandrian inheritance regarding the role of the Word. They were both products of an Origenist theological formation that insisted on God's radical freedom in creation and salvation, and on the fundamental distinction between God as the one, self-subsistent, spiritual source of all and the material and multiple creation. In their inherited cosmology, God's relation to a material cosmos must be secured by a mediating figure who is both like and unlike each of them—the Logos.[8] The Logos or Word, then, is the intermediary through whom God's creative and redemptive relations with the world are effected. Origen insisted that the work of the Word was in some sense the work of God. But he left unresolved a central theological question: Does the mediatorial *work* or *role* of the Word indicate that the Word's *identity* also is

---

7. "Sed aliter mittitur ut sit cum homine; aliter missa est ut ipsa sit homo" (Augustine, *De Trinitate* 4:20.27), http://www.thelatinlibrary.com/augustine/trin4.shtml (accessed July 20, 2015).

8. David H. Kelsey, *Eccentric Existence: A Theological Anthropology* (Louisville: Westminster John Knox, 2010), 52.

intermediate? On which side of the divide between Creator and creature does the Word fall?

It seemed obvious to Arius that the Word must fall on the creaturely side. To put the Word on the divine side would undercut the real distinction between the Son and Father witnessed to in the Gospels, and compromise divine aseity by associating God too closely with the dependence of creaturely life. Arius found numerous New Testament texts to support his argument, but his ace in the hole was Prov. 8:22: "The Lord created me at the beginning of his work, the first of his acts of long ago." The Word of God, here identified with Wisdom, has a source. God by definition is unbegotten, having no source. Therefore the Word cannot be God: the Word is the one created at the beginning of God's work, who comes into being on the occasion of and as the condition of the creation of the world. The Word's role in the economy of creation in turn helps explain the role attributed to the Son in the economy of redemption: as a dependent creature, he was capable of suffering and dying.

By contrast, at the heart of the story of redemption for Athanasius is God assuming humanity's alienated and sinful reality and healing it by union with God's own reality. Only God can do this work; it cannot be performed by some creaturely intermediary. So the Word who is incarnated in Jesus Christ must be on the divine side of the divide between Creator and creature. The Son is co-eternal with the Father. His begetting is separated conceptually from God's act of creating the world through him. For Athanasius, the logic of the economy of salvation guides what must be said of Woman Wisdom. Driven by soteriological convictions and concerns, Athanasius argues that what admittedly looks like a parallel construction—Wisdom being created at the beginning of God's work (Prov. 8:22), and Wisdom being brought forth before God had shaped the earth and the hills (Prov. 8:25)—is actually not, as really two very different things were being stated. According to Athanasius, Proverbs' affirmation that Wisdom was created refers to the creation in time of the *human* nature of Jesus Christ—it is a reference to the incarnation. When Proverbs says she was brought forth, that refers to the eternal existence of the *divine* Word with God. In the tortured sequence of Athanasius's interpretation, verse 22 refers to the Word's assumption of our human nature and verse 25 refers to the Word's being eternally begotten of the Father, and therefore, as the Creed will say, of one substance with him. As Athanasius sums up his interpretation of Prov. 8:22-25, God's Son was *begotten and then made*, that is, made flesh for our salvation, whereas human creatures were *made and then begotten* through Christ, becoming children of God by grace.[9] The growing understanding of the soteriological stakes of belief in Christ pressed the early church towards appropriating the biblical wisdom traditions in ways that identify Christ with Woman Wisdom and affirm Christ's full divinity.

Contemporary Considerations: Wisdom and Creaturely Dependence

We have been considering what Marcus Bockmuehl has called the "effective history" of Proverbs 8, the history of the Christian community's response to and interpretation of its canonical texts.[10] But this still leaves open the question of how to construe the connection between Christ and Woman Wisdom today. In her analysis of the Arian controversy over Proverbs 8, Frances Young provides a way forward by advocating what she calls an ethical reading of texts. This means for her that "readers have a responsibility

9. Athanasius, *Four Discourses against the Arians*, in *Nicene and Post-Nicene Fathers*, vol. 4, trans. J. H. Newman and A. Robertson (Grand Rapids, MI: William B. Eerdmans, 1957), 381-82.
10. Marcus Bockmuehl, "Reasons, Wisdom and the Implied Disciple of Scripture," in *Reading Texts, Seeking Wisdom: Scripture and Theology*, ed. David F. Ford and Graham Stanton (Grand Rapids: Eerdmans, 2004), 53.

to the text, but also to themselves." Ethical reading thus requires both distance and appropriation. Distance is required to respect the text's own claims and context and to provide critical leverage on far-fetched or over-confident interpretations. According to Young, recognizing the distance of the interpreter from the text will require allowing multiple readings in different communities across space and time. On the other hand, Young insists on "a recognition that a Christian reading of the Bible has to wrestle with issues of its unity and the ways in which it points to a reality beyond itself.... A Christian ethical reading also has to do justice to 'ourselves', and that includes the tradition of reading in which we stand."[11]

To most contemporary Christian sensibilities, Athanasius's christological interpretation of Prov. 8:22-25 seems far-fetched. Young notes that Athanasius assumes that his interpretation of the Proverbs 8 passage is its timeless, universal meaning, placed there by the Holy Spirit for him as an exegete to uncover. Thus, he is not cognizant of how his particular community of interpretation is influencing his textual assumptions about the text. Yet Athanasius's insistence that "what God is, the Word is" has become established Christian teaching, and Wisdom still remains a powerful and multivalent biblical metaphor for Jesus Christ. The "ethical reading" attempted in this essay affirms both the appropriateness of Word and Wisdom as christological metaphors and the hard-won results of the church's Trinitarian reflection.

Athanasius and Arius approach personified Wisdom from within the narrative frame of God's reconciliation of sinful humanity, and this has been the dominant way that canonical wisdom traditions have been appropriated christologically. However, it is generally

---

11. Frances Young, "Proverbs 8 in interpretation: wisdom personified," in *Reading Texts, Seeking Wisdom: Scripture and Theology*, ed. David F. Ford and Graham Stanton (Grand Rapids: Eerdmans, 2004), 114-15.

agreed upon by contemporary biblical scholars that the theological framework of the biblical wisdom books is creation.[12] The horizon of Proverbs, along with Ecclesiastes and Job, is humanity's ongoing relation to God in the ordinary, day-to-day network of life-giving and life-orienting relations with the physical world and with various human communities. The figure of Woman Wisdom in Proverbs functions as a trope for the relationship between God and creation. Respect for the claims of the text encourages developing an "ethical reading" of canonical wisdom texts that adheres to this framework.

Though I do not follow Athanasius in assuming a straightforward identification of Jesus Christ with the figure of Woman Wisdom in Proverbs, I do follow him (rather than Arius) in affirming that in Jesus Christ the very life of God takes on the dependence and finitude of creaturehood. At the heart of the doctrine of creation is a profound asymmetry: all creation depends on God for its very existence but God does not depend on it. God would be God, even without the world. Creation is thus an act of sheer grace. What God creates and delights in is finite creation—dependent, mortal, vulnerable to injury and harm, in short, radically contingent. It is this creation that God values and calls good. It is this creation whose flourishing God seeks for its own sake. God's loving self-determination in creation is to establish an ongoing relation with what is not God, a reflection of God's inexhaustible generosity. It is a mark of this supreme divine graciousness that in Christ God takes on the creaturely dependence of a fully human life.

The patterns of creaturely mutuality and dependence displayed in Jesus' life are woven into the fabric of creation. They are part of the wisdom by which the earth was founded (Prov. 3:19). All creatures

12. Walther Zimmerli, "The Place and Limit of the Wisdom Literature in the Framework of the Old Testament Theology," in *Studies in Ancient Israelite Wisdom*, ed. Harry Meyer Orlinsky (New York: KTAV, 1976), 316.

belong to an interconnected system of life, in which they flourish only in a sustainable interdependence. As an earth creature, Jesus is, from his gestation until his death, part of the earthly biome in which creaturely receptivity and dependence is the sine qua non of existence.[13] Throughout his whole earthly life, Jesus is the receiver of gifts, most fundamentally from God but also from his fellow creatures.

Dependence—unlike suffering, conflict, and death—is a dimension of the human condition that is not progressively overcome across the course of Jesus' human life. To be sure, the competition and predation that characterize aspects of creaturely interdependence contribute to the earthly suffering that Christ as Savior overcomes. Yet, creaturely dependence *per se* is not something to be defeated, but instead reflects in an appropriately human way the shape of the Trinitarian life. As Rowan Williams notes, "What sets Christian faith apart most decisively from even its closest religious relatives, is this picture of the divine life involving receiving as well as giving, depending as well as controlling." What Jesus Christ shows us is that "what we understand by 'God' can't just be power and initiative; it also includes receiving and reflecting back in love and gratitude." The eternal perfection of God's Trinitarian life is both a sending and a being sent, initiative and dependency.[14] There is an eternal pattern of dispossession and receptivity in God. In the creaturely dependence of Jesus, this eternal pattern of divine life is recapitulated.

For the most part in canonical wisdom literature, this creaturely dependence on God's continuing, life-giving relation of blessing is simply assumed. The world across the entirety of its existence

---

13. For theological reflection on Jesus' gestation and birth, see Elizabeth O'Donnell Gandolfo, "A Truly Human Incarnation: Recovering a Place for Nativity in Contemporary Christology," *Theology Today* 70, no. 4 (2014): 382-93.

14. Rowan Williams, *Tokens of Trust: An Introduction to Christian Belief* (Louisville: Westminster John Knox, 2007), 66, 68.

is utterly dependent on God. There is no hint in the canonical wisdom books of a deistic scheme whereby the world is increasingly distanced from the creative activity of God, and ultimately left to run on its own. From time to time, the assumption that God is Creator of all is spelled out a bit. In Ecclesiastes, it is God who gives human beings the few days they enjoy under the sun, and from whose hand they receive their daily food and drink. In Proverbs, God is the Maker of all, and those who mock the poor insult their Maker. God's gracious generosity towards the creation and creation's utter, continuing dependence on God for its very existence are the operative background beliefs in the wisdom books, the warp and woof of their theology.

In the second half of Proverbs 8, this background belief is foregrounded. It is as if a light shone briefly from behind an opaque scrim, illuminating what is generally hidden from view: the ceaseless, wise, delighted work of God the Creator, whose loving energy is behind every manifestation of life. God is here presented, in Tanner's phrase, as "the comprehensive productive principle."[15] Woman Wisdom speaks of a "time" when there were no springs abounding with water, no bits of soil. God's creating is not a manipulation of some pre-existing matter—God is the sole source of all that exists. As medieval theologians would later work out, God is not a kind of thing; God does not belong to a generic category populated by other items on the inventory list of the universe. God does not stand at the top of a great chain of being with some parts of creation in closer ontological relation to God than other parts. And therefore God is appropriately portrayed in Proverbs 8 as the Creator of all—mountains and hills, the fountains of the deep—not just of the

15. Kathryn Tanner, "Is God in Charge?," in *Essentials of Christian Theology*, ed. William C. Placher (Louisville: Westminster John Knox, 2003), 120. For a contemporary theological reading of Proverbs 8, see Amy Plantinga Pauw, *Proverbs and Ecclesiastes*, Belief: A Theological Commentary on the Bible (Louisville: Westminster John Knox, 2015).

bits of reality that we might deem most like God. *Pace* Arius's reading of Proverbs 8, there is no "buffer zone" between God and the world, no need for God to be protected from compromise and corruption when coming into contact with finite reality. As Tanner states, "If God is not a kind of thing, then the one God can be directly and intimately involved with the production of the world in all its aspects, without threatening to compromise or dilute either God's divinity or the natures of any of the things in the world."[16] In creation as well as redemption, God's self-determination is to be the One who is "for the world."

Woman Wisdom portrays herself in Prov. 8:30-31 in images of delight and rejoicing: "I was daily [God's] delight, rejoicing before him always, rejoicing in his inhabited world and delighting in the human race." As a trope for the relationship between God and creation, Woman Wisdom portrays both the mode of God's relationship to creation and of creation's relationship to God. In both directions, this relationship is characterized by a delighting and rejoicing in the presence of the other. God rejoices and delights in creaturely life that exists only by God's loving gift. Creatures, in turn, who have their life and find their fulfillment only in God, are called to a joyful embrace of their dependence on God and to interdependent existence with their fellow creatures.

Denying Dependence: Karl Barth as Cautionary Example

This creaturely joy is in fact what surfaces in the accounts of Jesus' life in the Gospels. Here Jesus' life is characterized by what David Kelsey has termed "doxological gratitude,"[17] an embrace of the gift of creaturely existence. Indeed, as we shall see, wisdom Christology developed within a creation framework comes into focus in a feature

---

16. Tanner, "Is God in Charge?," 121.
17. Kelsey, *Eccentric Existence*, 333.

of Jesus' ministry that is found in all four canonical Gospels: Jesus giving thanks to God. But a creation framework also emphasizes that Jesus' creaturely life is marked by profound interdependence with fellow creatures, both human and non-human. Here theologians focused solely on Christ's reconciling work tend to stumble. Jesus Christ for them is only the giver of gifts, not the receiver of gifts. Instead of affirming the dependent character of Jesus' full humanity, they replicate the essential asymmetry between God and creatures in their accounts of Christ's earthly life.

Karl Barth is a typical case. For him, what distinguishes Jesus from other human creatures is his lack of dependence. Human creatures as such are bound up in relations by which they both assist and are assisted by one another in the realization of their proper creaturely humanity. In Barth's words, "The minimal definition of our humanity, of humanity generally, must be that it is the being of the human in encounter, and in this sense the determination of humanity as a being with the other."[18] To be God's human creature is to be "able and ordained to render assistance to fellow creatures and to receive it from them."[19] According to Barth, however, such mutuality does not apply to the human being Jesus: he enhances the humanity of others but his humanity is not enhanced by them. As Barth notes, "God alone, and the man Jesus as the Son of God, has no need of assistance, and is thus able to render far more than assistance to humanity, namely, to represent them. For us, however, humanity consists in the fact that we need and are capable of mutual assistance."[20]

---

18. Karl Barth, *Church Dogmatics*, III.2, trans. Harold Knight, G. W. Bromiley, J. K. S. Reid, and R. H. Fuller (Edinburgh: T&T Clark, 1960), 247. I am grateful to Bill Werpehowski for conversation on this point. All quotations from the *Church Dogmatics* in this essay modify the male language of the original English translation.
19. Ibid., 262.
20. Ibid.

Barth's portrait of Jesus cannot be reconciled with the Gospel accounts, which depict him as needing and receiving assistance from others, starting with his infancy and moving throughout his adulthood. Jesus "grows in wisdom and stature" (Luke 2:52) only in the company of others. Moreover, Jesus' human dependence extends beyond fellow human beings to the earth and all its living creatures. In contrast to the sin and alienation of human life which Jesus takes on in order to heal them from within, the dependence and receptivity of his earthly life is part of the way in which he models the Trinitarian life we are to participate in. Barth's concern to affirm Christ's reconciling work on our behalf leads him to deny in the case of Jesus the mutuality that is at the heart of creaturely existence. This is a mistake. Christ's divinity is revealed *in* his human interdependence. Jesus is *for* others as Savior only as he is *with* others, and dependent on them.

Giving Thanks

As noted above, wisdom Christology developed within a creation framework comes into focus in a feature of Jesus' ministry that is found in all four canonical Gospels: Jesus giving thanks to God. The setting for this giving thanks is always a meal, either among the hungry multitudes or at an intimate table with his disciples. In giving thanks, Jesus affirms both the shared human need for physical nourishment and God's faithful provision for that need in community. There is no artificial distinction between nature and culture in God's gifts to creatures: just as God supplies the food needed to nourish bodies, so God also supplies the social networks of care within which human beings feed each other both spiritually and materially.

In the New Testament accounts of Jesus' giving thanks to God for food, the act of giving thanks (εὐχαριστέω) is interchangeable with the act of blessing (εὐλογέω). This is seen first of all in the Gospel scenes of feeding the multitudes. Matthew and Mark both recount two such stories: in the first story Jesus blesses the loaves (Matt. 14:19; Mark 6:41), and in the second story he gives thanks for the loaves (Matt. 15:36; Mark 8:6) and blesses the fish (Mark 8:7). In Luke's feeding story, Jesus blesses the loaves (Luke 9:16), while in John Jesus gives thanks for them (John 6:11).

Likewise, in the accounts of the Last Supper blessing and giving thanks are again interchangeable. In Matthew and Mark, Jesus blesses the loaf and gives thanks for the cup (Mark 14:22-23; Matt. 26:26-27). In the Lukan account, he gives thanks for both the cup and the loaf (Luke 22:17), and in the table scene at Emmaus the risen Jesus blesses the bread (Luke 24:30). In Paul's summary of the Last Supper (1 Cor. 11:23-26), Jesus gives thanks before feeding his disciples. When Paul calls the communion cup "the cup of blessing which we bless" (1 Cor. 10:16), he is calling the community to a grateful recognition of the way God provides for them.

Both God and human beings bless in Scripture. These parallel constructions in the Gospel accounts of Jesus' giving thanks for and blessing a meal suggest that in these stories his blessing should be interpreted as a human act of giving thanks. As Claus Westermann notes, when Jesus blesses the bread and cup, he is continuing the traditional Jewish practice of giving God thanks for the nourishment of food. He observes: "The blessing of a meal has two functions. It brings those who eat into a community in the sight of God, and it offers the praise and thanksgiving of the community to God."[21] Blessing the meal is a human way of acknowledging divine blessing: "the fruits of the field that have grown through the power of God's

21. Claus Westermann, *Blessing in the Bible and the Life of the Church*, trans. Keith Crim (Philadelphia: Fortress Press, 1978), 114.

blessing are received from the Creator in humble thankfulness."[22] Jesus' act of blessing a meal is both an acknowledgment of human dependence of God and a celebration of God's generosity. In these meal stories, gratitude for creaturely life and praise to God for giving and sustaining this life are at the center of Jesus' actions. Jesus in these stories shows us what union with God in human form looks like. He shows this union not only in acting to share God's good gifts with others, but also in living himself in grateful dependence on these gifts.

In these stories, Jesus also lives in grateful interdependence with other creatures. The bread he blesses was baked by others. The fish he distributes were caught and prepared by others. The wine for which he gives thanks was made from grapes that others grew and crushed. Even as he feeds others, his own body is being nourished by the plants and animals he eats. To be human is to depend on others, to receive from others. Though Proverbs can wax overconfident about the earthly benefits of following Woman Wisdom, it is clear that human attempts to be wise are not an escape route from the vulnerability and dependence that are intrinsic to creaturehood. Jesus lives wisely by embracing the mutual assistance required for human existence.

Following Christ's Example of Interdependence

In the feeding stories, Jesus insists that the disciples give the hungry crowds something to eat. Christian communities of faith continue to respond to Christ's demand with a commitment to a just provision of bread for a hungry world. It is not enough to recognize with thanksgiving that God is the wise and generous provider of sustenance. Human beings are also called to act wisely on behalf of their fellow creatures in acknowledging their common need and

---

22. Ibid., 90.

distributing God's generous provision. As Tanner puts it, "One with Christ through his Spirit we are bound together to be a community with a Trinitarian form of life in service to others."[23]

In Karl Barth there is a similar move from Christology to ecclesiology. Just as Christ is *for* humanity, so the community of his followers is to exist *for the sake of the world*. This is an important theological move in avoiding what Barth ridiculed as "pious egocentricity," according to which Christians rejoice in being the recipients of an "indescribably magnificent private good fortune, permitting them to obtain and possess a gracious God, opening to them the gates of Paradise which are closed to others."[24] A gift-oriented Christology properly invites a task-oriented ecclesiology, because Christ's gifts are for the whole world. However, Barth's ecclesiology exhibits the same troubling asymmetry as his Christology. The Christ who "has no need of assistance" becomes the model for the life of the Christian community, obscuring the dependence that Christians have on non-Christians, on other fellow creatures, and on the rest of creation. A church that exists only *for* the world, and not also *with* the world, risks becoming a church that proclaims but does not listen; a church that gives but is not willing to receive; a church that teaches, but makes no effort to learn from others. Here, too, communities of Christian faith must affirm their creaturehood by acknowledging their ongoing interdependence with other human communities and with all living things.

For communities of Christian faith, the feeding of the multitudes and Christ's Last Supper with the disciples are not ordinary meals. They are about creaturely nourishment and the celebration of God's ongoing sustenance of creaturely life, but they are not only about

---

23. Tanner, *Christ the Key*, 281.
24. Karl Barth, *Church Dogmatics*, IV.3.2, trans. G. W. Bromiley (Edinburgh: T&T Clark, 1962), 567.

that: these meals are also taken up into God's promises of reconciliation and eschatological consummation. In the feeding stories, the modest provisions of bread and fish are multiplied to feed a huge crowd with plenty left over. Here God's eschatological promise to relieve the physical suffering intrinsic to creaturely human life is glimpsed. This eschatological blessing is not experienced as continuously realized—the people in the crowd will be hungry again the next day. But God's promise of lifting the burdens of earthly finitude (while still preserving creaturely finitude itself) is made tangible. In the stories of the Last Supper, the disciples receive from Christ's hand not only the physical sustenance they need, but also the assurance that their brokenness and alienation from God and each other are healed through Christ's gift of himself.

Human brokenness and alienation are still very much in evidence in the Last Supper accounts. Jesus' meal with his disciples on the night of his arrest was a costly act of solidarity in a setting fraught with betrayal and impending violence. In the hours that followed, Jesus' dependence on his disciples would be frustrated, and even his trusting dependence on God would be put to the test. Only on the other side of Jesus' resurrection and glorification do the stories of the Last Supper become the foundation for the most profound enactment of Christian dependence on Christ for ongoing spiritual nourishment. As Tanner describes the Eucharistic movement, "The good things of the earth in forms that nourish our bodies—bread and wine—are first offered up in thanksgiving by us to the Father in Christ's own movement to him, and then received back from the Father as new Spirit-filled nourishment for new life in the form of Christ's own body and blood, through the power of the Spirit that makes those elements one with them."[25] The Eucharistic table is also

---

25. Tanner, *Christ the Key*, 200.

the paradigmatic site for Christian acts of communal sharing. Feeding each other with what Christ has provided affirms the intrinsic interdependence of Christ's body, in which no member can say to another, "I have no need of you" (1 Cor. 12:21).

Likewise, it is only on the Easter side of Christ's earthly story of struggle and seeming defeat, when his risen humanity fully manifests his dependence on the Father in the power of the Spirit, that the words from the Wisdom of Solomon quoted at the beginning of this essay can be seen to make sense of his earthly life as a whole: he is "the breath of the power of God, a pure emanation of divine glory, a reflection of eternal light, a flawless mirror of divine workings, and an image of God's goodness" (Wisd. of Sol. 7:25).

5

The Chief Point of Our Faith: Christ's Saving Death in Selected Greek Fathers

George Hunsinger

A certain puzzlement seems to recur about how Christ's saving significance was understood by the Greek Fathers. To what extent did they ascribe saving significance to Christ's incarnation and to what extent, if any, to Christ's death on the cross? Did they place most of their emphasis on the incarnation while allotting the cross only a minor role, or did they see the cross as somehow essential to the incarnation's saving significance? Did the two stand in disjunction so that the salvation was essentially independent of the cross? Or was there an inseparable connection between them in the accomplishment of salvation?

This dilemma appears in a recent essay by Brian Daley. He suggests that patristic soteriology was focused not on Christ's work but on Christ's person. "The soteriology of the early church," he writes, "most commonly understands redemption or salvation as being *achieved in Jesus' identity* rather than *accomplished as* his work."[1] This is a claim that the incarnation bears saving significance in itself, and that it does so essentially apart from the cross. "Patristic soteriology, both Eastern and Western," Daley explains, "tends to see redemption as already achieved in that personal *union* of God and a man—a union beginning in Jesus, uniquely rooted in him, but ultimately involving every human being."[2] The divinization of Jesus' human nature as rooted in the hypostatic union is ultimately extended to the whole of humanity. The role of the cross is minimal in the event of salvation as divinization. According to Daley, it plays little more than a symbolic role in reminding us of how deeply God entered into the human plight. This is a subtle version of the disjunctive view.

In what follows, I will attempt to defend the contrary proposition. At least for selected Greek Fathers, the cross is central not only to Christ's accomplishment of salvation but also to the form taken by the Christian life. The thesis of this essay is that for them the cross is the divinely ordained fulfillment of the incarnation while the incarnation is the necessary premise of the cross. The incarnation has no saving significance that can be separated from what took place in Christ's death, which is integral to the whole work of salvation. As seen by these patristic theologians, there is no cross without the incarnation, and no incarnation without the cross. The cross plays a fundamental role in the achievement of salvation.[3]

---

1. Brian Daley, "'He Himself Is Our Peace' (Ephesians 2:14): Early Christian Views of Redemption in Christ," in *The Redemption*, ed. Stephen T. Davis et al. (Oxford: Oxford University Press, 2004), 149-76 (151), italics original.
2. Ibid., italics original.
3. Although Daley does not neglect the role of the cross in patristic theology, it seems that he effectively marginalizes it.

Irenaeus of Lyons

As is well known, Irenaeus presents his understanding of salvation largely in terms of "recapitulation." Although this is a complex idea, for him recapitulation is essentially a process of reversal or undoing. Two things are happening in Christ at the same time: the past is undone while our human relationship to God is re-done, and this time rightly. What is reversed and renewed is not restricted to the level of spiritual inwardness, but is embodied in the flesh of the incarnate Son so that its implications are cosmic in scope.

Recapitulation means not just reversal and re-enactment, but also removal. Sin and death are undone and removed by the embodied obedience of the Son. The idea of an exchange, such as we will encounter again in later Fathers, is adumbrated. Jesus Christ takes our plight to himself in order to overcome it. He destroys our bondage to sin and death so that we might be restored to righteousness and life. He enters into in our corruption to destroy it from within so that, in and through him, we might become what he is. We are made to be children of God (by adoption) who may enjoy communion and eternal life—with the Father through the Son and in the Spirit. "In his immeasurable love, he became what we are in order to make us what he is" (*AH.* V, preface).[4] This is the patristic theme of the great and saving exchange.

For Irenaeus, the undoing of our corruption, which begins with the incarnation, does not reach fulfillment without the cross. There is no separation between the cross and the incarnation. They represent one integral process. Recapitulation through the incarnation as fulfilled in the cross involves participatory, victorious, and expiatory elements (though the latter is not always recognized by scholarship).

---

4. Translation as found in Hans Urs von Balthasar, ed., *The Scandal of the Incarnation: Irenaeus against the Heresies* (San Francisco: Ignatius Press, 1990), 54.

The Son reconciles us to God through his obedience unto death, by which the disobedience of Adam is undone. Based on this reversal, he elevates human beings to eternal life, which they enter by participating in his incarnate Person as glorified through his resurrection and ascension. Elevation to immortality and incorruptibility is understood as divinization.[5]

The cross, then, is the precondition of divinization. In it, all corruption is abolished that the corrupt may be transformed into incorruption, the sin of the world is expiated that the guilty may be divinely forgiven, and death is trampled out by death that the mortal may put on immortality. There is no separation between the person and the work. The person of Christ is always in his saving work, and the saving work is always in his person. Irenaeus takes the integral view.

Incorruptibility and immortality are not granted apart from the cross: "There was no other way for us to receive incorruptibility and immortality than to be united to them." But how could we be united to them, Irenaeus asks, without divine incorruptibility and immortality first becoming what we are—that is, without the Lord, incorruptible and immortal as he is, assuming to himself our mortal flesh (*AH.* III.19.1)?[6] He notes:

---

5. T. F. Torrance once told me in conversation that he saw a parallel between the Greek patristic idea of "divinization" and the traditional Reformed idea of "glorification." In his writings (following Athanasius and the early Cyril) he seemed to prefer the term *theopoeisis* as a way of keeping the divine and the human truly distinct. The standard account of *theosis* in English has been written by Norman Russell, who is excellent though perhaps at times overly schematic. A discriminating overview has been published by Donald Fairbairn, which is especially useful for Protestants. See Myk Habets, *Theosis in the Theology of Thomas Torrance* (Farnham, England: Ashgate, 2009); Norman Russell, *The Doctrine of Deification in the Greek Patristic Tradition* (Oxford: Oxford University Press, 2004); and Donald Fairbairn, "Patristic Soteriology: Three Trajectories," *Journal of the Evangelical Theological Society* 50 (2007): 289-310. For the traditional Reformed view, see Heinrich Heppe, *Reformed Dogmatics* (London: Allen and Unwin, 1950), 695-712, esp. 701.

6. Translation as found in D. J. Unger et al., eds., *St. Irenaeus of Lyons: Against the Heresies*, Book 3 (Mahwah, NJ: The Newman Press, 2012), 93 (translation revised).

In fact, it was not possible for humankind, which had once been conquered and dashed to pieces by its disobedience, to refashion itself and obtain the prize of the victory. Again, it was not possible for the human race, which had fallen under sin, to receive salvation. And so the Son, Word of God that he is, accomplished both, by coming down from the Father and becoming incarnate, and descending even to death, and bringing the economy of our salvation to completion (*AH*. III.18.2).[7]

Human salvation is not perfected by the incarnation alone, but ultimately in the Lord's death:

By his passion the Lord destroyed death, dissipated error, rooted out corruption, and destroyed ignorance, while also displaying life, revealing truth, and bestowing the gift of incorruption (*AH*. II.20.3).[8]

Recapitulation could be described by recourse to the image of the tree. The tree present at Adam's fall is reversed, Irenaeus suggests, by the tree on which Christ died. Adam's disobedience in the garden is undone by Christ's obedience "outside the gate" (Heb. 13:12). The Lord united himself to us and us to himself, not only by his incarnation (*AH*. V.16.2), but also by his passion and death (*AH*. V.16.3). It was a matter of dissolving Adam's disobedience, which was originally committed in respect of a tree, and healing it by Christ's obedience as triumphant on a tree (*AH*. V.16.3).[9] As by the one tree we became debtors to God, so by the other we receive remission of sins (*AH*. V.17.2). The cross is integral to the process of recapitulation.[10]

---

7. Ibid., 88.
8. Translation as found in H. E. W. Turner, *The Patristic Doctrine of Redemption* (London: Mowbray, 1952), 76 (translation revised).
9. Ibid., 65.
10. Note the hymn appointed to be sung for Holy Friday (actually sung Thursday night) in the Orthodox Church: "Today he who hung the earth upon the waters is hung upon a tree." This is a line that appears in the 2nd cent. Melito of Sardis's *Peri Pascha*, which is the earliest known Christian sermon on Pascha (although the rest of the hymn is later). It has a correlate in the liturgical cycle of Christmas, which is modeled on the Holy Week hymn. The connection to

Commenting on Paul, Irenaeus again sets forth the incarnation and the cross as inseparable. There is "one Jesus Christ," he notes, "who was born and who suffered" (*AH.* III.16.9). He continues:

> It was Christ who suffered.... He is the Son of God who, at the time fixed beforehand, died for us and redeemed us by his blood.... The same one who was captured and suffered, shedding his blood for us, was Christ, the Son of God, who also rose and was taken into heaven.... Christ Jesus, the Son of God, is one and the same, who through his passion reconciled us with God, and rose from the dead, and is at the right hand of the Father, having been perfected in all respects" (*AH.* III.16.9).[11]

The Lord's reconciling death on the cross was not without a priestly element. Although such a theme is not prominent in Irenaeus, he also affirms the cross as an act of intercession. The Son offers and commends to his Father the whole of humanity which he regained by his cross (*AH.* III.19.3). He redeemed us by his blood (*AH.* V.2.2). By his obedience on the cross, he propitiated the Father against whom we had sinned (*AH.* V.17.1). No one can forgive sins but God alone (*AH.* V.17.1). Anticipating Anselm, remarkably, Irenaeus states that only because Jesus Christ was both God and man could he receive the power to forgive sins from the Father: "Since as man he suffered with us, so as God he might take pity on us and forgive us the debts we owe to God our Creator" (*AH.* V.17.3).[12] God was pleased "to offer up . . . his own beloved and only-begotten Son, as a sacrifice for our redemption" (*AH.* IV.5.4).[13]

the cross is very firm in the Orthodox liturgical tradition. (I am grateful to the late Matthew Baker for this information.)

11. Unger et al., *St. Irenaeus of Lyons: Against the Heresies*, Book 3, 84 (translation revised).
12. Balthasar, *Scandal of the Incarnation*, 47-48.
13. Translation as found in *The Ante-Nicene Fathers*, vol. 1, trans. A. Roberts et al. (Grand Rapids: Eerdmans, 1987), 467.

Moreover, forgiveness by the cross is a reality that determines the Christian life, according to Irenaeus:

> Now, by the fact that the Lord said on the Cross, *Father forgive them, for they know not what they do*, Christ's long-suffering, patience, compassion, and goodness are shown forth inasmuch as he himself who suffered also excused those who had treated him wickedly. For the Word of God who told us, *love your enemies and pray for those who hate you*, did just that on the Cross, loving the human race so much that he prayed even for those who put him to death (*AH*. III.18.5).[14]

Because God did not use violence (*AH*. IV.37.1-2), but suffered for Adam and all humanity on the cross, the Lord's followers were to act accordingly by loving and forgiving their enemies without resorting to retaliation (*AH*. III.18.5).

In short, for Irenaeus, as Hans Urs von Balthasar urges, redemption depends on more than just the incarnation. It depends on three things: "the real Incarnation, the real suffering on the Cross, and the real resurrection of the flesh."[15] "The Cross," adds John Behr, "is *the* definitive event [for Irenaeus] in the revelation of God, occurring within our history yet with a significance that is eternal; the only perspective from which one can speak of the Word of God is that of the Cross."[16] Finally Denis Minns concurs that for Irenaeus the cross and the incarnation are integral to the work of salvation: "It was the incarnate Word who suffered and died on the Cross,... and it was the incarnate Word who conquered, endured, rose and ascended."[17] Reconciliation as accomplished by the cross was the precondition for divinization through the incarnation.

---

14. Unger et al, *St. Irenaeus of Lyons: Against the Heresies*, Book 3, 90 (italics original).
15. Balthasar, "Introduction," *Scandal of the Incarnation*, 3.
16. John Behr, *The Way to Nicaea*, vol. 1 (Crestwood, NY: St. Vladimir's Press, 2002), 122 (italics original).
17. Denis Minns, *Irenaeus: An Introduction* (London: T&T Clark, 2010), 111.

Athanasius of Alexandria

Elevating the incarnation at the expense of the cross was as foreign to Athanasius as it was to Irenaeus. Nevertheless, it is not uncommon for the disjunctive view to be ascribed to the great Alexandrian. According to J. N. D. Kelly, for example, "[T]he dominant strain in Athanasius's soteriology is the physical theory that Christ, by becoming man, restored the divine image in us."[18] Here the incarnation is seen as predominant, while the cross and resurrection are downplayed.[19] Or again, we read in R. P. C. Hanson: "One of the curious results of this theology of the Incarnation is that it almost does away with the doctrine of the atonement. Of course Athanasius believes in the atonement, in Christ's death as saving, but he cannot really explain why Christ should have died."[20] Regarding what is said in *On the Incarnation* about why the cross has saving significance, Hanson insists that Athanasius has little more than "a series of puerile reasons unworthy of the rest of the treatise." He concludes: "The fact is that his doctrine of the Incarnation has almost swallowed up any doctrine of the atonement, [rendering] it unnecessary."[21] Interpretations like these, while not uncommon, have been carefully refuted by patristic scholars like Weinandy, Anatolios, and Behr.[22]

Three main themes may be singled out from Athanasius's doctrine of salvation. First, through his cross, the Lord not only destroyed death by death but also (though again not widely recognized)

---

18. J. N. D. Kelly, *Early Christian Doctrines* (London: A. & C. Black, 1958), 377. As cited by Thomas G. Weinandy, *Athanasius: A Theological Introduction* (Farnham, England: Ashgate, 2007), 43.

19. Weinandy, *Athanasius*.

20. R. P. C. Hanson, *The Search for the Christian Doctrine of God: The Arian Controversy, 318–381* (Edinburgh: T&T Clark, 1988), 450. As cited by John Behr, "Introduction," in *Athanasius, On the Incarnation* (Yonkers, NY: St. Vladimir's Press, 2011), 37.

21. Ibid.

22. Ibid. Also, Weinandy, *Athanasius,*, and Khaled Anatolios, *Athanasius: The Coherence of His Thought* (London: Routledge, 1998), 67–84.

expiated our sins by his blood. Second, through his bodily resurrection he restored incorruption to all those united with him through faith. Third and finally, by revealing the truth of the Father, he restored us to the image of God. All these elements were essential to the goal of divinization.

At least four additional themes, moreover, stand out more sharply in Athanasius than in Irenaeus. First, in his account of the great and saving exchange, Athanasius incorporates substitutionary elements in a way that goes beyond Irenaeus. Second, the theme of Christ as the great High Priest emerges as a notable counterpoint to that of *Christus Victor*, thus combining cultic with royal elements. Third, Christ's death in its universal scope gains more prominence in Athanasius than in Irenaeus. Fourth and finally, more richly than in Irenaeus, Athanasius develops nonviolence and nonretaliation as implications of the cross for the Christian life.

Athanasius is famous for stating of the Word that "he became human that we might become God" (*Inc.* 54). The Greek original, however, is not easy to capture in its subtlety. The construction is actually more verbal.[23] It might better be rendered that "he was humanized (*enēnthropēsen*) that we might be divinized (*theopoiēthōmen*)."[24] Divinization would then, in effect, be something like the incarnation in reverse (when allowances are made for the difference between being God's Son by nature and being God's adopted children by grace).[25] Descent by incarnation takes place for the sake of the ascent, so to speak, by divinization.

23. The Greek text is given along with an English translation in Behr, *Athanasius, On the Incarnation.*

24. In context, *enēnthropēsen* actually implies the cross, not just incarnation, because Athanasius stresses throughout the mortal character of the humanity assumed by the Son.

25. Allowance would also need to be made for the difference between the hypostatic union (which is incommunicable) and the mystical union between Christ and his church. Divinization, properly conceived, does not "extend" the hypostatic union, nor does it "repeat" the Son's relationship to the Father. These relationships are unique in kind.

As Weinandy urges, the cross is fundamental to the whole process. He writes:

> It would ... be erroneous to interpret Athanasius' soteriology as merely incarnational, that is, by merely assuming our humanity he divinized it and made it incorruptible, thus diminishing the significance of the cross and the resurrection.... [Divinization is] achieved only through the whole of the soteriological economy—the Incarnation of the Word and the salvific actions that he undertakes as man, especially his death on the cross.[26]

"The primary cause of the Incarnation," urges Athanasius, is the death of Christ (*Inc.* 10).[27] His death is indeed "the chief point of our faith" [*to kephalaion tēs pisteōs*] (*Inc.* 19). The death of death takes place in the death of Christ for the sake of all (*Inc.* 25):

> Both things happened together in a paradoxical manner: the death of all was completed in the lordly body, and also death and destruction were destroyed by the Word in it.... The Word, although he was not able to die—for he was immortal—took to himself a body able to die that he might offer it as his own in the place of all [*anti pantōn*] and as himself suffering on behalf of all [*huper pantōn*], through coming into it (*Inc.* 20).[28]

The Lord's death is set forth, most especially, in victorious, substitutionary, sacrificial, and universal terms. He dies in the stead of all by offering himself up for the sake of all. He not only removes sin, but also destroys death as the two great obstacles to divinization:

> And thus taking from our bodies one of like nature, because all were under penalty of the corruption of death, he gave it over to death in the stead of all [*anti pantōn*], and offered it to the Father—doing this, moreover, of his loving kindness, to the end that, firstly, all being held to have died in him, the law involving the ruin of human beings might

26. Weinandy, *Athanasius: A Theological Introduction*, 43.
27. Behr, *Athanasius, On the Incarnation*, 71.
28. Ibid., 95 (translation revised).

be undone (inasmuch as its power was fully spent in the Lord's body, and had no holding power against human beings, his peers) and that, secondly, he might turn them again to incorruption, and quicken them from death by the appropriation of his body and by the grace of the resurrection, banishing death from them like straw from fire (*Inc.* 8).[29]

Athanasius stresses how great a reversal this salvation brings to the form of Christian life. Warfare is linked in his mind with dispositions and worship. Those whose dispositions are brutal are the very ones who worship demonic powers. They rage against each other "and cannot bear to be a single hour without weapons." It is to "barbarians" such as these, he writes, that the gospel is addressed (*Inc.* 52):[30]

> When they hear the teaching of Christ, they immediately turn from war to farming, and instead of arming their hands with swords they lift them up in prayer; and, in a word, instead of waging war among themselves, from now on they take up arms against the devil and the demons, subduing them by their self-command and integrity of soul (*Inc.* 52).

What this moral revolution proves, Athanasius suggests, is the Savior's Godhead: "What human beings were unable to learn from idols they have learned from him" (*Inc.* 52). The Lord's followers have ceased from mutual fighting. By their renewed hearts and peaceable lives, they oppose the demonic powers of death: "When they are insulted, they are patient, when robbed they make light of it, and most amazingly, they scorn death in order to become martyrs of Christ" (*Inc.* 52). Athanasius affirms that believers are those who would prefer to die "rather than deny their faith in Christ" (*Inc.* 27). In this way they show their love for him who "by his own love underwent all things for our salvation" (*Inc.* 52).

29. Weinandy *Athanasius*, 32-33 (translation revised).
30. All material excerpted from *Incarnation* 27 and 52 here and immediately hereafter is translated by a "Religious of C.S.M.V" as found in *St. Athanasius on the Incarnation* (Crestwood, NY: St. Vladimir's, 1989), 90-91.

Gregory of Nazianzus and Cyril of Alexandria

Were space to permit, similar trajectories of thought could be traced through other Greek patristic theologians. The great and saving exchange, the centrality of the cross, and most especially its victorious, sacrificial, substitutionary, and universal elements—as preconditions to divinization and eternal life—these themes became standard items in what Georges Florovsky liked to call the "patristic synthesis."[31] The suffering of the impassible God, a paradoxical theme broached by Athanasius,[32] was particularly carried forward and profoundly deepened by Gregory of Nazianzus[33] and Cyril of Alexandria.[34]

Gregory of Nazianzus, much like Irenaeus and Athanasius, set forth the cross as essential to salvation.[35] "We are saved," he taught, "by the sufferings of the impassible one" (*Oratio in laudem Basilii* 30). The impassible Lord was "made passible for our sake against sin" (*Or.* 30). He died that our sins might be forgiven (*Or.* 33). Echoing Irenaeus, Nazianzus could write: "He is brought up to a tree and nailed to it—yet by the tree of life he restores us" (*Or. 29*). A *Christus Victor* note is sounded—"He dies, but he vivifies and by death destroyed death" (*Or. 29*)—while a priestly counterpoint accompanies it: "He is called 'Sheep,' because he was sacrificed.... He is the 'High Priest,' because he presented the offering" (*Or.* 30). He continues: "The one who releases me from the curse was called 'curse' because of me; 'the

31. See Paul Gavrilyuk, *Georges Florovsky and the Russian Religious Renaissance* (Oxford: Oxford University Press, 2014): 261–63.

32. See Anatolios, *Athanasius*, 142–50.

33. See Christopher A. Beeley, *The Unity of Christ: Continuity and Conflict in Patristic Tradition* (New Haven: Yale University Press, 2012), 186–93.

34. See Paul L. Gavrilyuk, *The Suffering of the Impassible God: The Dialectics of Patristic Thought* (Oxford: Oxford University Press, 2004), 133–75.

35. All passages quoted from Gregory of Nazianzus, *On God and Christ: The Five Theological Orations and Two Letters to Cledonius*, trans. Fred Williams and John Behr (Yonkers, NY: St. Vladimir's Press, 2002).

one who takes away the world's sin' was called 'sin'" (*Or.* 30). In short, Nazianzus teaches that "you may ascend from below to become God, because he came down for us from above" (*Or.* 30), to die for us on the cross.

The situation is no different for Cyril of Alexandria. He, too, sees the cross as integral to the incarnation. He, too, makes no separation of Christ's person from his work of salvation on the cross. As he stated in his famous Twelfth Anathema against Nestorious:

> If anyone does not confess that the Word of God suffered in the flesh, and was crucified in the flesh, and tasted death in the flesh, and became the first-born from the dead, since he is life and life-giving God, let him be anathema.[36]

In his Isaiah commentary, Cyril links Isa. 53 with Hebrews 13: "Jesus suffered outside the gate to sanctify the people through his own blood" (Heb. 13:12). As Wilken observes, what interests Cyril is the point that Christ died on behalf of others, and that he was "wounded for our transgressions" (Isa. 53:4). Like Athanasius and Gregory of Nazianzus (but unlike Irenaeus), Cyril granted prominence to 2 Cor. 5:14. He especially emphasized the statement that "he died for all" (2 Cor. 5:14), one of the great universalizing verses in the New Testament: "Rightly then the prophet says: 'This one was stricken, for he knew that he was to bear our infirmities . . . and he suffered for us.'" As the one without sin (2 Cor. 5:21), he suffered and died for all.[37]

For Cyril, the divinizing purpose of the incarnation was closely aligned with the cross. Reminiscent of Athanasius and Gregory, the

---

36. Cyril of Alexandria, Letter 17 to Nestorius, in *Letters 1-50*, trans. John I. McEnerney (Washington, DC: Catholic University of America Press, 1985), 92.

37. Commentary on Isa. 53:4-6, as cited by Robert Wilken, "Cyril as Interpreter of the Old Testament," in *The Theology of Cyril of Alexandria: A Critical Appreciation*, ed. Thomas G. Weinandy and D.A. Keating (London: T&T Clark, 2003), 1-21(8).

reason for the incarnation was "that being by nature God and of God, the Only-begotten has become man; namely with the intent to condemn sin in the flesh, and by his own death to slay death, and to make us sons of God, regenerating in the Spirit those on earth to receive supernatural dignity."[38] He continues:

> For this cause, though he is Life by nature, he became as one dead; that, having destroyed the power of death in us, he might mold us anew into his own life; and being himself the righteous God, he became sin for us (2 Cor. 5:21).[39]

Weinandy concludes:

> While Cyril was concerned with upholding the impassible divinity of the Son as God, his interest in this was primarily for incarnational and soteriological reasons. He wished to assure that it was actually the divine Son who lived a full human life and so the Son who was impassible as God is the same Son who could truly experience human suffering and death.[40]

In short, although for significant stretches it can seem that for Cyril divinization takes place only through the incarnational union, he always comes back to the cross: "The Lord of Glory is himself the crucified one.... He suffered in the flesh for us, and on our behalf."[41] He continues: "Our Savior ... gave his blood" for us through "his sufferings on the Cross."[42] When "he wrapped himself in flesh that was capable of suffering," it was "a matter of the salvation of the whole world."[43]

---

38. Commentary on John 14:20 (translation revised), as cited by Thomas G. Weinandy, "Cyril and the Mystery of the Incarnation," in Weinandy and Keating, eds., *Theology of Cyril of Alexandria*, 23-53 (25).
39. Ibid.
40. Ibid., 51.
41. Cyril of Alexandria, *On the Unity of Christ*, trans. John Anthony McGuckin (Crestwood, NY: St. Vladimir's, 1995), 116.
42. Ibid., 112.
43. Ibid., 118.

Conclusion

The patristic doctrine of redemption was a complex matter in which royal and priestly elements were focused on the incarnation and fulfilled in the cross.[44] On my reading, the saving significance of Christ's cross is not fully developed in Kathryn Tanner's theology, although she is sympathetic to the early Greek Fathers and apparently takes the integral view argued in this essay. For example, Tanner writes:

> The incarnation is not, then, to be identified with one moment of Jesus' life, his birth, in contradistinction from his ministry, death, and resurrection. The incarnation is, to the contrary, the underlying given that makes all Jesus does and suffers purifying, healing, and elevating.... Jesus does not heal death until the Word assumes death when Jesus dies.... Here is a solution to the common problem of integrating the incarnation with the rest of those aspects of Jesus' life and death deemed to be saving—particularly, with the crucifixion. Here the saving power of the cross is a product of the incarnation, as its effects are actualized over time and in and through Jesus' actual dying.... The cross is a sacrifice but only in the same sense that Jesus' whole life is a sacrifice of love. Following Cyril of Alexandria, the sacrifice here is a sacrifice of incarnation.[45]

For the Greek patristic theologians we have considered, there was no future redemption without reconciliation, no regeneration without vicarious shedding of blood, and no divinization without the Lord's victory over death by death. This essay has thus more fully fleshed out a key point central to Tanner's Christology: by viewing his incarnate person as always in his work, and his saving work as always

---

44. In interpreting the Greek fathers (not to mention Luther), Gustaf Aulen was mistaken to elevate the royal elements above all else while throwing the priestly elements into almost total eclipse. See Aulen, *Christus Victor* (New York: Macmillan, 1969).

45. Kathryn Tanner, *Jesus, Humanity and the Trinity: A Brief Systematic Theology* (Minneapolis: Fortress Press, 2001), 28-29.

in his person, these patristic theologians took the integral not the disjunctive view for soteriological reasons.[46]

---

46. I would like to thank Kathleen McVey, Paul Molnar, and Deborah van Deusen Hunsinger for helpful comments on this essay. I dedicate it to the blessed memory of my friend and colleague Matthew Baker, who helped me greatly as I was preparing it.

6

On Making Christology Look Too Easy: A Dialectical "Rejoiner" to Tanner's Lineage

William A. Wright

The first time I read Kathryn Tanner, I was flummoxed. I had become infatuated with dialectical thinking, whether in Paul, Chalcedon, Dionysius, Luther, Hegel, or Barth. But here was brilliant theology that had no need of dialectical counterpose. Instead, the whole seemed to flow smoothly from a central insight into the noncompetitive relation between God and humanity. So was all of my self-gratifying intellectual handwringing quite unnecessary, after all? Kathryn graciously and supportively advised my dissertation—essentially a comparison of the dialectics of Calvin's soteriology, Hegel's *Logic*, and Derrida's deconstruction of Hegel—without ever betraying a note of distaste. I was left to ponder, and continue to do so here, what those 500 overwrought pages on dialectic really had to add to the elegant work of Kathryn Tanner.

"Dialectic" is a regrettably slippery and multifaceted word, due to the many avenues by which something called "dialectic" has insinuated itself into theology. In fact, Tanner's theology often follows one kind of dialectical format by which she surveys the history of theology according to certain aporias and then seeks to solve them. Thus, *God and Creation* considers the modern theological contradance between those insisting on grace alone and those trumpeting free will; she argues that this impasse is "dissolved" by considering the inner coherence of classical Christian formulations, and thus the choice is unnecessary.[1] In *Christ the Key*, Tanner wends her way through the longstanding disjuncture between Catholic and Protestant theologies of grace; and again in chapter seven, she considers "the split or bifurcated understanding of how the Spirit works that is typical of modern Christian thought and practice," namely, between those who see the Spirit working directly and instantaneously versus gradually and through ordinary processes.[2] This time, Tanner essentially sides with the latter option. Finally, and central to this essay, in *Jesus, Humanity and the Trinity* Tanner identifies two seemingly bedrock principles (divine non-competitiveness and transcendence) and applies them to "resolve christological conundrums," particularly the classical dispute between Alexandrian and Antiochene Christologies, a dispute regrettably sharpened by tendencies in modern theology.[3] In these helpful uses of dialectic, Tanner shows how a careful application of theological principles can either undo theological aporias or direct us to the correct side.

1. Kathryn Tanner, *God and Creation in Christian Theology: Tyranny or Empowerment?* (Minneapolis: Fortress Press, 2005), 8.
2. Kathryn Tanner, *Christ the Key*, Current Issues in Theology (Cambridge: Cambridge University Press, 2010), chs. 2, 3, and 7.
3. Kathryn Tanner, *Jesus, Humanity and the Trinity: A Brief Systematic Theology* (Minneapolis: Fortress Press, 2001), ch. 1.

The kind of dialectical theology I advocate for—hesitantly, given the power and utility of Tanner's theology—takes a more thoroughgoing dialectical form. The classical aporias of theology are not regrettable moments of confusion that await conceptual clarification, but are signposts to the inevitably dialectical content of theology. The purpose of systematic theology, then, is not to resolve theological conflict, but to show how it is inevitable and illuminating. Or again, the goal of theology, when it can afford the luxury of theory, is not to establish theological principles that can govern Christian language, but to collect and order the pluralism that results as Christian language through the ages falls out into conceptual conflicts—the proper product of theology being a dialectical *taxis*.[4] While I have come to believe in the value of this understanding of systematic theology, it brings with it disadvantages—primarily, a tendency to theoretical excess—and I am not prepared to assert its demonstrable value over Tanner's approach. Nor, as I shall show by closely examining her Christology, do I wish to cast Tanner's theology as a rigidly thetic and linear system. Rather, I believe that my more dialectical direction deviates only modestly from Tanner's already subtle use of conceptual principles; and however great the deviation, my hope is that it proves to be only a detour that ultimately can "rejoin" and defer to her insights.

Pragmatic and Apophatic Sensibilities

There are two global and general ways that Tanner's theology militates against any triumphalism of conceptual rule. There is, first, her strong grasp of the practical and contextual nature of theology, which lends all her work a deftly pragmatic bent. In particular,

---

4. See William A. Wright, "A Trinity of Non-Univocal Persons: Towards a Model of Doctrinal Writing," *Journal of Reformed Theology* 5 (2011): 129-58.

Theories of Culture argues that cultures are always plural and always contested; therefore theology cannot address some purportedly universal culture, as classical academia pretended to do. Eschewing universality and *its* university, theology should be located on a particular place in the cultural map and be a part of "everyday Christian practice."[5] Theology is a practical endeavor rather than a purely theoretical one. Even "systematic theology" is "an attempt to meet an essential demand of everyday Christian living."[6] While contextually oriented, Tanner, maintaining the tradition of university theology, upholds a commitment to studying the whole history of theology, but not to the end of establishing universal conclusions about Christian history. Rather, she turns to the history of theology as a resource for seeing how the Christian message has varied across a diversity of practical situations and cultural differences.[7] In sum, Tanner aligns theology explicitly with the pragmatist tradition.[8]

Tanner's theology also resists the straightforward application of principles, secondly, by a strong dose of *apophaticism* that is well-grounded in classical orthodoxy. The apophatic orientation to divine transcendence that she first elucidated in *God and Creation*[9] is even more at the fore in her recent article on creation *ex nihilo*: "[Divine transcendence] signals a general linguistic disturbance, the failure of all predicative attribution, in language about God."[10] Discourse about

---

5. Kathryn Tanner, *Theories of Culture: A New Agenda for Theology*, Guides to Theological Inquiry (Minneapolis: Fortress Press, 1997), 67, 71. See also Kathryn Tanner, "Theology and Cultural Contest in the University," in *Religious Studies, Theology, and the University*, ed. Linell Cady and Delwin Brown (Albany, NY: SUNY Press, 2002), 199-212.

6. Tanner, *Jesus, Humanity and the Trinity*, 13.

7. Ibid., xvii-xviii.

8. See her indirect alignment with pragmatism (and analytic philosophy) in Tanner, *God and Creation*, 11; cf. 13, 16.

9. Tanner, *God and Creation*, 12: "On this apophatic or agnostic reading, theological statements are not conveying information about God so much as they are suggesting how to talk in circumstances where we do not pretend to understand fully what we are saying."

God violates the way language usually works. God is not a *type* of thing, and so violates the normal way that placing something in a type automatically excludes it from a different type. That God is not a body, for example, does not mean God is a spirit. Putting it with verve: "God is identified ... by this very failure to mean," a failure that "haunts" all theological discourse.[11] "God becomes the paradigmatic inassimilable Other, the (paradoxically non-predicatively grounded) paradigm for all that remains indigestible to sense-making practices that insist on the exhaustive, homogenizing subsumption of particulars under general concepts." Here Tanner might be confused for the deconstructive theologians in the heady days of the 1980s and 1990s! Unlike this group of theologians, however, Tanner yokes apophaticism to the aforementioned pragmatic orientation for theology, as again in "Creation *Ex Nihilo*": the way theological concepts violate normal patterns of thought, she notes, makes these concepts exceptionally flexible in practical applications.[12]

In line with her pragmatic and apophatic commitments, Tanner draws on conventional designations to distinguish formal theological discourse from ordinary Christian language. In *God and Creation*, she employs the terms found in George Lindbeck, as well as others, to distinguish "first order" theological claims from the "second order" status of the peculiar type of theological rules that she will formulate

10. Kathryn Tanner, "Creation *Ex Nihilo* as Mixed Metaphor," *Modern Theology* 29, no. 2 (2013): 138.
11. Compare Tanner, *God and Creation,* 26, with Tanner, "Creation *Ex Nihilo*," 140. In the former document, Tanner applies language similar to what I cite above to finger not God as the basic problem of discourse, but the sedimented meanings in language that theology borrows: "The appearance of inconsistency that haunts theological statements is the result of this struggle *with previous linguistic habits.* The expectations of linguistic practices the theologian is working to revise always suggest that theological statements violate the canons of good sense" [emphasis added]. In the latter document, God's being beyond categories is the primary cause for a failure to make sense; the problem of linguistic sedimentations is a "subsidiary" cause.
12. Tanner, "Creation *Ex Nihilo*," 140; she makes the point more thoroughly, emphatically, and "conservatively" in *God and Creation,* 12.

(and which may sound like conceptually adjudicatory claims). These rules help in forming first-order statements, but the latter will vary with context.[13] In *Theories of Culture*, however, she subjects this distinction to rigorous critique, wishing neither to separate academic theology from practice (including its own "material social process") nor to dissemble the constructive and contestable character of theology under the pretense that "second order" theology simply defers to first-order practices.[14] Nonetheless, she continues even most recently to describe the principle of transcendence as a "grammatical remark."[15]

That Tanner practices, in all these ways, an attentiveness to primary communities of theology distinguishes her from those whose theology remains embedded within a theory-to-theory engagement, whether this means self-indulgently innovating on tradition or officiously exposing and refuting the heterodoxy of these innovations. While firmly orthodox, her work has nothing of the clamor nor the sprawling genealogies of such *defensores fidei* as John Milbank, David Bentley Hart, or Paul Molnar. Still, she is not beyond ruling innovations out of bounds. While Tanner can use her theological principles or rules as a "force for theological diversity"[16] by showing how they render a variety of theological expressions coherent, she readily abjures certain views, especially the suffering of God espoused by Jürgen Moltmann and others. Bad thinking, of course, deserves rigorous critique; Tanner's defrocking of the

---

13. Tanner, *God and Creation*, 27.
14. Tanner, *Theories of Culture*, 73-76. The entire section through p. 92 is a goldmine, to which I have failed to do justice in my forthcoming book's analysis of academic theology in relation to Christian practice. However, I wonder if Tanner's recent work, which is so intertextually engaged with early Christian theology, has moved away from the Bourdieu-inspired reflexivity so carefully explicated in *Theories of Culture*.
15. Tanner, "Creation *Ex Nihilo*," 138.
16. Tanner, *God and Creation*, 104. I can do no brief justice to the extremely subtle and insightful analysis and genealogy of traditional and modern theology in *God and Creation*.

political conclusions Moltmann draws from the Trinity is exemplary.[17] And to be sure, Moltmann, brandishing his own conceptual excess, has hastily extended his own experience and analysis of "twentieth century culture" into a speculative impugning of key tenets of classical orthodoxy. For her part, Tanner dismisses divine suffering universally, often under the assumption that a suffering God cannot save. In this case, she is willing to rule out a position without regard to contextual possibilities. It may be, however, that the extremes of suffering from the Shoah and other oppressions call forth radical "first order" expressions that ordinary experience would not need to countenance. If so, evaluating such expressions from a theoretical position betrays an excessive confidence in conceptual, academic discourse.

Of course, there is no sure path toward evaluating whether a given body of theology contains such an excess. Much depends on how we understand the theoretical jurisdiction of theological work; Tanner's overall position is very subtle.[18] It seems to me that in practical contexts, strong theological judgments may be called for, but it is also possible that a circumspect reserve would be appropriate. On the other hand, it is possible that strong theological judgments would be appropriate in the most theoretical and systematic contexts. I will suggest later how I see a dialectical theology to be a useful guide amidst these possibilities.

The Use of Conceptual Principles in Tanner's Christology

In the meantime, I can attempt to do some justice to Tanner's specific use of concepts, both forceful and nuanced, within her Christology.

---

17. See Tanner, *Christ the Key*, ch. 5.
18. Tanner notes, "One cannot appeal to something underlying or behind the surface of these changing patterns of actual uses [of Christian practice] that will sort out in advance which new uses of Christian notions will turn out to be right or wrong" (Tanner, *Theories of Culture*, 79).

Tanner begins her brief systematic theology with a bold and succinct doctrine of God: God is "the giver of all good gifts." While she foregoes many of the classical components of this locus, such as proofs for God's existence and divine attributes such as aseity (although she notes that God is "already abundant fullness"), included already in this spare but rich claim is the distinctness of God from creation and the goodness of God.[19] She also briefly indicates something about creation as the recipient of God's giving. The world does not receive gifts from God in the way rain falls from the sky, but "good gifts" here correspond to relations with God and the gradual "perfection" of creation.[20] Using flexible terminology, she states that perfection is achieved by "closer relations" with God, in "union" with God, in "being brought near" God.[21] This perfection happens gradually, certainly because of the struggle to overcome sin, but also because of a gradual increase in capacity for divine union over the course of a person's life and, on a larger scale, of history.[22]

Having set out briefly a view of God's purposes with creation, Tanner then identifies the two important principles that "underlie" it. The first concerns the relationship between God and creation; the second, while it is the "precondition" for the first, is more abstractly concerned with God's own being. The first principle, then, concerns the non-competitive relation between creatures and God. That is, God, in order to increase (so to speak—God's existence is replete),

19. Cf. Tanner, *Christ the Key*, 53.

20. Tanner, *Jesus, Humanity and the Trinity*, 2. There is a certain ambiguity detectable here in the nature of God's gifts. Are the gifts created goods, such as means of sustenance or even feelings of joy, or are they the divine presence itself? It is of course possible that Tanner's claim about the non-competitive relationship between God and creation could render this distinction meaningless. Perhaps my confusion stems from expecting the divine presence to imply personal categories; Tanner, responding to Ian McFarland, at least argues explicitly for the superiority of impersonal categories for grace. See Kathryn Tanner, "Author Response," *Theology Today* 68, no. 3 (2011): 344-45.

21. Tanner, *Jesus, Humanity and the Trinity*, 2.

22. See ibid., 41-46. See Tanner, *Christ the Key*, 34, on the idea that human beings are created immature.

does not need the creature to decrease (to twist the saying of John the Baptist); conversely, to be full of God does not equate to a diminishing of the creature's own existence and dignity—quite the opposite. Otherwise put, God's activity does not require the creature's passivity.

Since God does indeed give to creatures, but within a non-competitive relationship, then it must not be that God gives "on the same plane of being and activity as creatures."[23] Human beings, by contrast, when aiding each other on the same "plane" must either split the activity (co-operate) or act in someone else's stead.[24] We conduct our operations always upon a limited expanse of the world, which we competitively carve out for ourselves or cooperatively append to someone else's limited expanse. God's operations, however, have no such limit but include the entirety of existence. God's acting both on a different plane and all-inclusively point to the second principle of divine transcendence.[25] At its most abstract, this principle concerns

23. Tanner, *Jesus, Humanity and the Trinity*, 3; cf. p. 16: "Jesus' life as a whole is both divine and human but on different planes of reality, one being the source of the other."

24. An apt exception is the work of a teacher who brings out the student's own activity. It seems that the human plane is not closed off from participating in the divine form of non-competitive giving; indeed, Tanner's whole theology is directed toward elevating the human in this direction.

25. I say "both" without being sure whether there are two distinct things being said. The language of a different "plane" of causality, for instance, could mean that the cause of something can be described from two distinct but non-competing perspectives. Thus the same finite action could be the result of my virtue, from the human view, as well as God's inspiration from the divine view, without these two perspectives detracting from one another. (Cf. again, Tanner, *Jesus, Humanity and the Trinity*, 16, on the assumption: "The same human features and effects of Jesus' life may be attributed to Jesus as both divine and human since Jesus' divinity, the Word's assumption of his humanity, is the immediate source of his whole human life.") In this way, God could be said to be the cause of a finite action. But as for the point about God's bringing about the whole of creaturely action, the claim here could allow for a more robust but also equivocal sense of divine cause, one that not only parallels the creature's actions but is all-inclusive of them. In that case, explaining how God is the cause of finite events becomes potentially difficult. Ambiguity related to divine causality shows up when Tanner states, "Assumption by Christ cannot be identified with discrete moments of our lives in which we are merely passive," followed soon after by: "Unlike the case with Christ himself, our assumption by Christ can be indexed to some extent to certain discrete moments in our lives" (Ibid., 72–73). Representing her overall tendency, the remarks on Tanner, *Jesus, Humanity and the Trinity*, 3–4, favor the

the categories of identity and difference as they apply between God and the world: talk about God should avoid "either simple identity or contrast with the qualities of creatures." Tanner already more expansively treated this notion of divine transcendence in *God and Creation*, where she argued that a notion of transcendence that contrasts God with the world, characteristic of Greek philosophical thought, will inevitably bring "God down to the level of the non-divine to which it is opposed."[26] The result of this narrow view of transcendence is that God is denied any direct involvement with the world, something left to mediators.[27] To say in a more "radicalized" way that God is beyond any simple contrast with the world allows also for the opposite extreme: "a divine involvement in the form of a productive agency extending to everything that is in an equally direct manner."[28]

While there is much more to be said, these two principles lend her theology a conceptual power that is immediately evident and highly useful, especially for understanding—or better, not misconstruing—the incarnation. With Tanner's principles in place, the incarnation is not a freakish exception to the normally extrinsic relation between God and creatures.[29] It is just thus that modern

---

second, more robust relation of divine and creaturely causation. Perhaps she would want to say that the former relation can only be consistently made sense of by way of the latter. Or it could be that Tanner's overall approach is too committed to apophaticism, pragmatism, or both, to offer a more robust theoretical explanation; see Tanner, *God and Creation*, 26 (cited below). Her countering of "theological occasionalism" on pp. 86-90 is also relevant.

26. Tanner, *God and Creation*, 46.

27. Tanner's critique of this notion of transcendence may imply a rejection of the rich legacy of mediator Christologies. She does not address this issue directly, as far as I know. Certainly, she sees no need for the mediation characteristic of Anselmian theories of atonement, in which the Son mediates to satisfy the Father (Tanner, *Jesus, Humanity and the Trinity*, 29; Tanner, *Christ the Key*, ch. 6). Rather, she holds on to mediation language by transmuting it into the hypostatic union: "Jesus therefore mediates divinity and humanity because he unites both and not because he is something in between" (ibid., 157).

28. Tanner, *God and Creation*, 46.

29. In her own fine words: "Rather than coming at the expense of divinity, incarnation is the very thing that proves divinity" (Tanner, *Jesus, Humanity and the Trinity*, 11).

thought, both secular and Christian—and in either case more Deistic than it realizes—tends to view the incarnation, and as a result finds Christology fundamentally paradoxical at best and irrational at worst. But Tanner's principles establish precisely that *in principle* there is nothing impossible about the co-inherence of divinity and humanity in one person. Moreover, Tanner uses these principles to vindicate the fundamental correctness of Neo-Platonic-influenced[30] classical Christology as represented by Athanasius, the Cappadocians, and Aquinas.[31] In the process she resolves the long-festering dispute between Alexandrian and Antiochene Christologies, largely siding in favor with the former.[32] What matters about Jesus is not his possession of an intact human self like ours, but his being the Word of God united with humanity in the person of Jesus. Beyond simply vindicating the dominant strand of classical Christology, she constructs a way to correctively reconcile classical Christology with historically realistic accounts of Jesus' humanity, most notably through her understanding of the incarnation as a process of the elevation and perfection of Jesus' humanity through the Spirit.[33] Other scholars have more capably noted the significance of these achievements than I am able to do here. We only wish that more

---

30. I detect a shift in tone—subtly more positive—when it comes to Tanner's treatment of Neo-Platonism on its own terms; compare her critical comments in Tanner, *God and Creation*, 42–45, with her similar argument, published in 2013, in Tanner, "Creation *Ex Nihilo*," 144–46.

31. Care should be taken when pinning the blame for christological problems on "modernity," especially given the ideological resonances inherent in any talk of "modernity" and, in particular, the abuse of genealogy, however interesting and insightful, by figures like John Milbank. I believe Tanner could do more to subject classical Christian thinkers to critical scrutiny; more often she simply cites pearls of wisdom approvingly. But she, unlike Milbank, also values and cites Reformation theologians, as well as not only early postmodern theologians like Barth and Rahner, but also Schleiermacher.

32. Again, rather than see Tanner's achievement as a blow to modernity on behalf of a mythologized ancient Christian synthesis, I think it more accurate to see a corrected and improved version of the dominant strand of Orthodox theology, which was never uncontested in the ancient world and which can stand to be improved by new questions and thoughts proposed by modern thinkers.

33. Tanner, *Jesus, Humanity and the Trinity*, 26–32, 51–52.

non-professional theologians were aware of the powerful conceptual resource Tanner has made available.

Critical Scrutiny of the Principles

Naturally, questions remain about these principles themselves. Steffen Lösel claims to find a paradox in how Tanner applies these principles to overcome the Alexandrian-Antiochene conflict. Essentially, his point comes down to this: Tanner sides with a strong Alexandrian position (endorsing its anhypostatic-enhypostatic Christology) but refuses the statements of Cyril which affirm that the divine Son suffers in Christ.[34] He does not say as much, but it would appear that the principle of non-competitive relation, when it comes to Jesus' suffering, trumps the hypostatic union on this point.

Lösel's brief essay, perhaps too eager to allege contradiction in order to vindicate Pannenberg, could do more to probe the workings of Tanner's theology. To make a very basic gesture in this direction, I would venture that Tanner's christological discourse follows a pattern in which the leading claim asserts a strong ontological difference between God and creation, as in the phrase "a difference of planes." At the same time, there is a commitment to some kind of causal influence running only in one direction, from the divine to creation; God is a "giver" and "provider." When Tanner responds to Lösel, we see both elements. Tanner restates her position in *Jesus, Humanity and the Trinity*, clarifying that the divine and human natures of Jesus should not be seen to exist "on the same ontological plane"—the source of many traditional confusions and errors. This fundamental of transcendence is followed by the overtone of causality: Jesus' human

---

34. Steffen Lösel, "You Can't Have Cyril's Cake and Eat It, Too: Christological Conundrums in *Christ the Key*," *Theology Today* 68, no. 3 (2011): 330-39. I am more ambivalent about his other concerns—briefly: to preserve the "independence" of Jesus' humanity from his divinity and to resist a Christology from above.

nature is "thoroughly shaped ... in and through union with the second person of the Trinity."[35] In *Jesus, Humanity and the Trinity*, the element of causality especially moves to the fore when Tanner articulates an anhypostatic-enhypostatic understanding of the union of natures in Jesus.[36] There is nothing odd about this. These same twin elements of transcendence and causality are found in Aquinas; I suspect what Tanner would spell out by "causality" would be no less straightforward than what we find in Aquinas, since the causation principle is conditioned by the principle of transcendence, though she would presumably lean more toward Platonic participation than Aquinas does.[37] While there is a certain depth or obscurity, depending on how we see it, with regard to how transcendence and causality cohere, it seems precipitous to conclude with Lösel that a contradiction evidently results between the hypostatic union and divine impassibility. Tanner is clear that the causation runs one way only, and for the purpose of elevating the human into the divine. Her claim is motivated by both theological and soteriological convictions, namely: God is beyond suffering, and it wouldn't save us if the opposite were true. And so Jesus' human struggles, including suffering and death, are very real, because while the Word assumes

---

35. See Tanner, "Author Response," 340.

36. Tanner, *Jesus, Humanity and the Trinity*, 24 (with added emphasis): "One should seek an explanation [for the unity of natures in Jesus] instead in the divine *cause* of the togetherness of divine and human functions in Christ." There are several mentions in the ensuing pages of her book of causal concepts, especially God or the Word "effecting" the humanity of Jesus.

37. Tanner, *Jesus, Humanity and the Trinity*, 24-25, briefly considers some options, especially Aquinas, Rahner, and Barth, for understanding the relation of divine and human causality with regard to Christology. In a crucial passage on p. 26 she invokes the non-competitive principle to correct an Alexandrian mistake. While the Alexandrians are right about the Word's having "primacy" as the cause of Jesus' humanity, they contrast the activity of the Word with the activity of the human being, as if these are exclusive (or competitive). Non-competitiveness functions expressly as an *apophatic* principle here. To set Jesus' divine and human action in contrast, as the Alexandrians sometimes did, is "to bring divinity down to the human level." While insightful, Tanner's point comes among at least some degree of such contrast. The principle of non-competition only works in Tanner within a framework of absolute difference between God and creation.

the whole person of Jesus on the divine side, the elevation of the human can only transpire through normal human temporality. Presumably this elevation of the humanity of Jesus reaches a completion with the resurrection, since Tanner's soteriology is very much anchored in our participation in the completed union of divine and human in Jesus.[38] *Pace* Lösel, it is only if the causality between divine and human runs both ways that we would have to conclude, as Cyril apparently later did, that the divine must suffer along with the human in Jesus.

Still, well short of precipitously finding Tanner guilty of contradiction, I wonder if there is not more tension in the two principles than Tanner admits. I do not doubt that she could clear up the relationship between divine transcendence and causality, specifically: how exactly does God act on a "different plane?"[39] Assuming clarification is possible, still the principles invite a little deconstructing. Tanner repeatedly explains the principle of transcendence by saying that God cannot be held to "simple contrasts" between divine and human characteristics.[40] This idea has a rich history and deserves more attention than I can give it. Its explication by Tanner spans spare claims that God is "beyond kinds"—a type of conceptual rule—as well as the more dramatic, narrative language of Karl Barth in which God has overcome the contrast of divine and human in the Christ event.[41] Foregoing for

38. Tanner explores the continuing perfection of Jesus' humanity beyond his glorification, citing Barth's late and unfinished work: "The humanity of Jesus *per se* might continue to grow in perfection" (*Jesus, Humanity and the Trinity*, 52). Does this continuing perfection have anything to do with our participation in Jesus' humanity? Tanner suggests it does: "Christ's life is extended in new directions as it incorporates our lives within it" (ibid., 74).

39. In *God and Creation*, Tanner suggests a severe limit to clarification: "One cannot pretend, for instance, to reconcile God's agency with the creature's active powers through any material explanation of the actual mechanism found in some 'causal joint' between the two" (*God and Creation*, 26). In this context apophaticism holds sway.

40. Tanner, *Jesus, Humanity and the Trinity*, 4, 12; also "simply opposed" on pp. 10, 11. Obviously, not all contrasts are ruled out.

41. As Tanner quotes Barth, "[God] embraces the opposites of [divine attributes] even while he is

now this interesting complexity, it may seem that the principle of non-competition trades precisely on such a simple contrast of divine and human, especially when elaborated by the phrase "difference of planes." The tension is perhaps avoided if that phrase, and the "non-competitive principle" itself, be understood as fundamentally apophatic; that is, it can simply be denying the identity of divine and creaturely properties, consistent with the principle of God's radical transcendence. The language of a "difference in planes," however, sounds like a positive assertion of precisely a simple difference in divine and human properties. It even alludes to a more robust claim about the divine-human difference, as when Tanner asserts in the *Theology Today* review that God and humanity exist on a different "*ontological* plane."[42] For its part, the transcendence principle is not as conceptually simple as it sounds; it denies both identity and contrast between creaturely and divine attributes. Its structure therefore seems to be a dialectical neither-nor, obliquely pointing the way toward an apophatic middle ground.

Whatever it is worth, the preceding analysis may justly be accused of nitpicking. Language can hardly be expected to bear the scrutiny of this kind of deconstructive analysis, and especially not language as subtly apophatic and pragmatic as Tanner's.[43] Moreover, I suspect I

---

superior to them" (*Jesus, Humanity and the Trinity*, 12). While Tanner sometimes elides what I think is a significant difference between a conceptual rule and a divine act of overcoming, she is well aware of the issues raised by Barth with regard to whether the incarnation continues or exceeds a general idea of God founded on some other basis (see ibid., 6n7).

42. I confess here my predilection for Barth's narrative-dialectical approach to the divine-human relation; that is, salvation history involves unexpected reversals in divine properties. Tanner is clearly indebted to Barth here but dampens the dramatic (and perhaps dialectical) element in Barth. Might we go further still and wonder whether in the incarnation God is reversing the non-competitive relation and assuming the conditions of competitive relationships inherent to embodied humanity, so as to overcome them? Such an idea is not far from what Tanner has already claimed. I do not know whether this move could provide harbor for the dubious notion of divine suffering, but I believe a divine assumption of competitive relations would allow for a (chastened) re-reading of sacrifice and atonement. These thoughts run close to one of the concerns of Michael Root, "The Wrong Key," *First Things* 208 (2010): 63-64, who argues that a non-competitive relation cannot do justice to the divine-human interaction in the Bible.

have misunderstood Tanner in one way or another; or perhaps she has not had the occasion to clarify some of these finer points. Because of all these possibilities, I am not convinced that Tanner's principles in their stated form are in need of serious revision. But espying some possible unacknowledged tension, I am prompted to wonder what her theology would look like if the fundamental conceptual principles were not connected linearly through presupposition, but as principles counterposed—that is, statements that doctrine seems to dictate, but which cannot be easily affirmed together, nor reduced to some overarching singular principle. In other words, what if the fundamental principles had an explicitly dialectical shape? Or what if the principle of non-competition were seen as an eschatological outcome that here and now can only be conceived of partially or as a possibility? What if the principle of transcendence were couched in terms of a tension between identity and non-identity of divine and worldly attributes, such that God can be said both to act directly in the world but also to defy this description? The incarnation may then become the place at which the tension in these principles both comes to a head and is overcome, in a very complex movement.

Tanner's Counter-Thetic Movements

It would be premature to follow these questions to an alternative view. I must first examine the twists and turns in how Tanner carries forward her Christology from these two principles. Early on in *Jesus, Humanity and the Trinity*, Tanner disavows any attempt to deduce Christology from the two principles; moreover, new stages in salvation history "are not predictable from previous ones."[44] Here she

---

43. Cf. Tanner's diagnosis of the modern tendencies toward "referential adequacy of discourse" by decontextualizing theological claims, and to "reifying the distinctions of abstract analysis" (*God and Creation*, 155–56). My analysis could be accused of participating in similarly misleading modern linguistic tendencies.

44. Tanner, *Jesus, Humanity and the Trinity*, 6; see also p. 9. Predictability may be beside the point;

sides with Barth and against Rahner, though her reading of the latter is nuanced. It is worth asking, what is wrong with the principles that they must be in some sense exceeded en route to a developed Christology? Why could she not fully embrace the principles as a skeleton for a Christology that only needs more detail? As her argument goes, Tanner, augmenting her principle of transcendence, cites Barth's rather dialectical reversal of divine attributes in Christ: "[God] is absolute, infinite, exalted, active, impassible, transcendent, but ... He is all this as the Lord, and in such a way that He embraces the opposites of these concepts even while He is superior to them."[45] Yet I am not sure that this particular passage in Barth is so congenial to Tanner; it could indeed play into the hands of a Moltmann or others who, eager to go beyond Barth, "historicize God" by making God a dramatic character—precisely those whom Tanner is here critiquing. More generally, she does not follow the narrative-dialectical shape of Barth's soteriology, structured around the inverse yet singular movements of "the Lord as Servant" and "the Servant as Lord."[46] Moreover, Tanner shares little of Barth's existentialist-era rhetoric that the Word of God must continually break in upon the human; nor do we find in Tanner his dialectic of judgment and grace.

Setting Barth aside, Tanner's main stated reasons for insisting on a disjuncture between the incarnation and a general concursus of divine and human action are "soteriological": Jesus' grace would be external to him, as it is for us; it "might therefore be lost" and

---

who tries to retrospectively predict the incarnation? Tanner concedes as much: the general principles "came to be formulated as much in response to Christ as the reverse." Indeed, "Christ is their proof."

45. Ibid., 12, citing *Church Dogmatics* IV/1, 186-87.

46. But cf. Tanner, *Jesus, Humanity and the Trinity*, 17n31: for Barth "the exaltation of the human *is* the humiliation of God's becoming human." Hans Frei has a helpful description of how Barth's theology is primarily narrated, with "dialectic" acting secondarily in conjunction with "analogy" (Hans Frei, *Types of Christian Theology* [New Haven: Yale University Press, 1992], 160-61).

Christ would no longer provide "a more secure stage of God's graciousness."[47] For this reason, she contrasts in a variety of ways the hypostatic union with the general concursus of divine and human.[48] The "more" of the incarnation is the unique singularity of the subject Jesus Christ, who is (or can be described as) both divine and human. To arrive at this singularity, Tanner openly prefers the Alexandrian path of designating the Word as "the one subject of all that Jesus does and suffers."[49] Thus, in contrast to a human-divine concursus, she invokes the divine cause as the overriding cause.[50] She also endorses *enhypostatic* Christology—that Jesus' humanity has no existence outside of the Word. Indeed, Tanner affirms Alexandrian Christology because she shares its soteriology, that Jesus' union with the Word makes a more complete union with God possible for us. Of course, it is then incumbent on her to explain *how* the benefits of the hypostatic union translate to us.[51]

The claim that the divine Word is the true "cause" is once again the sticking point, if we insist on transparent clarity. Why would it be necessary or advantageous to attribute a singular divine cause (the Word) to Jesus when her principle of non-competition obviates any need or even ability to contrast a divine cause with a human cause?[52] A divinizing soteriology seems to lead to a need to have the divine override the human.[53] We find in Tanner some significant

47. Tanner, *Jesus, Humanity and the Trinity*, 22. Moreover, it would be wrong for Christians to worship Christ.
48. Ibid., 21-22; see also pp. 49-50.
49. Ibid., 25.
50. Ibid., 26: Jesus' life is "the effect … of the Word's primary agency." Further down: "The human being Jesus acts but these are God's own works."
51. Ibid., 9, cf. chs. 2 and 3.
52. We could flesh this out by saying that the Word is the formal and perhaps efficient cause, while the humanity is the material cause. Thus the healing and elevation of Jesus' humanity requires time, which concerns only how the divine cause is effected (see ibid., 27-28).
53. A parallel concern about Tanner's Christology can be found in Michael Horton, *Lord and Servant: A Covenant Christology* (Louisville: Westminster John Knox, 2005). For an appreciative defense of Tanner, see David P. Henreckson, "Possessing Heaven in Our Head: A Reformed

movements to the contrary. Notably, Tanner is careful to acknowledge and account for the historicity of Jesus as revealed by modern critical methods; ingeniously, she does this in a way that finds soteriological purpose in Jesus' historicity.[54] Beyond that, she several times invokes, now more reminiscent of Barth, a dual movement in the incarnation by which the divine becomes human and the human divine.[55] Yet, this dual explication of Christology at other times seems easily left out,[56] and it is not clear to me that the divine becoming human is thoroughly integrated into her soteriology. But again to the contrary, we find another movement promoting divine-human distinction, stemming from Tanner's invocation at several junctures of dual Trinitarian principles taken from Rahner: the Trinity itself is characterized by unity and differentiation, and these find their culmination in Jesus.[57] Union with God therefore need not be the only purpose of the incarnation; nonetheless, Tanner's tendency is to see unity as the overriding soteriological purpose.

Toward a More Dialectical Christology

It is possible to introduce a more dialectical structure to Tanner's

---

Reading of Incarnational Ascent in Kathryn Tanner," *Journal of Reformed Theology* 4, no. 3 (2010): 171-84.

54. Tanner helpfully tempers Alexandrian Christology by showing how only in being incarnate, and by undergoing a genuine process of perfection, could the Word save us; see Tanner, *Jesus, Humanity and the Trinity*, 30.

55. See ibid., 17-20. The two movements are in essence equated: "God becomes human—that is, God assumes the human ... [T]he human becomes God—that is, the human is assumed by God...." And already the overriding divine cause is signaled: "Both at once—God become human and the human become God—because the second ... is the direct result of the first." Tanner further states that "Jesus performs divine works in a human way... and performs human works in a divine way" (ibid., 21). This is the one location where she mentions the saving effect of "God's dying on a cross" (as a human being).

56. Ibid., 24. It is noteworthy that the corollary to "everything about Jesus' humanity is God's own" is confined to parentheses. Also, Tanner criticizes Barth for projecting the subordination of the incarnate Word into the immanent Trinity; ibid., 50n47, 52n54.

57. Ibid., 25n54, citing Karl Rahner, "Current Problems in Christology," *Theological Investigations*, vol. 1, trans. C. Ernst (New York: Crossroad, 1982), 181.

Christology by drawing out Rahner's Trinitarian principle, which allows Jesus' expression of the Trinity to result not only in union but also differentiation. That is, alongside of a soteriology of deification, we could posit a soteriology of humanization, whereby Jesus is not only the one uniquely and authentically united with God but is also the one uniquely and authentically distinct from God. This line of thinking could exploit an observation on the Trinity strikingly articulated by Tanner: the persons of the Trinity are absolutely distinct in their unity.[58] Unlike the human relation of children to parents, in which a child can in turn become a parent, the relation of Parent and Child in the Trinity is irreversible. The Trinitarian persons alone are absolutely distinct, and are the ground of all finite distinction. Extending this Trinitarian pattern into Christology would make Jesus the one who effects true humanity in distinction from God, whereas all other attempts to be human suffer either from usurpation or falling away into an empty, sinful non-relatedness to God.[59] (Sin here would best be understood privatively, which Tanner is congenial to, rather than as a wayward form of self-realization.) As the one authentically distinct from God, Jesus' identity as a human being remains the most singularly memorable and perpetually valid among all human beings. In its own way, this humanization Christology can help make sense of the co-inherence of divine and human properties, particularly if we do not consider the primary divine attributes to be omniscience or omnipotence, with the conundrums that arise when these are applied to Jesus' human nature, but perfect love as both differentiation and unity. Thus Jesus,

58. Tanner, *Christ the Key*, 226-27. See also Tanner, *Jesus, Humanity and the Trinity*, 13, where she extends this Trinitarian insight into Christology.

59. Cf. Rahner, "Current Problems in Christology," 163-65. Rahner espouses the idea that the hypostatic union of Logos and human nature must be supplemented by a statement that Jesus "is supremely creaturely and free;" and all other realities distinct from God are "deficient modes" of the Christological mode.

precisely in his perfectly distinct human existence, reveals the divine triune nature. Rooted in Trinitarian attributes, the distinctiveness of Jesus' humanity comes not at the expense of the hypostatic union but precisely as one way to express that union.

I have no intention of supplanting the Alexandrian divinization Christology with some sort of humanization Christology. I believe the latter is best left sitting awkwardly and in an unresolved dialectic next to the former. In this way, a dialectical systematic theology cedes to practical and pragmatic theology more options to draw on for a helpful soteriological effect—keeping in mind that, as Tanner skillfully demonstrates, contextual factors make possible a great variety of ways to apply any one theological position. But for instance, as important as the impetus is in Tanner's soteriology for shaping personal life and even a society's economics by divine Trinitarian relations (as embodied by Christ),[60] the dialectical scheme I suggest could create more room to embrace our mere humanity in its very humanness.[61] Without this counteractive possibility within soteriology, Tanner's divinizing soteriology might fail to yield a sufficient this-worldly place for love of the human as such[62] and for respite from the daunting task of perfecting ourselves and the world, which the Reformers might see as a cause for "despair."[63]

---

60. Tanner, preferably in my mind to those she critiques, invokes the Trinity as a pattern for ethical and political life, but only as mediated in Christ.

61. A nice precedent here is a direction in Luther's thought whereby justification by faith restores us to the good of our natural humanity; see Mark C. Mattes, *The Role of Justification in Contemporary Theology* (Grand Rapids: Eerdmans, 2004), 187. We may also think of Pannenberg's Christology based on Jesus' self-distinction from God, but his use of the resurrection and retroactive divinity seems to overcome the practical value of the dialectic I propose.

62. In practice, much of the effect of a humanization Christology could be achieved by attending to the continuing effect among human beings of the "created, non-divine goodness" that is common to all creation (see Tanner, *Jesus, Humanity and the Trinity*, 42). Our continuing participation in the goods of creation would need to be integrated into the theological anthropology found in *Christ the Key*. A humanization Christology might, in the very least, help keep this perspective from slipping into the periphery.

63. Tanner, *Jesus, Humanity and the Trinity*, 71: Assumption by Christ sets us a "hard task."

Aside from encouraging a wider array of practical options, a dialectical form is generally useful, I believe, to counter the tendency of academic theology to stake out opposed positions in a contest of theory-against-theory. This contest of positions can very easily lose sight of the concrete and variegated nature of theology on the ground. But precisely here, some will resist a dialectical theology in the sense I am suggesting because it weakens the power of theology to arbitrate the faith and practice of the church. To be sure, there is much bad non-scholarly as well as academic theology that deserves to be publicly critiqued. But academic theology, when not crossing over into particular contexts and practical concerns, can too readily see its role to be policing lines and closing off theological options, universally. Rather, theology, at some level, should strive to open up conceptual space for theological variations. To a great extent, Tanner's theology welcomes just such an open conceptual space; nonetheless, her formulation and use of theological principles can easily work in the opposite direction.

Likewise, we might wonder whether classical debates like that between Antioch and Alexandria, while certainly amenable to clarification and significant conceptual remediation as Tanner has done so well, are finally meant to be solved. Rather, academic theology, finding itself at a certain enforced leisure to survey and revisit the whole scope of historical theology, could draw out from such disputes the dialectical dimensions for precisely the open conceptual space mentioned above. Instead of posing at the heart of Christianity the existence of thetic principles or rules, we could

---

Significant also is the treatment of grace in Tanner, *Christ the Key*, 60: "The very created character of our existence, the fact, that is, that we are not divine, forms the major impediment to our receiving what God intends to give to us in creating us, and constitutes therefore the major impetus behind the gift of God's grace." Compare the "differentiated account" of how Jesus relates to humanity and the Trinity (ibid., 244-45); here Tanner's Christology is more dialectically described in a way perhaps conducive to my proposal.

see dialectical principles, characterized by a tension between a centripetal, orthodox tendency and a centrifugal, heterodox variation. In the case of Christology, the centripetal force is the union of divine and human in Jesus. All of what Tanner says about an incarnational Christology and the non-competitive relation of human and divinity in Jesus would fit here. But all of this remains in tension with the centrifugal minor premise, so to speak, of the difference between human and divine natures in Jesus. All that Tanner excludes or minimizes in terms of the differentiation of God and humanity belongs—or better, finds an opening—here, perhaps including the implicit competitive relation of humanity and divinity that finds an unstable place in sacrificial atonement as well as contemporary theories of divine suffering.[64]

This *more* dialectical approach, in line to be sure with Tanner's apophatic and pragmatic sensibility, would result in a greater theoretical openness to aberrant theological formulations. Its approach to the history of theology would not be restricted to looking for interesting contextual and practical flesh to drape upon the same orthodox skeleton, but would scour the history of theology—and why not the history of religion?—for the workings-out of a dialectics that defies any simple theoretical formulation. (To be sure, this work in the history of theology would have the option of judging that certain stagings of the dialetics of theology, including quite orthodox ones, violate its texture in practice.)

Whatever its potential merits for dealing with doctrine and the history of theology, such a dialectical approach would face the danger of choking on its theoretical excess, thereby failing to hold together theoretical and practical theology in the way Tanner has done.[65] This

---

64. Steffen Lösel finds Tanner's dismissal of contemporary German Hegelian theologians too brief. My hope is that a theology more dialectical in form could find room for some of the speculative conclusions about the historicized God—however peripheral that gentile court be in relation to the Orthodox sanctuary.

is perhaps her finest and most important gift to us, one that should be duly prized before we long for the academic fleshpots of a hopelessly theoretical dialectical alternative. It is this gift that still calls me, after so much dialectical peregrination, to rejoin her.

65. Tanner, *Theories of Culture*, 85: "No academic theology stands a chance of influencing the directions of everyday Christian life unless it makes some sense to people from their own theological outlooks."

7

Tanner's Non-Competitive Account and the Blood of Christ: Where Eucharistic Theology Meets the Evolution of Ritual

Eugene F. Rogers, Jr.

Kathryn Tanner's non-competitive account of divine and creaturely agency elegantly dissolves problems in Christology, anthropology, and ethics. Does it also generate interesting theses where sacramental theology meets the evolution of ritual, specifically, when it comes to the Eucharist? Because "blood" is succeeding "the body" as a central theme of the humanities, and because rituals such as the Eucharist have recently attracted the interest of evolutionary anthropologists and cognitive scientists, questions about "the blood of Christ" and how it functions are gaining importance outside the theological guild—across the humanities and even among some natural scientists. The new interest in blood raises a theological question ripe for

Tanner's non-competitive solvent: How can the blood of Christ do divine things socially and social things divinely?

Tanner's account of how God and creatures do not compete gains three advantages here. First, it allows theology to absorb more evolutionary science of religion, such as costly signaling, niche construction, and hyper-active agency detection devices, allowing those theories to show, some less reductively than others, how God can use natural means to build up society. Scientific theories of religion do not have to be used to explain God away, even if—like the objections in a Thomistic article—they can be so used.

Second, Tanner's non-competitiveness principle shows how the doctrine of God resists such reductions. Tanner's principle holds even, as Aquinas says, "If our opponents believe nothing of divine revelation, there is no longer any means of proving the articles of faith by reasoning, but only of answering their objections."[1] The principle holds because, for those open to theological argument, Tanner's principle reveals evolutionary theories of religion as what Aquinas would call *solubilia argumenta,* or "difficulties that can be answered." That is, the non-competitiveness principle serves both *ex professo* dogmatics and *ad hoc* apologetics.

The third advantage is harder to state; it reveals a similarity between nineteenth-century lives of Jesus and current neo-Darwinism. In both cases, external critics of Christianity can take the invisibility of God and the salience of creaturely agency—whether in the life of Jesus, or in the evolution of religion—as an argument against God's agency. They apply Occam's razor to suppose that alternative explanations eliminate one another: *either* God explains

---

1. Thomas Aquinas, *Summa Theologiae* Part I, question 1, article 8, corpus, hereafter cited in text as follows: I.1.8c. Here and hereafter I modify the "Benzinger edition" (so called after its longtime publisher) first translated by the Fathers of the English Dominican Province in 1911; the most recent edition is Allen, TX: Christian Classics, 1981.

the actions of Jesus, *or* his humanity does; *either* God's revelation explains the existence of religion, *or* human evolution does. By contrast, Tanner's principle says no, God and creatures do not compete in that way. Occam's razor does not apply, because God's agency operates on a different level that transcends creatures by lying more deeply within them, so that God can move them more intimately than they move themselves. Even though God's union with the humanity of Christ is more intimate than God's agency in other created things, Tanner's principle is powerful enough to expose that what is wrong with modern arguments about Jesus and what is wrong with modern arguments about Darwinism share an explanation: Godself is not made visible to us through any created thing.[2] Occam's razor, as used by reductionist evolutionary science, says that alternate theories eliminate each other; Tanner's solvent, on the other hand, says that God's agency does not displace creatures, but operates deep within them.

In two ways, therefore, those questions are not new. First, they follow the same pattern as the nineteenth-century controversy that divided the historical Jesus from the Christ of faith. Second, because the new evolutionary theories of religion like humanities theories of religion take culture seriously, they follow the pattern according to which Religious Studies and then theology of the Yale school learned to use cultural anthropology as a conversation partner. In this respect, it is not so much that theologians and humanists are being taken in by reductive Darwinian explaining–away, as that evolutionists are taking a real interest in culture and coming, therefore, more to resemble humanists. That move gains theology a new way of absorbing natural science. Tanner's non-competitive account supplies a theological

---

2. With more metaphysical and psychological commitments, Aquinas makes a similar argument in I.12.2: "Whether the essence of God can be seen by the created intellect through an image," to which the answer is no.

rationale for why this new and sacrament-oriented way of "absorbing the world" belongs to the doctrine of God.

The Eucharist makes a good test case for these issues, because Eucharistic theology has almost always insisted that the elements retain the salience of creaturely form (in an Aristotelian scheme, the "accidents" of bread and wine), while they convey to faith the agency of divine grace. And the exception proves the rule: the persistently red and flowing reliquary blood of the late medieval German *Dauerwunder*, which claimed to be the physical blood of Jesus miraculously preserved, slowly lost in its rivalry with the institutional eucharistic blood of the hierarchy, so that the blood with the accidents of wine eventually prevailed over the blood of putative miracle to convey the agency of God and retain the title of God's blood.[3]

Why Does Blood Seep in Where it Hardly Seems to Belong?

Appealing to Abraham's sacrifice, Jewish, Christian, and Muslim rituals all use blood as a tool to think with: circumcision thinks with biological blood, the Eucharist with metaphorical blood, the Eid al-Adha with blood transcended and returned. But the story of Abraham's son never mentions the word "blood." Focusing on Christianity, I ask why blood-talk dominates when other explanations would do, why blood seeps in where it hardly belongs.

Consider the text, "Abraham built an altar there, and laid the wood in order, and bound Isaac his son, and laid him on the altar, upon the wood" (Gen. 22:10). Different versions of that story generate indigenous theories of sacrifice in Judaism, Christianity (where Isaac prefigures Jesus), and Islam (where Abraham binds Ishmael). The

---

3. The burden of Carolyn Walker Bynum's *Wonderful Blood: Theology and Practice in Late Medieval Northern Germany and Beyond* (Philadelphia: University of Pennsylvania Press, 2007).

original story foresees a burnt offering, and an angel stops the knife. Yet, rituals in all three religions commemorate the sacrifice and initiate male children with a substance named nowhere in the story: blood. In minority rabbinic accounts, it is the blood of Isaac that Israelites paint on their doors so the Angel of Death will pass over.[4] Although the Qur'an criticizes sacrifice, Muslims at Mecca and at home annually kill and bleed ten million animals to commemorate Abraham's binding of his son for Eid al-Adha. Christians make Christ the Isaac figure and state as a general principle: "Without the shedding of blood, there is no remission of sin" (Heb. 9:22), thereby interpreting Christ's death as bloody even though crucifixion kills by suffocation. After all, hands and feet can be lashed to a cross without nails, and the wound in Christ's side, delivered after his death, would pump out little blood. Gospel writers responded to oral traditions about Jesus's references to blood at the Last Supper, and to the need, after the destruction of the Second Temple, to find a replacement for animal sacrifice. Jews and Muslims initiate their sons into community with the son of Abraham by drawing blood in circumcision, while Christians compare baptism to washing in Christ's blood, even though they baptize in water. In Leviticus, the altar needs "daubs" or "sprinkles" of blood to clean the horns of the altar; in Revelation, blood floods. Why does blood seem to burgeon at need? Early images portray Jesus intact and victorious on the cross; later, medieval angels collect his blood in cups. Blood exercises such fascination that Judaism, Christianity, and Islam race to read it in even where texts leave it to go without saying. Readers magnify blood in texts that hardly mention it (e.g., focusing on blood when crucifixion suffocates). Christians conduct disputes in blood-language, even far from blood's reality: they portray their opponents

---

4. Jon Levenson, *The Death and Resurrection of the Beloved Son: The Transformation of Child Sacrifice in Judaism and Christianity* (New Haven: Yale University Press, 1993), 193-94.

as offending Christ's blood. Scholars of religion have written shelves of books on sacrifice. But why do Christians, Jews, and Muslims bring up "blood" when other explanations would suffice? Why does blood seem to explain *too much*? Why does blood seep in even where it hardly seems to belong? This seems to call for an *anthropological* explanation before we ever get to the theological question why does *God* seem to rely on blood?

For a generation, humanists have talked about "the body": the human body, the social body, the medicalized body, the body and its instruments. They have imagined "the body" bounded as an envelope not alarmed with a fluid to redden its vulnerabilities . In Bynum, Biale, Bildhauer, and Anidjar, "the body" has yielded to blood. Historians or critics, those scholars hardly address the anthropological problem that blood *persists*. It persists because it provides a fluid to think with, and a language in which to disagree. Internal and external critics of Christianity have protested for half a century that Christian blood-signaling is dangerous. Yes, it is dangerous, but the protest has been anthropologically naïve. I intervene in their critique to say that Christian blood-signaling is not going away, and that the options are not exhausted by leaving it unchanged, on the one hand, or deploring it, on the other. A third option remains: to repeat blood's language subversively, to free it from contexts of oppression or violence. This option reclaims or "mobilizes the signifier for an alternative production."[5] Take, for example, the Gospel writers who show Jesus at the Last Supper queering a structure of violent oppression (crucifixion) to make it a repeated feast (communion). They show Jesus redeploying blood language, saying over the wine, "this is my blood; do this to remember me." Bynum, Biale, and

---

5. Judith Butler, "Contingent Foundations," in *Feminist Contentions: A Philosophical Exchange*, ed. Seyla Benhabib et al. (New York: Routledge 1995), 51–52.

Bildhauer work historically; Anidjar polemically: none mobilizes the discourse for social repair.[6]

Blood is apt for signaling in societies that model themselves on the human body. Blood may be red because iron compounds make it so, but societies draft its color and stickiness for multiple purposes of their own. We imagine individual, social, and animal bodies as securely bounded. Inside, blood carries life. Outside, it marks the body fertile or at risk. Society's work to maintain bodily integrity thus takes place in blood.[7] The body's permeability leaves us bloody-minded. It becomes a membrane to pass when it breathes, eats, perspires, eliminates, ejaculates, conceives, or bleeds. Only bleeding evokes so swift and public a response: blood brings mother to child, bystander to victim, ambulance to patient, soldier to comrade, midwife to mother, defender to border. This constellation of blood-signals helps define our society and our cultural niche.

Since Durkheim, students of religion have called the totem "the elementary form of religious life." Since Maximus Confessor, and reaching high points in Thomas Aquinas and in the twentieth century, theologians have insisted on working by "analogy." In Christian theology, "analogy" is no literary comparison, but names competing accounts of the largest repeating structures that hold the symbol system together. But theologians and anthropologists need not quarrel over terms. "Analogy" is just the theological word for "totemism." Aquinas and Durkheim would agree that Christianity paints a pattern according to which the body of Jesus is the body of Christ; the church is the body of Christ; the bread of the Eucharist

6. Bynum, *Wonderful Blood*; David Biale, *Blood and Belief: The Circulation of a Symbol between Jews and Christians* (Berkeley: University of California Press, 2007); Bettina Bildhauer, *Medieval Blood* (Cardiff: University of Wales Press, 2006); and Gil Anidjar, *Blood: A Critique of Christianity* (New York: Columbia University Press, 2014). Bildhauer is far and away the best of all the books I have read on blood.
7. Bildhauer, *Medieval Blood*, 1–7.

is the body of Christ; the believer represents the body of Christ; the crucifix around a neck displays the body of Christ; and the body of Christ is the body of God. No Christianity exists without some version of this pattern, which theology calls "analogy" and Durkheim "totemism."

Closely allied with the body of Christ is his blood, which the New Testament cites three times as often as his "cross" and five times as often as his "death."[8] The blood from the cross is the blood of Christ; the wine of the Eucharist is the blood of Christ; the means of atonement is the blood of Christ; the unity of the church is the blood of Christ; the kinship of believers is the blood of Christ; the cup of salvation is the blood of Christ; icons display the blood of Christ; and the blood of Christ is the blood of God. [9]

"The blood of Christ" works by analogy in Christian theology and as totem in Christian practice. It names a large-scale structure that holds together cosmology, fictive kinship, gender roles, ritual practices, atonement for sin, solidarity in suffering, and recruits history and geography to illustrate its purposes. Unlike cleansing/defiling and inside/outside, the analogical or totemic structure escapes the binary, although it can uphold or undermine binaries at need. When conflict reveals the body as penetrable, we glimpse that the body does not define *itself*, but society uses its bleeding to redline its borders. Lately, issues as diverse as atonement, evolution, women's leadership, and same-sex marriage disturb and revive the symbol system that the blood of Christ structures, cleanses, and unites. In theology and anthropology, blood outside the body is matter out of place: Abel's blood cries out from the ground. But menstruation and

---

8. Vincent Taylor, *The Atonement in New Testament Teaching*, 2nd ed. (London: Epworth, 1950), 177.

9. The previous four paragraphs appeared to a different purpose in my review of Gil Anidjar's *Blood* in *The Theology Syndicate* (February 23, 2015), https://syndicatetheology.com/commentary/genre-book/ (accessed July 20, 2015), and are reused with permission.

childbirth make gendered exceptions where outside blood promises new life. Exegetes argue whether the blood of Christ means life or death, but *blood* provides the language *within which* they disagree.[10]

That's why historical explanations only push the question back. If we say, Christians talk about blood because Second Temple Judaism did, then the question remains, why did Second Temple Jews talk about blood? Why, for example, animal sacrifice? The origin of sacrifice, of course occupies shelves and shelves of books. Blood became a cultural symbol in multiple societies around the globe, especially in those societies that modeled themselves as a social body on the human body. Blood became a means of communication and a technology for costly signaling. Blood is meaning made with bodies on the line; on the line that marks the frontier between enemies, the line that marks the division of the sacrificial lamb, or the line between inside and outside when a human body bleeds or gives birth. Blood is not just any signal, but a costly signal. And that language—"costly signaling"—opens up a new field, that of evolutionary anthropology of religion, which seeks, as its name implies, to see how religion evolved.[11]

10. Much of the last two paragraphs appeared to different effect in Eugene F. Rogers Jr., "How Blood Marks the Bounds of the Christian Body," *Zygon* 49 (2014): 540-53 (543). Exegetes disagree. For a tendentious example, see Alan M. Stibbs, *The Meaning of the Word Blood in Scripture*, 3rd rev. ed. (Oxford: Tyndale Press, 1963).

11. See for example Candace S. Alcorta and Richard Sosis, "Ritual, Emotion, and Sacred Symbols: The Evolution of Religion as an Adaptive Complex," *Human Nature* 16 (2005): 323-59; Lee Cronk, "Evolutionary Theories of Morality and the Manipulative Use of Signals," *Zygon* 29 (1994): 32-58; Richard Sosis, "Religion and Intragroup Cooperation: Preliminary Results of a Comparative Analysis of Utopian Communities," *Cross-Cultural Research* 34 (2000): 70-87; Richard Sosis, "Why Aren't We All Hutterites? Costly Signaling Theory and Religious Behavior," *Human Nature* 24 (2003): 91-127; Richard Sosis and Candace S. Alcorta, "Signaling, Solidarity, and the Sacred: The Evolution of Religious Behavior," *Evolutionary Anthropology* 12 (2003): 264-74; Richard Sosis and E. Bressler, "Cooperation and Commune Longevity: A Test of the Costly Signaling Theory of Religion," *Cross-Cultural Research* 37 (2003): 211-39; Richard Sosis and B. Ruffle, "Religious Ritual and Cooperation: Testing for a Relationship on Israeli Religious and Secular Kibbutzim," *Current Anthropology* 44 (2003): 713-22; and Ibid.,"Ideology, Religion, and the Evolution of Cooperation: Field Experiments on Israeli Kibbutzim," *Research in Economic Anthropology* 23 (2004): 87-115. In conversation at the Center

Even theologians and humanists know a simple version of costly signaling. Peacocks grow tails and antelopes antlers at a high cost to signal their evolutionary fitness. Their ornaments supposedly help them compete among their own gender for the favors of the "opposite" gender. Religion, meanwhile, seems hard for evolution to explain: religious people do things that *sacrifice* their reproductive fitness, like joining a monastery, taking a vow of celibacy, or martyring themselves. Instead of dying out, even martyr-religions seem to flourish. But a more sophisticated application of costly signaling tries to explain this. Costly signaling explains not only sexual selection, but how social animals gain fitness by sacrificing themselves *for their group*. The monk or martyr loses his or her own children but secures social cohesion. Jesus was a martyr without children, and Paul advised celibacy, but between them they founded a successful and cohesive group (Christianity). Among humans, the costliest signaling takes place in blood. Blood is meaning made with bodies on the line. For that reason both "without shedding blood there is no forgiveness" (Heb. 9:22)—and suicide bombings continue.

Evolution itself is good at sorting costs and benefits. Some animals even seem to deliberate on cost. Is this display worth it, or does the animal withdraw? Other animals mislead with signaling that appears more costly than it is. Humans do something more distinctive than count or counterfeit the cost. They use gesture and ritual, image, symbol, and language to *magnify* blood's power to signal while *lowering* its cost, ratcheting their cultural niche to more and more subtle and effective signaling. ("Cultural niche" is more evo-speak: beavers, when they build dams, make environmental niches for

of Theological Inquiry, I suggested to Sosis that what he meant by an "adaptive complex" sounded like Lindbeck's cultural-linguistic account of religion—and Sosis began to read *The Nature of Doctrine* with graduate students in evolutionary anthropology at the University of Connecticut.

themselves; humans build cultural niches for themselves, including distinctive human practices like religion.) The eucharistic ritual is powerful; many Christians find it more powerful than biological blood, because it is the blood of God. But in evolutionary terms, it is a whole lot cheaper. The eucharistic wine is no counterfeit: no one is misled by it, even if they disagree on what theory makes it God's blood. It is something else that marshals humans' distinctive ability to imagine and live into alternative futures and virtual worlds. Multiple societies have cultural niches in which blood matters in more ways than one. Despite its ties to oppression and war, blood-signaling, in our cultural niche, also fosters virtue, cooperation, and gratitude—and thus persists.

Meanwhile, evolutionary ritual theory and cognitive science explain why ritual evokes emotion and changes affect. Some Christians, accustomed to ascribing emotional effects directly to divine agency, may find such theories threatening; yet, they too belong to Tanner's pattern according to which God remains invisible among created effects. It keeps happening: evolutionary scientists suggest that believers "detect" God as a kind of "hyperactive agency detection," which saved more active hominid detectors of agency from predators by inclining them, on hearing a rustle in the bush, to suspect lions first and investigate later—but this is what Rahner already dealt with in *Hearers of the Word*, where God graciously provides the means for God's own detection. Nothing prevents God from using created means to bring human beings to Godself.

Because Christians worship a Logos made flesh and blood, God's own costly signaling, they ritualize growth and gratitude in blood's terms. With "My Lord and my God," Doubting Thomas put his fingers in the wound to make belief red and sticky. Blood images sustain the sacraments, where Christians find sacrifice and wisdom, grace, and gratitude in bread and wine. "Taste and see that the Lord is good" (Ps. 34:8), which used to invite one to communion, makes the throatiest of costly signals, where God became a costly signaler in the blood of the executed Word.

Tanner's Non-Competitive Account

Tanner learned the non-competitive principle, she says, from Richard Norris.[12] "What makes God *different* from every creature … is … precisely what assures [God's] direct and intimate *relation* with every creature."[13] Tanner turned Norris's historical observation into a conceptual tool of profound power.[14] Once stated, the principle is evident in the Bible, where the metaphors are notably embodied: "Neither is there any creature that is not manifest, in his sight, but all things are naked and opened unto the eyes of him with whom we have to do" (Heb. 4:13). "Wisdom in justice envelopes and penetrates all things" (Wisd. of Sol. 7:24). Although those metaphors are sexual, other biblical metaphors for the intimacy of divine agency name bones (in Ezekiel), flesh (in the incarnation), heart, and blood (Gen. 9:4; Lev. 17:11, 14; Deut. 12:23; John 6:53-54), until the Gospel of John makes blood a principle of divine intimacy: "Those who eat my flesh and drink my blood abide in me, and I in them" (John 6:56).

In *Christ the Key*,[15] Tanner makes several observations about blood and the Eucharist that comport well with the non-competitive principle, but she does not invoke it explicitly:

12. See Kathryn Tanner, *God and Creation: Tyranny or Empowerment?* (Oxford: Blackwell, 1988), 56, 174n7, 175n21.
13. Richard Norris, *God and World in Early Christian Theology: A Study in Justin Martyr, Irenaeus, Tertullian, and Origen* (New York: Seabury, 1965), 84-86. For more on Norris's use of this principle, see Eugene F. Rogers, Jr., "Believers and the Beloved: Some Notes on Norris's Christology," *Anglican Theological Review* 90, no. 3 (2008): 527-32.
14. Tanner, *God and Creation*, 56-58; Tanner, *Jesus, Humanity and the Trinity* (Minneapolis: Fortress Press, 2001), 2; and Tanner, *Economy of Grace* (Minneapolis: Fortress Press, 2005), 23-29, 75-84, 104-109, 135-39; and elsewhere.
15. Kathryn Tanner, *Christ the Key*, Current Issues in Theology (Cambridge: Cambridge University Press, 2010).

In general, we bring to the Eucharist gifts we have already received in order to get them back transformed from the Father as a conduit of further gifts.[16]As a repeated act of worship, the Eucharist continues the circle—from ascent to descent to re-ascent.[17]

She goes on to suggest that "Blood purifies and reconnects across separation because of its life-giving powers—'the life is in the blood' (Lev. 17:11)."[18] In addition, she notes the eucharistic roots of remarks that God takes our infirmities and returns gifts,[19] or that "to overcome … corruption at its root requires a comparable natural participation in what is essentially life-giving and good … with [which] humanity … might be physically intertwined."[20] A clear if implicit invocation of the noncompetitive principle appears once with respect to Christ's (human, not eucharistic) blood:

Christ works the salvation that only God can bring, but in a thoroughly human way—through his speech, spit, touch, his blood poured out. The divine and human operate in Christ at the very same time in the very same way.[21]

We will see that Thomas Aquinas does apply a Christology like that to the blood of the Eucharist.

The first remark cited above—that "we bring to the Eucharist gifts we have already received in order to get them back transformed from the Father as a conduit of further gifts" —might sound Protestant in tone. It sounds as if it plays down divine initiative *in the sacrament* in favor of divine initiative *in the mind*. It sounds as if the causation of eucharistic grace may run through the faith of the believer while bypassing the material elements. But Tanner's remark does not, in

16. Ibid., 203.
17. Ibid., 202.
18. Ibid., 267.
19. Ibid., 201.
20. Ibid., 75.
21. Ibid., 297.

fact, necessitate such a narrowing, but remains open to both Protestant and Catholic accounts. In Thomas Aquinas, as we shall see, faith both prepares for and results from the reception of the sacrament, because the reception must count as a human act. Thus, the reception must be intentional and voluntary: the believer must receive the bread as the Eucharist (no particular theory required, just intention), and Aquinas picks out the voluntary aspect of the act (digestion does not count, but eating does). Many if not all eucharistic theories expect that taking communion worthily will, by grace, eventuate in supernatural virtues of faith, hope, and love, whether the theory is transubstantiation, memorial, something else, or none.

In the Eucharist, the power of the Holy Spirit in conforming the believer and the sociological human facts about the effectiveness of ritual, "moral effervescence," memory, and so on do not conflict. God remains free to use human, social, evolutionary means—costly signaling, niche construction, hyperactive agency detection, ritual effects, whatever—however God likes. (The pattern follows Barth's *Aufhebung* of religion,[22] without the anti-Judaism.)

As a theological matter, "the blood of Christ is the blood of God" has to be a true statement on various analogical levels, even if we do not know *how* the statement is true. Aquinas's account of the Eucharist in his Commentary on the Gospel of John provides a good example:

> Even [Christ's] flesh is life-giving, for it is an organ of his divinity (*organum divinitatis*). Thus, since an instrument acts by virtue of the agent (*cum instrumentum agat virtute agentis*), then just as the divinity of Christ is life-giving, so too his flesh gives life (as Damascene says)

---

22. Karl Barth, *On Religion: The Revelation of God as the Sublimation of Religion*, trans. and introduced by Garrett Green (Edinburgh: T&T Clark, 2005). This is a retranslation of *Church Dogmatics* §17.

because of the Word to which it is united. Thus Christ healed the sick by his touch. So ... "I am the living bread" pertained to the power of the Word; but ... the communion of his body (*communionem sui corporis*) [pertains] to the sacrament of the Eucharist.[23]

That passage models God's use of the eucharistic elements on God's use of Christ's historical human body, quoting John of Damascus, that the "body of Christ" (in Jesus or in communion) is God's "instrument." Aquinas uses first *organum*, speaking in his own voice, and then *instrumentum*, quoting Aristotle about how an agent expresses *virtus*. This remark is helpful *above* the level of eucharistic theory—transubstantiation is not in the context, and Aquinas's remark can explain memorial theories as well. On Aquinas's account, the Eucharist extends the pattern of God doing divine things humanly and human things divinely in "the body of Christ." The pattern extends up and down the analogical series that runs on the body or the blood of Christ. We do not need to choose a theory about *how* this happens. We only need to observe the conjunction.

Although God can of course do what God likes, nevertheless, because God is invisible and incomprehensible, we should not expect to see "magic" effects from the Eucharist.[24] Thus, Aquinas avoids nutritive or humoral theories of the Eucharist in favor of ones that engage the human will: so *taking* the Eucharist voluntarily (an act of the will) differs from *digesting* the Eucharist involuntarily (an action of the intestines). Aquinas distinguishes between *actus*, which are

---

23. Thomas Aquinas, *In Ioannem* 6:56, in *Commentary on the Gospel of John,* trans. by Fabian Larcher and James Weisheipl (Washington, DC: Catholic University of America Press, 2010), paragraph 959, modified in accord with the Latin texts at http://www.corpusthomisticum.org/ (accessed July 20, 2015).

24. So in the *Summa Theologiae* II-II.1.4, "Whether the object of faith can be seen," the answer is no, and the standard example is Doubting Thomas, who, saying "My Lord and my God," "saw one thing" (the humanity of Christ) "and believed another" (that the humanity of Christ was the humanity of God) (*ad* 2).

voluntary, and *actiones*, which are bare movements, although the boundary shifts and is not reflected in translations.

Aquinas avoids the nutritive or humoral route not only because human agency requires a movement of the will, but also because *grace* requires—not as a precondition, but as an inevitable concomitant—a movement of the will.[25] This happens because grace moves more interiorly than we are to ourselves, like romantic love: grace moves and changes our desires, so that what we do, including the movements of our will, are in accord both with our willing and with grace. Love, in short, moves the heart; and grace puts us in the position of "love God and do what you will." The trouble with nutritive or humoral theories is not that they work like magic—that would be a false dichotomy. Rather, the trouble is that they seem to work by human movements that are not voluntary, as digestion or a shot of adrenaline is not. They bypass the will. A human action without intention is not, technically speaking, a human *act* or *actus*; it is not the having-been-done by a human agent. Aquinas distinguishes terms just here, as translators fail to do: human *actions* (*actiones*) are raw movements; human *acts* (*actus*) are intentional. Of course, acts are made up of actions, and actions unify acts, and a lot depends on how you break them up in analysis.[26] Yet, while eating is an act, digestion is only an action. In his own terms, Aquinas is right to hang the effect on eating, which is an intentional human act, as opposed to digestion, which is not.

How can the efficacy of the Eucharist depend on eating but not digestion, on drinking but not infusion? Because it depends on the *voluntary* act, not the involuntary action. *If* by grace I eat, then God

---

25. *Summa Theologiae* II-II.2.

26. I owe the observation to remarks by Victor Preller. For more on the distinction, see Eugene F. Rogers Jr., *Aquinas and the Supreme Court: Race, Gender, and the Failure of Natural Law in Thomas's Biblical Commentaries* (Oxford: Wiley-Blackwell, 2013), 66–68, 82, 85, 239.

takes the occasion of my eating, by a kind of divine irony, to be the cause of my salvation. This works like intercessory prayer. God *takes* my prayer as the cause of someone else's good. God need not do so; but God can set chains of cause and effect so that my prayer counts as the cause even of what God would do anyway, because that *involves me* in charity toward others, which is good for both of us. Thus God draws creatures Godward.[27]

The requirement of human voluntariness means that transubstantiation theories, memorial theories, and those in between *concur* in recognizing that God uses sacraments as a means, does so invisibly, and engages human acting. Transubstantiation theories emphasize God's commitment to a particular means. Memorial theories emphasize God's engagement of human memory, devotion, and so on. Both insist that God's acting is invisible in the wine.

For example, in his *Meditation on Human Redemption* (the eucharistic version of his atonement theory, a short communion meditation), Anselm fares well in Catholic circles because he emphasizes God's commitment to eucharistic means—but he fares well in Protestant circles because his folding in of atonement appeals to memory, love, devotion, and other human acts.[28] Protestants appreciate Anselm's appeals to human memory and fervor. Note the verbs: "Christian soul . . . rouse yourself and remember ... realize

27. *Summa Theologiae* II-II.82.1-2: "Divine Providence disposes not only what effects shall take place, but also from what causes and in what order these effects shall proceed. Now among other causes human acts are the causes of certain effects. Wherefore it must be that human beings do certain actions. Not that thereby they may change the Divine disposition, but that by those actions they may achieve certain effects according to the order of the Divine disposition: and the same is to be said of natural causes. And so is it with regard to prayer. For we pray not that we may change the Divine disposition, but that we may obtain by asking that which God has disposed to be fulfilled by our prayers in other words 'that by asking, human beings may deserve to receive what Almighty God from eternity has disposed to give,' as Gregory says (*Dial.* i, 8)" (82.1c).

28. I am not trying to defend or deny Anselm's theory. I am just observing something about its popularity in Catholic and Protestant theology alike.

that you have been redeemed and set free. Consider.... Meditate....
Delight in the contemplation of it. Shake off your lethargy and set
your mind to thinking over these things."[29] Yet right beside these
appeals to human memory and will, act and affect, are concrete
appeals to the physical realities of wine and wafer. Immediately after
"set your mind," Anselm continues without a break: "Taste the
goodness of your Redeemer.... Chew the honeycomb of his words,
suck their flavor which is sweeter than sap, swallow their wholesome
sweetness. Chew by thinking, suck by understanding, swallow by
loving and rejoicing. Be glad to chew, be thankful to suck, rejoice to
swallow" (ll.7-12).

To "accept Jesus," in Anselm's *Meditation on Human Redemption*,
is to accept him *into your mouth*. "See, Christian soul, *here* is the
strength of your salvation" (holding a cup or a wafer), "*here* is the
cause of your freedom, *here* is the price of your redemption.... Chew
this, bite it, suck it, let your heart swallow it, when your mouth
receives the body and blood of your Redeemer" (ll.163-69, emphasis
added). The word "faith" never appears. Because God became flesh
to save, the saved accept God in the flesh. It is because God uses
the flesh of Jesus to pay the debt (in a third version, the dowry) of
honor that God uses the bread and wine to honor the communicant.
And yet the appeals to memory, to arousal, to action are present.
The bridge, in Anselm as in Tanner, is divine intimacy, closer to
us than we are to ourselves, which Tanner expresses in logical and
Anselm in erotic language. When, in *Oration II*, Anselm shifts from
"debt" language to "dowry" language, Anselm describes himself as by
baptism "betrothed to Christ" and therefore "dowered with the Holy
Spirit," in the technical sense of a widow receiving an inalienable

29. Anselm of Canterbury, *Meditation on Human Redemption,* in *Prayers and Meditations of St Anslem
with the Proslogion,* trans. Benedicta Ward (New York: Penguin, 1973), 230-37, cited by line
number; here: ll.1-7.

share of her dead husband's property. There the erotic and marital metaphors displace those of slavery and satisfaction.[30] But even in the context of debt, in the *Meditation on Human Redemption* the closing eucharistic language of desire swamps the language of debt: "By you I have desire; by you let me have fulfillment. Cleave to him, my soul, and never leave off. Good Lord, do not reject me; I faint with hunger for your love; refresh me with it. Let me be filled with your love, rich in your affection, completely held in your care. Take me and possess me wholly, who with the Father and the Holy Spirit are alone blessed to ages of ages. Amen" (ll.265-71).

---

30. Anselm of Canterbury, *Oration II* (formerly *Oration III*) in *Opera Omnia*, vol. III, 80, ll.7f. For more on an erotic-marital atonement theory open to same-sex couples, see Deirdre Good, Willis Jenkins, Cynthia Kittredge, and Eugene F. Rogers Jr., "A Theology of Marriage Including Same-Sex Couples," *Anglican Theological Review* 93 (2011): 51-87, esp. 81-87.

PART III

Christianity as Culture: A Gift to Theology

8

Creative Christian Identity: Christianity and Culture Reconsidered

Mary McClintock Fulkerson

After reading the Exodus account of the Ten Commandments at the worship service, the minister at Good Samaritan United Methodist Church asks for responses from the congregation. Sketching pictures of lightning and clouds on a whiteboard, he asks for people who are afraid of thunder to raise their hands, then asks them to raise their hands if lightning makes them afraid. Both questions get lots of noisy responses and hand-waving, and one member comes to the front to share at the minister's invitation. Invoking heaven, angels and God, Bob starts talking about these images, saying that when you lay "on your back, the clouds above roll by." The pastor goes on to draw stone tablets on the board, asking folks to name the commandments and this generates a lot of excitement. Most of the responses are vibrant raising of fingers to identify the numbers: "first!", "two!", "second!" One participant says "Love me as you love your neighbor." Some of the participants are non-respondent during the verbal interaction. Terry sits frozen in her wheelchair when the pastor is speaking, but squeals loudly when the others respond. Tim is also in a wheelchair. He does not talk, but trembles, also making guttural noises that appear to convey pleasure in response to some of the performances.[1] Piano music for hymns generates even more response even by those who are not able to sing.

Chan has cerebral palsy and is profoundly intellectually disabled. He cannot understand or produce words or sentences and lives in a group home. Despite cognitive limitations, however, Chan does have significant abilities. "Primary among them is Chan's ability to express himself in a variety of ways and to interact with the world around him. The caregivers in Chan's group home have noticed that when Philip enters Chan's room in the morning to bathe, dress, and transfer him to the wheelchair, Chan exhibits more 'awake behavior." When his wheelchair is placed near a group playing volleyball with a balloon, "Chan begins to vocalize, his head flexes forward and backward, and the motor activity of his arms and legs increases . . . Chan is able to participate through his presence as he responds to the game being played with changes in his behavior, which Philip and the others interpret as Chan's interest in the activity."[2]

Generating Creativity

Attention to a wound can generate creativity. If theologians simply depended upon the explicit beliefs which shape us as Christians—for example, what counts in "the tradition" as correct Christology, or

---

1. Mary McClintock Fulkerson, *Places of Redemption: Theology for a Worldly Church* (New York: Oxford University Press, 2007), 110-13.
2. Molly C. Haslam, *A Constructive Theology of Intellectual Disability: Human Being as Mutuality and Response* (New York: Fordham University Press, 2012), 57-58, 61.

specific "sins" or moral behaviors—that would definitely limit the parameters of what should and sometimes does catch our attention. Of course, noticing or caring about something as a wound has very much to do with how we are shaped by our normative vision of God's ways of being present in the world. Yet "noticing something" is not limited or reducible to specific orthodox lenses, so to speak. One of the significant ways that new dilemmas, questions, and insights are generated is through a kind of general interest in or compassion for *all* of creation. When shaped by that kind of compassion, what catches our attention are the ways in which that creation is diminished or harmed—what I am calling a "wound." The communicative modes of people designated as disabled or, in the past, "mentally retarded," have long been overlooked and disregarded in most of society *but also in churches*, to the detriment of us all. The first opening anecdote in this essay tells of a regular service in a church that is specifically designed for people from group homes.[3] Good Shepherd UMC is an unusual church that regularly welcomes such people, relying upon a minister who works to do his best at creating worship that honors their skills and needs. The second story of Chan and his communicative abilities illustrates the change in this understanding of people with disabilities—at least for some kinds of caregivers. Clearly, the more focus there is upon persons with different communicative capacities, the more possibilities emerge for enhancing our abilities to honor one another, regardless of our differences. Addressing the continued wound found in what is

---

3. The first story comes from my ethnographic study of a church that regularly serves people with disabilities. I chose Good Samaritan UMC for an ethnographic study because of its significant racial diversity, which is still unusual in mainline denominational churches. Among other surprises I experienced in my participant observation in this church was the discovery of this other wound besides racism that was being addressed by the community—attention to persons with disabilities. Fulkerson, *Places of Redemption*.

typically the larger social *lack* of awareness is an important move toward creativity.[4]

This chapter explores ecclesial attention to honoring persons with disabilities as an example of creativity. To foreground such attention first requires a brief consideration of inadequate accounts of theology and "culture" and alternative definitions of these categories such as developed by Kathryn Tanner. A look at two approaches to this wound shows the importance of Tanner's "New Agenda for Theology" with regards to culture, as she argues for three crucial themes: first, the omnipresence of culture in faith, second, the need to de-reify "tradition," and third, the crucial need that Christian identity be defined as a *task*.[5]

Defining the Wound

The wound of obliviousness to persons with disabilities does not mean that we who are considered "normate" typically define such persons as sinful or unfaithful. Rather, it has to do with forms of life that have simply been pretty much off the radar screen of most faith communities and certainly outside of my own awareness as well. Good Samaritan Church's inclusion of persons from group homes embodied another feature in addition to its racial diversity that is very unusual in faith communities. The church not only regularly included people with disabilities, but it also did not require them to "behave" like so-called "normal" congregants. The disabilities were mental as well as physical, and there were a range of folks who came—from people with Down's syndrome and autism to people with a variety of conditions for which I had no categories.[6] Some

---

4. Even as I avoid the outdated phrase "mentally retarded," I must confess that the descriptors of these folks are still problematic, insofar as they appear to be reductive adjectives.

5. Kathryn Tanner, *Theories of Culture: A New Agenda for Theology*, Guides to Theological Inquiry (Minneapolis: Fortress Press, 1997).

6. The U.S. Department of Education lists the following under the category of disability: speech

of them did not have language while some had limited linguistic capacities, but the majority of them responded to worship in quite visible ways. Importantly, as my opening examples illustrate, the minister's worship practices and their responses were not the standard behaviors that are expected and usually required in most worship services because he took their different modes of "knowing" seriously. As a result, he received vibrant and enthusiastic responses.

According to a standard theological view, faithfulness requires, at least minimally, some correct beliefs as well as a transformed life. For example, a faithful Christian needs to have a proper Christology, including a Trinitarian view of God, defined by the Nicene and Chalcedonian creeds. Necessarily related to such beliefs, of course, is the proper understanding of redemptive life in these Protestant churches, such as justification by grace through faith rather than by works. To be sure, no theologian would expect all of this to be understood in its full and nuanced way by most ordinary Christians. The complexities of *homoousios* and the details of the immanent Trinity, for example, are rarely part of popular Christian awareness. However, beliefs are typically a boundary-setting qualifier for theology, given the assumptions that faithful participation does entail the cognitive.[7] This view, then, would appear to exclude such persons as Tim, who was a regular attendant at Good Samaritan Church's worship services. There were others, like Tim, who did not have

or language impairments, learning disabilities, mental retardation, emotional disturbance, and diverse disabilities such as hearing, orthopedic, visual impairments, autism, traumatic brain injury, delayed development and deaf-blindness. See Ann P. Turnbull, Rud Turnbull, Marilyn Shank, Sean J. Smith, eds., *Exceptional Lives: Special Education in Today's Schools,* 4th ed. (Upper Saddle River, NJ: Prentice Hall, 2003), 2-39.

7. The clearest example of this would be orthodox theologies. However, liberal theologies still assume cognitivity as a primary element of faith. Thomas Aquinas makes rationality central to the *imago Dei,* but seems to allow those with lesser rational abilities to participate in the image, just not as fully. See Molly Haslam's discussion of these theologies (*Constructive Theology of Intellectual Disability*).

language, even as they were clearly responding to music and enthusiastically clapping in the services.

Theologians with an account of faith requiring the cognitive would certainly not say that these people are going to hell or that these human beings do not matter to God. However, given the minimal appearance of people with disabilities in the average church, they do not appear to be on most churches' radars. Nor do they seem to shape most theologians' definitions of faith.[8] And with no categories other than sympathy and, perhaps, pity, such care seems to have little if any effect on the categories of theology. Even if most Christians would certainly want to say that God loves them, minimally such persons are viewed as disruptive. And by failing to alter theological categories for faith—both "academic" and ordinary—such an approach, however well-intentioned, diminishes their status as *imago Dei*. It does so by ignoring the ways in which their experiences are real and should matter. Responding to music, clapping, and making noise all indicate real religious experience. Taking intellectual disability seriously creates an important challenge to what counts as "faith" and proper relation to God, not simply with regard to the person with ostensible "disabilities" but also to those of us considered "normate" as well.[9]

Faith Intertwined With Culture

While an alternative theological anthropology that fully attends to the categories of intellectual disability—adequately redefining the *imago Dei*, sin, and redemptive existence sustained by God—is too complex to be fully explored in this essay, some important insights

8. There are a number of exceptions, such as Nancy Eiesland, Molly Haslam, John Swinton, Hans Reinders, Amos Young, and Jean Vanier.

9. I am not addressing all forms of so-called disability. For the crucial role of the visual, see Temple Grandin's writing on autism: *Thinking in Pictures and Other Reports from My Life With Autism* (New York: Vintage, 1995).

are made possible by Tanner's view of theology and culture and her consistent reminder of our theonomous existence, that is, that we are the creatures of a transcendent, redemptive God. Indeed, I begin with her claims about the inextricable intertwining of the cultural and the theological itself to further pursue the concerns I am raising.

This first insight into the unavoidable intertwining of culture and "the Christian" signifies the crucial recognition that Christianity is *never* disconnected from the worldviews, codes, languages, and pre-reflective assumptions that attend a particular time and place, what we can generally construe as "culture." Indeed, Tanner's attention to culture theory and theological accounts of Christianity leads to her judgment that we must reject accounts that treat culture and Christianity as "independently specifiable wholes."[10] Tanner presses this issue in important ways as she insists that it is not simply particular beliefs that define and distinguish Christianity. Furthermore, Christian faith is not distinguishable from culture as a literally separate social reality or a "community," nor are there clearly demarked Christian practices that incorporate and alter the so-called culture. Even as some postliberal theologians such as George Lindbeck do acknowledge the role of culture in Christian formation, they still assume that something evaluative, like a theological "grammar," is supposed to be controlling culture in a normative way.[11]

Tanner rejects the frequent ways in which Christian community and the "world outside" are defined so as to communicate some sort of normative distinction between the two worlds, even when culture is recognized as part of Christian communities. "Christian community" is ideally *the* normative reality that exists over against the ostensibly secular world. In short, it is easy to assume that "the

---

10. Tanner, *Theories of Culture*, 107-19.
11. Ibid., 104ff.

world" is a reality that intersects only with the secular community. To accept such distinctions, however, suggests that the God that Christians worship ceases to be the God of creation. The distinction can be made, Tanner says, "between a life lived with Christ and life lived without him, but what makes the difference is a new relationship with what lies beyond the Christian community itself, a new orientation of standards and values around, not simply being the Christian community itself, but that to which the community witnesses—the free grace of God in Christ."[12]

To be oriented toward God through Christ cannot entail an escape from place and culture—after all, do Christians quit using the language of their society? Do they cease navigating the geography they occupy? They may alter some of the culture, but they can never simply escape it. The behaviors of the Pastor at Good Samaritan UMC would not strike many typical Methodists as explicitly Christian. Although he does invoke the Ten Commandments, he does not discuss them. The Pastor and the participants are employing images and topics that would most likely be perceived as coming from the local culture rather that from Scripture or the creeds. Thus, Tanner rightly refuses the distinctions that define our difference in terms of an absolute difference or a kind of superiority, a superiority that assumes cultural and locational distinctions that simply do not exist. That error, Tanner argues, is quite simply idolatrous.[13]

Challenging Christian Identity

Secondly, assumptions regarding how we are *imago Dei*—created in the image of God—offer a crucial clue regarding what *kind* of creatures qualify. Is it our gendered bodies where being male is the

12. Ibid., 101f.
13. Ibid.

more valorized version of theonomous creatureliness that make us more or less *imago Dei*? Is it our whiteness? These characteristics have certainly functioned in North American Christianity as qualifiers for full status and participation. Perhaps it is our capacity for rationality that makes us *imago Dei*, as a theological view requiring correct belief might well assume. Thomas Aquinas, among other "classic" theologians, considered our intellectual ability to be the crucial marker of the *imago Dei*. As Tanner continues to refuse definitions of Christianity that require uniformity of belief or practice, she reminds us of the inevitable results of taking cultural change and difference seriously.

One such result is that there will always be different forms of Christian faith, and there will always be disagreements. The honoring of inevitable difference as constitutive of human life is part of Tanner's insights into redefining Christian identity. Refusal to insist upon identity around the same beliefs or the same practices indicates her grasp of the radical way that God's redemptive presence entails recognition of difference as a good in the finite, fallible world. While this honoring of difference is not about the rejection of anything shared, it does redefine what is shared in constructive ways. Tanner points out that faith communities share Scriptures, creeds, and rituals, for example, although not in the exact way they are interpreted or practiced; they share the passion to figure out what faithful discipleship looks like, but not exactly what qualifies.

Task of Mutual Recognition

Such sharing is real and significant, but definitely does not require unanimous views or practices.[14] Thirdly, and more importantly, it is about sharing a *task*, the task of faithful discipleship, but one

14. Ibid., 151–55.

"sustained by a continuity of fellowship, by a willingness, displayed across differences of time and space, to admonish, learn from, and be corrected by all persons similarly concerned" with true Christian discipleship.[15]

Given that the honoring of disagreement can still connote cognitive abilities, another crucial feature of human life foregrounded by Tanner is essential. A profound beginning for a shift to alternative images for faith communities that are able to take seriously the inevitability of difference and disagreement is that of "mutual recognition."[16] Mutual recognition entails a form of relationality that is much broader than cognitive awareness. When we consider honoring persons with disabilities, the identification of relationality appears to be a much more compelling and expandable feature of creatures understood as *imago Dei*. Relationality is a deep and wide experiential element of created life, and it would seem that any creature capable of response is relational.[17] While this is a promising way to imagine the *imago Dei*, it is important to recognize the need for more clarification. Some versions of the *imago Dei* as relational refer primarily to the relationship between creatures and God. Using Martin Luther as an example, Molly Haslam points out that, for Luther, relation to God is defined by the "intellectual ability to believe in the existence of God and trust in the faithfulness and goodness of God."[18] Thus, relationality can sometimes continue to require a particular capacity that rules out a variety of creatures. Here we turn to Tanner's quite relevant insight that idolatry can take many forms.

15. Ibid., 155.
16. Ibid., 172.
17. The use of relationality to indicate the basic feature of creation as *imago Dei* might be understood to also include animals, a topic for further exploration. What I do not know how to address is an adequate way to image the created world beyond human beings and animals as God's creation—a topic certainly addressed by environmental theologies.
18. Haslam, *Constructive Theology of Intellectual Disability*, 95.

Tanner's refusal to allow the idolizing of any human construction of faithfulness is a reminder that a theocentric view of Christianity demands a willingness to rely upon what Tanner calls the Word, as opposed to our contextual definitions of the faith. The Word invokes the "sovereignty" of the Divine over human realities; or, as Tanner puts it, "making Christian identity a matter of allegiance to certain meanings threatens to put human ideas about God in the place that only God should fill in Christian life."[19] So, relationality cannot be reduced to certain meanings in the sense of beliefs. Furthermore, since Christian identities are neither "self-contained" nor "self-sufficient,"[20] they require inevitable change that may require learning from other disciplines, from other communities and non-normate worldviews. Theology in its many forms needs to learn from caregivers who work with people with disabilities as well as from scholars who research topics on the ways in which communications occur with various developmental differences.

Creativity beyond the Word

Now there appears to be a contradiction in the claims being made here. Is there not something odd about the imperative to value the non-cognitive forms of experience of many people and to critique overly intellectualist approaches to worship and faith, but nonetheless continue to rely upon intellectualist claims and resources to make this call? Yes, it is important to acknowledge the inevitable difference in the ways that we all experience and display realities of the world and the disconnects that are typically entailed in those differences. While an excessive emphasis on the cognitive can contribute to obliviousness about these realities, it does not have to lead to such blindness. Surely, Tanner's primary images for Christian identity

19. Tanner, *Theories of Culture*, 126.
20. Ibid., 152.

as task, openness, and relationality, as well as change, are radically inclusive of different kinds of experiences and abilities. However, she also identifies the need for theology as an intellectual endeavor along with its other functions. Theology is to be "a specialized practice of intellectual production with some autonomy from the immediate demands of everyday practice." However, even this intellectual vocation "is to remind people making such judgments about the need for openness to a free Word." Moreover, we must all "remain open for new movements of faithfulness to a free Word."[21] Crucially, theology is about radical openness to change given its grounding in the radical graciousness of God, an openness by so-called ordinary people of faith and by intellectual theology as well.

Given the importance of this openness in academic theology, I must close by noting that "the Word" is not an adequate image for God's transcendent, redemptive presence, especially in light of the compelling need to honor persons such as Terry, Tim, and Chan. The Word obviously connotes the linguistic, and the linguistic points to the cognitive. Importantly, an inherent openness to change is entailed in this theological insight. As Tanner concludes, "since the Word of God is a free Word, the meaning of discipleship—what it really means to be a Christian—cannot be summed up in any neat formula that would allow one to know already what Christian discipleship will prove to include or exclude over the course of time."[22] Tanner provides deeply insightful accounts of the combination of God's transcendence and immanence in the life of faith, insights that are to be communicated by invoking of the Word of God in order to invite just the kind of openness and willingness to change that is needed. We must, as she says, make "God, rather than some human account of God, the center of our lives," and that

21. Ibid., 155.
22. Ibid.

constitutes an inherent challenge as we are confronted with the new and the surprising. While attention to a variety of aesthetic modes of relating to persons without high level cognitive skills is one of the next steps, new pictures of the holy and the Divine also would be creative for persons with autism, as suggested by Temple Grandin.[23] Images of the Divine that communicate redemptive disruptions to the larger communities and our cultures are worth considering as well, such as the profound representation by Nancy Eisland of the "Disabled God."[24] So, even as I push against this primary linguistic image for the Divine, I commend Kathryn Tanner's wisdom as she invites ongoing redemptive change within her theological work, reminding us again and again of the never-ending creativity of the grace of God in Christ.

23. Grandin, *Thinking in Pictures*.
24. Nancy Eisland, *The Disabled God: Toward a Liberatory Theology of Disability* (Nashville: Abingdon Press, 1994).

9

Inculturation as Theology of Culture: Exploring Kathryn Tanner's Contribution to Intercultural Theology

Jan H. Pranger

In her 1997 book *Theories of Culture* Kathryn Tanner has provided the theological community with what is arguably one of the most probing theological discussions of culture.[1] Yet her work has drawn little attention from fields of theology that traditionally have been involved in the study of culture and theology, that is, intercultural theology, missiology, and ecumenism. However, Tanner's theology of culture not only has important implications for intercultural theology, it is also informed by intercultural theological insights. This essay explores the intercultural dimensions and ecumenical

---

1. Kathryn Tanner, *Theories of Culture: A New Agenda for Theology*, Guides to Theological Inquiry (Minneapolis: Fortress Press, 1997).

implications of Tanner's proposals for Christian interactions with culture in the context of postcolonial Christianity.

I will begin with a brief overview of Tanner's contribution to the theology of culture, especially focusing on the way her theological-methodological perspective on culture is informed by postmodern anthropology. Next, I will explore the potential of Tanner's work for understanding "inculturation," the missiological concept used to indicate how in the postcolonial church Christians construct theologies in the particularity of their cultural situations. Tanner argues that theology always works with and on the cultural materials available in the culture at large, and this perspective can help better understand the nature and aims of theological inculturation. Tanner's theology of culture can also help missiological discussions overcome the unproductive preoccupation with syncretism as well as bridge the divide between theologies of inculturation and contextualization. Finally, this essay will explore the significance of Tanner's understanding of Christian identity as participation in communication about discipleship amidst the diversity of ongoing cultural and intercultural theological articulations of global Christianity.

Culture as Agenda for Theology

Tanner pursues the significance of culture for theology along two broad lines. First, echoing H. R. Niebuhr's classical study she raises the question of the relationship between Christian theology and human culture, or, more specifically, how to understand Christian identity in relation to culture.[2] As Tanner takes up this classical question, she enhances its discussion by problematizing the concept of culture itself, specifically by introducing postmodern theories of

2. H. Richard Niebuhr, *Christ and Culture* (New York: Harper & Row, 1951).

culture. Meanwhile her second line of inquiry concerns the theological-methodological implications of culture as she explores theology as a form of cultural construction in light of the postmodern concept of culture.

The roots of Tanner's interest in culture may be traced back to her training at the Yale Divinity School, where the then reigning postliberal paradigm championed by theologians Hans Frei and George Lindbeck built on a theological methodology that employed the notion of culture for its articulation, especially in the work of Lindbeck.[3] Yet Tanner's interest in culture has clearly also been fostered by the important role that this concept has come to play in feminist theology, gender studies, literary theory, and other areas that have attracted her attention.[4] The shifting understanding of culture in these fields, especially when compared to the culture concept underlying the postliberal paradigm, led to Tanner's 1997 book on theories of culture.[5] However, postliberal theology is not Tanner's only discussion partner. Her conversation partners also include theological constructivists such as Gordon Kaufman, correlationist theologians such as David Tracy, radical orthodox scholars such as John Milbank, and modern theologians such as Schleiermacher, all of whom in one form or another have given important consideration to the relationship between Christian theology and culture.[6]

3. George A. Lindbeck, *The Nature of Doctrine* (Philadelphia: Westminster Press, 1984).
4. See for instance Kathryn Tanner, "Social Theory Concerning the New 'Social Movements' and the Practice of Feminist Theology," in *Horizons in Feminist Theology : Identity, Tradition, and Norms*, ed. Rebecca S. Chopp and Sheila Greeve Davaney (Minneapolis: Fortress Press, 1997).
5. This book also exposes some significant differences between Tanner's theological insights and postliberal theology, especially in terms of how culture is understood and applied theologically. Without eclipsing the postliberal project into its theological assumptions about culture, it is nevertheless clear that, in Lindbeck's work especially, methodological reflections on the modern concept of culture help set important theological parameters. Tanner herself calls it a "defining moment of the postliberal stance" *Theories of Culture*, 183n7.
6. Gordon D. Kaufman, *In Face of Mystery* (Cambridge, MA: Harvard University Press, 1993); John Milbank, *Theology and Social Theory : Beyond Secular Reason*, Signposts in Theology (Oxford: Blackwell, 1991); Friedrich Schleiermacher, *On Religion : Speeches to Its Cultured*

Tanner's approach differs from these theologians in significant ways. First, Tanner takes as point of departure that cultures only exist as specific historical, diverse, and ultimately contingent human realities. Culture as a universal phenomenon is an abstraction derived from the fact that humans everywhere are part of *particular* cultures. Culture in a universal or generic form does not exist, and is therefore not available as horizon for theological construction.[7] Thus Tanner insists that theological constructions should only be considered in relation to *particular* cultures and communities.[8] Second, Tanner insists that cultures cannot be objectified for the purpose of theological methodology. Cultures are not engaged as wholes from a position over and against them, but only from within culture, in concrete historical practices that engage specific cultural elements piecemeal.

Postmodern Concept of Culture

A further important difference between Tanner and her conversation partners lies in the concepts of culture that they employ. The engagement with culture by theologians such as Lindbeck and Tracy all takes place in reference to a modern concept of culture, which Tanner describes as "self-contained and clearly bounded units, internally consistent and unified wholes of beliefs and values, which are simply transmitted to every member of their respective society or social group as principles that maintain the social order and ensure the regular functioning of the organized behaviors characteristic of the group."[9] Following postmodern anthropology and cultural studies

Despisers (Louisville: Westminster John Knox Press, 1994); and David Tracy, *Blessed Rage for Order* (San Francisco: Harper & Row, 1988).

7. Tanner, *Theories of Culture*, 64–66.

8. Ibid., 67.

9. Kathryn Tanner, "Cultural Theory," in *Oxford Handbook of Systematic Theology*, ed. John Webster, Kathryn Tanner, and Iain Torrance (New York: Oxford University Press, 2007), 530.

Tanner critically reviews each of these characteristics, instead arguing for the porous and intercultural character of cultures. Such cultures are internally contested and dynamically changing due to the same social processes that also provide coherence, namely through the exercise of power. These postmodern characteristics of culture lead Tanner to develop new perspectives regarding Christian identity and theological construction as cultural process.

Christian Identity and Interactions in the Wider Culture

Methodological reflections on theology and culture often assume a clear boundary between Christianity and its wider culture. They usually also portray Christianity as a community with its own unique culture. Tanner challenges both these assumptions. Sociologically speaking, Christian communities share the cultures of the societies of which they are part. To presume otherwise only makes sense if Christians live in isolation from other communities or the larger society—socially, economically, linguistically, and so on—a situation not characteristic of the large majority of Christians, past or present. Moreover, in contemporary postcolonial and globalizing societies, social and cultural boundaries clearly no longer coincide.

Christians thus only mark certain elements of the cultures within which they participate as social and cultural boundaries, and never the totality of a culture. Which particular elements come to form these boundaries is a historically contingent outcome of particular social processes rather than something that is determined for all times and places. Tanner rejects the idea that some inherent essence or identity resides within Christianity that guides Christians in identifiable ways in their encounters with cultures. Instead it is in the encounters with cultures—or better, with elements of cultures—that Christians construct Christian identities using those cultures. Tanner refers to this as the relational character of Christianity, thereby expressing the critical insight that Christianity in some important ways is as culturally contingent as the cultures of which it is part and in relation to which it identifies itself.[10] She thus rejects both the fundamental premise of postliberalism that sees Christian culture generate its own meaning independent of anything outside of itself, and correlational theology's insistence that the classics of the Christian tradition generate a Christian culture prior to the engagement with a specific culture.[11]

Because Christian identity is constructed locally and relationally, establishing Christianity's cultural boundaries cannot be a matter of including uniquely Christian elements or rejecting others as not Christian. Indeed, in a postmodern view "cultural elements may cross the boundaries between cultures without jeopardizing the distinctiveness of those cultures."[12] Christians can thus incorporate elements of their wider culture without this practice threatening Christian identity. Instead, Tanner shifts the discussion to the *use* of cultural elements as the way by which groups distinguish themselves from others: cultural difference is established more often by how cultural materials are used than by their presence or absence.[13] The existence of particular Christian cultures is thereby not denied, but the idea that such boundaries would take the form of unique cultural content is.[14] According to Tanner, "Christian culture is formed through the reworking of borrowed materials; it is the culture of others made odd."[15]

Christianity thus exists without cultural essence. Nor has it ever existed in a pristine or original cultural form that warrants its truth

---

10. Ibid., 537.
11. Ibid., 538.
12. Ibid., 537.
13. Ibid.
14. Ibid.
15. Ibid., 539.

or forms its revelatory standard.[16] Instead it is a cultural hybrid—or better, a process of ongoing hybridization—that uses differently some of the elements of the historical cultures of which Christians have been part. Tanner understands "use" in a variety of ways. It can include affirmation of cultural forms on different grounds, such as gender equality in light of Christ's love for all, or may reverse cultural forms, for example when honor before God is established by humility rather than by glory.[17] Moreover, the transformation of another culture is a selective and fragmentary process, not something in which a whole culture is taken on but only some of its forms and practices.[18] In sum, then, Christian culture is relational to its host culture, marking itself only partially from the larger culture and society, and creating a hybrid with that larger culture in a messy historical and cultural process through different uses of its elements.

It is important to note that this non-essentialist account of Christian identity is foremost theological in origin. While Tanner's arguments clearly track with the postmodern theories of culture that she employs—emphasizing the indeterminacy and contested character of culture—they are fundamentally rooted in the transcendent and eschatological character of the Word of God that never coincides with the cultural forms in which it comes to be expressed.

Theology as Cultural Construction

Tanner's use of the postmodern concept of culture also has methodological implications for theology understood as a form of cultural construction. Christian cultures do not take the form of shared beliefs and values, nor do they form consistent or coherent

---

16. Tanner, *Theories of Culture*, 148.
17. Tanner, "Cultural Theory," 539.
18. Ibid.

systems. Instead it is in the nature of Christian beliefs that they are contested and need to be articulated, that is, selected, weighted, and organized into more or less coherent but particular and conditioned perspectives.

Underlying these viewpoints is the idea that any Christian culture that is the product of largely contingent social and historical processes comprises materials of which the "various elements are not likely to show a great deal of consistency among themselves."[19] In the process of Christian intercultural communication and relational, cultural articulation of Christian identities, elements of host cultures are brought in relation to elements of cultures that have been previously engaged by Christians, that is, to cultural elements that have come to be accepted as "Christian." But in their loosely organized state these previously adopted cultural elements cannot themselves give coherent or unambiguous guidance in the engagement of new social and cultural situations.

Thus, on the one hand, the elements that make up Christian culture are in themselves ambiguous and therefore need to be interpreted and developed. As Tanner puts it, "the rather vague beliefs that all Christians share—for example, that Jesus saves—need to be elaborated if they are to influence the shape of Christian life."[20] On the other hand, these elements are part of a much larger set of materials in relation to which they take on much of their meaning, but with which they sometimes are in tension or even contradiction. The task of the theologian, and in some way of each believer, is to select certain elements among these materials, interpret them, give them prominence, and connect them with other elements to put all of this together as a more or less coherent way of understanding Christian faith. Only in this way can the loosely connected materials

19. Ibid.
20. Ibid., 540.

of Christian culture become sufficiently meaningful to determine a Christian way of life.[21]

Complementary to this underdetermined character of Christian culture is the insight that it encourages the development of alternative perspectives—using the same set of materials. Tanner observes that "cultural elements that are not selected for inclusion or are under-emphasized in a given construction of Christian culture remain resources for radically different views of what Christianity is all about."[22] Christian culture is thus always bound to be internally heterogeneous with regard to Christian beliefs and practices, and it is thus in the nature of Christian culture itself that it generates alternative, diverse, and conflicting perspectives on what it means to be Christian.[23]

Tanner's non-essentialist accounts of Christian identity and theological construction make her theology of culture particularly intriguing for intercultural and missiological scholars, who in their study of Christianity's cultural plurality often ponder similar methodological questions. Tanner herself incorporates an important intercultural insight: "When Christian culture meets a particular historical context, no single understanding of Christianity naturally arises from their confluence; instead, an argument usually breaks out over the meaning of Christian culture for that time."[24]

Theology as Inculturation

Yet most theologians with whom Tanner is in discussion focus implicitly or explicitly on the particular relationship between Christianity and Western culture, understanding the latter as having

---

21. Ibid.
22. Ibid.
23. Ibid.
24. Ibid.

been deeply (and often adversely) affected by modernity. These theologians are usually not directly concerned with the interaction between cultures, relationships with postcolonial or non-Western cultures, or with questions of power and inequality. However, such issues have been the central concerns of intercultural, ecumenical, and Third World theologians, many of whom have focused explicitly on social change and cultural diversity. Two particular theological concepts have been especially important in the work of these theologians, namely, theology as inculturation and theology as contextualization. Both explicitly address theological articulation in situations of social change and cultural diversity, as well as issues of inequality within and between cultures. However, inculturation and contextualization perform these analyses along somewhat different lines: while inculturation tends to approach theology in terms of "culture," that is, in relation to patterns of cultural differences and similarities, contextual theologians generally perform their analyses in terms of social, political, and economic inequalities among people and communities.

In this chapter I focus primarily on theology as inculturation because its programmatic concern with culture shows affinity with the cultural agenda for theology described by Tanner. I argue that theology as inculturation can greatly benefit from her extensive exploration of the implications of postmodern concepts of culture for the relationship between Christian identity and culture as well as for theological construction. Moreover, with regard to theology as contextualization I argue that many of its sociopolitical concerns can be subsumed in the cultural-theological agenda of inculturation if the latter employs Tanner's postmodern analysis of culture.

The concept inculturation emerged in response to the deep inequalities that existed during European colonialism between colonized and colonizing communities and cultures, and, above all, in response to the identification of Christianity with European cultures. During the decolonization process, in which nationalistic and anti-colonial sentiments were often championed by indigenous religious communities, the identification of Christianity with European cultures became an embarrassment and source of alienation for Christian communities in formerly colonized societies. In the postcolonial period, therefore, Christians in the global South argued for the common task of building up the new nations together with the theological cultural policy of inculturation that emphasized Christian engagement with the cultures of the postcolonial nations. As a result, inculturation "has become one of the most prominent themes of the Asian, African, Pacific, and Latin American theologies."[25]

Inculturation as Theological Concept

In theological discourse inculturation thus refers to the insight that the Christian gospel is or should be articulated *by means of* a particular culture's symbolic and linguistic order, and *in relation to* the cultural, historical, and social circumstances of a (local) community. One of the first definitions of inculturation stems from Pedro Arrupe, who defined it as "the incarnation of Christian life and of the Christian message in a particular cultural context, in such a way that this experience not only finds expression through elements proper to the culture in question but becomes a principle that animates, directs and unifies the culture, transforming it and remaking it so as to bring about a 'new creation'."[26] Like the concept contextualization, inculturation emphasizes the need for what Robert Schreiter has called "local theologies," thereby challenging the assumption of

25. Brian Stanley, "Inculturation: Historical Background, Theological Foundations and Contemporary Questions," *Transformation* 24, no. 1 (2007): 22.
26. Pedro Arrupe, "Letter to the Whole Society on Inculturation," *Aixala* 3 (1978): 172.

universality on the part of modern theology.[27] Instead, inculturation highlights the historical and cultural particularity of Christian practices and beliefs. This is first a theoretical insight, in the sense that it is supported epistemologically by contemporary models of human understanding and production of meaning such as hermeneutical and cultural anthropological perspectives. Like Tanner's theology of culture, these perspectives all depict human meaning and understanding as contextual, that is, they must be seen in the context of a particular historical and cultural symbolic and linguistic system. Hence, Christian beliefs and practices are always conditioned by, and must be interpreted in relation to, the particularity of their situation described in terms of cultural, historical, social, economic and other factors—even when past and present processes of (global) intercultural exchange clearly demonstrate that cultures and communities do not exist in isolation but are in continuous interaction with each other.

The concept of inculturation also expresses theological grounds for the articulation of Christian theology in the local cultural idiom and in relation to local social and religious concerns. The word inculturation itself combines the idea of incarnation—that is, the theological notion that the Word of God becomes embodied in Jesus Christ and thus in the concreteness and particularity of this world—*and* the anthropological concept of enculturation—that is, the intercultural process in which elements of one culture are assumed within another culture. In this light incarnation is understood as an ongoing historical process. Inculturation thus expresses the theological belief that God's healing and saving activity takes place within the concrete historical and cultural realities of humanity, and that this perspective should inform the Christian engagement with cultures.[28] In fact, advocates of inculturation usually consider God

27. Robert J. Schreiter, *Constructing Local Theologies* (Maryknoll, NY: Orbis Books, 1985).
28. There is a similar theological argument underlying the idea of contextualization. However, this

to be at work in traditional cultures and religions, before, and independent of, the arrival of Christianity.

It will be clear that Tanner's argument that Christians create their own Christian culture through selective and transformative appropriation of elements of the cultures to which they belong shows important theoretical affinity with the idea of inculturation. Indeed, I argue that Tanner's theology of culture can make important contributions to the understanding of inculturation. This certainly does not mean that the two can simply be equated. To mark one significant distinction upfront, inculturation expresses an explicit theological motive for the engagement with particular cultures. Interestingly, in her theology of culture Tanner seems to embrace the anthropological inevitability of culture rather than view culture itself theologically as the stuff in which God engages humanity. Generally speaking, Protestant theologians have been wearier than their Roman Catholic counterparts to consider culture theologically in a constructive way because of their concern with the corrupting influence of sin. In Tanner's case, however, what can be considered to be at work here is her principle of non-competiveness between divine and human agency. Rather than see divine and human agency as inversely related, Tanner sees divine and human agency as non-competitive. Seen in those terms, then, while Tanner may not directly address the question how and where God is at work in human cultures, this does not mean that God is not at work in human cultures, but rather that God's activity in cultures should be understood in a non-competitive way.

Inculturation as Theology of Culture

Apart from this theological difference, there are also other important

argument is related to the theological framework of *Missio Dei*, and does not see God's activity in the culture but in the processes of social change—often seen to disrupt the former.

differences between Tanner's theology of culture and inculturation as it is commonly understood. Many of those differences relate to Tanner's use of the postmodern concept of culture, and its implications for the relationship between Christianity and culture and for theological articulation as cultural process. Indeed, I argue that Tanner's theology of culture can in important ways help rethink the theology of inculturation, and especially some of its methodological concerns.

Inculturation and Postmodern Concepts of Culture

The understanding of inculturation is often inscribed explicitly or implicitly in the conventional, static, bounded, and integrated concept of culture that postmodern anthropology critiques. It cannot be held against Arrupe that he used a modern understanding of culture in his 1978 contribution to the theology of inculturation.[29] However, his presupposition that cultures are defined by unique and clearly determined characteristics that unify these cultures and organize them as consistent wholes still characterizes much contemporary discourse about inculturation. For instance, a recent article describes inculturation as the "process by which the Christian gospel, so to say, infuses itself into a new culture; transforming it on some levels and, at the same time, taking on the unique characteristics and concerns of a particular culture."[30] Another, frequently used image for inculturation sees the gospel as a plant that, when planted as a seed in the soil of a particular culture, will organically grow to maturity, taking on the unique characteristics of this culture.[31] This image not only sees the inculturated gospel as an integrated and

---

29. Arrupe, "Letter to the Whole Society on Inculturation," 172.
30. Richard A. Pruitt, "Contemplating the Inculturation of the Christian Gospel among the Igbo of Southeastern Nigeria," *Missiology* 40, no. 4 (2012): 425.
31. For instance, see Gerald A. Arbuckle, *Earthing the Gospel: An Inculturation Handbook for the Pastoral Workers* (Maryknoll, NY: Orbis Books, 1990), 3.

static whole, but, because of the way in which the culturally specific soil enables a unique inculturation, it also implies the particular, determined, and coherent character of culture itself. Moreover, much discourse about inculturation still presupposes unique, isolated, and static cultures rather than recognize that cultures emerge from, and are continuously shaped by, historical intercultural interactions—as is certainly the case in the present age of technological, economic, cultural, and religious globalization.

Finally, the inculturated gospel is itself often seen as an internally coherent whole, which can "infuse" an entire culture, or can "direct and unify" it, so that this culture becomes, in its totality, a "new creation." In other words, the inculturated gospel, in its unity, relates to the totality of a culture.[32] These ideas not only presuppose that cultures can be engaged in their entirety, but also set unrealistically high expectations of the interactions of Christians with their cultures, namely, to reshape them in their totality. Instead, the theology of culture suggests that inculturation is a more modest process: Christians transform and reorient only elements of their cultures in messy and ambivalent social practices. In light of the postmodern notion of culture, then, it is necessary to consider more closely how inculturation relates to culture, and how inculturation itself is understood as a process of cultural construction.

Inculturation: Universal or Postcolonial?

To further conceptualize inculturation it may be helpful to explore an apparent contradiction within the discourse of inculturation. On the one hand, advocates of inculturation often state that all theology is the result of inculturation. In other words, they make the argument that inculturation is not a modern innovation but consistent with the

---

32. Arrupe S.J., "Letter to the Whole Society on Inculturation," 172; and Pruitt, "Contemplating the Inculturation of the Christian Gospel," 425.

tradition of Christianity. Yet, on the other hand, these proponents make their case explicitly because they argue that forms of theology exist—specifically in colonial Christianity—that are not inculturated and for which inculturation is presented as a necessary correction.

According to the theology of culture, Christian theology has throughout its history been borrowing and reusing cultural elements from the cultural worlds of which Christians have been part. Proponents of inculturation may therefore use Tanner's portrayal of the 'normal' process of hybridization and reappropriation of cultural forms that occurs throughout Christian history as an ongoing or universal process of inculturation, that is, as *theologia semper inculturanda*. Yet, this begs the question: what then characterizes the situation of particular concern to theologies of inculturation, namely, the construction of theology in the postcolonial world? In what way is theology from the colonial period in the majority world different from this universal process of inculturation? And how shall these two forms of inculturation be distinguished if they are indeed different?

It is important to recognize that the ongoing process of cultural reappropriation and hybridization has also characterized the creation of Christian cultures in the majority world during colonial times. The intercultural processes by which Christianity spread in the global South have been deeply impacted by local communities and cultural systems. For instance, in his classic study *Translating the Message*, Lamin Sanneh has shown how deeply Africans have shaped African Christianity.[33] Even if Sanneh's claim of reciprocity between the European missionaries and African Christians is a rather one-dimensional characterization of a very complex situation, there can be little doubt that European missionary Christianity was never in control of the process by which Christianity came to be adopted

---

33. Lamin Sanneh, *Translating the Message*, American Society of Missiology Series (Maryknoll, NY: Orbis Books, 1989).

in Africa.[34] This is not only the case in African Initiated Churches that associated historically Christian and traditional African cultural elements free from missionary oversight, but also in the mission churches themselves.[35] Kwame Bediako, too, in what he calls "grassroots theology," has shown how African Christianity related the figure of Jesus Christ in complex ways to the traditional cultural and religious worlds of Africa.[36] What these theologians recognize is that in colonial Christianity, too, the "normal" process of hybridization and reappropriation of cultural elements—or universal inculturation—has been going on.

At the same time the colonial situation was unique because indigenous cultural forms were often rejected as incompatible with elements of the Christian culture that had been inserted through missionary activity. In colonial Christianity, theology was usually constructed relational to the colonial culture rather than to the culture of the colonized. This outside Christian culture was moreover considered superior. Local cultural elements were rejected because they were seen as indigenous (for example, as "African") or were seen as belonging to other religions, that is, as "syncretism." Moreover, the power to reject or accept such cultural elements was, at least in the mission churches, in the hands of cultural outsiders, that is, missionaries and missionary organizations who demanded conformity to their own theological constructions.

---

34. Ibid., 173. Tanner refers to some of these discussions when she brings up the ambiguity of the relationship between African Christianity and traditional African religions: "When the God of Christians is identified with the high God of African religions, is the African high God assimilated to a Christian outlook, or the reverse?... When African Christians identify the spirits in control of everyday life with demons and Jesus Christ as the only antidote to their pernicious influence, which is absorbing which–African religious practices or Christian ones" *Theories of Culture*, 148-49.

35. Allan H. Anderson, *African Reformation: African Initiated Christianity in the 20th Century* (Trenton, NJ: Africa World Press, 2001).

36. Kwame Bediako, *Jesus and the Gospel in Africa: History and Experience*, Theology in Africa Series (Maryknoll, NY: Orbis Books, 2004), 8-15.

The latter situation constitutes what Tanner's theology considers an improper limitation of "the exercise of theological creativity by demanding conformity with … human authority deemed a pure … stand-in for God's Word itself."[37] Furthermore, even if specific cultural elements are rejected as Christians articulate ways of Christian living in their particular culture, according to the theology of culture such a rejection—uncommon occurrence as it is—needs to be argued relationally to that culture, and not primarily in relation to forms of Christianity negotiated in other cultures. As Tanner observes, the distinctiveness of Christian culture is formed not *by* but *at* the boundaries of cultures.[38] Thus, while in intercultural processes such as Christian mission cultural elements from other cultures clearly play a role, local Christian articulations are primarily relational to their own cultural context. Rejection of elements because they belong to a particular culture makes cultural boundaries the issue rather than the *use* of specific cultural elements. A rejection of cultural elements should therefore not be based on interculturally given criteria. Underlying Tanner's theology of culture is a fundamental insight with important intercultural implications: "Christian identity hinges on remaining open to direction from the free grace of God in Christ; that is the organizing principle for its use of borrowed materials."[39] Moreover, the improper use of borrowed materials is not determined by "whether those materials seem to threaten the established character of Christianity," but rather by "whether that use distorts that to which Christians are trying to witness, and there is no easy test for that."[40] Finally, no elements of a culture can be rejected because they are considered inherently un-Christian. While there

37. Tanner, *Theories of Culture*, 163.
38. Tanner, "Cultural Theory," 537.
39. Tanner, *Theories of Culture*, 150.
40. Ibid.

are things all Christians should reject for good reasons, for example, slavery or racism, the relational character of all Christian articulation cautions against considering cultural elements incompatible with Christianity outside of specific cultural contexts.

The colonial reality in which improper intercultural arguments did negatively impact emerging forms of Christianity further points to the problematic inequality between cultural outsiders, who sought to control cultural articulations of Christianity, and those who adopted Christianity in their culture. As a result, indigenous Christians were taught to be suspicious of their own cultures. In these regards, then, the postcolonial situation of Christianity in the majority world does pose a particular set of problems that theology as inculturation seeks to correct. In situations in which such improper intercultural arguments and power inequalities between native and outside participants are being critically addressed one may speak of *postcolonial inculturation*, and distinguish it from the cultural reappropriation and hybridization, or *universal inculturation*, that is always going on, including in colonial situations.

The question remains how postcolonial inculturation addresses these problems. Because Christian colonial cultures in the majority world were often constructed over and against the cultures they engaged, theologians such as Bediako argue that the issue of cultural identity is at the heart of theology in Africa. To him the central question is what it means "to be African *and* Christian."[41] Echoing Bediako, Brian Stanley observes that the "quest for inculturation is a quest for a secure and integrated identity, motivated by a concern to find ways of being both authentically Christian and authentically Chinese, Indian, African,… so that … we do not feel torn apart by two mutually contradictory allegiances."[42]

41. Bediako, *Jesus and the Gospel in Africa*, 53.
42. Stanley, "Inculturation," 22.

The goal of postcolonial inculturation is thus not to infuse the entire culture with the values of the gospel, but the more limited task of restoring a sense of cultural dignity and continuity. This is done most effectively by engaging elements associated with cultural identity, and especially those elements that in the past have been rejected without valid theological reasons, that is, without arguments relational to the culture. Such a re-engagement seeks to restore cultural integrity by positively engaging these cultural elements within Christian culture. As Edward Fasholé-Luke observed, "African theologians have … to draw together the various and disparate sources that make up the total religious experience of Christians in Africa into a coherent and meaningful pattern."[43]

This intentional engagement with indigenous culture cannot be an isolated process, but needs to take place in the context of cultural changes and intercultural processes that affect the community, culturally, socially, and economically. Moreover, postmodern cultural theory does not understand cultural identity as an essence but as a contested label that is an important stake in communities' cultural negotiations about the proper ordering of social relations. This implies that Christians should not adopt elements associated with cultural identity without considering their use in the larger culture. What does the agenda of inculturation mean, for instance, for Christians in countries like Uganda where agendas profoundly hostile towards homosexuals are pursued in the name of traditional African culture—as well as in the name of Christianity?

Finally, postcolonial inculturation seeks to overcome the binary opposition between traditional or non-Christian and Christian cultures. Unfortunately this binary is alive and well in those theological discussions that continue to reject cultural elements

---

43. Edward W. Fasholé-Luke, "Quest for an African Christian Theology," *Ecumenical Review* 27, no. 3 (1975): 259–69. Quoted in Bediako, *Jesus and the Gospel in Africa*, 65.

because they belong to traditional cultures or religions. The mutual exclusionary character of being Christian and being African, is still used by those who do not care for inculturation. Ironically, however, the discourse of inculturation itself also runs the danger of prolonging the circulation of this binary, namely, when it assumes that only theologies incorporating traditional cultural elements are truly inculturated. According to the theology of culture, Christian culture always (re)uses the cultural elements it encounters. Thus, the fact that something is Christian without, on the face of it, being African or Indian does not mean this particular theology is not the result of a process of inculturation. The real question is whether this theology is constructively linked to important cultural elements of the community. Moreover, while theologies deliberately engaging cultural elements formerly rejected maybe most effective in restoring a sense of cultural continuity, no one form of inculturation organically flows or grows from the encounter with a culture. Hence, the ways in which Christians choose and use the elements of the culture in relation to which they define themselves is open to debate among them, and inculturation can subsequently take many forms.

Christ as Ancestor

A brief illustration of the complex cultural negotiations involved in inculturation may be in order. In light of the rejection of honoring ancestors in most missionary constructions of African Christianity, and in light of the continued cultural significance and status of ancestors to many Africans, African theologians have extensively explored the idea of Christ as Ancestor.[44] The importance of the ancestors in many traditional African worldviews derives from their role as source and mediator of life in its biological, material, social,

---

44. Among the theologians exploring Christ as Ancestor are John Pobee, Charles Nyamiti, Bénézet Bujo, and François Kabasélé.

and spiritual dimensions—which they pass on from the highest God—as well as from their function as guardian of the community.[45] Yet, while restoring a sense of continuity between African cultures and Christian identity, the re-appropriation of these ideas by African Christians also significantly shifts their use. For instance, in many African cultures ancestors must have been married and had progeny. They must also have died well—that is, of natural courses and in old age—rather than young or as the result of conflict, which is often associated with distorted relationships within the community or with witchcraft.[46] There are thus clearly important divergences between African ideas of ancestors and their use in relationship to Jesus Christ. In African Christianity the notion of Christ's offspring is understood spiritually rather than biologically. Moreover, Christ's death was a violent one, taking place at a young age and within the context of social and political conflict. But rather than making ideas of ancestry unfit to be applied to Jesus Christ, these divergences bespeak a tension with traditional understandings of ancestors that sets the Christian use of the term apart, and may also stir debate among African Christians about the appropriateness of traditional or Christian conceptions. Should the lack of biological offspring indeed be seen as a tarnish or even curse upon a person? Is conflict in the community always necessarily negative or can it also lead to a more just and equal society? Why is it unthinkable for Jesus to have had progeny? Can Christians imagine the afterlife in community with the living? African theologians have also challenged the singular affirmation of familial or ethnic affiliations in traditional African notions of ancestry, instead emphasizing the universal nature of Christ's ancestry, which unites all of humanity into one family.[47]

45. François Kabasele Lumbala, "Christ as Ancestor and Elder Brother," in *Faces of Jesus in Africa*, ed. Robert J. Schreiter, Faith and Culture Series (Maryknoll, NY: Orbis Books, 1991), 117-18.
46. Ibid., 118. See also Diane B. Stinton, *Jesus of Africa : Voices of Contemporary African Christology*, Faith and Cultures Series (Maryknoll, NY: Orbis Books, 2004), 113.

In short, then, appropriating African notions of ancestors leads theologians to a cultural hybridization that, rather than simply affirming existing cultural or religious notions, challenges both traditional African and existing Christian cultural articulations. Rather than seeing this process as a threat to the purity and integrity of Christian faith, a theology of inculturation informed by Tanner's theology of culture sees these challenges positively in accordance with the transcendent character of God's Word that cannot be contained in any cultural form. However, while the idea of Christ as Ancestor has shown to be an important proposal for inculturation in African cultures, claims of other Christians that the idea of ancestors is not helping them express their faith as Africans do not necessarily mean their proposals are incompatible with inculturation.[48]

Syncretism

Tanner's perspective on the relationship between Christian identity and cultures also sheds light on longstanding discussions about inculturation and syncretism. Clearly, most of what is presently readily recognized as "Christian" has it origin in other cultures and religions, and at some point came to be reused and accepted as part of Christian culture. In spite of this history discussions about inculturation and syncretism abound. Stanley asks, "what are the boundaries which separate legitimate inculturation from syncretism?"[49] He continues, "the question is often posed in the form: "Is there an irreducible core of Christian truth that should be universal in its application to all contexts and cultures, and if so, what is it?" Steve Bevans, similarly refers to syncretism as the

---

47. Bediako, *Jesus and the Gospel in Africa*, 31–32.
48. For some arguments African Christians make against the idea of Christ as Ancestor, see Stinton, *Jesus of Africa*, 131–35.
49. Stanley, "Inculturation," 24.

"danger in contextualization ... that one ... mix Christianity and culture in a way that does not enhance but compromises and betrays Christianity."[50]

Tanner's understanding of the interaction between Christianity and cultures voids many of the answers and perspectives traditionally given in relation to these issues. Cultures are not primarily distinguished by different cultural forms but foremost by different uses of the same cultural forms by different groups, which interpret these forms in line with their particular activities.[51] There is thus nothing particular surprising or alarming about the use of other cultural or religious elements in Christian culture. In fact, if the *presence* of "other" cultural or religious elements is to be the criterion Christianity always has been "syncretistic." But making the presence of such elements the issue misdirects the theological task of engaging one's culture, or misdirects judgments concerning inculturation in other cultures. The fundamental theological question is how elements of cultures and religions are interpreted and aligned within a Christian cultural horizon. This question, however, can only be considered as these elements are made part of a particular cultural articulation of Christian identity and beliefs. According to the theology of culture, questions of appropriate use are considered primarily in relation to the social and cultural reality being engaged. Unlike forms of inculturation that work with a model of translating theologies from one culture into another, and therefore locate the criteria for appropriate use in incultured forms of Christianity found previously or elsewhere, the theology of culture considers the question of "fit" relationally to the culture being engaged. This does not mean that "fit" is based on criteria derived from this culture,

50. Stephen B. Bevans, *Models of Contextual Theology* (Maryknoll, NY: Orbis Books, 1992), 17.
51. Tanner, "Cultural Theory," 534.

but that arguments are made in relation to the use of elements in a culture's social and symbolic practices.

The question of proper inculturation can also not be an issue of including essential core beliefs or practices. The question is not merely what these essential beliefs are. Understanding theology as cultural construction implies that essential beliefs have very limited significance. The meaning of these beliefs depends upon how they are articulated in particular cultures as they are selected, weighed, and linked to other materials of those cultures as well as to previous Christian materials. Finally, Tanner's theology of culture resists articulating cultural norms for proper inculturation on theological grounds. Efforts to maintain Christian identity and guard against syncretism can easily subordinate the Word to human words. Tanner maintains that "Christianity does not need to keep the upper hand when using borrowed materials; the Word does."[52] The real danger does not come from syncretism but from looking for easy answers where answers must remain elusive for methodological and especially theological reasons.

Meanwhile few would contest that Christianity can be "betrayed." However, there is usually far less agreement on what constitutes or causes such betrayal. Nor is it clear how insisting on core essentials, or keeping elements of other cultures or religions at bay, guarantees fidelity to Christianity's true identity. Even in cases where, in hindsight, most Christians agree that Christian faith was corrupted, such as the Christian sanctioning of the institution of slavery or the nazification of theology by the German Christians, it is difficult to see the inclusion of external cultural elements as the root cause. Although Christian arguments for slavery did indeed sometimes borrow from classical Greek culture, they also found ample support within the

---

52. Tanner, *Theories of Culture*, 149.

Hebrew Bible and the New Testament themselves. Similarly, the racial antisemitism of the Nazi church—sometimes portrayed as "syncretism"—was built on an anti-Judaism that is deeply engrained in the history and textual sources of Christianity. Indeed, the "othering" of Judaism has often been constitutive of Christian identity.

The importance of avoiding such distortions of Christian beliefs and practices is obvious, but the answer cannot be found in including essential beliefs or excluding elements of other cultures. Instead, the answer must be found in the practice of explicitly including within the Christian community and its communication those who are being marginalized by cultural and social practices, including Christian beliefs and practices themselves.

Inculturation or Contextualization?

Inculturation and contextualization both express that Christian theology should be articulated in relation to the cultural, historical, and social circumstances of a community, but do so in different ways.[53] However, while it is neither judicious nor necessary to play inculturation off against contextualization, this often has been the history of these two concepts. Some of these divergences should be traced to different theological and institutional orientations. But the most contentious issue has been the social analysis of the reality in which Christian communities exist. Specifically, proponents of theological contextualization have critiqued inculturation for being

---

53. The concept of contextualization typically relates theology to the notion of *Missio Dei*—God's mission within the history of humanity and especially in those sociocultural movements that are "making history," that is, producing social change and creating an awareness of historical agency. For instance, Shoki Coe defined contextualization as "that critical assessment of what makes the context really significant in light of Missio Dei. It is the missiological discernment of the sign of the times, seeing where God is at work and calling us to participate in it." See Shoki Coe, "Contextualizing Theology," in *Mission Trends No. 3*, ed. Gerald H. Anderson and Thomas F. Stransky (New York: Paulist Press, 1976), 21-22.

focused on static cultures rather than being concerned with social justice.

One of the great advantages of incorporating into the theology of inculturation a postmodern concept of culture is the potential it has to overcome the differences between these theological approaches. The postmodern understanding of culture emphasizes that meaning and identity are never simply given. Instead, they are the (temporary) results of ongoing processes of production of meaning and identity that make up cultures. Postmodern anthropology takes its cue from poststructuralism according to which the meaning of a cultural form "is not fixed by a transparent reference to reality," but instead is "plural and shifting, always different and deferred, in keeping with the ever-changing, multivalent circumstances of its historical production."[54] Meaning and identity thus drift unless they are fixed and stabilized by social forces that advance such outcomes. Postmodern anthropology therefore does not assume the stability of cultures, nor does it understand cultural change as the result of forces external to a culture. Instead, cultures change because they consist of "fluid forms susceptible of varying interpretations, loosely connected elements that can therefore be ordered and reordered to support or contest various social arrangements."[55] Such elements include "logically incompatible beliefs or values that might be pushed and pulled ... or the potentially subversive remains and traces of alternatives to now-dominant cultural forms, interpretations, or arrangements."[56]

This characterization of culture importantly informs Tanner's understanding of theology as cultural construction. However, it also opens up important possibilities for the analysis of culture within

54. Tanner, *Theories of Culture*, 46.
55. Ibid., 51-52.
56. Ibid.

processes of inculturation, namely, with a critical eye to the cultural processes that exercise social power. Postmodern anthropology criticizes the modern concept of culture for disregarding the role of conflict and how power is negotiated through cultural processes.[57] In the postmodern understanding of culture power is "at stake in the interpretation of beliefs, values, or notions with a cultural currency. Struggles over power become enacted in struggles over meaning. In that space ... between a cultural form and the multiple possible meanings of it, contests over power are engaged."[58] This analysis of power at work in and through culture is essential for a theology of inculturation that seeks to be a force for social transformation and for greater justice in societies. It opens up critical spaces to challenge dominant cultural formations that are oppressive to groups within the community, as well as creative spaces to propose alternative Christian interpretations.

Furthermore, as culture is the meaning dimension of social practices, the unjust practices that are the main concerns of theological contextualization also have a cultural dimension. Social practices of exclusion or discrimination on the basis of race, gender, or other social identities are all accompanied by cultural values that express the meaning of these practices. Hence, with the right tools for cultural analysis the theology of inculturation can critically engage discriminatory or oppressive practices in societies. Similarly, socio-economic injustice is not just the result of social and material practices, but also directly correlated to cultural values, symbols, and ideas. Social analysis thus needs to be married to cultural analysis. For instance, liberation theologians have rightly challenged cultural notions that poverty is part of the God-given order, that the market is the divine instrument to organize resources most efficiently, that

57. Ibid., 46.
58. Ibid., 47.

material needs are meted out deservedly by the capitalist economy, or that U.S. international policies are justified by the American way of life.

In conclusion, then, a theology of inculturation that is informed by Tanner's theology of culture can help to include the social justice agenda typical of contextual theologies into a cultural approach to theology. The postmodern understanding of culture, specifically, opens up the theological analysis of culture for the assessment of mechanisms of oppression, disenfranchisement, and exclusion, and makes available to theologians of inculturation a set of tools that can encompass the concerns of contextual and liberation theologians.

Christian Identity as Participation in Communication

The understanding of theology as inculturation emerged in response to the cultural diversity of postcolonial Christianity and has important implications for ecumenical discussions about Christian unity and identity. If Christian culture itself does not provide such an identity in the form of shared Christian beliefs and values, and if, moreover, local articulations of Christianity are relational to their particular cultures, where then is Christian identity to be located? Tanner's answer to this question is very relevant for intercultural theological discussions. Rather than seeing certain elements or practices of Christian culture as maintaining Christian identity, Tanner argues that this identity is located in the commitment to discipleship: "What Christians have in common, what unites them ... is concern for true discipleship, proper reflection in human words and deeds of an object of worship that always exceeds by its greatness human efforts to do so." [59] Yet Christians are not bound together by agreement regarding practices and beliefs marking discipleship, but by a "shared sense of the

59. Ibid., 153.

importance of figuring it out."[60] Being Christian means: the committed participation in a communicative process that, by its nature, will not be concluded through consensus at any time in history. The character of human cultural processes and especially their eschatological relationship to the Word of God imply that this communicative process will always remain open-ended.

Participation in this process is marked by a mutual accountability to learn from and be criticized by others as well as to contribute to and challenge all others with a similar commitment to Christian discipleship.[61] Tanner anchors these commitments in "theological affirmations" presumed by the communicative process, as well as by "standards of argument" that are themselves theologically informed.[62] While not regarding such affirmations as essential—if only because they have no circumscribed meaning outside of particular articulations—Tanner argues that Christian practices revolve around certain "claims and ritual actions that because of their lack of definition amount in practice to a similar set of questions to be answered in the effort to be true to God."[63] An example of such a theological affirmation is a belief in the significance of Jesus strong enough to orient one's life around figuring out the ground and meaning of this significance.[64] However, such a theological affirmation should be understood as a "project requiring a solution," rather than as establishing a given identity.[65]

While such affirmations provide the basis for the Christian "community of argument," Tanner argues that it is also possible to discern certain "standards of argument" based on the mutual

---

60. Ibid.
61. Tanner, "Cultural Theory," 540.
62. Tanner, *Theories of Culture*, 153-54.
63. Ibid., 153.
64. Ibid.
65. Ibid.

accountable commitment of the participants in the communication about discipleship.[66] Among these standards Tanner lists the need to take seriously the arguments supporting Christian claims; to offer interpretations for consideration and judgment by other participants; and to include everyone else engaged in the same project in an extended argument.[67] These standards of argument are also informed theologically, in that the seriousness of sin should encourage each participant to challenge others and be willing to stand corrected oneself.[68] Finally, Tanner emphasizes the ecumenical character of the mutually accountable communication about discipleship, which should ideally include "all Christians in every historical and geographical location."[69]

Christian unity and identity is thus provided by the ongoing intercultural communicative process about discipleship that is mutually compelling as well as open-ended. As Tanner puts it concisely, "Christianity has its identity as task."[70] Yet this identity must not be understood in a self-referential sense, but always in light of Christianity's eccentric and eschatological orientation to the Word of God. This orientation leads one to be bold in obedience to the demands of the Word as well as to be open to the Word's freedom.[71]

To understand theology as an ongoing process of inculturation in a cultural pluralistic world affirms, highlights, and complicates Tanner's non-essentialist understanding of Christian identity. The amount of cultural materials reused and hybridized will be very extensive, lack coherence, and will often be difficult to interpret and assess beyond the cultural situation in which particular Christians use

66. Ibid., 154.
67. Ibid.
68. Ibid., 154-55.
69. Ibid., 155.
70. Ibid.
71. Ibid.

them. However, in no way does this delimit the importance of the intercultural communication about discipleship. Moreover, while this complexity may lead to a certain privileging of local communities to assess the appropriateness of their understanding of Christian discipleship—after all, such communities are seen to be more internally diverse and conflicted than previously understood—it is still important that the suitability of these understandings, but also their significance beyond their own culture, are assessed as extensively as possible. Thus, African understandings of Christ as Ancestor may inspire Christians elsewhere to imagine discipleship in new ways, for example, by emphasizing our indebtedness to previous generations or inherited institutions and material distributions, or by highlighting the reciprocity by which previous generations challenge us to guard the interests of future generations.

Theology as inculturation also complements Tanner's understanding of Christian identity, especially if it incorporates concerns for social justice. These concerns have implications for the inclusive character of the community of argument as well as for the importance of social practices in relation to communication about Christian discipleship. Tanner argues for the inclusive and ecumenical character of the communicative process and sees the eschatological character of God's Word as warrant against human authority usurping its critical function.[72] However, are these important insights sufficient in light of Tanner's understanding of human sin and of the power inequalities at work in cultural and communicative processes? Instead of being willing to stand corrected by God's eschatological Word, its status in the communication about discipleship can also tempt Christians to try to determine, assert, and control what the meaning of the Word is, and to try to exclude whoever contradicts this assertion. This temptation is most likely to

72. Ibid., 163.

affect those already in positions of power and privilege. In order for all voices to be included in the communicative process it is therefore important to explicitly privilege those who are marginalized or excluded by the power structures in their communities and cultures. This privileging of the marginalized thus follows from the need to complement, challenge, and correct the most dominant articulations of Christian beliefs and practices, and to respect the freedom of the Word of God. It may also be supported theologically by important elements of historical Christianity, among which are included the Hebrew Bible's prophetic materials as well as Jesus' historical ministry to the poor and marginalized.

Discipleship, moreover, is foremost a way of being and of acting. It is therefore necessary to spell out more clearly the role of social practices in relation to communication about discipleship. Christians try to figure out what discipleship means as they reflect with their cultural materials on the social practices in which they are involved as Christians. Discipleship implies being affected by and involved with God's salvation as it is seen to relate to the world in which Christians live, regardless of how precisely "salvation," its relationship to the world, or the role of human agency in salvation are understood. Christians are therefore involved in figuring out what it means to be disciples while they engage themselves in their practices with God's healing and redeeming participation in the world. Such social practices should especially include practices of resistance and transformation by those who are marginalized and oppressed socially, or by those who are in solidarity with the oppressed. It is important to consider involvement in these practices to be part of Christian identity. Moreover, the involvement in practices of discipleship relates to communication about discipleship as part of a hermeneutical circle. Christians move continually between social practices they regard as forms of discipleship in their societies, and communication in which the meaning of these practices is spelled out in Christian terms in relation to the most inclusive and diverse Christian community.

10

Creative Appropriation and Interreligious Respect: Applying Tanner's Account of Christian Identity to an Interreligious Context

Hugh Nicholson

This essay examines some of the issues that arise when the conception of Christian identity that Kathryn Tanner presents in *Theories of Culture*[1] is applied in an interreligious context. In *Theories of Culture*, Tanner creatively draws on postmodern culture theory to offer a fresh perspective on the familiar and rather timeworn "Christ versus culture" problematic that has dominated discussions of theological method. There she develops a compelling account of Christian

---

1. Kathryn Tanner, *Theories of Culture: A New Agenda for Theology*, Guides to Theological Inquiry (Minneapolis: Fortress Press, 1997).

identity that calls attention to the distinctive ways in which Christians appropriate the cultural practices of others. Against the understanding of Christianity as a self-contained and self-generated cultural formation that enters into relation with other cultural formations only after it has already been formed, she argues that Christian identity is internally constituted by the non-Christian cultural forms that Christians continually confront and consume in forging a distinctively Christian way of life.

To the extent that religion represents a dimension of culture, this understanding of Christian identity suggests that an engagement with other religions is integral to the Christian theological task. The extension of Tanner's relational account of Christian identity to a specifically interreligious context, however, brings to the surface several implications of that account that stand in tension with other emphases in her work. In particular, applying the notion of a creativity of cultural consumption to Christian relations with non-Christian religions threatens to transform what was intended as a tactic of popular resistance against the imposition of elite cultural productions into an imperialistic model of Christian expropriation. An interreligious application of a notion of Christian identity based on the notion of creative appropriation would therefore seem to violate the principle, which Tanner eloquently defends elsewhere in her oeuvre, of respecting the cultural-religious other *as* other. Moreover, the obligation to respect the religious other as other presupposes the formation of a religious boundary, thereby suggesting a return, at least in the interreligious sphere, to a basically postliberal conception of Christian identity in virtue of cultural-religious boundaries.

We can, of course, reconcile the ethic of respecting religious difference with a relational concept of Christian identity easily enough by simply distinguishing, as Tanner in fact does, between cultural boundaries and notions of intrinsic identity. While cultural-religious boundaries are, in practice, often sustained by the misrecognition of these as marking a set of intrinsic cultural properties, there is no reason in principle why this has to be so. And yet, the notion of religious boundaries is problematic even when dissociated from essentialist notions of intrinsic identity. In the absence of a notion of intrinsic identity, the formation of religious boundaries implies an element of formal opposition—that is, the rejection of a belief or practice, not because it is morally or intellectually inconsistent with a Christian worldview, but simply because it defines another religious tradition. Tanner, no less than the liberal and postliberal theologians she critiques, is reluctant to concede formal opposition in her normative account of Christian identity. This reluctance, I suggest, manifests itself in a couple of apparent lapses into the notion of intrinsic identity. For example, Tanner appeals to a distinction between, on the one hand, matters of internal importance for Christian practice, and, on the other, situationally determined matters of importance for marking Christian distinctiveness.

Christian Identity Is Essentially Relational

Tanner develops her distinctive conception of Christian identity in the context of an effort to rethink theological method in light of postmodern critiques of the classic anthropological concept of culture. The latter informs a wide spectrum of theological positions, including those of R. H. Niebuhr, George Lindbeck, David Tracy, and Gordon Kaufman.[2] She observes that the longstanding debate between liberal and neo-orthodox theologians—continued by their respective revisionist and postliberal heirs—on the stance Christians

2. Ibid., 62-63.

should take vis-à-vis the wider society has reached an impasse. Neo-orthodox and postliberal theologians accuse their liberal and revisionist adversaries of compromising the distinctiveness and authenticity of the Christian message in the latter's apologetic effort to establish that message on presuppositions shared by the wider culture. Liberal theologians counter that their adversaries' refusal to engage in cultural apologetics effectively concedes the marginality of Christian faith in the modern world. Given the way the debate has been framed, it would seem that the theologian can avoid the twin pitfalls of accommodation and irrelevance only by muddling through with a series of never fully satisfying, ad hoc compromises.[3] Tanner gets around this impasse by observing that the framework of this debate presupposes a conception of the two entities whose relationship is at issue—namely, Christianity and the wider culture—that postmodern culture theory has shown to be problematic. Both liberal and postliberal camps conceive "Christianity" and "culture," like cultures in classic anthropology, as self-contained systems of belief and practice that enter into relation only after they have been formed.[4] Against the essentialist understanding of cultures as homogeneous and autonomous formations whose identities are based on a set of intrinsic properties, anthropologists and cultural theorists since the late 1970's have emphasized the ways in which the social formations conventionally designated as cultures achieve a sense of identity through a continual process of confrontation, appropriation, and negotiation with their surroundings. This postmodern perspective on culture suggests that the interactive processes by which Christians relate to the various others with whom they share a cultural space in the contemporary world are continuous with those by which Christianity emerged as

---

3. Kathryn Tanner, "Two Kinds of Apologetics," unpublished manuscript, 13-14.
4. Ibid., 15-16.

a distinctive way of life in its formative period. Having called into question the notion of Christianity as a pre-given and independently existing form of life, the task of relating Christian claims of meaning and truth to the wider culture cannot therefore be regarded as a secondary and perhaps optional matter of apologetics.[5] Nor does interaction with the wider culture necessarily threaten the distinctiveness of a Christian way of life if, in fact, Christians achieved a distinctive sense of identity through relational processes from the start. Tanner's analysis thus calls into question an underlying assumption of the "Christ and culture" problematic, namely, that Christians engage with the wider world only at the risk of losing their distinctive identity. The above-mentioned impasse on the question of theological method—that one avoids the pitfall of accommodation only at the cost of becoming irrelevant, and vice versa—therefore rests on a false dilemma. Tanner's thesis that relationality "goes all the way down" constitutes a powerful argument in favor of Christian engagement with the wider world, even if that engagement occasionally takes the form of opposition and confrontation.[6]

Even if Tanner's critique of the assumption of intrinsic Christian identity applies to classic liberal and correlationist theologies as much as postliberal ones,[7] the weight of her critique falls most heavily on the latter. Postliberalism epitomizes the conception of Christian identity in terms of a self-contained and bounded cultural unit modeled on the classic anthropological concept of culture. Nowhere is this conception of Christian identity more evident than in George Lindbeck's advocacy of the formation of close-knit Christian enclaves preserving a distinctively Christian way of life against the

---

5. Tanner, *Theories of Culture*, 115.

6. See, e.g., ibid., 152: "[P]rophetic objections to the wider society are maintained, not by isolation, but by the indefinitely extended effort to alter, where necessary, whatever one comes across through sustained engagement with it, in and out of church."

7. Ibid., 107, 115-16.

encroachments of an assimilative secular culture.[8] The main thrust of Tanner's postmodern critique, to repeat, is to challenge the assumption upon which this vision of Christian sectarianism rests, namely that Christians risk losing their identity if they engage with wider culture.[9]

On my reading of *Theories of Culture*, Tanner's critique of postliberalism under the heading of "Christian identity in virtue of a cultural boundary"[10] goes a step beyond the postmodern critique of the conception of cultures as reified, self-contained entities defined by a set of intrinsic properties. While the postmodern critique of intrinsic identity calls into question the notion of *naturalized* boundaries—that is, boundaries misrecognized as passive markers of supposedly innate cultural properties[11]—it does not exclude, as Tanner duly concedes,[12] the idea of boundaries as socially constructed markers of difference.[13] Tanner's critique of postliberalism marks an almost imperceptible shift from a descriptive analysis of how Christian communities have, in fact, forged a sense of identity to a normative proposal of how Christians in the contemporary world ideally should think about Christian identity.[14] She finds theoretical support for her theological proposal in theories of popular culture, such as those of Stuart Hall and Michel de Certeau, that emphasize the

---

8. See George Lindbeck, "The Sectarian Future of the Church," in *The God Experience: Essays in Hope*, ed. Joseph P. Whelan (New York: Newman, 1971), 226-43; cf. idem., "Ecumenism and the Future of Belief," *Una Sancta* 25, no. 3 (1968): 3-18.

9. Tanner, *Theories of Culture*, 104-5, 114-15.

10. Ibid., 104-19.

11. Ibid., 110.

12. Ibid., 114; cf. 152.

13. See, e.g., Arjun Appadurai, *Modernity at Large: Cultural Dimension of Globalization*, Public Worlds (Minneapolis: University of Minnesota Press, 1999), 13; and Bruce Lincoln, *Discourse and the Construction of Society: Comparative Studies of Myth, Ritual, and Classification* (New York: Oxford University Press, 1989), 9-10.

14. She acknowledges this normative character explicitly in "Theology and Popular Culture," in *Changing Conversations*, ed. Dwight N. Hopkins and Sheila Greeve Davaney (New York: Routledge, 1996), 117.

creative agency of ordinary people vis-à-vis the cultural productions of the elite.[15] These theories highlight the ways in which socially subordinate subcultures that are deprived of the means to create their own cultural productions nevertheless maintain their difference by consuming the cultural productions of the dominant social classes in ways unintended by their producers.[16] De Certeau draws an illuminating analogy between, on the one hand, the subversive consumption of the cultural products of the elite and, on the other, the cunning tactics of a militarily disadvantaged adversary forced to maneuver on terrain controlled by a militarily dominant power.[17] This concept of popular culture in the sense of the popular use or consumption of the cultural products of the elite[18] provides the model for Tanner's conception of Christian identity formation.[19] The concept of popular culture not only applies to popular religious practices that "make do" with available beliefs and ritual forms in addressing practical religious needs. It also provides a model even for elite forms of theology to the extent that these must work with popular beliefs and practices in order to win a broad base of popular support.[20] An understanding of theological activity modeled on the operations of popular culture highlights the ways in which Christian theology creatively appropriates or ironically tropes the discourses of others.[21] Put differently, the concept of popular culture encourages an understanding of Christian identity in terms of use rather than of substance. What makes a Christian way of life distinctive is not an

---

15. Ibid., 103-107.
16. Michel de Certeau, *The Practice of Everyday Life*, trans. Steven Randall (Berkeley: University of California Press, 1984), 30-34 and passim; and Stuart Hall, "Notes on Deconstructing 'the Popular'," in *People's History and Socialist Theory*, ed. Raphael Samuel (London: Routledge, 1981), 232-33; cf. Tanner, *Theories of Culture*, 112.
17. De Certeau, *Practice of Everyday Life*, 36-39.
18. Tanner, "Theology and Popular Culture," 105.
19. Ibid., 114, 116.
20. Ibid., 111-17.
21. Ibid., 114; cf. *Theories of Culture*, 116.

inventory of beliefs and practices not shared with the wider culture but rather the distinctive use that Christians make of the discourses and practices of others.[22] To the extent that the "placeless" tactics of popular consumption provide the model for Tanner's conception of Christian identity, it presents a stark alternative to the postliberal understanding of Christian identity in virtue of a cultural boundary. There can be no question of cultural boundaries as long as we operate "tactically" or interstitially in the cultural spaces of the other.[23] Expressed the other way around, the presence of a cultural boundary presupposes a place from which our relations with others can be "strategically" managed.[24]

Tanner's understanding of Christian identity in terms of popular culture thus represents a specification of her broader thesis that Christian identity is essentially relational. This point will be important to keep in mind as we explore the interreligious implications of her theory below. In the next section, I argue that the broader "relationality" thesis implies that an interreligious moment is integral to Christian identity formation. And yet, we shall see that the more specific understanding of this process in terms of creative consumption is problematic when applied in an interreligious context.

The Interreligious Dimension of Christian Identity Formation

Although Tanner does not develop the implications of her theory of Christian identity for the question of Christianity's relations with other religions, her thesis that Christian identity is essentially relational clearly implies that an engagement with religious others is integral to Christian identity formation. The principle that Christians

22. Ibid., 112–13 and passim.
23. De Certeau, *Practice of Everyday Life*, 37: "The space of the tactic is the space of the other."
24. Ibid., 36.

achieve a distinctive sense of identity in relation to the cultural activities of others applies, *a fortiori*, to the specifically religious discourses and practices of others. The notion that religion represents a subset or dimension of the broader category of culture has been a commonplace in anthropology and the history of religions. Its classic expression is Geertz's once immensely influential essay, "Religion as a Cultural System." Subsequent critiques of Geertz's understanding of religion in terms of the broader concept of culture have only radicalized his insight into the close connection between the two concepts. Scholars like Talal Asad and Bruce Lincoln no longer follow Geertz in theorizing religion as a specific type of cultural formation distinguished from others by a definable set of intrinsic properties—in particular, a set of symbols that refer to a cosmic order of existence.[25] Rather, they regard religion as a kind of meta-discourse that authorizes or recodes a particular cultural content—in principle, *any* cultural content—as having a transcendent or more-than-human status.[26] To exclude specifically religious formations from those cultural formations in relation to which Christians mobilize a sense of identity would be wholly arbitrary from either the perspective of the classic Geertzian definition of religion "as a cultural system" or, *a fortiori*, from the perspective of postmodern critiques of the notion of religion as an autonomous cultural sphere. An understanding of Christian identity like Tanner's that acknowledges and affirms the differential and hybrid nature of Christian identity is therefore obliged to recognize a specifically interreligious dimension to Christian theological reflection. John J. Thatamanil eloquently argues this point in making the case for the

25. Talal Asad, "The Construction of Religion as an Anthropological Category," in *Genealogies of Religion: Discipline and Reasons of Power in Christianity and Islam* (Baltimore: Johns Hopkins University Press, 1993), 36-37, 50-52 and passim; and Bruce Lincoln, *Holy Terrors: Thinking about Religion after September 11* (Chicago: University of Chicago Press, 2003), 1-3, 5-8, 51-61.
26. Lincoln, *Holy Terrors*, 6, 55-56.

theological subdiscipline of "comparative theology." Alluding to Paulo Gonçalves's critique of the theological representation of religious traditions as "homogeneous narrative worlds," a critique that runs along the same lines as Tanner's critique of postliberalism, Thatamanil argues that,

> [Gonçalves's "carnivalesque vision of theology"] can help disrupt and deconstruct the idea that comparative theology is a special but marginal brand or subdiscipline within theology proper. When we realize that theology has always been "messy, agonistic, creative . . . multiple," the term "comparative theology" begins to sound more like a redundancy rather [than] an oxymoron. How could theology be anything other than comparative? The call for a robust and interreligious comparative theology must be, on this account, understood as a call for reflection that lives into and thinks out of the inherent creative multiplicity of tradition(s), a multiplicity that already bears within it the mark of tradition's encounters with difference.[27]

The basic principle that Christian identity is essentially relational thus implies that the task of relating Christian claims of meaning and truth to those of other religions is integral to Christian identity formation. Yet, Tanner's more specific understanding of this process in terms of the concept of a creativity of cultural consumption becomes problematic when applied to an interreligious context. This point becomes clear when we recognize that creative consumption is theologically appropriate only when applied against a cultural power gradient. As we have seen, the model for this particular conception of Christian identity formation is the concept of popular culture, understood in terms of the creative ways that groups deprived of the means of cultural production still manage to preserve their difference in a cultural field dominated by elites. The power differential implicit in this concept of popular culture could not be more starkly expressed

---

27. John J. Thatamanil, "Comparative Theology after 'Religion'," in *Planetary Loves*, ed. Stephen D. Moore and Mayra Rivera (New York: Fordham University Press, 2007), 252.

than in the military metaphor invoked by de Certeau's distinction between tactics and strategies: creative consumption corresponds to the placeless tactics of the weak over against the strategies employed by an established military force. Cultural consumption takes on a completely different aspect, however, when it is employed by a culturally dominant power or faction. Then it easily becomes an instrument of cultural expropriation and repression. Thus the notion of Christians ironically troping the cultural practices of others is all well and good when the Christians in question belong to a relatively disadvantaged religious minority asserting itself over against a dominant culture; for example, when early Christians trope imperial discourse in speaking of Jesus Christ as Lord.[28] The notion becomes considerably less appealing, however, when the Christians are the members of an established imperial church seeking to expropriate the sacred tradition of a relatively weak and dispersed community like the ancient Jews.

Tanner's conception of Christian identity formation in terms of the concept of popular culture is appropriate in the contemporary North American, European, and Australian contexts to the extent that Christian communities there no longer enjoy cultural hegemony vis-à-vis the pluralistic or secular surrounding culture.[29] The cultural gap between Christian communities and the wider culture in places like North America, Europe, and Australia greatly diminishes, however, when we widen our angle of vision to include Christianity's relations with other religions in a global context. From

---

28. Cf. Tanner, *Theories of Culture*, 121.

29. Even in these contexts, however, the dominance of secular culture vis-à-vis Christianity is relative and ambiguous, particularly if we compare the situation of Christian communities there to their Islamic, Jewish, or Hindu counterparts. Any evaluation of the cultural power dynamics in such contexts, moreover, must take into account the tendency for Christians to exaggerate their minority status, whether as the innocent by-product of a laudable effort to identify with the underprivileged, or out of a less innocent interest in concealing the privileges they currently enjoy in order to extend their influence over public life.

a global perspective, Christianity retains, for good or for ill, its historical connection with a globally dominant Western culture. Any consideration of "Christ and the religions" has to be sensitive to the fact that Christianity typically relates to other religions along a descending power gradient. Even when Christianity fails to win converts, its presuppositions are carried along with the global hegemony of Western culture, as seen, for example, in the phenomenon of "Protestant Buddhism," that is, the transformation of Buddhism in Southeast Asia in accordance with an imported Protestant model of religion.[30] In light of the long history of European colonialism in the parts of the world where non-Christian religions form a constitutive part of the indigenous culture, any talk of Christianity creatively appropriating the beliefs and practices of other religions in those contexts smacks of cultural imperialism. We see exactly the same difficulty in applying a properly intracultural concept to a global, interreligious context with George Lindbeck's concept of intratextuality, a key concept in his postliberal theological program.[31] As I understand it, the point of this notion of redescribing the world in terms of the biblical narrative is to resist or contain Christianity's loss of hegemony in post-Enlightenment Western societies. The concept gives expression to the refusal to allow the wider culture set the standards of meaning and plausibility for Christian claims such that the latter have to be translated into a secular idiom in order to be intelligible and relevant. However, the application of this notion of untranslatability to interreligious relations in a global context—where the interpretive movement from text to world now follows along with, rather than against, a power gradient—can result in statements that have a decidedly imperialistic

30. Richard Gombrich and Gananath Obeyesekere, *Buddhism Transformed: Religious Change in Sri Lanka* (Princeton: Princeton University Press, 1988), 202-40.
31. George Lindbeck, *The Nature of Doctrine: Religion and Theology in a Postliberal Age* (Philadelphia: Westminster Press, 1984), 113-24.

ring. For example, Lindbeck speaks of using the Bible "to assimilate by redescription all the worlds and world views which human beings construct in the course of history."[32] The history of European colonialism testifies to the vulnerability of indigenous religious beliefs and practices to the potentially destructive power of redescription at the hands of a militarily and economically more powerful culture.[33] One thinks of the effacement of innumerable indigenous religious practices invidiously redescribed in terms of the biblical category of "idolatry."

Here Tanner's notion of creatively troping or ironically redescribing the cultural practices of others comes into tension with her understanding of tolerance, eloquently defended in her earlier book, *The Politics of God*, as respect of the other *as* other. There, she contrasts this conception of tolerance to an Enlightenment model of tolerance premised on an underlying similarity of beliefs or norms.[34] Tanner notes that the latter concept of tolerance, precisely by making similarity a condition for respect, finds itself in disconcerting proximity with the colonialist (and neo-colonialist) project of cultural assimilation.[35] She applies this critique to theologies of religions that posit a universal religious experience or common reference to Ultimate Reality (for example, John Hick's concept of "the Real") as the basis of relations of mutual respect among the religions. Such theologies are implicated in colonialist forms of discourse to the

---

32. Lindbeck, "The Gospel's Uniqueness: Election and Untranslatability," in *The Church in a Postliberal Age*, ed. James J. Buckley (Grand Rapids: Eerdmans, 2002), 235. Postliberals owe their confidence that the Christian interpretive framework will retain the upper hand over the cultural and religious materials it absorbs to the global hegemony of Western culture. See Hugh Nicholson, "Comparative Theology after Liberalism," *Modern Theology* 23, no. 2 (2007): 238.

33. On the potentially destructive effect of redescription more generally, see Richard Rorty, *Contingency, Irony, and Solidarity* (Cambridge: Cambridge University Press, 1989), 89-90.

34. Kathryn Tanner, *The Politics of God: Christian Theologies and Social Justice* (Minneapolis: Fortress Press, 1992), 202-19 and passim.

35. Kathryn Tanner, "Respect for Other Religions: A Christian Antidote to Colonialist Discourse," *Modern Theology* 9, no. 1 (1993): 6-9; cf. *Politics of God*, 208-14.

extent that they make the other worthy of respect *in spite of*, rather than in virtue of, their differences.[36] Such theologies thus fall short of her ideal of tolerance by failing to take the other on their own terms. Although Tanner's conception of Christian identity formation in terms of creative consumption rests on very different presuppositions than the pluralist and inclusivist theologies she criticizes, it arguably ends up with the same result: a description of the religious other—or, more precisely, a redescription of the other in Christian terms—that violates their own self-understanding. To be presented with a redescription of oneself in another's terms does not have to be an unwelcome thing. In principle, the experience of being redescribed can perhaps serve as a salutary occasion for critical self-reflection or as a necessary moment in a process of mutual understanding. When such redescriptions have a long history of oppression or colonial domination behind them, however, they are apt to be greeted with suspicion. Nowhere are such suspicions about the prospect of Christian theological redescription more acute—and more understandable—than in the sphere of Christian-Jewish relations. Jews are all too familiar with the denigratory effects wrought by Christian re-readings of Jewish tradition in light of the Christ event.[37]

We can safely infer, however, that Tanner expects and indeed hopes that the cultural-religious contents redescribed or creatively troped by Christians will preserve their original identity. Indeed, the transformed meaning those contents thereby receive depends, paradoxically enough, on the ability of the contents redescribed to assert and maintain their original meaning, just as the emergent meaning of metaphor is sustained by the literal meanings of its juxtaposed terms.[38] I do not want to argue, then, that Tanner's theory

36. Tanner, "Respect for Other Religions," 9-12.
37. Marianne Moyaert, "Comparative Theology after the Shoah: Risks, Pivots, and Opportunities of Comparing Traditions," (paper presented at the "Methods and Criteria for Comparative Theology" conference, University of Paderborn, Germany, August 10, 2014).

of Christian identity is implicated in larger discourses of cultural imperialism. My point, rather, is simply that her theory requires restrictions or qualifications if it is to be applied interreligiously.

A Return to Postliberalism?

It might seem, then, that the safest strategy for Christians would be to exclude the specifically religious discourses and practices of others from creative appropriation. Here a contemporary sensitivity to the insidiousness of imperialism coincides with a traditional concern with avoiding syncretism. In the latter context, the propriety or impropriety of appropriating the discourse or practice in question is precisely what is at stake in defining it as religious practice, or, conversely, in decoding it as "merely" a social custom.[39] Thus Roberto Nobili's missionary strategy of adopting Brahmanical customs rested on a distinction between social customs and religious ceremonies; when Brahmanical practices were defined as the former, they could be safely adopted by the missionary or retained by the Indian convert.[40] Contemporary Christians make a similar determination, even if implicitly, when they adopt the spiritual practices of yoga or Zen meditation.[41]

The analogy that Tanner draws between the operations of elite and popular theologies breaks down when we consider their respective stances towards specifically religious contents. Above, we saw that Tanner emphasizes the ways in which elite forms of theology mimic the strategies of their popular counterparts in creatively appropriating

---

38. Tanner, *Theories of Culture*, 116, 121; cf. "Theology and Popular Culture," 106, 114.

39. Tanner, *Theories of Culture*, 108.

40. Wilhelm Halbfass, *India and Europe: An Essay in Understanding* (Albany, NY: State University of New York Press, 1988), 4–42.

41. I take as an almost random example Robert E. Kennedy's remark about Catholic appropriation of Zen practice: "Zen Buddhism need not be looked at as a religion at all, but as a way of seeing life that can enhance any religious faith" (Robert E. Kennedy, *Zen Spirit, Christian Spirit* [New York: Continuum, 1999], 14).

available cultural elements. While popular forms of religion and theology are syncretistic or "hospitably inclusivistic" with regard to religious beliefs and ritual forms,[42] elite forms of theology, as we have just seen, must be circumspect out of a postcolonial concern with avoiding cultural imperialism about appropriating the specifically religious beliefs and practices of others. Elite forms of Christian theology must therefore operate with this additional constraint. We could perhaps say that one of the consolations of belonging to a subaltern group is the freedom to appropriate available cultural and religious practices without arousing suspicions of imperialism.

The recognition of a discourse or practice as religious—an act implying a respectful "letting be" of that discourse or practice—at once presupposes and sustains a religious boundary. Expressed in terms of de Certeau's distinction between strategies and tactics, the question of Christian relations with religious others presupposes a place, "delimited as its own," from which those relations can be strategically managed.[43] The recognition of the other *as* other—thus Tanner's ethic of tolerance—belongs to the realm of de Certeau's strategies, not tactics. "Strategic" relations between religions do not exclude a "tactical" and pragmatic dimension of interreligious encounter in which Christians make judgments about specific practices.[44] Nonetheless, as the example of Nobili shows, these judgments are usually made with a clear sense of Christianity as a way of life clearly delimited from others. Indeed, often what motivates the appropriation of outside cultural practices in a distinctive way is a formal interest in differentiating one's community from others.[45]

---

42. Tanner, "Theology and Popular Culture," 102-103.

43. De Certeau, *Practice of Everyday Life*, 36.

44. Tanner, *Theories of Culture*, 117-19.

45. The analysis of popular culture actually supports this point: if it is impossible to determine, on the level of descriptive content, where the popular ends and the elite begins, it nevertheless remains the case that the cultural field is structured by the opposition between the "popular" and the "not-popular" or elite (Hall, "Notes on Deconstructing 'the Popular'," 234).

In her laudable effort to foreground the variety of forms of creative appropriation that tend to be obscured in attempts to characterize Christian attitudes towards "culture" in terms of one type of relation,[46] Tanner downplays, almost to the point of elision, this "strategic" dimension of intercultural interaction. As I have been arguing, this strategic dimension comes insistently to the fore in the realm of specifically interreligious relations.[47]

When we consider Christian relations to specifically religious beliefs and practices, Tanner's theory of Christian identity, to the extent that it presupposes religious boundaries, begins to look not all that much different from postliberalism, specifically, a more refined kind of postliberalism that acknowledges outside influences on a Christian way of life.[48] The ethic of respecting religious others as other evokes a Herderian vision of interreligious harmony in which the religions each represent a distinctive way of life with its own integrity. Such a vision need not exclude the culturally mixed character of the discourses and practices of each religion so long as the basis of the identity of each—ultimately that which one respects as other—is not mixed. Yet, as we have seen, Tanner also criticizes this refined version of postliberalism for preserving a self-originating and self-contained conception of Christian identity. While postliberals like Lindbeck are willing to concede the culturally mixed character of Christian beliefs and practices, they nevertheless exempt the Christian semiotic system or interpretive framework itself—that which imparts a Christian interpretation to the appropriated cultural contents—from

---

46. Tanner, *Theories of Culture*, 119.
47. There is a close connection between, on the one hand, the meta-discursive "coding" of a cultural discourse or practice as "religious" (see Lincoln, *Holy Terrors*, 6) and, on the other, the "strategic" dimension of intercultural relations in which those relations can be consciously managed.
48. Tanner, *Theories of Culture*, 105.

outside influence.[49] Even this refined version of postliberalism is still vulnerable to postmodern critiques of intrinsic identity.

Elsewhere, however, there are indications that Tanner herself may not have entirely abandoned the notion of intrinsic Christian identity, and to that extent has not broken free of a basically postliberal conception of Christian identity vis-à-vis non-Christian religions. For example, in one of her arguments against the conception of Christian identity in virtue of a cultural boundary, she appeals to an apparently commonsensical distinction between internal and external matters of Christian identity, that is, between what is distinctively Christian in a particular context and what belongs to the essential character of Christianity.[50] She argues that the beliefs or practices that distinguish Christianity in a particular cultural context—she gives the example of Indian Christians eating beef to distinguish themselves from their Hindu neighbors[51]—may not coincide with what is most important for a Christian way of life. To be sure, she will qualify this distinction: sometimes matters of external and internal importance to Christians do coincide, and in these cases, moreover, the contrast with a discourse or practice on the other side of the boundary does have the virtue of precluding the notion of intrinsic identity that she criticizes elsewhere.[52] Nevertheless, the force of this argument against boundaries rests on a basically essentialist notion of Christian identity that is not conditioned by situational factors and therefore is not, strictly speaking, essentially relational.[53]

I would argue that Tanner's appeal to the notion of style as a model

49. Ibid., 105; cf. 107, 114.
50. Ibid., 108.
51. Ibid., 109; cf. 121.
52. Ibid., 121. This concession actually supports the point I am making here.
53. In *Theories of Culture* (ibid., 108), Tanner contrasts "situational factors" with "arguments about the essential character of Christianity."

for Christian identity also suggests a conception of Christian identity that in the end is not all that different from a refined version of postliberalism. The notion of style functions as a metaphor for the distinctive way Christians make use of borrowed cultural materials.[54] The concept of style highlights the elusiveness of the patterns of Christian use. Unlike specifiable rules or principles of appropriation, style can only be recognized *a posteriori* in a set of Christian practices that somehow hang together.[55] If the notion of style is to be more than simply a label for what is *de facto* recognized as Christian, however, it names a kind of situationally enacted practical sense, which, although antecedently unspecifiable, is functionally equivalent to the postliberal concept of an interpretive framework. In other words, the notion of cultural style, insofar as it is not reducible to a placeholder for whatever is conventionally taken as Christian at a particular time and place, preserves a trace of intrinsic identity.

Would it be fair, then, to compare Tanner's complex relationship with postliberalism to what has been said about Aristotle's relationship to Plato, namely, that the former's thought "is always struggling against Platonic influences, which nevertheless generally emerge triumphant in his ultimate conclusions"?[56] While a consideration of Tanner's account of Christian identity in the context of interreligious relations brings to the surface tensions and ambiguities in that account, I remain convinced that a vital distinction remains between Tanner's account of Christian identity and postliberalism. Nowhere is this distinction more stark than in her specifically theological objection to the implicit postliberal argument that Christianity can preserve its distinctiveness in the midst of intercultural interaction only if its interpretive framework (that is, the

---

54. Ibid., 58, 144–45.
55. Ibid., 147.
56. G. P. Goold, "Introduction," *Aristotle's Metaphysics, Books I-IX*, Loeb Classical Library (Cambridge, MA: Harvard University Press, 1933).

biblical narrative) is exempt from outside influence. Tanner appeals to the sharp Barthian distinction between, on the one hand, Christianity as a *religion*, understood as the product of human activity and aspiration, and, on the other, the Word of God addressing humanity from without. She argues that the postliberal preoccupation with preserving the purity and authenticity of the Christian interpretive framework, despite being well-intentioned, ultimately betrays an idolatrous confusion between a human creation and the Word itself as the guarantor of Christian identity.[57] Ultimately what sustains her argument that Christian identity is relational "all the way down"—and thus her critique of postliberalism—is the theological conviction that Christian identity be founded upon a continual openness to God's free Word. Tanner's theological vision thus excludes any qualification of her thesis that Christian identity is essentially relational. Any notion of intrinsic Christian identity, even in more nuanced versions of postliberalism, would interfere with the radical openness to God's Word.[58]

---

57. Tanner, *Theories of Culture*, 148-53; cf. 114.
58. Perhaps we can understand the ambiguities that appear when Tanner's proposal is transposed into an interreligious sphere in terms of W. C. Smith's distinction between faith and religion, that is, between a personal response to God (or, in Smith's more inclusive idiom, "the Transcendent"), on the one hand, and a consideration of Christianity as a sociological *cum* theological entity. Smith himself appeals to Barth when drawing this distinction; see, e.g., *Towards a World Theology* (Philadelphia: Westminster Press, 1981), 100 and passim; cf. idem., *The Meaning and End of Religion* (Minneapolis: Fortress Press, 1991), 124, 304-305, n.19. A consideration of Christianity's place among the religions would presuppose what Smith terms "reification," a perspective on human religiosity that betrays a falling away from the properly theological stance of continual openness to God's Word. Only with this shift in perspective from faith to religion do the ambiguities recounted above come into view. Tanner's decision to bracket a consideration of specifically interreligious relations in formulating her account of Christian identity, then, may be more than a simple matter of pragmatics. Given her commitment to the radical Barthian disjunction between Christianity and the Word, between religion and faith, that decision might ultimately reflect an unwillingness to abandon the latter "faith" perspective.

Formal Opposition

How, then, might we explain the lingering traces of intrinsic identity, noted above, in Tanner's account of Christian identity? I suspect that these reflect an underlying reluctance to countenance one of the implications of an essentially relational conception of Christian identity, namely, formal opposition. If we reject the naturalized conception of cultural boundaries as markers of the allegedly intrinsic properties of groups (where the latter are conceived on the model of material substances), then we must acknowledge a *formal* element at work in the recognition of the social differences that constitute cultural boundaries. The drawing of social borders, in other words, is not simply a matter of taking note of the material differences among groups. A formal element is present even in the mere selection of the particular cultural contents that will serve, like the phonemes of language,[59] as symbolic markers of socially significant difference. Going further into admittedly controversial territory, I suspect that many Christian doctrines began their careers as little more than tokens or rationalizations for relations of formal opposition. For example, the concept of consubstantiality in the original Nicene creed was arguably little more than a political token to justify the neutralization of the "Arian" threat to early fourth century episcopal authority—"an apotropaic formula for resisting Arianism," as Richard Hanson aptly puts it.[60] While no one can reasonably deny the role of formal opposition in the history of

---

59. Pierre Bourdieu, *Language and Symbolic Power*, trans. Gino Raymond and Matthew Adamson (Cambridge, MA: Harvard University Press, 1991), 237.

60. R. P. C. Hanson, *The Search for the Christian Doctrine of God* (London: T&T Clark, 1988), 172. See Athanasius's first hand, although likely prejudicial, account of the proceedings at Nicaea (*De decretis*, 19-20; cf. *Ad afros*, 4-5). According to Athanasius, the bishops deliberately introduced the *homoousios* into the creed in order to thwart the Eusebians' attempts to reconcile the creedal draft with their heretical view of the Son. However vague and ambiguous the *homoousios* was in terms of positive content, it was chosen precisely because it was a formula that the "Arians" could not accept.

Christian identity formation, few seem willing to countenance formal opposition in a *normative* account of Christian identity. It is difficult to justify the notion that Christians should oppose a discourse or practice, not because it is morally or intellectually incompatible with a Christian form of life, but simply because it defines a non-Christian community. Similarly, it is difficult to accept that whatever theological or ethical justifications are given for this exclusion are rationalizations after the fact. Social opposition should follow ethical or doctrinal conviction, not the reverse.[61] Tanner is willing to concede opposition to some particularly noxious practices—slavery, infant sacrifice, Nazi genocide[62]—but seems to regard formal or situational efforts at differentiation—the Christian rejection of Hindu dietary restrictions, for example[63]—as theologically insignificant.

To countenance formal opposition in Christian identity formation would thus be to concede an element of arbitrariness in the concept of Christian identity. More precisely, it would be to admit that the beliefs and practices taken to define a Christian way of life are determined in no small part by the particular constellation of rival forms of life present in a particular historical context. A corollary to this thesis that Christian identity is environmentally determined is that notions of Christian identity can change abruptly with major changes in the cultural-religious environment. In his fascinating sociological analysis of the history of philosophy, Randall Collins shows how the identity of the ancient Greek philosophical schools

61. Paradigmatic of such a refusal to countenance formal opposition is the distinction John Henry Newman draws between the orthodox and the Arians in the fourth century. Taking the diversity of non-Nicene theological trajectories in the fourth century as evidence for an indifference to matters of faith on the part of a self-conscious party motivated by a craven quest to win imperial favor, Newman concludes that for this alleged party, the so-called Arians, "the party was prior to the creed" (John Henry Newman, *The Arians of the Fourth Century* [London: Longmans, Green and Company, 1901], 259). This attitude contrasts with that of the orthodox, for whom partisanship was an unintended by-product of prior theological conviction.

62. Tanner, *Theories of Culture*, 118-19, 154.

63. Ibid., 109.

changed dramatically with the profound environmental changes accompanying the transition to the Hellenistic and, later, Roman periods. In the former transition to the Hellenistic period, Aristotle's Peripatetic school, for example, veered towards a more extreme materialist position in response to the Stoics' usurpation of a middle position between materialism and idealism.[64] In the latter transition to the Roman period, Aristotelianism tacks in an idealist direction, becoming more or less a variant of the Platonic variety.[65] To be sure, there are things that intellectual traditions can do to maintain a sense of continuity. For example, in the history of the early church, there is a tendency to assimilate present heresies to those of the past.[66] Nevertheless, to the extent that Christian identity is driven by social identity processes, a Christian community can find itself committed to positions that previous generations of Christians could scarcely have imagined. I suspect that a second-century theologian like Irenaeus would have been surprised, to say the least, to learn that an originally Gnostic concept like consubstantiality was destined to become a mark of Christian orthodoxy. And any ancient Christian would have been surprised to discover that slavery would become the paradigmatic example of an institution unambiguously opposed to the spirit of Christianity.[67]

I suspect that this formal dimension of social identity formation is an important factor in the unpredictable zig-zag course that intellectual traditions follow through time. And this formal dimension goes a long way towards explaining why, as Tanner notes, the consistency—or inconsistency—of a belief or practice with

64. Randall Collins, *Sociologies of Philosophies: A Global Theory of Intellectual Change* (Cambridge, MA: Harvard University Press, 1998), 107.

65. Ibid., 109, 111.

66. John B. Henderson, *The Construction of Orthodoxy and Heresy: Neo-Confucian, Islamic, Jewish and Early Christian Patterns* (Albany, NY: State University of New York Press, 1998), 27.

67. Tanner, *Theories of Culture*, 154; cf. Lindbeck, *Nature of Doctrine*, 85–86.

a Christian way of life often cannot be predicted in advance.[68] The dynamics of formal opposition explain how, more broadly, the significance of a cultural movement like Christianity appears only in retrospect, when it can be incorporated into a narrative leading up to, and explaining, the present. Thus, for example, Christianity, to quote a memorable remark of Richard Rorty, "did not know that its purpose was the alleviation of cruelty."[69]

Although an account of Christian identity directed by social identity processes is, on one level, decidedly secular, it nevertheless coheres, ironically enough, with the theological principle to which Tanner appeals in her argument against an understanding of Christian identity based on the putative continuity of tradition, namely, the freedom of God to intervene in human history in unprecedented and unexpected ways.[70]

68. Tanner, *Theories of Culture*, 136.
69. Rorty, *Contingency, Irony, and Solidarity*, 55.
70. Tanner, *Theories of Culture*, 135-38.

PART IV

The Gift of Theology to Praxis

11

Closed Eyes and Blocked Vision: Gendering Tanner's Theology of Sin and Grace

Joy Ann McDougall

In an essay written fifteen years ago, Rebecca Chopp observed that few feminist theologians of her generation were engaging with classical Christian symbols or doctrinal issues in their work.[1] Whereas "second-wave" Christian feminists had done the initial spadework of critiquing, mining, and reinterpreting their confessional traditions, so-called "third-wave" Christian feminist theologians had become occupied elsewhere—in digesting secular feminist theories and incorporating their sophisticated gender frameworks and analyses of social location into their methodologies. Feminist theology, Chopp lamented, appears to have become captive to the atheological (and at times anti-theological) limits of secular feminist theory.

---

1. Rebecca S. Chopp, "Theorizing Feminist Theology," in *Horizons in Feminist Theology: Identity, Tradition, and Norms,* eds. Rebecca S. Chopp and Sheila Greeve Davaney (Minneapolis: Fortress Press, 1997), 215-31.

As an academic and a church theologian, deeply invested herself in critical feminist theories and indeed methodological questions, Chopp's remarks were hardly condemnatory. Rather she was issuing a challenging invitation to her colleagues—to use feminist theories not only to address methodological questions but to do constructive theological work. Just as Aquinas and Schleiermacher had done with the revolutionary philosophical systems of their day, Chopp encouraged contemporary feminist theologians to deploy the insights gained from new gender theories along with their theological imaginations to "transform theological symbols and visions."[2] In short, she was asking the next wave of feminist theologians to do what she felicitously describes elsewhere as "saving work:" to offer bold interpretations of Christianity that revitalize the life of the church and its public witness to the world.[3]

Chopp was not alone at the time in recommending that feminists return to the task of interpreting and reformulating Christian doctrines and confessional traditions. In a subtle and provocative essay in the same anthology—an essay that has received scant scholarly attention—theologian Kathryn Tanner lent support to Chopp's invitation by contributing a distinctive take on the nature and authority of past theological traditions for contemporary feminist work.[4] Tanner anchors her view of theological traditions in a political theory of culture, one in which past cultural and symbolic resources are not ultimately fixed in terms of their meaning, but instead gain and lose their significance as they are deployed in particular configurations to support different social and political ends. In more

---

2. Ibid., 230.
3. Rebecca S. Chopp, *Saving Work: Feminist Practices of Theological Education* (Louisville: Westminster John Knox Press, 1995).
4. Kathryn Tanner, "Social Theory Concerning the 'New Social Movements' and the Practice of Feminist Theology," in Chopp and Davaney, eds., *Horizons in Feminist Theology: Identity, Tradition, and Norms*, 179-97.

familiar terms, Tanner argues that past theological traditions are not a stable homogenous "deposit of faith" that can be transmitted without change or remainder to different times and contexts. Christian theological traditions are always and everywhere a "social construction"—a selection and an interpretation of heterogeneous past cultural resources in support of certain hegemonic understandings of Christian identity and social order. Note that Tanner does not intend to utterly relativize the truth-claims or the authority of appeals to tradition, but rather recognizes that all such appeals to past traditions involve acts of political, imaginative, and indeed theological judgment. All Christian systematic theologians—and feminists in this regard are no different—assemble, order, and elucidate a range of diverse cultural resources in support of their particular vision of Christian identity. Indeed, Tanner expects feminist theologians to assume the same demanding intellectual effort at historical inquiry that she first articulated in her programmatic work, *Jesus, Humanity and the Trinity*, namely, of weighing the different ways that Christians historically have made sense of the whole of Christianity in order to argue persuasively and prophetically for one's contemporary vision of what Christianity is all about. Such historical inquiry into Christianity, Tanner avers, can be both "freeing and empowering" for it "expand[s] the range of imaginative possibilities for theological construction in any one time and place, a way of expanding the resources with which one can work."[5]

Building on this understanding of Christianity's traditions and their authority, Tanner urges Christian feminist theology to remain "traditional." Specifically, she advises her feminist colleagues to appropriate "as many elements as possible from patriarchal discourse" and to "rearticulate" them "to a feminist purpose."[6] At the same

---

5. Kathryn Tanner, *Jesus, Humanity, and the Trinity: A Brief Systematic Theology* (Minneapolis: Fortress Press, 2001), xvii, xviii.

time, feminist theologians should actively "counter," "interrupt," and "disarticulate" patriarchal Christian traditions that "serve the interests of men at the expense of women," "supports sexist institutional structures," and "social practices that demean and exclude women."[7] Tanner further argues that Christianity's "valued past" should be a veritable "site of political contest" for feminist theologians today. This is not least because appeals to "a valued past" in Christian theology authorize present and future Christian practice: "Whoever controls the interpretation and designation of the past that authorizes present practice," she reminds her feminist colleagues, "gains ... the power to delimit what is authentically Christian, what is appropriate for a Christian to say or do."[8]

On a first hearing, Tanner's approach to theological traditions may appear purely pragmatic—and smack of raw power politics at that. But, what lies just beneath the surface is a firm conviction that Christianity's symbolic resources are *not* irremediably patriarchal. For Tanner as for Chopp, Christian theological traditions present a rich reservoir of past and present symbolic resources that can be loosened from their moorings to patriarchy (at least most of them!), and be redirected in support of just and life-giving feminist visions of God, self, and the world. Although Tanner never quite puts this into words, as a Christian and a feminist, she possesses a reasoned faith, resolute hope, and a deep love for the treasures of these Christian traditions.

A quick glance at recent publications in Christian feminist theology suggests that the current generation of feminist theologians heeded Chopp's and Tanner's advice. Over the past fifteen years, an impressive number of feminist proposals have burst on the scene

---

6. Tanner, "Social Theory," 189.
7. Ibid., 186.
8. Ibid., 193–94.

that constructively engage core Christian doctrine, even the sacred cows of particular Christian traditions. These include an anthology of feminist/womanist Reformed dogmatics, as well as major feminist interpretations of the Reformed doctrines of justification and sanctification, sin and grace, and ecclesiology; the Lutheran theology of the cross; Anglican theologies of the Trinity, the incarnation, and spirituality; and a host of Roman Catholic proposals in Mariology, theological aesthetics, and sacramental theology, to offer just a sampling.[9]

Significantly, none of these works are feminist apologetics focused on defending the orthodoxy or the confessional loyalty of their respective proposals. These are also not "add and stir" projects that simply add experience from women's life-worlds and gender justice concerns to contribute a feminist flavor to a traditional theological recipe. Rather, these are constructive feminist systematic theology works in which each author appeals to her central doctrinal traditions as the key to mount her constructive feminist agenda. Moreover, with the help of critical feminist theories and theological imagination, each offers creative and often unexpected interpretations of these familiar doctrines. In so doing, each paves a way to keep feminist faith with their respective ecclesial traditions.

This is not to suggest that this particular group of feminist

---

9. See, for example, Amy Pauw and Serene Jones, eds., *Feminist and Womanist Essays in Reformed Dogmatics* (Louisville: Westminster John Knox Press, 2006); Serene Jones, *Feminist Theory and Christian Theology: Cartographies of Grace* (Minneapolis: Fortress Press, 2000); Deanna Thompson, *Crossing the Divide: Luther, Feminism, and the Cross* (Minneapolis: Fortress Press, 2004); Sarah Coakley, *Powers and Submissions: Spirituality, Philosophy and Gender* (Oxford: Blackwell, 2002); Sarah Coakley, *God, Sexuality, and the Self: An Essay on the 'Trinity'* (Cambridge: Cambridge University Press, 2013); Elizabeth Johnson, *Truly Our Sister: A Theology of Mary in the Communion of Saints* (New York: Continuum, 2003); Laurie Cassidy and Maureen H. O'Connell, *She Who Imagines: Feminist Theological Aesthetics* (Collegeville, MN: Michael Glazier, 2012); Susan Ross, *Extravagant Affections: A Feminist Sacramental Theology* (New York: Continuum, 1998); and Susan Ross, *For the Beauty of the Earth: Woman, Sacramentality, and Justice* (New York: Paulist Press, 2006).

theologians view their past theological traditions as an unequivocal blessing. While these inherited traditions may offer symbolic resources for supporting women's (and men's) flourishing and contemporary gender justice concerns, they also bear a history of damaging effects and ongoing potency for distorting women's identity, deflating their agency, and diminishing their well-being. Hence, these authors approach their Christian traditions with what Serene Jones has aptly called "double-visions"[10] or what I describe as sophisticated two-fisted strategies of theological reform and innovation. On the one hand, they seek by various interventions to contest and to disarm patriarchal interpretations of their traditions. On the other, by appealing to feminist theories and women's lived experiences in order to elucidate their scriptural and doctrinal traditions, these feminist authors claim, construct, and renew the authority of their Christian theological traditions to support the well-being and flourishing of women.

Despite the fact that Tanner has urged feminist theology to lay claim to their theological traditions for feminist ends, she has—except for a couple of occasional essays that she has penned herself—left the task of doing constructive feminist systematic theology to others.[11] Perhaps even more surprising is the fact that there has been little feminist reception of Tanner's major work, *Jesus, Humanity and the Trinity* (2001), the work in which she herself most clearly assembles, re-orders, and deploys both patristic and Reformed theological traditions to develop her constructive theological stance. This essay

---

10. Serene Jones, "Glorious Creation, Beautiful Law," in *Feminist and Womanist Essays in Reformed Dogmatics*, Pauw and Jones, eds., 38.

11. Tanner's most substantial engagement with feminist theological issues thus far has been her chapter "Death and Sacrifice" in *Christ the Key*, Current Issues in Theology (Cambridge: Cambridge University Press, 2010), 247-73. Here she directly addresses feminist and womanist critiques of classical theories of the atonement. See also her chapter, "Gender," in *Oxford Handbook of Anglican Studies*, ed. Mark Chapman et al. (Oxford: Oxford University Press, forthcoming).

seeks to address this lacuna. In particular, I seek to demonstrate how Tanner's vision of a radically transcendent gift-giving God, along with her notion of sin that she develops *in nuce* in this work, provides a powerful set of traditional resources to develop a robust feminist theology of sin and grace.

This essay aims not only to expose the feminist possibilities latent in Tanner's work, but also to call for a change of course in contemporary Christian feminist discourse about sin. Here, my theological hunch and admittedly my discontent about the current state of play in Christian feminist theology is that it has too precipitously abandoned the classical notion of a transcendent and sovereign God as the foundation for constructing their feminist proposals. Feminist theologians have largely steered clear of appealing to this traditional God-concept on the faulty assumption (taken over mainly from modern theology's depiction of divine transcendence and its antinomy with human freedom) that such a move automatically reintroduces a dangerous hierarchy of divine-human relations that eviscerates women's agency, and offers divine legitimacy to sexist and patriarchal patterns of domination and subjugation in the creaturely realm.[12]

At the same time that Christian feminist theologians have largely stopped speaking about sin in terms of a distorted or ruptured relation to an almighty and transcendent God, they have gravitated towards immanent analyses of sin, anchored solely in the creaturely realm, for example, in one's psychological or moral development, the

---

12. For a classic if also powerfully argued example of this feminist theological position, see Daphne Hampson, *After Christianity* (Valley Forge, PA: Trinity Press International, 2002), esp. 119-69. For a sophisticated critique of Hampson's argument, particularly with respect to the notions of kenosis and vulnerability, see Sarah Coakley, "Kenosis and Subversion: On the Repression of 'Vulnerability' in Christian Feminist Writing," in *Swallowing a Fishbone?: Feminist Theologians Debate Christianity*, ed. Daphne Hampson (London: SPCK, 1996), 82-111; and a slightly revised version in Coakley's *Powers and Submissions: Spirituality, Philosophy and Gender* (Oxford: Blackwell, 2002), 3-39.

interpersonal realm, or else various forms of inequity and exploitation in institutional structures.[13] Let me be clear on this point: such feminist immanent analyses of sin have been well-targeted and essential in order to expose and to redress the highly particular "faces" of gender oppression that course through our ecclesial bodies and other social institutions in our contemporary society.[14] Moreover, they have provided a much needed corrective to modern theology's individualistic and spiritualized paradigms of sin against which feminist theology originally objected. And yet, such immanent analyses of gender oppression often jettison altogether an appeal to sovereign and transcendent God, or, if they retain the notion of a transcendent God, it does not figure into their interpretation of sin.[15] Either way, in my view feminist theologians forfeit their distinctive contribution beyond that of secular feminist analyses both to diagnose and to denounce the evils of gender oppression. Feminist theologies of sin may still lend moral urgency or personal piety to secular critiques of women's oppression, but they cede the theological ground upon which to mount both an idolatry critique and a vision of a way out of this patriarchal order.[16]

Against this feminist theological backdrop, Tanner's tradition-rich

13. For a more detailed and nuanced account of these various migrations of the doctrine of sin in second and third wave feminist theology and their contributions as well as my critiques, see my chapter, "Feminist Theology," in *The Oxford Handbook of Systematic Theology*, eds. John Webster, Kathryn Tanner, and Iain Torrance (Oxford: Oxford University Press, 2007), 670-87, esp. 673-80.

14. Jones, *Feminist Theory and Christian Theology: Cartographies of Grace*, 79.

15. On this point I agree with Alistair McFadyen's sympathetic but also critical reading of the lack of *genuinely* theological foundations undergirding many feminist theologies of sin. See especially his discussion of "pragmatic atheism" in contemporary feminist theologies of sin in his *Bound to Sin: Abuse, Holocaust and the Christian Doctrine of Sin* (Cambridge: Cambridge University Press, 2000), 10.

16. The most notable exception on this issue (and one to whom my theology of sin is deeply indebted) is Serene Jones, *Feminist Theory and Christian Theology: Cartographies of Grace*. Jones appeals in a nuanced way to God's sovereign grace to anchor her feminist notion of sin as "grace denied," and which she uses to critique the different faces of gender oppression. See especially pp. 94-125.

concept of a radically transcendent God as the giver of all good things and her accompanying doctrine of sin—that she weaves together from patristic and Reformation theological traditions—suggests another way forward for feminist theologians today. In what follows, I sketch what such an application of Tanner's theology of sin might entail. I turn first to demonstrate how Tanner's vision of an absolutely beneficent and radically transcendent God contests the feminist charge that appeals to a transcendent and sovereign God always come at the expense of women's agency, ensnaring them into structures of domination and subjugation. On the contrary, I suggest that Tanner's vision of this gift-giving God creates the theological foundation for affirming God's enduring and empowering presence in women's lives, and for critiquing the subjugation of women's agency, the diminishment of their gifts, and the deprivation of their flourishing.

In a second step, I contend that Tanner's theological paradigm for sin as "denial of or opposition to God's gift-giving," which she spells out with two major metaphors for sin— "blockage" and blindness or "closing one's eyes" to God's gracious and abundant gift-giving—offer a more incisive resource for feminist theology than the usual analytic of sin as the "will to power" or lack thereof. In particular, I suggest that Tanner's root paradigm for sin can analyze the complex dynamics involved in sexism and gender oppression, and resolve some of the unhappy binaries that have emerged in feminist theologies of sin; for example, sinner versus sinned against, and personal versus structural sins. As such, this concept of sin can at once disclose the depth dimensions of the sin of patriarchy, human beings' universal solidarity in it, and their common responsibility for ameliorating it.

In the concluding section of this essay, I take Tanner's theology of sin a constructive step farther—what I describe as gendering her theology of sin. Such a step is critical to the feminist task of naming the actual gender injustices that afflict contemporary women's lives and analyzing the insidious hold that they have on all of our lives. Here, I propose to re-conceive the classic notion of "the bondage of the will" as a twofold "bondage of the Eye/I." With this double-edged metaphor, I describe how women and men become ensnared in and also pass on oppressive gender roles, cultural scripts, and systemic structures—not always of their deliberate choosing. The first part of the metaphor, "the bondage of the Eye," signifies the common human predicament, which is "our solidarity in sin" created by the sins of patriarchy: both men and women possess distorted visions of a true, just, and life-giving economy of gender relations, and therefore participate together, albeit differently, in the gendered bondage to sin. The other half of the metaphor, "the bondage of the I," points to the shared fallout for women and men from gender oppression: both are accorded prescriptive gender identities and social roles that diminish their individual God-given gifts, their particular vocations, and collective flourishing. My theological wager here is that sexism and many subtle forms of oppression that accompany a patriarchal social order can be more adequately analyzed as profound deceptions about oneself, the relations with others, and cultural and institutional realities.

Divine Beneficence and Sinful Realities: Resources for Re-envisioning a Feminist Theology of Sin

A feminist theology of sin and grace can be anchored in human beings' dynamic and dependent relationship to a transcendent and beneficent God. As I suggested above, Kathryn Tanner's *Jesus, Humanity and the Trinity* offers a powerful rereading of classical theological resources, particularly focusing on a theology of creation and providence for pursuing such a project. The fundamental premise of Tanner's work is her vision of God as the "giver of all good gifts, their fount, luminous source, fecund treasury and store house."[17] For Tanner, God's entire providential purpose in creating the world, and humankind in particular, is the communication of divine goodness. God takes delight in creation and works tirelessly for its full flourishing. Correspondingly, the whole of God's creation find its telos, its true and proper end, in unity with and dynamic participation in the divine life of gift-giving.

Especially instructive for my purposes about Tanner's vision of an utterly beneficent gift-giving God is that she cuts the knot that feminists usually tie between a transcendent sovereign God and a divine economy of domination. She does so through two intertwined principles that govern her theological argument. The first one is that God and human beings exist in a non-competitive relationship to one another; and the second, that God is radically transcendent of the creaturely realm. Note that Tanner is appropriating and re-deploying here a classical view of divine transcendence, namely, that God is the source of all goodness, and that God operates on a different order or plane of causality from that of humanity. Since divine agency operates on a different plane than human agency, God's agency *transcends* rather than *competes* with humankind. In this divine economy of grace, the more the creature depends on God, the more empowerment she receives for her good. As Tanner puts it, "the fuller the giver the greater the bounty to others."[18]

At this point, we can already detect how Tanner's vision of a radically transcendent and utterly beneficent gift-giving God allays feminist worries that affirming a transcendent sovereign God will necessarily come at the expense of women's agency. In Tanner's schema, the divine-human relationship is from one perspective

---

17. Tanner, *Jesus, Humanity and the Trinity*, 1.
18. Ibid., 3.

unilateral: God is utterly self-sufficient while human beings depend entirely on God's beneficence for their very existence. Yet, this divine-human relationship does not entail domination, that is, power being exerted over and against and at the cost of the finite agency of human beings. Instead, this relationship consists entirely out of God's gracious and ceaseless self-giving and human beings' gracious reception of those gifts. In short, human beings' dependency on a transcendent and beneficent God becomes the very source of human empowerment, which issues forth in gratitude for the gifts received, and in the finite agency to share these gifts with others.

Note that Tanner's construal of the inviolable covenant between this gift-giving God and human beings not only clears away feminist objections about women's dependency on an utterly transcendent God, but it supplies a theological rationale for Christian feminists' agenda, namely, that Christian communities should denounce and actively resist all forces and structures that exploit, do violence to, or in other ways diminish the flourishing of women's identities. As human beings created by this gift-giving God, we are all, on Tanner's account, called and enabled to shine forth the goodness of God, that is, to be an image of God, in and through fostering beneficent relations with others.[19] Given this vocational charge, we have a specifically theological imperative to counter any and all forces that distort the economy of gift-giving that God has willed for all of creation, including any and all forces of "deprivation" and "depravation" that patriarchy brings in its wake.[20]

In line with this powerful vision of God's gift-giving economy of creation and providence, Tanner sketches in *Jesus, Humanity and the Trinity* a theological concept of sin that can be turned to feminist

19. Ibid., 69-70.
20. Rebecca S. Chopp, "Feminism and the Theology of Sin," *The Ecumenist* (November-December 1993): 12-16 (13).

ends. Unsurprisingly, she defines sin in theocentric terms, that is, as the denial of or opposition to God's gift-giving nature. In sin, human beings enact the very opposite of this divine self-communication of goodness: they either intercept or block the gratuitous flow of divine gifts to themselves or to others in the world and, in so doing, they turn away or act contrary to God's beneficent will for the world. As Tanner puts it, sin is a "deliberate failure of humans to reflect God's intentions for the world, the human refusal of God's hopes for the world as a place where God's perfect triune self-communication of goodness might be imitated. Human beings in this way sin, by closing their eyes to and blocking the reception of God's gifts to themselves and others."[21]

Here and elsewhere, Tanner invokes two major metaphors to describe the reality of sin. Her primary metaphor is that of blockage. Human beings block divine gift-giving by refusing to receive the gifts, by separating themselves or others from the gifts, or else by refusing to share God's good gifts with others. In all these ways, we stop the free flow of God's plenitude. Tanner's second metaphor for the reality of sin is that of blindness or closing one's eyes to the reality of God's good gifts. Here, sin assumes the form of either a profound mistake or a self-deception about one's creaturely status and our true identity. In sin, human beings blind themselves (along with perhaps others) to the boundless receiving of God's good gifts and their vocation of distributing these good gifts to others. With this second metaphor of blindness, Tanner reminds us that sin is a lie or delusion about our true condition. Of course, our failure of vision does not mean that God halts the flow of good gifts; God continues to shower us with good gifts regardless of whether we deserve them or receive them with gladness of heart.

---

21. Tanner, *Jesus, Humanity and the Trinity*, 46.

At this point, we can espy several key dimensions of Tanner's notion of sin that are salutary for developing a feminist theology of sin. First, Tanner's account of sin precisely weds the divine and the human, the transcendent and the immanent, dimensions of sin, without sacrificing one or the other. When we sin, we do so against God, for sin violates God's deepest desire for sharing good gifts with creation. At the same time, sin disrupts the economy of right relations in the created realm and causes moral evils. To borrow Tanner's terms, our blockage and blindness to gracious God's gift-giving blocks ourselves, separates other individuals, and isolates social structures from the reception of the good gifts. By interlocking the divine and human dimensions of sin in this manner, Tanner's account does not fall prey to a perennial temptation of theocentric approaches to sin, namely, that an individual's alienation from God overshadows the particular ways in which human beings perpetrate evils against one another. Nor does she fall into the opposite problem that many feminist immanent analyses of sin suffer from, namely, that such attention is given to structural sins that the theological dimensions of sin, the ways in which we distort God's abundant gift-giving towards us, disappear from sight. In contrast, in Tanner's robust theological account of sin, there can be no competition between the transcendent and the immanent planes of sin, and hence no risk that attending to the one will come at the expense of the other.

Second, Tanner's root theological paradigm for sin is capacious enough to account for individual, cultural, and structural sins. This is a crucial feminist good once we recall the diverse array of actual sins to which feminist theologians have been drawing our attention. To give just one example, while a refusal or blockage of God's good gifts might very well refer to concrete goods, such as bodily health or living wages, it can also illuminate injustices that arise from sexist gender roles; for example, the denial of adequate educational opportunities for girls, or lack of public recognition for women's work. So, too, blindness or closing one's eyes to God's good gifts can also take on the guise of women's lack of self-worth or else false guilt arising from their gendered socialization as the primary caregiver and nurturer of relationships in their families and in the larger communities at the expense of their own desires and self-care.[22] Indeed, Tanner's rubric for sin is all the more powerful because it lends a theological depth-charge to these psychological ills and social inequities. Such gender issues truly emerge as sins since they blind or block women from receiving their God-given gifts of grace and pursuing their unique vocations for their full flourishing.

Third, Tanner's concept of sin admits of both active and passive interpretations. We can speak of "refusing" and "being refused," of "blocking" and "being blocked from the flow of good gifts." Such active and passive descriptions of human sin are more than a rhetorical flourish in feminist theology. They are essential in order to address the complex interplay of gender constructions and social structures in a given situation, where it is often difficult to determine individual agency and therefore to assign personal responsibility for gender injustices. Stated differently, the language of "blockage" or "blindness" highlights human solidarity in the sinful predicaments of patriarchy: both perpetrators and victims, sinners and sinned against, possess distorted visions of the proper economy of gender relations, and therefore both participate, albeit in radically distinct and incommensurate ways, in patriarchy's productions.

Fourth and finally, Tanner's theological account of sinful realities

---

22. For an excellent overview of the feminist discussion about women's socialization to relationality and its implications for pastoral care practice, see Christie Cozad Neuger, "Women and Relationality," in *Feminist and Womanist Pastoral Theology*, eds. Bonnie J. Miller-McClemore and Brita L. Gill Austern (Nashville: Abingdon, 1999), 113-32; see also Brita L. Gill-Austern, "Love Understood as Self-Sacrifice and Self-Denial: What Does it Do to Women?," in *Through the Eyes of Women: Insights for Pastoral Care*, ed. Jeanne Steven Moessner (Minneapolis: Fortress Press, 1996), 304-21.

overcomes the logic of divine retribution that many feminist criticize as often accompanying classic paradigms of sin. Tanner overturns this logic by primarily using root metaphors for sin that do not rely on a forensic model of sin and justification. Here, sin is not defined as disobedience to a moral law; nor is there a judgment and punishment (even a stayed one) by a divine lawgiver. This is not to say that sin does not have deadly serious consequences. Note how Tanner describes them: "Our sins interrupt the reception and distribution of God's gifts, bringing suffering and death in their train."[23] Such sufferings do not represent, however, a divine punishment for our actions, but are the natural consequences of having disrupted the economy of grace. In other words, we bring suffering on ourselves and on others by blocking the reception of God's beneficence. In response to our sinful realities, God does not ruthlessly punish, but instead acts in perfect beneficence. God keeps on showering good gifts on sinners and their victims alike in order to heal their situations, and, even more, so that they may receive, more fully enjoy, and share God's gifts with others.

The Bondage of the Eye/I: Gendering a Theology of Sin and Grace

While Tanner offers a robust theological framework for diagnosing and denouncing gender injustices, her work can take us only so far in constructing a feminist theology of sin. As I suggested earlier, specific gendered discourse about sin remains essential if we are to expose those various faces of oppression that women experience and to which they become readily captive. And Tanner has left that task, at least for the time being, for others to take up. In that spirit, let me propose one step towards developing such gendered discourse about sin: to re-craft the classic metaphor for the condition of sin,

23. Tanner, *Jesus, Humanity and the Trinity*, 86.

"the bondage of the will," in terms of "the bondage of the Eye/I." One of my primary aims in making this move is to displace the will as the privileged site for diagnosing gendered realities of sin. While the will is certainly involved in the predicament of sin—the language of refusing either to receive or to share God's good gifts makes that readily apparent—the will has too long occupied center-stage in contemporary Protestant analyses of sin. This is especially true in the wake of modern theologies' androcentric model of sin as pride and possessive individualism. In my view, titrating the dynamics of the will—either too much or too little—is particularly ill-suited for identifying the social or structural dimensions of gender injustice, which often resist the assignment of individual agency and therefore of culpability. Furthermore, describing women's condition as "the bondage of the will" risks reinforcing the double bind of either blaming women for their own victimization or else sapping them of the personal agency necessary to resist patriarchy's force. Hence, by shifting the locus of sin to the visual sphere, gender oppression can be better understood as a profound blindness or distortion in one's perception of oneself, one's resources, and the relationships and structures in which one lives, moves, and has one's being. Indeed, my feminist wager is that "the bondage of the Eye" better captures how personal agency, gender constructions, and social structures often collude together in order to deceive women concerning their grace-filled identities. Meanwhile, the other side of this metaphor, "the bondage of the I," draws into clear sight the inevitable fallout of gender oppression—the captivity of oneself to the desires, the expectations, and the needs of others.

We might well interject at this point: why retain the language of bondage at all in a feminist theology? Why try to wrestle a blessing from an aspect of the Christian tradition that has so plagued women's lives with false guilt and paralyzing self-doubt? Why not instead follow the path taken by many other feminist theologians and abandon altogether the analysis of the human condition as ensnarement in sin? A critical reason for retaining the notion of bondage to sin is to underscore the gravity of gender injustices. The image of being held captive depicts the intractable and insidious hold which gender constructions—that mélange of gender expectations, stereotypes, and power relations—have upon women's and men's bodies, their minds, and their souls. In short, bondage language underscores that the problem of sexism is not a mere matter of ignorance or a denial of certain rights (although it surely includes both of these aspects). Rather, sexism is a radical distortion that cuts to the core of individual's graced identities and society's perceptions and prejudices.

By shifting the metaphor of bondage from the will to the visual sphere, we can also attend to both the individual and the social dimensions of sexism. For example, "the bondage of the Eye" describes most obviously the predicament of an individual who fails to see through the androcentrism that distorts his perception of women's desires, needs, and gifts of grace. This term can speak equally well to institutions that turn a blind eye to their sexist structures. We can easily name blatant examples of such distorted vision, such as the significant wage disparities between men and women in most professions. Yet, we can also think of social forces that are harder to spot, for example, the nearly impossible demands placed on working women who must juggle childcare and professional responsibilities. Or, the stained-glass ceiling that women in the ministry regularly encounter in their churches as they experience the subtle (or not so subtle) resistance of laity or denominational leaders to women in positions of pastoral leadership. I would argue that the notion of "the bondage of the Eye" seems particularly well-suited to name structural sins such as these—sins which might be called sins of omission in which persons fail to look at or are unable to recognize gender inequities for what they are.

Beyond describing such failed individual and institutional sight, "the bondage of the Eye/I" metaphor can also point to cultural forms of gender oppression. To take just one example: this metaphor can be used to describe how women's identities are trapped by the colonizing gaze of the visual media in our culture. Curiously enough, in a "post-feminist" age we see more examples than ever of the use of videos, television, and billboards to turn women into objects of others' visual pleasure. The power of this colonizing gaze becomes apparent when we consider how women subject themselves to body management practices from workout regimens to fat-reduction programs in order to meet our culture's beauty myths. For years now, feminists have pointed out that such normalizing practices are not a matter of choice for women, but instead manifest a cultural bondage in which women police their bodies in accordance with desires and standards not of their own making. In sum, speaking of women's predicament as "the bondage of the Eye/I" at once highlights the distorted cultural vision that women participate in when they conform their bodies to sexist images, and underscores how such gendered body ideals possess a colonizing power over women, transforming them into shadows of their true identities.

Given what I have suggested here about the radical depths of gender oppression that resides in individuals, cultural forms and practices, and our social institutions, we might ask: what might redemption look like from this predicament? To keep with the visual metaphor, what might it take to clear women's and men's vision today and free them from the captivity of the gendered bondage to sin? Let me suggest first that clearing one's sight requires developing spiritual practices that help strip away false gender prescriptions and women's distorted self-images while also creating space for women's flourishing through strengthening their relationship to the divine. Christian theologians have long held that knowledge of sin requires purging oneself of false views of the self in order to gain insight about one's true identity and vocation as *imago Dei*. And yet, feminist theologians have been quick to point out that those whose selves have already been stripped away by patriarchy have to travel a different *via purgativa* than the tradition has often instructed them in.[24] Simply stated, feminist spiritual practices must offer women positive images and experiences of the self while helping them to identify and to resist destructive ones. Just as important to feminist spiritual care is engaging women in critical analysis of social structures, for example, of the child-care arrangements or their work-place environment, so as to the stop the pernicious cycle of self-blame and isolation that women experience in situations of gender injustice.[25] Moreover, feminist spiritual practices must also help women to come to their senses, that is, to engage in embodied practices that help women overcome their alienation from and distrust of their minds along with their bodies. As theologian Stephanie Paulsell reminds us, women today need to rethink even the most ordinary of practices—eating, bathing, and resting—so as to celebrate the body's pleasures and to protect its sacred vulnerabilities.[26] While the Christian tradition may hold precious spiritual resources for the interior journey at hand, it has a terribly long way to go in formulating spiritual disciplines and liturgical practices that cultivate reverence for women's bodies.

Clearing one's sight also requires face to face confrontation with the political and the material sources of women's oppression. Put

24. Mary Grey, *Redeeming the Dream: Feminism, Redemption and the Christian Tradition* (London: SPCK, 1989), 86-89.

25. On balancing contemplative attention to their intrapsychic and interpersonal relations with analysis of social structures in women's spiritual care, see Elizabeth Liebert, "Coming Home to Themselves: Women's Spiritual Care," in Moessner, ed., *Through the Eyes of Women*, 257-84.

26. Stephanie Paulsell, *Honoring the Body: Meditations on a Christian Practice* (San Francisco: Jossey-Bass, 2002).

another way, women's redemption from "the bondage of the Eye/ I" calls for linking spiritual practices with consciousness-raising and engaged social and political action. To this end, feminist theologians need more than the treasures of their theological traditions and the spectacles of faith to clear their sight. They need the help of feminist critical theories as well as the galvanizing force of the global women's movement to gain the power to see what has been eclipsed in theological discourse. Just as much, however, feminist theology needs vibrant communities of faith that will act as a prophetic witness to the world by incarnating new possibilities for just gender relations in the family, the workplace, and the life of the church.

Within this proposed theological framework, Christian feminist theology must ultimately treat redemption from the gendered bondage to sin as an eschatological goal; for women and men see their God-given gifts now only in a glass darkly, and await the day when they will delight in them fully. To recall the eschatological dimension of this framework is not to quell feminist passions about the present injustice of gender inequities, but simply to acknowledge our finite vision. Contemporary feminist proposals like my own cannot see through the gendered bondage to sin or its redemption once and for all. Moreover, feminist models of redemption remain eschatological because they do not seek to restore what once was, but to create what has never been. Therefore, gaining true feminist insight into sin requires ongoing discernment, vigilant critical inquiry, and visionary hope that women and men might one day discover and delight in the fullness of their life together.

12

Creation as Gift: Tanner's Theology of God's Ongoing Gift-Giving as an Ecological Theology

Hilda P. Koster

> *[The] relationship of total giver to total gift is possible ... only if God and creatures are, so to speak, on different levels of being, and different planes of causality—something that God's transcendence implies.*
>
> – Kathryn Tanner[1]

This essay draws out the rich promise of Kathryn Tanner's theology of God's ongoing gift-giving for a contemporary eco-theology.[2] While Tanner has articulated the implications of her early work for a

---

1. Kathryn Tanner, *Jesus, Humanity and the Trinity: A Brief Systematic Theology* (Minneapolis: Fortress Press, 2001), 3.
2. I thank my friend and colleague Dr. Alfhild Ingberg for her careful reading of this essay and for offering very helpful comments.

non-anthropocentric theology of creation and an ethics of ecological justice,[3] to my knowledge her theology has not been mined as a resource for ecological theology. One obvious reason is that Tanner's theology is not an ecological theology in an explicit sort of way; the environmental crisis simply is not the organizing principle of her theological work in spite of the fact that concerns for ecological justice do inform *The Politics of God* and *Economy of Grace*.[4] From the perspective of most ecological theologies, moreover, there is something oddly counterintuitive to Tanner's theological scheme. In an effort to overcome oppressive notions of a distant, yet all-powerful Creator, eco-theologians typically stress God's immanence in and to the world and recast God's power as love. By contrast, Tanner's theology of creation hinges on a dual theological principle—namely, of God's non-contrastive and non-competitive relation to the world—which strengthens, not diminishes, divine transcendence and sovereignty. In addition, Tanner defends creation *ex nihilo*—albeit not as a doctrine of origination—which arguably is *the* doctrine *non grata* of ecological theology. And whereas her early work in *God and Creation in Christian Theology* presented a creation-centered theology, the strong focus on God's grace in Christ in her most recent books, most notably *Christ the Key*, seemingly pushes a concern for creation to the periphery. Tanner herself acknowledges as much: "*Christ the Key* ... is not a very creation-centered theology: it primarily focuses on a grace beyond that of creation per se—the grace of God's own life."[5]

3. Kathryn Tanner, "Creation, Environmental Crisis, and Ecological Justice," in *Reconstructing Christian Theology*, ed. Rebecca S. Chopp and Mark Lewis Taylor (Minneapolis: Fortress Press, 1994), 99–123.
4. Kathryn Tanner, *The Politics of God: Christian Theologies and Social Justice* (Minneapolis: Fortress Press, 1992), chap. 5; and Kathryn Tanner, *Economy of Grace* (Minneapolis: Fortress Press, 2005), 133–40.
5. Kathryn Tanner, "Author Response," *Theology Today* 68, no. 3 (2011): 341.

At first glance, then, Tanner is a somewhat unlikely conversation partner for an ecological theology. Yet the genius of her work is that it offers alternative, heretofore untried, solutions to theological problems, solutions that are not only persuasive in their own right, but also have rich promise for solving recurrent problems inherent in some prominent eco-theological models. Most notably, Tanner's dual principle of God's non-contrastive and non-competitive relation to the world allows her to maximize God's presence in and to the world *without* idealizing certain aspects of created reality or reducing God to a cause among causes, both of which, I believe, are stumbling blocks in eco-theological panentheism. Instead, Tanner offers a cosmic-theological scheme that affirms creation as God's gift, and God as the ongoing giver of life; a scheme that acknowledges the world's autonomy and God's radical otherness, without reinstalling oppressive accounts of God's relation to the world.

Tanner's theological principles further lead to a non-anthropocentric theology and ethics that situates human beings firmly within the community of creation and plays down their superiority vis-à-vis the rest of creation. Yet while most other ecological theologies fall back on some ontological resemblance between God and humans in order to articulate human beings' duty towards non-human nature, typically expressed by way of the *imago Dei*, Tanner's principle of God's radical transcendence prohibits such a move. Instead she proposes a prospective, Christ-centered reading of the *imago Dei*, which refers not to human beings but to the Word or the Son.[6] Assumed by the Word, human beings are given the gift of becoming images of God by serving the world. Tanner thus views Christian discipleship as a matter of grace, allowing ecological theology to call for bold action on behalf of the rest of nature, while

6. Kathryn Tanner, *Christ the Key*, Current Issues in Theology (Cambridge: Cambridge University Press, 2010), ch. 1.

remaining humble concerning humanity's place in the larger scheme of things and human being's ability to make things right. For while *hubris* about our place vis-à-vis the rest of creation arguably has led to our current crisis, *hubris* concerning our ability to solve this crisis may well lead to despair.

Finally, Tanner's theology is promising because it offers ecological theology an inclusive soteriology that does not water down the unique character of God's saving work in Christ. Like most other ecological theologies, Tanner casts salvation as part of God's ongoing creative involvement with the world. Salvation is not a response to an original fall into sin but is intrinsic to God's ongoing gift-giving in creation which culminates in the incarnation. It is moreover *this* world that is being perfected by God's ongoing gift-giving. Other than most eco-theological soteriologies, however, Tanner's model does not come at the expense of the uniqueness of God's giving in Christ. On the contrary, it is precisely because of her 'high Christology' that Tanner is able to defend an inclusive soteriology that is *cosmic* in scope.

This essay discusses these three aspects of Tanner's theology—her way of casting divine transcendence and God's general relationship to the world, her non-anthropcentric theology and ethics, and her cosmic soteriology—in more detail. While I argue that Tanner's theology has rich promise for ecological theology and indeed can *itself* be read as an ecological theology, certain difficulties remain. First, Tanner's principle of God's radical transcendence helps articulate God's intimate and immediate presence in and to creation; nonetheless, her theology ultimately fails to articulate a more sacramental understanding of the world. The emphasis on what God does for us in Christ in her recent work suggests a retreat to a more strictly Protestant position in so far as it implies that we can know God from nature only indirectly through Christ. Second, precisely because Tanner's most recent work on Christology in *Christ the Key* is less creation-centered, it is not always clear *how* God's ongoing gift-giving is extended to non-human nature. While the scope of Tanner's soteriology is cosmic and includes of all that is, God's salvific way of relating to the non-human world remains rather vague. Finally, Tanner's account of salvation casts finitude, most notably death, suffering and conflict, as a problem that is overcome by God's work in Christ. From a human perspective death and discord make life tragic, but when viewed from the perspective of evolutionary ecology they are essential features of the vitality of biotic communities.

In response to these questions and concerns the final part of this essay briefly engages the work of Catholic ecological theologians Denis Edwards and Elizabeth A. Johnson, who, like Tanner, have been deeply shaped by Thomistic theology, most notably the work of Karl Rahner, but are less dialectical in their soteriology. Their engagement with Wisdom Christology and the idea of "deep incarnation" is particularly useful in relation to Tanner's theological scheme: it allows for a soteriology that, rooted in the wisdom of the cross, embraces the tragic aspects of our finite lives more fully, tracing God's sustaining and redemptive presence in and through them. Before turning to these constructive possibilities, however, the essay first discusses the rich promise of Tanner's dual principles of God's non-contrastive and non-competitive relation to the world for an ecological theology.

Recycling Divine Transcendence and Sovereignty

Although divine transcendence is a central feature of her theology, Tanner would be the first to agree that certain portrayals of divine transcendence and power have desacralized the world and have risked positing God as a divine despot. Reflecting on our current environmental predicament, she insists that Christian beliefs of human beings' relations to the natural world "are determined in large part by Christian beliefs about the relations that God maintains with the various inhabitants of the world that God creates."[7] Indeed, according to Tanner it is exactly because Christians tend to model their own relationship to the world after God's *general* way of relating to the world, that viewing God as a distant ruler seems to legitimize the domination of nature by human beings in so far it places humans over and against the rest of nature as its lord and master.

Ecological theologians typically have responded to Christian theology's hierarchical dualism by embracing a form of pan(en)theism that plays up divine immanence and casts God's power as love. Tanner, however, urges us to leave the constraints of modern theological discourse behind and to entertain a very different understanding of God's transcendence, an understanding that she culls from discussions in the early church. Christian theologians of the early church came to defend a non-contrastive account of divine transcendence precisely because they sought to make sense of the seemingly contradictory claim that God is both transcendent and directly involved with the world—a claim which became extremely relevant in light of Christological debates on the question as to how God is fully present in the human Jesus without compromising God's divinity or Jesus' humanity.[8] Tanner argues, and has done so throughout her work ever since *God and Creation*, that this particular understanding of transcendence, namely, that God is beyond every kind of being, offers contemporary theologians a way of saying

7. Tanner, "Creation, Environmental Crisis, and Ecological Justice," 102.

8. Kathryn Tanner, *God and Creation in Christian Theology: Tyranny or Empowerment?* (Oxford: Blackwell, 1988), 39–44.

that God is immediately present to all without reiterating coercive accounts of God and world.

In order to fully understand Tanner's particular account of transcendence and its implications for ecological theology, it is instructive to briefly reconstruct her interpretation of early Christian debates on divine transcendence against the background of Hellenistic dilemmas concerning divinity.[9] Tanner explains, first of all, that within the Greco-Roman world, God was either a thing among other things found in the world, or God was utterly different from anything in the world. Both claims (Tanner calls them "horns") of this so called Greco-Roman dilemma assumed that like must be involved with like. If unlike things are intimately involved with each other—for instance, an eternal principle with a finite world—their respective natures are compromised. The first horn of this dilemma simply gives certain things within the world divine status. This move can be found both within popular Greco-Roman polytheism and within the more sophisticated rational theologies that criticize them. For instance, in the theologies of Plato, the Stoics, and Aristotle, divinity at times is "a class name, a sortal term, specifying those principles within the world that are responsible for order, pattern and regularity."[10] The second horn of the Greco-Roman dilemma, on the other hand, constructs divinity in radical opposition to anything in the world and casts transcendence as distance. The rationale here is that because like can only be involved with like, God cannot have anything directly to do with a finite world of death and decay.[11] Thus, the supreme God produces a chain of intermediary divine

9. This discussion can be traced in several places in Tanner's work, most notably in *God and Creation*. I am here mainly drawing on the account in her article "Creation *Ex Nihilo* as Mixed Metaphor," *Modern Theology* 29, no. 2 (2013): 138-55.
10. Ibid., 142.
11. Ibid., 143.

principles, which form a kind of "buffer zone" between God and world.

Tanner observes that the theologians of the early Church rejected both solutions to the Greco-Roman dilemma. They judged that these accounts conflicted with monotheism, and failed to offer a way of saying that God is involved with the world in an immediate and intimate way that did not compromise God's divinity or the finite character of the world. Early Christian thinkers were attracted, instead, to the Neo-Platonism of Plotinus. According to Plotinus, God simply is not a particular sort of thing that stands in contrast to other sorts of things; God is neither like nor unlike anything in the world.[12] In Tanner's analysis, Plotinus' account of divinity has three important implications: first, because God is beyond all contrasts, God no longer only produces what is most like God. Second, because God is not like anything in the world, God's productive capacity is no longer restricted. Whereas a God who is a kind of thing can only produce what is most like itself, a God beyond kinds of things can be the source of *all* that is. Finally, Tanner judges that Plotinus's account of God's relation to the world implies that divine transcendence no longer means distance.[13] For in order to be separate from something one needs to have a difference in itself—a difference that implies one is something in contrast to something else. Obviously, a God who is beyond being does not contain such a difference.

Plotinus thus demonstrates that when God is seen as beyond any of the contrasts that characterize finite being, God can be intimately involved with all that is, and can do so in a comprehensive manner. Interestingly, Tanner insists that, while Plotinus himself is not fully consistent in following through on this insight, early Christian theologians did realize that "Hellenistic ideas about God's radical

12. Ibid., 145–46.
13. Ibid.

transcendence suggest that ... God is intimately involved with everything."[14] She believes that this is already the point of Irenaeus's polemic against the Gnostics. Irenaeus argues that if the first God is indeed fullness without limit then nothing can be outside the direct influence of this God: there simply is "nothing that exists apart from God and nothing that is not subject to God's direct influence."[15] Indeed, because Irenaeus sees divine transcendence as beyond "all oppositional contrasts characteristic of the relations among finite beings," God also exceeds the duality between presence and absence. Accordingly, divine transcendence "allows for the *immanent* presence *to* creatures of God in his otherness."[16]

Tanner's assessment of Irenaeus differs from that of some eco-theologians, most notably Catherine Keller, who have blamed Irenaeus's doctrine of creation *ex nihilo* for introducing hierarchical and coercive accounts of divinity into Christian theology.[17] Tanner's analysis demonstrates, however, that God's immediacy does not have to come at the expense of the autonomy of finite creatures. Because Irenaeus situates God's relation with the world within the overall context of his non-contrastive account of divine transcendence, God can be intimately present without diminishing the creaturely character of created existence. The upshot of all of this is a rather

14. Ibid., 147. Cf., Tanner, *God and Creation in Christian Theology*, 56. In both cases Tanner refers to the second book of Irenaeus's *Against Heresies*.

15. Tanner, "Creation *Ex Nihilo* as Mixed Metaphor," 147.

16. Tanner, *God and Creation in Christian Theology,* 57. Italics added. The previous four paragraphs appeared in a different form and to a different effect in Hilda P. Koster, "Questioning Eco-Theological *Panentheisms*: The Promise of Kathryn Tanner's Concept of God's Radical Transcendence for Ecological Theology," *Scriptura: International Journal of Bible, Religion and Theology in Southern Africa* 111 (2012): 385–94, esp. 389–91. They are reused by permission.

17. For instance, Catherine Keller insists that Irenaeus's "hands-on immediacy strengthens the imaginary of unilateral, linear and masculine dominance," which she believes comes at the expense of finite contingency. Catherine Keller, *Face of the Deep: A Theology of Becoming* [New York: Routledge, 2003], 51. Keller's criticism is an important reminder of the continued need for a hermeneutics of suspicion when reading Christianity's early texts. Even when Irenaeus may not have intended to install a dominative theology, his particular notion of a God who creates *ex nihilo* has fed into oppressive accounts of God and world.

different account of creation *ex nihilo*. As Tanner sees it, within the early church the *ex nihilo* "developed in tandem with" a non-contrastive account of transcendence, and, hence, served to express the ineffectiveness of all familiar categories for talking about the creativity of a God who is beyond kinds.[18] For if God is beyond ordinary categories and distinctions of being there simply is no analogy between the divine creativity and the way finite causes can be said to be creative. The creation *ex nihilo* thus follows from the radicalization of God's transcendence and expresses the *apophatic* character of all God-talk.

Viewed this way, Tanner believes that creation *ex nihilo* makes sense of the biblical affirmation that "God is responsible, not just for those aspects of the world that are supposedly like God … but for the whole of the world, from the bottom up."[19] Because ordinary causes fall short when it comes to expressing such a comprehensive and immediate creativity, only a God who is beyond ordinary categories of being can be said to accomplish such a feat. This does not mean that God originated the world in terms of historical processes. According to Tanner, the creativity of a God who is beyond kinds does not work within ordinary processes of time and change. If anything, creation *ex nihilo* encourages us to strip our idea of God's creativity of all "ordinary ideas of time, change, and finite process."[20] The result is a rather "abstract idea" of "a relation of utter dependence on God that holds for the whole world, in every respect, across the whole time of its existence."[21]

---

18. Tanner, "Creation *Ex Nihilo* as Mixed Metaphor," 138.
19. Tanner, "*Is God in Charge?*," in *Essentials of Christian Theology*, ed. William C. Placher (Louisville: Westminster John Knox Press, 2003), 120.
20. Ibid., 124.
21. Ibid.

Implications for Ecological Theology

Tanner's reading of early Christian debates on divine transcendence and *ex nihilo* against the background of Hellenistic concerns yields important implications for an ecological theology. Her account demonstrates, first of all, that instead of introducing an oppressive account of divinity into theology, the idea of God's transcendence was in fact used to *block* hierarchical and coercive accounts of God and world. The power of a God who is beyond kinds simply is not in competition with created causality. What this means is that eco-theologians can affirm God as the source (or giver) of all that a creature is in itself, without being worried that this will take away from the creature's own power and agency. Claiming that God's power is constitutive of created existence does not imply that creatures are passive. God's creative power simply does not come at the expense of the active operations of a created cause. Moreover, the binary opposition between bad and good power—the power of control versus the power of love—does not apply when talking about God. Because God's agency is comprehensive and immediate, God does not work from the outside to redirect or manipulate the conduct of others, as ordinary forces do. While there are certainly many bad forms of power, God's way *with* the world simply is not like any of our ways *in* the world.

Tanner's account of divine transcendence further allows eco-theologians to radicalize God's presence in the world without requiring that the world somehow resembles the divine nature. This latter insight is especially significant in light of a tendency, prominent in eco-theological panentheism, to associate God most closely with those aspects of nature exhibiting a higher capacity for complexity and interdependence. For instance, drawing on the social doctrine of the Trinity, Jürgen Moltmann insists that God is present in the world as Spirit: it is as Spirit that God continuously creates egalitarian, loving relationship corresponding to the divine community or *perichoresis*. Moltmann affirms that the divine Spirit "is poured out on everything that exists."[22] All things are formed by way of the Spirit, and it is in the Spirit that they exist and are renewed. At the same time, however, Moltmann suggests that only those aspects of creation that correspond to the perfect *perichoresis* express God's presence most fully. Thus, he states: "Our starting point here is that all relationships which are analogous to God reflect the primal, reciprocal indwelling and mutual interpenetration of the Trinitarian *perichoresis*."[23] This raises the question whether God can be said to be truly present to all that is. For a God who is closest to what is supposedly more like God is at most partially present in nature.

A similar problem can be traced in process theological accounts of God's relation to the world.[24] According to process theology, the world's increasing complexity enables a greater self-actualization of God within the world. God is the "creative aim" or "lure" persuading the world towards higher levels of self-actualization.[25] Yet while this process allows for a more involved account of God's presence over time, pairing God's self-actualization with an increase in complexity implies that God is more present in and to forms of life with more

---

22. Jürgen Moltmann, *God in Creation: A New Theology of Creation and the Spirit of God* 1st ed. (San Francisco: Harper & Row, 1985), 10.

23. Ibid., 17.

24. See, for instance, John Cobb Jr. and David Ray Griffin, *Process Theology: An Introductory Exposition* (Louisville: Westminster John Knox Press, 1976); and John Cobb Jr. and Charles Birch, *The Liberation of Life: From the Cell to the Community* (Cambridge: Cambridge University Press, 1981). For reasons of clarity, I am limiting myself here to these early accounts of process theology. I realize that this fails to do justice to the development and rich nuance within process theology as a whole. Catherine Keller's work especially has complicated process theological renderings of God and world in tremendously rich ways, most notably by drawing on the tradition of negative theology. Cf. *On the Mystery: Discerning God in Process* (Minneapolis: Fortress Press, 2008); and her latest, *Cloud of the Impossible: Negative Theology and Planetary Entanglement* (New York: Columbia University Press, 2015).

25. Cobb and Griffin, *Process Theology*, 52-54.

complex self-actualization. The latter is problematic not just for what it implies about the fullness of God's presence, but also from the perspective of evolutionary ecology. After all, there is no reason to assume that more complex forms of life are the ones whose representation in nature is most important for the preservation of an eco-system. Less complex forms of life may have little richness of experience, but they are crucial to the health and continuation of an eco-system.

Assuming that my sketchy portrayal of these prominent panentheistic models is valid—even as it fails to do justice to their rich complexity—it is easy to see how Tanner's account of God's relation to the world holds strong promises for ecological theology. According to Tanner, the world does not need to be like God in order for God to be present to it in a most direct and intimate manner. This is the case precisely because God radically transcends all categories of being. Only when God is beyond all contrasts of being can God be present to all that is in an equally immediate fashion. Thus, while a mosquito may express the fullness of God's super-abundance in a different way than a human being, this says nothing what-so-ever about God's presence to it. And while it might be true that more complex forms of life experience God's presence more intensely, this too does not mean that God is present to them in a way different than God can be said to be present to less complex forms of life. In short, then, Tanner allows ecological theology to maximize God's presence in and to a finite world, without requiring that the world somehow resembles the divine nature.

A Non-Anthropocentric Theology of Creation

A final implication of Tanner's non-contrastive account of divine transcendence for ecological theology is that it leads her to defend a non-anthropocentric theology of creation. Tanner herself has articulated this implication in her 1994 essay "Creation, Environmental Crisis, and Ecological Justice," which, I believe, has received too little attention from ecological theologians to date. In light of current scholarship in Christian environmental ethics some of the essay's observations, such as the need for an eco-justice approach, now have been more widely accepted. Yet Tanner's approach is still compellingly ingenious in so far as it provides an orthodox argument—God's relationship to the world as Creator—for a progressive, namely radically non-anthropocentric, theology and ethics. She demonstrates moreover that all other more conventional models, such as the model of stewardship, not only re-inscribe human superiority over nature but, historically, have re-enforced social inequality.

Tanner argues that because God's radical transcendence prohibits drawing a likeness of sorts between God and creatures, there simply is no ontological resemblance between God and humans. A God who is beyond categories of being is not on the same plane with any aspect of creation, humans included. Unlike other strands of Christian thinking about creation—strands that see the relationship of human beings to the rest of creation in terms of stewardship, imitation of God's rule, or the great chain of being—Tanner sets "human beings within the world as fully natural beings in essential relations with others."[26] While human beings certainly have special capabilities, these capabilities do not lift them out of the created order or put them on the divine side of things: while human beings may be different from plants and other animals, their difference is a difference among creatures as creatures. From the perspective of a theology of creation, human beings' most important feature is *creaturehood*, something they share with all other creatures.[27]

26. Tanner, "Creation, Environmental Crisis, and Ecological Justice," 114.
27. Ibid., 117.

Within this scheme all creatures not only have *inherent* value as creatures of God, but also are *equally* valuable. From the perspective of an environmental ethics this means that all creatures are entitled "… due treatment that respects both the value of their continued existence as the beings they are and the value of those activities and achievements proper to them."[28] Indeed, Tanner asks us to make the value and entitlement of *all* lifeforms the overarching context of our decision making. At no point should non-human interests be subordinated to humans on the ground that they supposedly have "a lesser degree of entitlement."[29] While there certainly are many situations which require that we give preference to human interests over that of other species, the latter should never happen on the assumption that non-human life-forms have inferior status in the larger scheme of things.

Tanner's radically inclusive ethics is particularly powerful because it does not come at the expense of a concern for social justice. Today most ecological theologians, Pope Francis prominently among them, are aware of the multiple ways environmental diminishment and the plight of the poor are interconnected. Yet when it comes to wilderness preservation the need for environmental protection has often come at the expense of poor and disenfranchised communities.[30] It is significant therefore that Tanner's model draws together the preservation of nature with an abiding concern for social and economic justice. She demonstrates, first of all, that theologies that privilege humans over non-humans have been "implicated historically in non-egalitarian proposals for human relations."[31] For

---

28. Ibid.

29. Ibid., 119.

30. Thus Pope Francis in his encyclical *Laudato Si* writes "a true ecological approach always becomes a social approach; it must integrate questions of justice in debates on the environment, so as to hear *both the cry of the earth and the cry of the poor.*" The Holy Father Francis, Encyclical Letter *Laudato Si: On Care For our Common Home*, 2015, 49. Italics in original text.

31. Tanner, "Creation, Environmental Crisis, and Ecological Justice," 115.

instance, "the "great chain of being" strand of Christian theology of creation" insists that "hierarchical relations between human beings are established by nature just as they are throughout the entire chain of being."[32] Similarly, "the 'stewardship' strand of Christian theology has supported, and in turn been supported by, paternalistic relations between human beings of unequal social standing, for instance, relations with servants and laborers in one's employ."[33] Tanner, however, insists that a non-anthropocentric theology of creation blocks such a justification of unequal distributions of power and privilege. The recognition of shared *creaturehood* requires that we take the equal entitlement of all creatures into account. And because the equal entitlement of non-humans and the poor have been violated in different, yet interlocking ways, Christian environmental ethics needs to be concerned with eco-justice.[34] This means that issues of structural injustice are raised while discussing environmental issues: "[c]alls for the preservation of rain forests should ... lead immediately into questions of national and global economies and their possible restructuring towards more equitable distributions of income and opportunities."[35] Christians are further urged to "join efforts in their

32. Ibid.
33. Ibid.
34. The ethicist Cynthia Moe-Lobeda distinguishes two streams in the eco-justice movement: environmental racism and climate injustice. In both instances eco-justice asks questions concerning "ecological debt" and "environmental space." The latter approach is a "rights based and fair share based approach to eco-justice," arguing that "all people have rights to a fair share in the goods and services that the earth provides for human kind." See Cynthia Moe-Lobeda, *Resisting Structural Evil: Love as Ecological-Economic Vocation* (Minneapolis: Fortress Press, 2013), 40. Eco-justice focused on environmental space generally is the ethical position defended by eco-feminist theologians. See, for instance, Ivone Gebara, *Longing for Running Water: Eco-Feminism and Liberation* (Minneapolis: Fortress Press, 1999). Larry Rasmussen has done path breaking work articulating an eco-justice approach as the hallmark of Christian environmental ethics in his book *Earth Community, Earth Ethics* (Maryknoll, NY: Orbis Books, 1997), and of religious environmental ethics more broadly in his *Earth-Honoring Faith: Religious Ethics in a New Key* (Oxford: Oxford University Press, 2012). A fine example of an eco-justice approach in relation to climate change is James Martin-Schramm, *Climate Justice: Ethics, Energy, and Public Policy* (Minneapolis: Fortress Press, 2010).
35. Tanner, "Creation, Environmental Crisis, and Ecological Justice," 115.

communities to build coalitions across environmental groups and organizations working for minority and workers' rights."[36]

Tanner's theology of creation thus leads to a non-anthropocentric environmental ethics that advocates an eco-justice stance. As I indicated in the introduction to this chapter, however, it is important to acknowledge that Tanner anchors Christian responsibility for planetary well-being and the poor in Christ, and, hence, soteriology. On one level, human's responsibility vis-à-vis the rest of creation simply flows from human beings' created capabilities, most notably the ability to "imagine a universal community of moral concern."[37] Yet, while human beings have this capacity, they are either not using it or using it to ill effect. Indeed, if anything, our current predicament vividly demonstrates the failure of the human community to make decisions that include the well-being of all. On another level, therefore, Christian responsibility must be understood as an act of grace. This, I believe, is the significance of Tanner's Christ-centered reading of the *imago Dei* in *Christ the Key*.[38] According to this account, the *imago Dei* refers not to human beings but to the second person of the Trinity: the Son, or Word. Human beings become images of God only as their humanity is assumed by Christ, the Word incarnate. Tanner insists: "By the power of the Holy Spirit, the first person of the Trinity sends the second person into the world so as to be incarnate in human flesh, one with the humanity of Jesus. That same power of the Spirit comes to us through the glorified humanity of Christ in order to attach us to him, make us one with him, in all the intensity of faith, hope, and love."[39] In short, then, in the incarnation we are gratuitously given the capability of becoming an image of God, and, hence, of becoming responsibly engaged with the rest of

36. Ibid., 122.
37. Ibid., 119.
38. Tanner, *Christ the Key*, ch. 1.
39. Ibid., 14.

creation. While human beings by way of their created capacities have a special duty towards the rest of creation, the ability to exercise these capacities wisely is a matter of grace. Tanner's Christ-centered reading of the *imago Dei* thus calls us to act with a deep and abiding humility. Yet, act we must! Indeed, following Luther's theology of justification and sanctification, Tanner's Christology is a task-oriented one: assumed by Christ, we are called to *become* images of God by serving the world. [40]

Creation as Gift: Promises for a Green Soteriology

So far this chapter has sought to demonstrate that in spite of appearances to the contrary, Tanner's dual principle of God's non-contrastive and non-competitive relation to the world does in fact offer an attractive model for a non-dualistic, non-anthropocentric, and non-hierarchical theology of creation. A model that avoids some of the pitfalls of current eco-theologies and radically decenters human beings without jeopardizing their special responsibility towards the rest of creation and the poor. In her more recent writings on Christology, the full cosmic-theological vision of her theology is spelled out—a vision that brings together God's work in creation with God's work in salvation in a radically inclusive account of God's ongoing gift-giving.

In *Jesus, Humanity and the Trinity*, Tanner states that "at the heart of my theology is the idea that God is the giver of all good gifts."[41] The triune God is a source of self-communicating goodness. God does not need to share God's own perfect fullness with a finite world:

---

40. For a more detailed account of the eco-theological implications of Tanner's Christ-centered reading of the *imago Dei*, see my contribution to the Book Forum in *Theology Today*. Hilda P. Koster, "Greening the *Imago Dei*: The Promise of Kathryn Tanner's Christ-Centered Interpretation of the *Imago Dei* for Ecological Theology," *Theology Today* 68, no. 3 (2011): 317–23.
41. Tanner, *Jesus, Humanity and the Trinity*, 1.

"There is nothing yet to achieve beyond what God's own Trinitarian perfection already instantiates."[42] Instead, God shares God's abundant fullness with the world for the sole gain of God's creatures as an act of pure grace. Yet, because a finite world cannot receive all God wants to give it at once, God bestows God's gifts in stages, over time. Creation, covenant, and salvation must all be seen as stages or degrees, "representing a greater communication of goodness to the creature and the overcoming of any sinful opposition to these gifts' distribution."[43]

Within this context, creation is the stage in which God gives the creature itself: God provides the world with "its created, non-divine existence, and all that it includes: life, truth, beauty, goodness in their finite forms."[44] Whereas God gratuitously constitutes the world's very existence from the store of God's own Trinitarian fullness, God does not yet give God-self. The latter is the case *not* because God withholds this gift, but because the world is not yet able to receive it: "God's gifts come to it over the course of time in what God intends to be an unending expansion of its *ability* to receive created gifts from the Father's hands of Son and Spirit."[45] Indeed, even God's gifts of existence come to the world over time. Thus, drawing on Irenaeus, Tanner depicts creatures growing into God's gifts. And, referring to Gregory of Nyssa's notion of *epectasis*, she insists that a creature constantly moves forward "beyond itself into the boundlessness of God's fullness as the creature's capacities are stretched by what it receives."[46] By way of the gift of creation, then, God ceaselessly pervades the world with the created versions of God's own goodness.

God's gift-giving in creation and covenant culminates in God's

42. Ibid., 68.
43. Ibid., 2.
44. Ibid., 42.
45. Ibid. Italics added.
46. Ibid., 43.

perfect self-communication in the incarnation. While in Tanner's scheme the triune God moves beyond the general level of created gifts in so called covenant relations, it is only in the humanity of Jesus that what is other than God is united with God in such a way that it becomes God's own. This is the case because "[t]he perfections of Jesus' humanity and the perfect fellowship Jesus enjoys as a human being with the Father are *not* his as gifts (in a narrow sense).... They are instead his by *nature* since here God becomes human; they come to his humanity *not* by some external grant but because God unites with humanity in Jesus, and thereby communicates goods to it."[47]

Tanner's model thus casts God's redeeming work in Christ as integral to God's work as Creator. She is adamant however that the incarnation should not be seen as God's response to human sinfulness. This would make God's gift-giving in Christ *extrinsic* to creation. While Tanner fully recognizes the fact of sin and the need for redemption from sin, her theology of God's gift-giving implies that the incarnation was always intended by God. Creation and incarnation are two moments—if two differentiated moments—within the one process of God's self-giving and self-expression. This rather radical move makes Tanner's account of God's ongoing gift giving an attractive model for an ecological theology of creation and salvation. Instead of reducing creation to the mere backdrop for human salvation, creation as a whole is seen as an intrinsic part of God's salvific involvement with the world.

Yet what separates Tanner's account from some other integrative models in ecological theology is that it does not downplay the unique character of God's gift-giving in Christ. This does not mean, however, that Tanner is not sensitive to the concerns articulated by some feminist and ecological theologians about how one limited by

47. Ibid., 46-47. Italics added.

humanness, maleness, and a parochial spot on the planet (Galilee) can be said to save women and the earth.[48] Yet she insists that it is precisely because of the *hypostatic* union between Jesus' humanity and the second person of the Trinity that all of creation is able to fully receive God's superabundance. Because "Jesus is the human mode of the Son's own relation to the Father and the Spirit, it signals a level of covenant fellowship with God otherwise impossible for creatures."[49] In other words, Jesus' humanity is salvific *not* because the humanity assumed in Christ is common to both Christ and us, but rather because it is assumed by the Word. Accordingly, the inclusivity of salvation in Christ has nothing to do with what is or is not included in Jesus' humanity. Tanner's affirmation of God's comprehensive concern as Creator implies, moreover, that God's concern in Jesus is comprehensive as well. In Jesus, "God does not just save certain aspects of created existence, but rather brings total liberation, not just spiritual but physical healing, not just the liberation of individuals but of society, starting with the church, not just reconciliation among people but between them and the natural world."[50] In other words, Tanner's cosmic-theological scheme not

---

48. For instance, Rosemary R. Ruether has argued that because of the particularity of Jesus' historical form, Jesus should be seen as *a*, rather than *the*, revelation of redeemed and redeeming humanity; Rosemary Radford Ruether, *Sexism and God-Talk: Toward a Feminist Theology* (Boston: Beacon Press, 1983), ch. 5. Similarly, Elisabeth Schüssler Fiorenza proposed we view Jesus not as the Word incarnate but as a special kind of prophet "proclaiming a vision of the *Basileia* (kingdom/reign) of God that engendered a discipleship of equals;" see Francine Cardman, "Christology," in *Dictionary of Feminist Theology*, eds. Letty M. Russell and J. Shannon Clarkson (Louisville: Westminster John Knox Press, 1996), 4. Finally, Catherine Keller maintains that, whereas in Jesus the Logos has been realized in a unique way, intimate union or "sonship" is not an exclusive event. The incarnation seeks "materialization … not just in Jesus but always and everywhere." Keller, *On the Mystery*, 151.

49. Tanner, *Jesus, Humanity and the Trinity*, 50. While Tanner agrees that human and divine functions remain distinct in Christ's life, she does not see Jesus' unity with the Word as just a perfect fellowship. Unlike Barth but in agreement with the Fathers of the early church, she insists that the incarnation is "a higher form of unity than fellowship with God, and thereby the closest approximation to the Triune life that is possible for a creature."

50. Tanner, "Is God in Charge?," 122.

just allows ecological theologians to articulate the universal scope of salvation without jeopardizing the unique exclusivity of the incarnation, it also demonstrates that it is precisely because of the unique character of God's gift-giving in Christ that salvation is cosmic in scope.

A final important feature of Tanner's proposal is that salvation is understood as *deification*: in virtue of being drawn closer to God, the world is able to receive what God wants to give to it and hence *becomes* more God-like. Tanner insists that *all* of creation is being deified by way of God's gift-giving in Christ. The idea of salvation as deification has often been associated with other-worldly, body-denying tendencies in Christian thought.[51] Tanner is adamant, however, that, while the world is deified by way of God's gift-giving in Christ, it does not become divine. As demonstrated by Tanner's reading of the *hypostatic* union of divinity and humanity in Christ, the principle of God's radical transcendence holds true for God's redemptive relation to the world as well. Indeed, it is precisely because God and world are on different planes of existence that the world can be drawn ever closer to God without losing its quality as a finite creation. And, as implied by God's non-competitive relation to the world, the world does not lose its autonomy when being drawn close to God. On the contrary, the closer to God, the more the world can come into its own as God's good, but finite creation.

---

51. For instance, Ernst Conradie remarks that deification "can easily revert to a denigration of that which is material, bodily, and earthly." As such, Conradie feels that "it can breed contempt for the fragility and mortality of being embodied." Ernst M. Conradie, "Introduction: Doing Justice to Creation and Salvation," in *Creation and Salvation. Volume 2: A Companion on Recent Theological Movements*, ed. Ernst M. Conradie (Münster, DE: LIT Verlag Dr. W. Hopf, 2012), 3. A notable exception to the negative assessment of salvation as deification in ecological theology is the work of Denis Edwards, *How God Acts: Creation, Redemption, and Special Divine Action* (Minneapolis: Fortress Press, 2010), ch. 7.

It's Not Easy Being Green

So far we have seen that Tanner sketches a radically inclusive, this-worldly account of salvation in which God's ongoing involvement with the world is both creative and salvific. Being drawn closer to God, the world is able to more fully receive God's good gifts and, hence, becomes the perfect reflection of God's own superabundance. Positively, the groans of travail that are part and parcel of a finite world do not take away from the affirmation that the world is God's good creation here and now. Suffering and death do not signal that the world has fallen into sin—Tanner does away with a cosmic fall that casts death and suffering as the result of sin—nor do they indicate that the world is threatened by the forces of non-being as for instance is the case for Moltmann's *kenotic* reading of creation.[52]

One difficulty with Tanner's scheme is that, while she does not demonizes finitude, she does make finitude the problem addressed by the incarnation. For instance, she states that "[t]he primary problems addressed by Christ, on my account, are ones of death, suffering and conflict ... [which] are at root problems of finitude."[53] Granted that this interpretation works rather well when applied to human sinfulness—human beings can be said to act sinfully by virtue of their finite limitations—it falls short when applied to biotic communities. After all, from the perspective of evolutionary ecology, conditions such as death, predation, and disease—conditions Tanner sets out to remedy—guarantee the vitality and resilience of these communities. While I do not think Tanner is wrong in viewing these aspects of finite life as tragic, she risks projecting an eschatological vision that has rather little to do with the processes that give continuance to

---

52. Jürgen Moltmann, "God's Kenosis in the Creation and Consummation of the World," in *The Work of Love: Creation as Kenosis* (Grand Rapids: Eerdmans, 2001), 137-51; cf. *God in Creation*, chs. 4 and 8.

53. Tanner, "Author Response," 341.

earthly life. This is especially odd, given that she insists that even a redeemed creation—a creation fully open to God's gifts—is still finite.

Casting finitude as a problem may also feed into the tendency, characteristic of global capitalism, to deny the vulnerable ecological communities on which life depends. Writing from the slums in her native Brazil, the eco-feminist theologian Ivone Gebara insists that this denial comes at the expense of both non-human nature and the poor. In her view, our refusal to accept our finite limitations allows a global elite to dominate, to exploit the earth and the poor.[54] Similarly, Catherine Keller observes that one of the problems perpetuating the environmental crisis is the luxury of a privileged minority to insulate itself from the discomfort and vulnerability of the physical reality of life; a luxury that comes at the expenses of those humans who cannot "afford to experience nature as banal, outside of immediate bonds of dependency upon weather conditions."[55] Thus these theologians maintain that our theologies should name the tendency to flee finitude as our cardinal sin.

Finally, in addition to casting finitude itself as a problem, Tanner's theology of creation and redemption at times suggests that we can see the world as God's good creation only by way of God's giving of God-self in Christ. Indeed, she insists that, while God's intimate relationship with "a world of suffering, loss, and conflict" might not be very apparent, "the most intimate identity of God with the one, Jesus, who saves us out of the world of suffering, violence, and conflict by taking it all on himself, proves God's capacity to be in intimate relations with that sort of world."[56] Positively, the incarnation places us within a new relation to the world—as indeed we saw was the implication of Tanner's prospective, Christ-centered

---

54. Gebara, *Longing for Running Water*, 13.
55. Catherine Keller, "Postmodern "Nature," Feminism and Community," in *Theology for Earth Community: A Field Guide*, ed. Dieter Hessel (Maryknoll, NY: Orbis Books, 1996), 95.
56. Tanner, "Is God in Charge?," 122.

account of *imago Dei*. Nonetheless, I wonder whether this Christo-centric account does not hamper our ability of experiencing and knowing God from nature. As we have seen, part of the "green" promise of Tanner's theology of creation is that it maximizes God's presence in and to a finite world, without idealizing the world or identifying God more closely with a particular aspect of it. Her concept of radical transcendence thus opens up the possibility of reading created existence as a sacrament of God. Her work on Christology, on the other hand, seems to suggest, in a rather Barthian fashion, that we can only see nature as creation from the perspective of what God has already done for us in Christ. The dilemma then seems to be how to hold on to her soteriological scheme without casting finitude as a problem or watering down the sacramental quality of her earlier theology of creation. In order to point towards some constructive solutions, the conclusion of this essay briefly engages the eco-theological work of Denis Edwards and Elizabeth Johnson. On wisdom Christology and deep-incarnation as a viable route to address this question, especially in so far it draws out God's way with a finite world in light of the wisdom of the cross.[57]

The Wisdom of the Cross

Like Tanner, both Edwards and Johnson stress the significance of God's transcendence for a comprehensive theology of creation and redemption. Edwards, moreover, also views creation and redemption as a process of divine self-bestowal, and salvation in terms of a transformative deification. Unlike Tanner, however, both Edwards and Johnson choose to articulate the cosmic scope of the incarnation

---

57. I am drawing here on the following works: Denis Edwards, *Jesus the Wisdom of God: An Ecological Theology* (Maryknoll, NY: Orbis Books, 1995); Denis Edwards, *How God Acts*; and Elizabeth A. Johnson *Ask the Beasts: Darwin and the God of Love* (New York: Bloomsbury, 2014).

by turning to wisdom Christology. They further combine wisdom Christology with the idea of "deep incarnation"—an idea first articulated by the Lutheran theologian Niels Gregersen.[58] When viewed in light of the wisdom of the cross, "deep incarnation" allows for an inclusive soteriology that affirms the finite character of created existence—including its tragic ambiguity—more fully.

Edwards and Johnson agree that wisdom Christology is an important route for connecting God's redemptive work in Christ with God's work in creation. Wisdom Christology portrays Jesus as the personification of the wisdom figure (*Hokmah*) of the Hebrew Scriptures in whom God creates and sustains the universe. Johnson writes: "[t]he connection … between Jesus and wisdom was especially fruitful in that it began to identify the crucified prophet from Nazareth, localized in time and place, with a divine figure associated in the Jewish tradition with creating and governing the world."[59] As the wisdom of God, Christ is present at creation: all things are created in and through Christ. And because all things are created in and through Christ, all things are included in the transformation brought about by the incarnation (1 Cor. 8:6 and Col 1:16).[60] Wisdom Christology, then, is a cosmic Christology.

---

58. Niels Henrik Gregersen, "The Cross of Christ in an Evolutionary World," *Dialog: A Journal of Theology* 4, no. 4 (2001): 192-205.

59. Johnson, *Ask the Beasts*, 193.

60. Edwards draws on the work by biblical scholar Bruce Vawter, who traces Jesus identification with divine Wisdom in Paul and John back to pre-existent Christian hymns which are scattered throughout the Christian scriptures, including Phil. 2:6-11; Col. 1:15-20; Eph. 2:14-16; 1 Tim. 3:16; 1 Pet. 3:18-22; Heb.1:3; and John 1:1-18. Cf. Bruce Vawter, *This Man Jesus: An Essay toward a New Testament Christology* (Garden City, NY: Doubleday, 1973); quoted by Edwards, *Jesus the Wisdom of God*, 33. The most explicit identification of Jesus with the cosmic wisdom of God is in the Gospel of John. Scholars agree that the main influence behind John's *Logos* theology is that of *Hokmah* or *Sophia*. From a feminist perspective it remains problematic that the Gospel of John has replaced the feminine *Hokmah/Sophia* by the masculine *Logos*. The latter arguably has led later traditions to project the maleness of the human Jesus onto the Son or the Word. At the same time, Elizabeth Johnson has argued that the dissonance between the female *Hokmah/Sophia* and the male Jesus impedes the literal tendencies of much Son of God language, and, hence, *de facto*, blocks an easy identification between the second person of the

Because Tanner insists that the universality of the incarnation hinges on the assumption of Jesus' humanity by the Word, it seems to me that wisdom Christology would allow her to strengthen the non-anthropocentric and cosmic scope of her Christology. [61] Indeed it is precisely as a Cosmic Christology that wisdom Christology can connect the concern with God's grace in Christ in Tanner's more recent writings with her earlier theology of creation. In this context it is significant that both Edwards and Johnson combine their account of wisdom Christology with the idea of "deep incarnation." Deep incarnation indicates that by taking on flesh in Jesus of Nazareth, God becomes part of the interconnected eco-systems that support life on earth. The notion of deep incarnation allows us to see that, as human flesh, Jesus is the product of an evolving cosmos and thus interconnected with all other life-forms. As Johnson explains, "'deep incarnation' understands John 1:14 to be saying that the *sarx* which the Word of God became ... reaches beyond us to join him to the whole biological world of living creatures and the cosmic dust of which they are composed."[62] Edwards elaborates "to say that God became flesh is ... to say that God became an Earth creature, that God became a sentient being, that God became a complex Earth unit of minerals and fluids, that God became an item in the carbon and nitrogen cycles."[63] Deep incarnation, then, can be understood as "an incarnation into the very tissue of biological existence, and system of nature."[64]

Trinity and the masculinity of the human Jesus. In addition, she insists that the fact that the early church identified the male Jesus with the female *Hokmah* indicates that Jesus' maleness is not a constitutive element of his redemptive significance. See Elizabeth A. Johnson, *She Who Is: The Mystery of God in Feminist Theological Discourse* (New York: Crossroad, 1992), 164-67. Cf. Elizabeth A. Johnson, "Jesus the Wisdom of God: A Biblical Basis for a Non-Androcentric Christology," *Ephermerides Theologicae Lovanienses* 61 (1985): 216-94.

61. I have argued this point also in Koster, "Greening the *Imago Dei*," 322-23.
62. Johnson, *Ask the Beasts*, 197.
63. Denis Edwards, *Ecology at the Heart of Faith: The Change of Heart that Leads to a New Way of Living on Earth* (Maryknoll, NY: Orbis Books, 2006), 58-59.

When combined with the notion of deep incarnation, wisdom Christology further allows Tanner to embrace the finite conditions of life more fully without downplaying the sacramental potential of her theology. In this regard both Edwards and Johnson point to the potential of the theology of the cross. According to Edwards, the Wisdom incarnate at the heart of the universe is the wisdom of the cross.[65] This wisdom is not like worldly wisdom and revokes all conventional standards of purpose and power. Thus, while according to human standards and sensibilities the natural processes and systems of the world are violent, random, and even void of a deeper significance, in light of the wisdom of the cross they can be considered an expression of God's love as solidarity with the evolutionary suffering of life forms. Similarly, according to Johnson, the cross of Christ reveals that "[d]welling in the evolving world and acting in, with and under its natural processes, the Giver of life continuously knows and bears the cost of new life."[66] From the perspective of the cross, then, the world is a *sacrament* of God precisely *in* and *through* the trials of an evolving world. Combining wisdom Christology with the idea of deep incarnation, the cross signals the "infinitely compassionate presence,"[67] by which the gift-giving God accompanies the world in its pain. Indeed, it is this loving presence that draws us more fully into the web of life as well. For, as followers of Christ, we are called to grow into the image of the incarnated Wisdom of God by embracing the finite character of our lives in solidarity with all those life-forms—human and non-human—suffering from injustice and ecological destruction.

64. Gregersen, "Cross of Christ in an Evolutionary World," 205.

65. Edwards quotes 1 Cor. 1:21: "For since, in the wisdom of God, the world did not know God through wisdom, God decided through the foolishness of our proclamation, to save those who believe." *Jesus the Wisdom of God*," 72.

66. Johnson, *Ask the Beasts*, 205.

67. Ibid., 210.

13

From "Thrift Shop" to the Zero Waste Home: Popular Culture, Subversion of the Ordinary Economy, and *Economy of Grace*

Courtney Wilder

In her 2005 book *Economy of Grace,* Kathryn Tanner argues that Christian theology and practice ought to be, but are typically not, in deep tension with capitalist economic practices. In her analysis and critique of capitalist economies, Tanner offers an alternate proposal, a theological economy. Although this economy is not fully realized, the time is ripe for creating it, and it is visible in fragmentary form, disrupting the standard economy. Although Tanner does not make the connection explicit, her vision of theological economy has a sense of the already-and-not-yet. It resembles the Kingdom of God in Jesus' parables: as Jesus says in Matthew 13:32, "it is the smallest of all the seeds, but when it has grown it is the greatest of shrubs and becomes a tree, so that the birds of the air come and make nests in its branches."[1] Tanner argues that the "discipline of theology in a time of economic dead ends can work to open up the economic imagination"[2] and from there construct alternate economic systems that reflect a primary allegiance to God and reliance upon God's grace. Thus she envisions theological reflection transforming economic structures, but she also analyzes economic practices other than capitalism, and phenomena outside Christianity, for insight into God's gracious activity.

Tanner's primary examples of non-capitalist economic possibilities are the work of John Locke and anthropological analysis of gift-exchange practices in South Asia, both of which inform her description of a theological economy. She does not engage in *Economy of Grace* with existing Christian practice that runs counter to the dominant economic system, the Amish or Mennonite communities, for instance. She voices some reservations about a possible avenue for Christian economic practices: "With nothing to gain from attention to the capitalist system it hopes to escape, a theological economy might limit its purview to the Bible or to church practices, and model its self-reliant, small-scale communities on, say, the subsistence agrarian economies of ancient Israel or on the desert monasteries of the early church.... Pretending to self-sufficiency, an alternative theological economy might in this way cut itself off from any sophisticated theological analysis of the realities of today's world."[3] Instead, Tanner turns to economic principles outside the Christian tradition for new language and models for understanding God's grace and envisioning an economy grounded in that grace. Tanner writes, "Every theological category and claim,

1. My thanks to Jeremy Rehwaldt for this insight.
2. Kathryn Tanner, *Economy of Grace* (Minneapolis: Fortress Press, 2005), 33.
3. Ibid., 88.

no matter how basic and theologically primary ... might very well then be framed ... in response to these economic principles of the wider world; any theological category might take up these economic principles, in the effort to make sense of God, and by giving them an odd spin, offer, at least implicitly, a critical commentary on them."[4] Tanner thus uses the insights of Locke and South Asian gift practices to better understand God, and also to examine and transform those (or any) economic practices for Christian use.

What Locke provides for Tanner, she says, is an argument that "property rights are inclusive or common at their root: the world and everything in it have been given by God for the good of all."[5] This creates a model for theological anthropology; Tanner writes that Locke's emphasis on the inalienability of one's own body and one's capacities runs counter to capitalism, where "[f]ull liberty over oneself easily suggests ... that, should one feel like it, one can hand [oneself] over by contract to someone else."[6] For Locke, the human person remains under the auspices of God's ownership, and cannot properly be sold or exploited, which provides us with a strong rejection of the *de facto* practices of capitalism. But Tanner argues that Locke's theology does not include a robust account of God's grace, and so must be problematized and transformed by another model entirely.

Tanner turns next to theological analyses of "noncommodity gift exchange in non-Western locales not yet fully subject to market conditions."[7] In contrast to Western capitalist practices, these gift exchanges occur within the community "between familiars"[8] rather than among strangers; the purpose of exchanging gifts is to more firmly tie each participant to the community. Although sometimes

4. Ibid., 2.
5. Ibid., 40.
6. Ibid., 42.
7. Ibid., 49.
8. Ibid., 50.

the gifts are useful and ensure that the recipient's needs are met, the more important function of the practice is that the community determines the status of its members through their participation: "One's social standing goes up the more one gives away to others rather than the more one receives from them.... The goal of the exchange for the individual is to maximize what one puts out ... in contrast to commodity exchanges, where the goal is to accumulate or take in as much as one can for oneself."[9] Ultimately, these gift exchanges are not an adequate model for an economy of grace, because the giving has "mixed motives."[10] If one is giving to preserve one's social status, the gift is not pure. However, the analysis of these gift-giving practices provides a lens through which to understand God's gift-giving behavior, and to frame an appropriate human response. Tanner writes that God's gifts "efface themselves in their very occurrence by virtue of their difference from any other sort of gift exchange among creatures with which we are familiar.... God's act of giving is invisible."[11]

What of these human responses to God's gifts, responses that reflect the inalienable self-possession of each human being? More pointedly, how can Tanner's description of a theological economy work to reveal it emerging in the secular world? In *Economy of Grace*, Tanner suggests that a theological economy is visible, erupting into the dominant capitalist economy; aside from her analysis of Locke and South Asian gift-giving, she does not explicitly identify examples that might serve as models, or the beginning of models, for contemporary Christians. In the interest of further developing Tanner's concept of a theological economy and exploring how it might function outside of typical Christian practice, I will explore the emergence of economies

9. Ibid.
10. Ibid., 60.
11. Ibid., 71.

of grace in three popular cultural phenomenon: first, the book and blog Zero Waste Home, by writer Bea Johnson; second, Macklemore's chart-topping hip-hop song "Thrift Shop"; and third, the website "Unfuck Your Habitat," the online home of a community focused on mutual support for creating healthy and comfortable physical space in lieu of disorder or squalor.

These three examples of popular culture, different as they are from one another, illuminate Tanner's concept of a theological economy, and encountering them through the lens Tanner provides reveals similarities. In each case, there is shared rejection of false and even oppressive values, of aesthetic and economic ideals that harm individuals, communities, and the environment, in favor of reframing economic, social, and aesthetic practices in such a way that exploitation is reduced and individual and community health are prioritized. The work of Bea Johnson is pragmatic and practical as well as aspirational for the average American household. One of Tanner's critiques of capitalism, as we will see, is that it does not account for harm done to the environment. Tanner argues, "Those doing the damage or encouraging the damage by buying the products do not have to pay for it, and therefore the market does nothing to discourage forms of production with these environmental costs."[12] Johnson's Zero Waste Home approach rejects the capitalist economy at precisely this point, and maps out for her readers how their ordinary daily choices can affirm environmental health as well as improve the quality of their lives. The song "Thrift Shop" also provides a model of resistance to the demands of a capitalist economy that one be dressed in newly-manufactured clothing, at the expense of garment workers and one's own financial resources. Finally, the Unfuck Your Habitat site, in the creation of community around the shared goal of humane living spaces over and against despair or

12. Ibid., 133.

illness, engages in the sort of relationship-building that Tanner points to: "In keeping with the universal community of unconditional giving, when one gives, one has everything to do with what is unlike oneself—those who are not in one's circumstances, not in one's economic class or social bracket."[13] Although the giving of Unfuck Your Habitat denizens is not comprised of material goods, the participation and encouragement of the community has the effect Tanner argues is important to a theological economy. Tanner's description of a theological economy provides a means of recognizing each of these three phenomena as potentially theologically meaningful, as "formed in response to, a kind of vis-à-vis with, the economy [they contest]."[14] The three examples above, in turn, provide examples of an emerging theological economy.

Theological Economy

First, let's explore Tanner's critique of both capitalism and Christianity's response to capitalism. What is wrong with current global capitalist practices, from a theological perspective, and why aren't Christians more aware of the conflict between their religious beliefs and the living conditions of people around the world? Too often, Christians fail to engage in critique of oppressive economic systems at all. Tanner notes a dismaying conflation of economic prosperity, including social class, with favor from God. Especially problematic is the association of denomination, class status, and wealth with presumed divine blessing. From this perspective, "Those who have economic goods—those with money—also have grace or religious goods, and vice versa. If you have cornered the market in material goods, you have also done so for spiritual ones. The successful are God's favored ones; God's favored ones become

13. Ibid., 80.
14. Ibid., 88.

successful."[15] Once this relationship between success and divine favor has been established, "one or the other term—either grace or money, whichever one is viewed as the meaning of the other—is given automatic explanatory privilege.... What is really at issue in worldly success is grace, or what is really at issue in one's religious standing is money."[16] Regardless of whether the rich are favored by God or God's favorites become rich, the effect of such a theological position is to further legitimize the disenfranchisement of the socially and economically marginal; their lack of wealth can easily be construed as proof of divine disfavor. Such a system grossly misconstrues grace and neatly excuses the prosperous Christian from any obligation to those suffering the effects of poverty.

Another problematic effect of capitalism, Tanner argues, is that material goods are prioritized over human relationships: "Everyone is after *things* they want or need, and they enter into exchange relations with *people* just to the extent that those other people own those things."[17] This disregard for the well-being of others encourages those with wealth to pursue more wealth at the expense of the economically marginal members of the community:

> Having money or lacking it tends, in short, to become a cumulative condition. If you have money, on the one hand, you can make money—for example, by loaning it to people who don't have as much.... [The lives of the privileged] improve, while the others' lives decline even further.... If you lack money ... every problem likely snowballs into a crisis. You lack the money to get professional help for your child with a disability; you stay at home on an unpredictable basis to attend to her yourself; you lose your job as a result, and have to start over at the lowest rung of the employment ladder if you are ever employed again.[18]

15. Ibid., 9.
16. Ibid.
17. Ibid., 37.
18. Ibid.

Thus the problem is not simply that affluent people are encouraged to acquire more and more wealth and material goods, but that that wealth and those goods are obtained at great cost to non-affluent people.

Tanner argues for an alternative, a *theological* economy. She describes it as "a universally inclusive system for the increase and distribution of goods, one dedicated to the well-being of all its members and organized to ensure that what benefits one benefits all."[19] She holds that such a system is visible within Christian Scripture and the Christian tradition, although not as a dominant voice. Instead, Christian analysis of money and of economic practices tends to back away from any obligation to humble or disenfranchise oneself. Since Constantine, institutional Christianity has been content to see "power, privilege, and success" as signs of grace.[20] The possibility of God's preference for the poor remains a thread within Christian practice, but not a dominant theme. Tanner observes, "Direct attention to economic questions also emerges … piecemeal in Christian history, as occasions warrant, without any clear systematic connection among various Christian pronouncements and warnings."[21] However, liberation theologies tend to pick up the thread of God's grace: "[T]he religions of the oppressed are true to, are the saviors and keepers of, a neglected strand of thinking present in Christian history."[22] This is the idea of grace: God distributes the good of this world, and this good "is to be distributed by us in imitation of God, in an indiscriminate, profligate fashion that fails to reflect the differences in worthiness and status that rule the arrangement of a sinful world."[23] This practice of profligate giving,

19. Ibid., 92.
20. Ibid., 6.
21. Ibid., 3.
22. Ibid., 25.
23. Ibid.

mutual rather than competitive, has not dominated global economic practices, but it is visible within Christian teaching and—to some degree—within the broader, secular society: "The whole Christian story, from top to bottom, can be viewed as an account of the production of value and the distribution of goods, following this peculiar noncompetitive shape."[24]

Might Tanner's method of analysis also find meaningful alternatives to a capitalist economy, and thus fresh theological resources, in other places? And might the concept of a theological economy shed light upon secular practices that push back against capitalist practices? Tanner observes, "Theological economy seems a singularly peculiar, wild and unworkable ideal. It is very hard to conceive in practical terms how this theological economy would work, just because it doesn't correspond to anything with which we are already familiar."[25] Although it does not exist in a fully-fledged form, Tanner notes that aspects of it may "infiltrate and subvert" the capitalist system.[26] "Something about the workings of global capitalism hints at the principles of theological economy we have explored; these are points allowing an opening for theological economy. The hints might sometimes be positive intimations and at other times more like rifts or strains in the capitalist fabric."[27] Since *Economy of Grace* was published, the American economy (and the global economy) has been battered, and among the many creative responses to the current economic challenges are three distinctive popular cultural phenomena—rifts and strains in the capitalist fabric—that are the focus of this chapter. Although none are explicitly Christian, each of them rejects the values of consumer culture and thus provides a potential model for Christian theological reflection

24. Ibid., 27.
25. Ibid., 87.
26. Ibid., 90.
27. Ibid., 89.

on economics and on how to recognize and address the dissonance between Christian teaching and ordinary American living.

Zero Waste Home

The first resource to consider as a possible breaking through of theological economy into capitalism is the blog "The Zero Waste Home" (http//www.zerowastehome.com/), whose author, Bea Johnson, published a book of the same name in 2013. Johnson's blog documents the experience of her family and a growing cohort of like-minded households seeking to curb or eliminate their contribution to landfills; her book systematizes their experiences and provides an argument for readers that a Zero Waste household is practical, within reach for ordinary families, and will provide not only monetary savings but also bring dividends in health and richer family experiences.

Along with Johnson, her family (a spouse and two sons) has converted their household and family practices to minimize consumption; although they have a conventionally middle-class income, they own relatively little and are extraordinarily innovative in their daily living. The family does not own a trash can or have garbage collection.[28] They recycle as little as possible, preferring instead to reduce the household's intake of recyclables. Johnson posted on her blog about the contents of the family's quart-sized annual garbage collection; the items the family had been unable to refuse, recycle, compost, or reuse in 2014 included some Band-Aids (applied after vaccinations and a biking accident), the wooden portion of Bea's reusable mascara wand (she makes her own makeup), a passport cover (only the pages were recyclable), "a green plastic tie, found in my yard (dragged under a shoe from somewhere else,

28. Bea Johnson, *The Zero Waste Home* (New York: Scribner, 2013), 17.

maybe?), and the last dust mask we had (now, we use a bandanna instead),"[29] and various other items. Living without creating waste is serious business for Johnson and her family.

Johnson exhorts her readers to simplify their own lives by curbing their acquisition (and disposal) of material objects; her approach is to "refuse what you do not need; reduce what you do need; reuse what you consume; recycle what you cannot refuse, reduce, or reuse; and rot (compost) the rest."[30] In her book, Johnson provides detailed descriptions of how to simplify every area of one's life, from grocery shopping and cooking to entertaining to purchasing cosmetics. She argues for purchasing things that align with the objectives of her life, noting that choosing low-impact food, clothing, and household items is important for a range of reasons: "Where we spend the fruit of our hard labor should more than meet our basic need of filling a pantry shelf; it should also reflect our values. Because ultimately, giving someone your business implicitly articulates this message: 'Your store satisfies *all* my needs and I want you to flourish.' We can vote with our pocketbooks by avoiding wasteful packaging and privileging local and organic products."[31]

To what end does Johnson pursue a Zero Waste lifestyle? Johnson frames her Zero Waste life as one that emphasizes the well-being of her family and the environment over the acquisition of objects. Her book argues that her family's lifestyle subverts the existing capitalist economy, permits them to prioritize the relationships of the family over obtaining, caring for, and financing material goods, and to significantly reduce their environmental impact. Johnson confesses, "Okay, I'll be honest: my rebellious side also gets satisfaction from being able to make do without buying into corporations and their

29. Bea Johnson, "What's in our Family's Jar of Annual Waste?," http://www.zerowastehome.com/2014/11/whats-in-our-familys-jar-of-annual-waste.html (accessed July 20, 2015).
30. Johnson, *Zero Waste Home*, 14.
31. Ibid., 52.

marketing engines. It gives me a sense of freedom, knowing that I do not depend on them, feeling as though I am outsmarting the system in place."[32] This reflects the priorities that Tanner sets out for a theological economy.

Describing a noncommodity gift exchange, Tanner notes: "Unlike commodity exchange, which gives the impression that objects are being brought into relation via the people who own them, here persons are brought into relation by the objects they exchange."[33] The typical capitalist economy prioritizes obtaining objects (often to enhance one's status or comfort) over engaging with human beings or pursuing the well-being of all members of the community. A new outfit, and the status it will bring its owner, is more important in a capitalist system than the well-being of the garment worker or the lack of basic necessities in a poor household. The Zero Waste lifestyle, Johnson argues, permits her to renounce objects, and the capitalist web that brings objects into her ownership, in favor of the relationships in her family and in favor of choosing to buy things that support the livelihood of the farmer or producer, as well as minimizing her family's environmental impact.

How did this transformation occur for Johnson? She writes that her family's journey to a simpler life began with a move to a smaller, more urban home. She became dissatisfied with her comfortable, affluent lifestyle and decided to change the family's priorities. Johnson writes, "I was thirty-two, and deep down I was terrified at the thought that my life had settled and set."[34] She began to disrupt their existence; the couple agreed to move. After selling their large suburban California house, the family put furniture and other belongings in storage, rented an apartment, and began searching for

---

32. Ibid., 39.
33. Tanner, *Economy of Grace*, 51.
34. Johnson, *Zero Waste Home*, 3.

a house in an urban neighborhood.[35] She writes, "I came to realize that most of the things in storage were not missed, that we had spent innumerable hours and untold resources outfitting a house with the unnecessary. Shopping for the previous home had become a (worthless) pastime, a pretext to go out and be busy in our bedroom community.... We had placed too much importance on 'stuff' and we recognized that moving toward simplicity would provide us with a fuller and more meaningful life."[36] In 2008, the family began to change its practices. As Johnson began to focus on a simpler life, she formed the goal of "zero waste," a lifestyle with as little consumer consumption as possible. "I examined what was left in our trash and recycling cans as a directive for our next steps. In the waste bin, I found packaging of meat, fish, cheese, bread, butter, ice cream, and toilet paper. In the recycling, I found papers, tomato cans, empty wine bottles, mustard jars, and soy milk cartons. I set out to eliminate them all."[37] Soon the family's food came home from the grocery store or farmer's market in reusable bags and pre-weighed glass jars, with no packaging required.

Johnson also addressed the family's excess of clothing and other material goods. She recounts with some chagrin her earlier conversion to the marketing standards of the diamond industry; she persuaded her husband to upgrade her diamond engagement ring to one costing the prescribed two months' salary. "Blinded by greed, I gave too much importance to something that could vanish into thin air.... Last year, when I grabbed a flat of tomatoes from the coarse and hardworking hands of the vendor whose fair prices I had bargained, it caught his eye: 'Nice ring,' he said. At that moment, I realized that it no longer suited me.... I have since auctioned it

35. Ibid., 4.
36. Ibid.
37. Ibid., 7.

off which brought me an inexplicable sense of relief."[38] Along with shedding the expensive ring, Johnson reduced the family's wardrobe to what each person needed; the family generally shops at thrift stores for clothing.[39] Tanner argues that this choice supports the theological economy: "Cheap goods for consumers in the developed countries ... come at the expense of continued poverty in the underdeveloped world. Capital drains into the developed countries from the developing ones that need it most."[40] By focusing her family's spending on non-exploitative economic exchanges and resetting the family's expectations about how much is enough, Johnson provides a detailed, attainable model for the theological economy, despite not having been motivated by religious belief. Interestingly, Johnson's choices to reduce her family's waste were the cause of, rather than the result of, her environmentalist and ethical awakening.

In the weeks and months that followed, Johnson experimented with a variety of practices in the pursuit of Zero Waste. She made her own mustard and cheese from scratch; she eliminated both the microwave and the can opener.[41] Sometimes things got complicated: "One conversation with my girlfriend Karine led to kefir making.... Kefir grains are tiny; they look like grains of white rice. But they are high-maintenance and depend on regular feeding. They soon loomed large in our family's life. We came to consider their welfare along with that of our dog, Zizou: Did you feed the kefir grains today? Do we take them camping this weekend? A simple process had snowballed and complicated my life more than I cared to admit."[42] Johnson rejects the ongoing commitment to the kefir grains, and eventually composts them. She regards the experience as

38. Ibid., 114.
39. Ibid., 128-29.
40. Tanner, Economy of Grace, 114.
41. Johnson, Zero Waste Home, 45.
42. Ibid., 39.

useful and interesting, but draws a clear line when the Zero Waste practices begin to undermine her ability to spend time with her family or pursue other aspects of her chosen lifestyle.

Johnson's description of her Lenten practices is especially constructive for the reader interested in an economy of grace. She writes that what excites her about Easter "is the period that precedes it: Lent. Although I do not consider myself a religious person, I recently found that Lent satisfies my spiritual needs and presents and opportunity. It sets aside a forty-day period to test a sustainable idea, or to evaluate a personal attachment to a habit.... I am by no means suggesting that you convert to Christianity, but that you regularly set aside time to try something new every year."[43] For those already practicing Christianity, this renewed approach to Lent is both pragmatic and radical. Tanner points to the "voluntary abnegation of wealth, voluntary poverty, among ascetics and monastic devotees that becomes a sign of grace;"[44] Johnson provides a modern-day strategy for modern people, Christian or not, to open themselves up to this grace.

Thrift Shop

Another pop-culture phenomenon that illuminates the possibilities of a theological economy is the song "Thrift Shop" by the rapper Macklemore and his producer, Ryan Lewis. The song rose to the number one spot on the Billboard charts in January of 2013 and remained there for six weeks, making it Billboard Hot 100's top song of 2013,[45] but it offers a worldview openly critical of American consumer culture and is not typical of hip-hop culture. The song is

43. Ibid., 220.
44. Tanner, *Economy of Grace*, 6.
45. Jay Balfour, "Macklemore and Ryan Lewis' 'Thrift Shop' Billboard's No. 1 Song of the Year," Hip Hop DX, http://www.hiphopdx.com/index/news/id.26608/title.macklemore-and-ryan-lewis-thrift-shop-billboard-s-no-1-song-of-the-year (accessed July 20, 2015).

an unabashed celebration of thrift shopping, where the opportunity for unique self-expression and frugal spending practices are lauded over and against achieving an identity through excessive spending on new, brand-name clothing. The song features artist Michael Wansley, whose artist name is Wanz; prior to recording "Thrift Shop," he was a part time musician, and his full-time livelihood was working as a software test engineer.[46]

The video, produced by Jon Jon Augustavo, Ryan Lewis, and Macklemore,[47] opens with a group of people gathered along an ersatz starting line, presumably waiting for the local thrift shop to open. The crowd of about twenty people includes Macklemore and Lewis and assorted other people poised to shop, mostly young to middle-aged adults, many of whom have somewhat unusual means of conveyance. Macklemore rides a child's bike, Lewis is wearing roller blades, and various other people are perched on children's Big Wheel cycles, pushing a laundry cart, or riding on an office chair or in a child's stroller. Some are walking; one woman carries a large stuffed giraffe. The image of this group of people of varying races and clothing styles is both playful, even ridiculous, and perfectly serious; the parody of hip-hop videos is obvious and unselfconscious. The music begins as the group moves forward.

As the music continues, the scene shifts and heightens the parody: Macklemore, still riding the mint-green child's bicycle, is flanked by two women, and all three are earnestly drinking Slurpees (the Slurpee cups, the bicycle, and one woman's nail polish are all color-coordinated, emphasizing that the thrift-store fashion ethos is not

46. Steven J. Horowitz, "Wanz Q&A: Meet the 'F-ing Awesome' Singer in 'Thrift Shop'," *Billboard*, January 31, 2013, http://www.billboard.com/articles/news/1537520/wanz-qa-meet-the-f-ing-awesome-singer-in-thrift-shop (accessed July 22, 2015).
47. See the video "Thrift Shop," August 29, 2012, https://www.youtube.com/watch?v=QK8mJJJvaes (accessed July 20, 2015). Lyrics transcribed by author. All lyrics quoted with permission.

haphazard, but creative). Macklemore is wearing a highly recognizable and distinct coat made of faux leopard print fabric and what appears to be a real fur hood, which he describes in the song as "leopard mink." (At various points in the video, Lewis wears a full-length fur coat and Macklemore substitutes a fur coat for the leopard/fur coat; there is no shortage of second-hand luxury here.) The women escort Macklemore to a Delorean driven by Ryan Lewis. Its distinctive gull-wing doors open, Macklemore climbs into this obviously-used but still iconic car, and the two men drive to a nightclub. The video's scenes of thrift shopping are interspersed with scenes of Macklemore at the club, having mixed success promoting his thrift-shop style. He confides to the listener about his coat: "Probably shoulda washed this/smells like R. Kelly's sheets/Piss/But shit, it was 99 cents." At this point one of the women flanking him responds with a disgusted expression, unswayed by his frugality. Eventually, near the end of the video, Wanz is positioned in the club scene as the arbiter of cool, dressed in a second-hand peach-colored three-piece suit with darker orange piping on the lapels and singing the chorus, "I'm gonna pop some tags/Only got twenty dollars in my pocket/I, I, I'm huntin'/Lookin' for a come-up/This is fucking awesome." The song simultaneously holds up Macklemore as an alternative to standard hip-hop spending patterns, and slyly positions him as less cool than Wanz.

In the thrift store scenes, which were filmed at a variety of thrift shops in Macklemore's hometown, Seattle,[48] the standard music-video trope of backup dancers is replaced by dancers who are shopping in the aisles of the thrift store. Macklemore happily describes the various items he has purchased (including a kneeboard,

48. Shalini Gujavarty, "Macklemore's Thrift Shop Features Arcade Bar Narwhal," *Seattle Eater*, September 19, 2012, http://seattle.eater.com/2012/9/19/6543827/macklemores-thrift-shop-features-arcade-bar-narwhal (accessed July 20, 2015).

which is the lead-in to three brief scenes of Macklemore on a boat being driven by Wanz, another parody of more typical music videos.) The backup singers reflect a range of ethnic and aesthetic traditions: "sneakerheads" are young Asian men, depicted as awed by Macklemore's white Velcro sneakers. He sings, "I could take some Pro Wings, make them cool, sell those/The sneaker heads would be like 'Ah, he got the Velcros'."[49] When the lyrics next laud Macklemore's leather jacket with the claim "John Wayne, he ain't got nothing on my fringe game, hell no," the music is illustrated with a black child dancing joyfully in a field; a middle-aged, full-figured white woman wearing a polka-dot dress dances to the chorus, displaying a rockabilly aesthetic, and sings while flanked by two young, black men.

In scene after scene of the video, the various shoppers are depicted as joyfully and creatively reclaiming and reconfiguring clothing; despite only having twenty dollars, as the chorus emphasizes, the shoppers are successful in creating a self-presentation that they affirm vigorously. The economic critique of a materialistic culture—and perhaps especially of hip-hop culture, devoted to conspicuous consumption—is clear. The artist speaks from experience; Macklemore describes himself as a lifelong thrift shopper. As he says in an interview with *GQ*,

> When you walk into a thrift store, you cannot have any expectations. Like none of that "Oh, I'm looking for a rain jacket" stuff. Forget it. You're never gonna find a rain jacket that way. You have to be open-minded, and you've gotta dig around the entire store—not just the men's section. Hit up the shoe section, the women's section, the toy section. Some of my best finds have been in sections that weren't meant for me.[50]

49. "Thrift Shop" (see n. 47).
50. Andrew Richdale, "The Macklemore Bible of Thrift-Store Shopping," *GQ*, October 17, 2012.

The nature of thrift shopping, then, is that a person must be creative and diligent, must set aside narrow expectations about what is "meant for" him or herself, and, in so doing, he or she can work around, and even subvert, an economy that is designed to conflate conspicuous consumption of this or that specific item with a person's social status. The song emphasizes the average consumer's objectification and victimization in the standard economy when Macklemore responds to the possibility of buying a Gucci t-shirt for $50. He sings, "I hit the party and they stopped in that motherfucker/ They be like oh! That Gucci, that's hella tight/I'm like Yo! That's 50 dollars for a t-shirt/Limited edition, let's do some simple addition, 50 dollars for a t-shirt, that just some ignorant bitch shit/I call that getting swindled and pimped, shit/I call that getting tricked by business/That shirt's hella dough/and having the same one as six other people in this club is a hella don't."[51] Macklemore both rejects the status of victim to the desire-creating aspects of capitalism, and argues that having the same stuff as everybody else—as one would with a shirt purchased new at the high-end boutique—is actually less appealing and fashionable than having a distinctive shirt. One of the recognizable images on a garment in the video is a picture of Kurt Cobain on a t-shirt worn by a dancer in the thrift store scenes, although whether it is a nod to Cobain's influence on Macklemore, or a cautionary tale about having one's work co-opted and commercialized, or both, is unclear.

What are we to make of Macklemore's take on thrift shopping, and how does it illustrate Tanner's claim that a theological economy may be "peculiar" and "wild" and may emerge to "infiltrate and subvert" the capitalist economy?[52] Like Bea Johnson, Macklemore provides a rationale for a consumer practice that is subversive of

51. "Thrift Shop" (see n. 47).
52. Tanner, *Economy of Grace*, 87, 90.

the prevailing norms. He is less concerned with the environmental impact of shopping at a typical retail store, and focused instead on disconnecting the experience of fitting into a community, of establishing an identity, of being cool, from spending a great deal of money on clothing and other objects. This strategy, of establishing one's sartorial identity with used clothing, is one that the artist's fans are then free to take up. Tanner argues, "Human needs are social; what one needs to live is not equivalent to some bare level of subsistence but to the minimum standard of a good life in a particular society at a particular time."[53] This baseline, she argues, is manipulated by standard capitalist practices that keep consumers in a perpetual state of needing more than they have. What Macklemore's song does is to reconfigure the relationship between what one needs and what one can obtain, without sacrificing his listeners' desire to be part of a community and to represent themselves in that community as they wish.

One effect of this resetting of social norms is to make imitating one's favorite rap star much more affordable; Macklemore is advocating what Tanner describes as "noncompetitive property and possession."[54] Tanner writes, "In this noncompetitive understanding of things, being ourselves as the persons we are and having all that we have for our own good should not come, then, at the expense of our being other peoples' own in community with them."[55] By subverting the accepted competitive practices around owning a Gucci shirt, for example, Macklemore opens up the community of hip-hop fans to include people for whom paying $50 for a shirt would be unthinkable.

The artist appears to be speaking from experience. In

53. Ibid., 38.
54. Ibid., 80.
55. Ibid., 81.

Macklemore's interview with *GQ*, he elaborates on how thrift shopping works: "If anything gets over $12.99, then you really need to evaluate whether this is something you need in your life, because then it is turning into something that's not exactly in the thrift-shop price range, you know?"[56] This inversion of typical capitalist-driven values, where one's expensive possessions are associated with success and happiness and the envy of one's neighbors, creates a model for Macklemore's fans that is compatible with Tanner's vision for noncompetitive giving. She writes, "Without the danger of losing what we have by giving, we are freed up to give to others."[57] If one's (in the case of this successful hip-hop artist, rather high) status is not determined by what one owns, then other people are also invited into a relationship with material goods that is significantly less competitive. Seeing an expensive name brand as a swindle, rather than a status marker, and participating wholeheartedly in the donation and recirculation of goods practiced by thrift stores, permits a non-capitalist strategy for shopping, for establishing status, and for managing one's financial resources. The song's subversion of extremely powerful market forces—the arbiters of coolness—emphasizes creativity and frugality as supportive of human dignity, rather than affirming conspicuous consumption as the determining factor in establishing a person's worth.

Unfuck Your Habitat

A third example of popular culture that provides examples of theological economy is the Tumblr site and blog "Unfuck Your Habitat" (hereafter UfYH). The site, which includes testimonials, cleaning instructions, and responses to reader questions, offers motivation (often in the form of .gifs and photos of completed

---

56. Richdale, "Macklemore Bible of Thrift-Store Shopping."
57. Tanner, *Economy of Grace*, 85.

cleaning projects) and strategies for people with lives that do not conform to cultural standards, typically reflective of middle-class privilege, for housecleaning and home decoration.[58] UfYH offers practical strategies for cleaning, including a system of working and then taking breaks for prescribed periods of time (usually a "20/ 10" or a "45/15," where one works for twenty minutes and then takes a break for ten, or works for forty-five minutes and then relaxes for fifteen), and has cultivated a mutually supportive cleaning community. People submit questions, offer advice and commiseration, and encourage each other through difficult logistical, interpersonal, and emotional experiences. While it is somewhat unconventional, UfYH is an example of solidarity, which Tanner argues "need not have anything to do with physical proximity.... The sufferings or doings of others might also be felt as one's own; what happens to others or what they do becomes a part of one's own story as well."[59] Although the site began as a cleaning website, it has grown into an opportunity for community and a source of significant emotional and practical help for a range of people.

UfYH is emphatically not a glossy "better living" website; it rejects the basic premises of publications like *Martha Stewart Living*, *Dwell*, *Sunset*, or *Better Homes and Gardens*, or websites like Apartment Therapy. UfYH does not cajole readers to turn to Pinterest or HGTV for design or style ideas. In fact, the community grew in response to the overwhelming cultural demand for unattainably chic and expensive home décor. The site's author, a woman who in some posts uses the name "Rachel,"[60] writes,

> There's a weird sort of void in the "taking care of your physical surroundings" stuff, in the archaic 'how to keep a home' and "how to

58. Some UfYH material is also on the blog PersephoneMagazine.com (accessed July 20, 2015).
59. Tanner, *Economy of Grace*, 78.
60. See PersephoneMagazine.com for UfYH posts authored by "Rachel."

be domestic" arenas. It tends to ignore single people, or people without kids, or students, or people with pets, or people with roommates, or people with full-time jobs, or classes, or other shit going on. It assumes everyone is married with kids and one partner is around a lot of the time, and has a lot of time to devote to "housekeeping." Well, we don't all live that life. Very few of us do. Our lives are complicated and sometimes messy, and we're often distracted and overwhelmed and lazy.[61]

The UfYH author and by extension the community of the site represent, as do Macklemore and Bea Johnson, a deliberate rejection of a consumer culture that emphasizes new, expensive, visually appealing, and unattainable aesthetic standards. Instead, UfYH focuses on the power of an individual person to create healthy and supportive physical and emotional surroundings; the visual improvement in the before and after photos is only the most obvious indicator of the system's purpose for users.

UfYH targets people who are not wealthy and not benefitting significantly from a capitalist economy. Some participants are more socially marginal than others, but the common goal is to regain a sense of peace and functionality within one's living space, often against significant odds. Testimonials submitted by users of UfYH frequently describe situations of mental illness, of turmoil within the household, and precarious finances that lead to difficult living conditions. Significantly, the tools promoted on UfYH are not useful only for housecleaning. The site's "about" page notes, "And our homes aren't the only things that need to be unfucked. Our finances, our jobs, our relationships: there's no end to the things we can fuck up. The important thing to remember is that there is nothing that can't be unfucked."[62] The use of the word "our" here is reflective of the ethos of UfYH; a popular feature of the site is the "before" and "after" pictures submitted by users. One person comments along with

61. Unfuck Your Habitat, http://unfuckyourhabitat.tumblr.com/about (accessed July 20, 2015).
62. Ibid.

his or her before and after photos, "I've been living in this as my sick room, too sick to clean it, for at least four years. I'm recovering now, and this is one of the best signs yet—but I couldn't have done it without UfYH. Thank you, UfYH lady, you're the best!"[63]

Another community member writes and notes that, while the site's strategies for cleaning have worked in the past, "what I am having difficulties with now, where my apartment is HORRIBLY cluttered (and gross), is beating myself up, criticizing myself saying I'm a nasty slob etc. and that puts a damper on the energy.... And I end up only cleaning for 5 mins. Which isn't enough when my place is in this state. How do I deal with that? It's detrimental to progress."[64] While this experience may or may not be related to illness, the person is writing to express, and receive support in solving, a genuine problem related to his or her experience of basic household management. Rachel responds, "Negative self-talk is sometimes really hard to overcome. Tell yourself that I (the UfYH lady) know that you're not a nasty slob and that you can be helped and that I think you deserve to live in a place you love."[65] This is more than cleaning advice; it is firm rejection of an identity that reflects failure to meet a social standard that emphasizes appearance, affluence, and capability. This theme is recurrent in the comments and on the site's "about" page: UfYH provides tools that can be used by those struggling with mental illness. Rachel writes,

> Depression ... has its own set of related life issues that my poor arthritic knee has never caused. And one of those is the self-perpetuating cycle of depression and a messy home.... Things are awful. It's a struggle to walk to the bathroom. Making dinner seems more impossible than advanced

---

63. Unfuck Your Habitat, http://unfuckyourhabitat.tumblr.com/post/110721734388/candlesandfish-oh-my-gosh-guys-i-did-a-thing-the (accessed July 20, 1015).
64. Ibid.
65. Unfuck Your Habitat, http://unfuckyourhabitat.tumblr.com/tagged/getting-started (accessed July 20, 2015).

calculus. Anything that's not your couch or your bed might as well be hot lava. And so the mess builds around you. I purposely use the passive voice there because when you're depressed, it seems nearly impossible that you're contributing to the chaos of your house, because that would require energy, and you sure as hell don't have any of that to spare.[66]

What does this have to do with Tanner's envisioned theological economy? An important feature of Tanner's description of God's blessing on human beings is that it is gracious. She writes, "There just aren't any conditions for God's favor.... We are ransomed on the cross from the suffering and oppression in which a debt economy has thrown us; snatched out of a world of deprivation and injustice from which we suffer because of our poverty, our inability to pay what others demand of us; and returned to God's kingdom of unconditional giving."[67] The experience of needing help to manage one's life situation can cause shame and despair; the experience of joining a community that affirms one's capabilities is, according to the participants in UfYH, transformative. The community's central premise is that people who are struggling—with disability, with family or work circumstances, with motivation, with virtually anything—deserve support.

The experience of people living with mental illness, or other kinds of disability, is acknowledged specifically in the "About" section of UfYH:

If you are someone dealing with physical limitations, chronic illness, chronic pain, mental illness, or any other situation that makes getting your living environment under control difficult, please know that you are not lazy, and that we know that "getting off your ass" may not be easy or even possible sometimes. We encourage anyone who has limitations to modify challenges, suggest alternatives, and, above all, put

---

66. Unfuck Your Habitat, http://unfuckyourhabitat.tumblr.com/post/56181930156/the-depression-messy-house-cycle (accessed July 20, 2015).

67. Tanner, *Economy of Grace*, 65.

their health first. If you can only do five or three minutes of unfucking, that's worth celebrating. If you accomplish something that's been modified so you can do it seated or in shorter stages, we want to hear about it.[68]

This practice of modification is also represented under the heading, "Unfucking with a Chronic Illness or Chronic Pain," where the site author emphasizes, "Many members of Team UfYH are living with chronic conditions, mental illness, learning disabilities, physical limitations, and any number of factors that may make traditional 'cleaning' difficult. They've shared their methods of working within those limitations and still making progress on their homes."[69] A reader with significant impairment may take several things away from that statement. First, he or she can participate in this system and in this community. Second, other people with impairments or disabilities have already found ways for the system to work for them, and the modifications they used are available; it is not a solo venture. Third, and perhaps most important, the person learns that he or she has the opportunity to contribute constructively to help others. Tanner argues that this kind of experience is reflective of a theological economy: "When one accepts one's ownership by others, one's sense of self is expanded beyond anything simply one's own. One includes others, incorporates them, so to speak, within one's sense of self.... Knowing that we have ourselves as gifts from God and from all those others in who we are in a community of mutual benefit, we now give to others, rather than withhold from them, by holding what we have simply as our own."[70] The community need not be physical, it need not be comprised of one's neighbors or family members; the community does need to be welcoming, to offer constructive

68. Unfuck Your Habitat, http://unfuckyourhabitat.tumblr.com/about (accessed July 20, 2015).
69. Unfuck Your Habitat, http://www.unfuckyourhabitat.com/unfucking-with-a-chronic-illness-or-chronic-pain/ (accessed July 20, 2015).
70. Tanner, *Economy of Grace*, 82.

support, and to uphold the well-being and dignity of all members, regardless of circumstance.

Thus, the needs of a vulnerable group of people are addressed by the community of this site. As Tanner notes, this is how an economy of grace works: "Our lives as individuals should be constituted and enhanced in their goodness as we share our lives with others in community, identifying ourselves thereby as persons in community with others and not simply persons for ourselves. We perfect one another in community as our efforts to make the most of our own gifts and talents enter into and supplement the similar efforts of others in a combined venture for goods otherwise impossible."[71] Here, the "goods" are not material goods, even for the creator of the site (she offers apps and a donation button, but the site does not accept advertising). Instead the goods include clear strategies for return of one's physical space to a state of order, and a set of tools for managing one's life and tasks that is empowering and constructive.

Conclusion

Each of these popular cultural phenomena—the Zero Waste Home lifestyle that Bea Johnson advocates, the hip-hop song "Thrift Shop," and the lifestyle website UfYH—illustrates some aspect of an economy of grace, over and against a capitalist economy. This theological economy, in turn, reveals something about the nature of God: God provides enough, refusing excess can make one richer rather than poorer, and focusing one's life energy on relationships rather than objects demonstrates something of the love God has for human beings. Embracing an identity marked by repurposing used items rather than spending excessively on new ones reflects the human being's God-given capacity to be creative, and God's

71. Ibid.

provision of sufficient materials to sustain that creativity. Even when the experience of ordinary life feels overwhelming, God provides a community to rally around those who struggle and to remind individuals that they are not alone, that they are worthwhile, and that, whatever their capacities, they can create meaningful lives for themselves and can contribute to the meaning of others' lives. The richness of counter-capitalist popular culture is that it offers a reset baseline, where one's household possessions can be pared down, where one can strategize to live a good life while on the economic margins of a society, where one can say out loud that overspending reflects having been tricked by business. Tanner argues for an economy of grace, where private property is not presupposed and loans are replaced with gifts whose givers imitate the graciousness of God.[72] Johnson, Mackelmore, and Rachel of Unfuck Your Habitat provide an even broader set of possibilities for living out this notion of Christian identity.

72. Ibid., 56.

14

Placards, Icons, and Protests: Insights into Antiracist Activism from Feminist Public Theology

Rosemary P. Carbine

Julia Shields, a 45 year old white woman, went on a shooting spree in Chattanooga, Tennessee, the day after Christmas 2014. Wearing body armor and firing shots at people and at cars through her own vehicle's window, Shields gave chase with police officers in pursuit. She reportedly turned the gun on the officers, but was ultimately arrested without incident or injury. *New York Times* columnist Charles Blow recounted this case and commented that "The American mind has been poisoned, from this country's birth, against minority populations."[1] Racism as the original sin of America has produced a racially polarized nation, which is reflected in popular

---

1. Charles M. Blow, "Privilege of Arrest Without Incident," *The New York Times* January 5, 2015: A17.

perceptions about police treatment: a recent *Washington Post*-ABC News poll showed that while 63% of whites expect equal treatment by police, the majority of Latinos (57%) and blacks (77%) do not.[2] This public perception of racial bias in law enforcement is manifested in reality, and poignantly demonstrated by recent episodes of police brutality directed against black youth and especially but not only men in America.

Michael Brown, an 18 year old black teenager, was fatally shot by Ferguson, Missouri, police in early August 2014. Eric Garner, a 43 year old black man, died in July 2014 after a New York City police officer applied an illegal chokehold while arresting Garner for selling cigarettes. Both Brown and Garner were unarmed. In other cases, John Crawford, a 22 year old black man, held an air rifle (which fires BB pellets) in a Beavercreek, Ohio, Wal-Mart in August 2014, and Tamir Rice, a 12 year old black boy, played with a toy handgun in a Cleveland, Ohio, park in November 2014; neither pointed a gun at anyone or at police when officers shot and killed them both. In still other recent cases, black men like Antonio Martin in Berkeley, Missouri, and Jerame Reid in New Jersey either pointed or in other ways directed guns at police officers, who immediately shot them. Unlike Shields, as Blow notes, "none had the privilege of being 'arrested without incident or injury.' They were all black, all killed by police officers. Brown was shot through the head. Garner was grabbed around the neck in a chokehold, tossed to the ground and held there, even as he pleaded that he couldn't breathe; it was all caught on video. Rice was shot within two seconds of the police officers' arrival on the scene. Crawford, Martin, and Reid were also cut down by police bullets."[3] While an Ohio medical examiner described Rice's death as a homicide, grand juries in the Brown,

2. Ibid.
3. Ibid.

Garner, and Crawford cases decided not to indict the police officers, igniting both nationwide civic conversations and nonviolent protests that oppose the further reification or normalization of racist thinking and living.

This essay seeks to illuminate these conversations and protests sparked by police killings of black men in America in the light of feminist public theology, with particular reference to Kathryn Tanner's reflections on public theology. Stepping away from some social Trinitarian theologies which take immanent Trinitarian relations as a direct religio-political model for human social relations without attending to the differences between divine and human relationality or to the deeply fraught nature of human relations,[4] Tanner instead proposes public theology as a communicative process of religio-political discourse, which parallels her understanding of Christian tradition as a task of continued conversation. This essay addresses and presses beyond discursive public theology in Tanner by exploring rhetorical, symbolic, and prophetic practices of public engagement by nonreligious and interreligious groups in the aftermath of Ferguson, practices which *both* denounce racism and its dehumanizing, death-dealing forms, *and* proclaim black religio-political subjectivity and community.

Can We Talk? Public Engagement as Civic Conversation

In March 2008, then presidential candidate Barack Obama spoke against the backdrop of Independence Hall in Philadelphia not to pronounce a postracial or colorblind politics in America,[5] but to articulate the ways in which persistent racial tensions and

---

4. Kathryn Tanner, *Jesus, Humanity and the Trinity: A Brief Systematic Theology* (Minneapolis: Fortress Press, 2001), 77-83.
5. Obama rejects the description of the present-day U.S. as a colorblind society in *The Audacity of Hope: Thoughts on Reclaiming the American Dream* (New York: Three Rivers Press, 2006), esp. ch. 7.

polarizations tear at the fabric of the U.S. common good. Liberty, equality, and justice are enshrined in America's founding documents, but have not translated easily into American history and reality; the U.S. has witnessed civil war, civil disobedience, and court battles as a means to close the gaps between American political ideals and everyday citizens' experiences. Pointing at these political incongruities, a controversial sermon by Obama's pastor Rev. Jeremiah Wright at Trinity United Church of Christ on the South Side of Chicago surfaced, in which Wright invoked the biblical prophetic tradition of the jeremiad and called for divine retributive justice against America for its original sin of racism, for its broken covenant with its citizens.[6] In his speech, Obama distanced himself from black prophetic religiosity[7] (because Wright appeared to "commit the supreme sin of anti-Americanism") but not from the black church which confirmed and sustained both his own spiritual commitments and his community-based and faith-based organizing for social justice.[8] While jeopardizing the black prophetic tradition,

6. Rosemary Radford Ruether, "Damning America: Right and Left," *Religion Dispatches* May 27, 2009, http://religiondispatches.org/damning-america-right-and-left/ (accessed July 20, 2015).

7. As Cornel West has convincingly argued, "The great irony of our time is that in the age of Obama the grand Black prophetic tradition is weak and feeble.… There is the shift of Black leadership from the voices of social movements to those of elected officials in the mainstream political system.… This neoliberal shift … contains a vicious repressive apparatus that targets those strong and sacrificial leaders, activists, and prophetic intellectuals who are easily discredited, delegitimated, or even assassinated, including through character assassination. Character assassination becomes systemic and chronic, and it is preferable to literal assassination because dead martyrs … elevate the threat to the status quo." See Cornel West, "The State of Black America in the Age of Obama Has Been One of Desperation, Confusion, and Capitulation," *Salon* October 5, 2014, http://www.salon.com/2014/10/05/cornel_west _the_state_of_black_america_in_the_age_of_obama_has_been_one_of_desperation_confusion _and_capitulation/ (accessed July 15, 2015). For recent attempts to reclaim the black prophetic tradition, and to situate King, Wright, and Obama within it, see Angela D. Sims, F. Douglas Powe, Jr., and Johnny Bernard Hill, *Religio-Political Narratives in the United States: From Martin Luther King, Jr. to Jeremiah Wright* (New York: Palgrave Macmillan, 2014).

8. Ruether, "Damning America." Obama provides his religious autobiography with reference to the black church in *The Audacity of Hope*, esp. ch. 6. Since his progressive political campaign, Black scholars have increasingly appraised his two-term presidency critically in light of his policies—Wall Street bailouts, increasing drone military warfare and surveillance, and apparent indifference to rising incarceration rates of poor people. Compare Marvin A. McMickle, ed.,

Obama nonetheless urged a national conversation about race to confront and resolve entrenched and enduring post–Civil Rights era racial inequalities regarding broken schools, growing wealth and income gaps, lack of public services and spaces in urban neighborhoods, and the increased criminalization and incarceration of poor minorities. This conversation would enable all of "we the people" to deliberate and reach consensus about other overarching national issues about terrorism, education, the economy, healthcare, and climate change which touch and transcend racial lines:

> The issues that have surfaced over the last few weeks reflect the complexities of race in this country that we've never really worked through—a part of our union that we have not yet made perfect. And if we walk away now, if we simply retreat into our respective corners, we will never be able to come together and solve challenges like healthcare or education or the need to find good jobs for every American.[9]

From Obama's perspective, this conversation on race could potentially overcome the present U.S. "racial stalemate" if we diagnose both black *and* white resentments, and then build a coalition-based politics of solidarity across race, class, and gender lines around similar issues facing all Americans.

Yet, can elite white Americans even take what Obama identifies as the first step in this conversation on race, and comprehend as well as work to ameliorate the effective history of slavery, legalized segregation, and ongoing racial discrimination? One of the most recent versions of this conversation started in earnest after Ferguson in August 2014. *New York Times* columnist Nicholas Kristof wrote a multi-part series with an accompanying reader blog, which, on my

---

Audacity of Faith: Christian Leaders Reflect on the Election of Barack Obama (Valley Forge, PA: Judson Press, 2009) with Cornel West, *Black Prophetic Fire* (Boston: Beacon Press, 2014).

9. Barack Obama, "A More Perfect Union," March 18, 2008, http://my.barackobama.com/page/content/hisownwords/ (accessed July 20, 2015).

reading, spotlights wider trends in U.S. civil society discourse that hamper this conversation and thus perpetuate, rather than resist, racial inequality.

Parallel to the aftermath of Hurricane Katrina, the U.S. body politic confronted in Kristof's articles its systemic discrimination against (and subsequent disenfranchisement of) people of color through social structures such as healthcare, education, law enforcement and criminal justice systems, and jobs.[10] As a result of these deeply entrenched racialized structures, blacks have a shorter life expectancy, get less access to schools with advanced math and science courses, are suspended and expelled from school more often than whites, and earn about 59% of the median household income of non-Hispanic whites. Studies by the National Bureau of Economic Research have also shown that black men are more often imprisoned than employed: "nearly 70% of middle-aged black men who never graduated from high school have been imprisoned."[11] Also, "black families have on average only about 6% as much wealth as white households,... only 44% of black families own a home compared with 73% for white households."[12]

White folks responded to this portrait of persistent racial inequalities in post-Jim Crow, post-Civil Rights era America with what sociologist Eduardo Bonilla-Silva calls white habitus, or the socialized semantic strategies and styles that elite whites utilize in order to misrecognize or ignore racialized social structures of inequality and injustice, and thereby safeguard their racial group

10. Nicholas Kristof, "Is Everyone A Little Bit Racist?," *The New York Times* August 28, 2014: A25.
11. Nicholas Kristof, "When Whites Just Don't Get It," *The New York Times* August 31, 2014: SR11. For more on the racialization of mass incarceration in the U.S., see Nicholas Kristof, "When Whites Just Don't Get It, Part 3," *The New York Times* Oct. 12, 2014: SR1, and Michelle Alexander, *The New Jim Crow: Mass Incarceration in the Age of Colorblindness* (New York: The New Press, 2012).
12. Nicholas Kristof, "When Whites Just Don't Get It, Part 4," *The New York Times* November 16, 2014: SR1.

interests without sounding blatantly racist. These strategies and styles correlate with some signposts of American civil religion, such as appeals to equal opportunity (to erode affirmative action policies although many minorities are underrepresented in various jobs and schools), to freedom (to justify segregated neighborhoods and schools while not dealing with the multiple inequalities in those same neighborhoods and schools), to diversity (to associate certain family ideals, work ethics, and ways of life with minoritized cultures and thereby naturalize the racist status quo), and to progress (to minimize or outright deny the racist socio-economic and political systems in contemporary America).[13] For example, Kristof's white readers appealed to present-day personal responsibility rather than the socio-structural legacy of U.S. slavery and its effective racist history (such as segregation and the prison system) to account for racial economic and education gaps; pointed to Asian immigrant groups as model minorities for black educational success; invoked racial stereotypes of blacks (as lazy) as an explanatory myth for black unemployment and mass incarceration in Protestant "pull yourself up by your own bootstraps" work-ethic America; and, emphasized the progress in African American civil rights in the last 50 years epitomized by the election of President Barack Obama.[14] As one white reader commented, "I am tired of the race conversation. It has exasperated me. Just stop. In so many industries, the racial ceiling has been shattered. Our president is black. From that moment on, there were

13. Eduardo Bonilla-Silva, *Racism without Racists: Colorblind Racism and the Persistence of Racial Inequality in America*, 4th ed. (New York: Rowman and Littlefield, 2014), 73-78. See pp. 151-52, 171-72 on white habitus, and see also ch. 4 for an in-depth discursive analysis of these conversational styles which "show that whites explain the product of racialized life (segregated neighborhoods, schools, and friendship networks) as nonracial outcomes and rely on the available stylistic elements of color blindness to produce such accounts" (111). I associate these styles with elite whites, because, as Bonilla-Silva notes, white working class folks, in particular women, find common cause with blacks in resisting race and class-based inequities.

14. Nicholas Kristof, "When Whites Just Don't Get It, Part 2," *The New York Times* September 7, 2014: SR11.

no more excuses."[15] This reader, akin to others which Kristof described throughout this series, dismissed the multiple ways in which historic oppressions in the U.S. continue to complicate our present and steadily growing inequalities. In sum, white habitus means that most whites operate in what Bonilla-Silva terms "a world of racism without racists," that is, they agree with racial equality "but are quietly oblivious to injustice around them.... We are not racists, but we accept a system that acts in racist ways."[16] White habitus, or these conversational styles about race, thus erects seemingly insurmountable roadblocks to these national conversations.

At the conclusion of his multi-part series, Kristof supported the creation of an American Truth and Reconciliation Commission, modeled on the similar commission created in post-apartheid South Africa. This commission, recommended Kristof, should hold televised hearings and release a report with "evidence-based solutions to boost educational outcomes, improve family cohesion, and connect people to jobs."[17] Such a commission depends on a thriving political culture rooted in a deliberative model of democracy, in which all citizens engage in communicative practices of reasoned dialogue and debate about socially significant issues, eventually reaching consensus. Leading public theologians contend that Christians are better prepared to engage in this communicative practice of rational argument because they already constitute a community of shared inquiry, interpretation, and debate. The church expresses and

---

15. Kristof, "When Whites Just Don't Get It, Part 4."

16. Kristof, "When Whites Just Don't Get It, Part 3." See Bonilla-Silva, *Racism without Racists*, ch. 1. Kristof also describes white habitus as follows: "the presumption on the part of so many well-meaning white Americans that racism is a historical artifact. They don't appreciate the overwhelming evidence that centuries of racial subjugation still shape inequity in the 21st century.... One element of white privilege today is obliviousness to privilege, including a blithe disregard of the way past subjugation shapes present disadvantage." Kristof, "When Whites Just Don't Get It, Part 4."

17. Nicholas Kristof, "When Whites Just Don't Get It, Part 5," *The New York Times* November 30, 2014: SR 9.

embodies a community of inquiry that equips people with conversational practices consonant with dialogical practices of democratic debate in U.S. public life. Actively deliberating among alternative visions of religious life intersects with actively deliberating among alternative visions of public life.[18]

This communicative approach to U.S. public life and Christianity's contributions to it, as described above, correspond with and are advanced by Kathryn Tanner's notion of Christian tradition as an argumentative task. Tradition in recent theologies is defined in terms of both content (Latin: *tradita*) and process (Latin: *traditio*), that is, comprising both inherited Christian texts, beliefs, and practices as well as the actual transmission of these inherited texts, beliefs, and practices across different times and places. These two aspects of tradition, materiality and performance, have been characterized in various ways in the history of Christian thought. At times, tradition has been portrayed as a uniform, unchanging consensus about the materials that shape and determine the performance of Christian identities and ways of life. To disrupt this fixed, universalized content of tradition—this deposit of faith—associated with Western European Christianities, tradition has been construed at other times through the local, contextual, diverse, and divergent nature of Christian groups. Besides highlighting either the stability or the particularity of the material content of tradition, tradition has been treated at still other times in Christian thought as the dynamic performance of receiving and transmitting inherited Christian materials and ways of life in and in light of different socio-historical situations and issues. Invoking this post-modern Christian approach to tradition, Tanner regards tradition as style or as invention in order to emphasize the constructive role that agents (whether individuals or groups) play

---

18. See Rosemary P. Carbine, "*Ekklesial* Work: Toward a Feminist Public Theology," *Harvard Theological Review* 99, no. 4 (2006): 433-55, esp. 437-41.

in recrafting and reworking Christian materials and ways of life in response to particular times, places, and concerns.[19] Tradition is not simply fabricated, thereby undermining the importance of longstanding Christian beliefs and practices. Rather, according to Tanner, framing tradition as style and invention better situates Christianity as always already a cultural product and a part of culture—as a task that is part of our ongoing shared struggle to engage and make meaningful sense of the world from within a variety of inherited resources.[20] Tanner interprets this task of re/constructing Christian tradition and identity as "an argument over how to elaborate the claims, feelings, and forms of action around which Christian life revolves.... It is an argument that is engaged throughout the whole of Christian social practices, not just in some specialized intellectual sphere.... In order for such a common project of argument to be viable despite substantive disagreements among its participants, something like the community of solidarity and hope ... may be required."[21] Christian communities, understood by Tanner as communities bound together by argument, socialize their members with certain conversational, or better disputational, virtues, such as humility and open-mindedness (to listen to and entertain all interpretations and claims), mutual accountability (to correct and be corrected by others), responsibility (not only for embracing conflict but also continuing the conversation with others across different times and places), and courage and hope (for recognition amid conflict).[22]

---

19. Tanner, *Theories of Culture: A New Agenda for Theology*, Guides to Theological Inquiry (Minneapolis: Fortress Press, 1997), 87-92, 144-51. Moreover, an emphasis on style and invention reinforces the inherent interactions of different religions and cultures within Christian tradition; in other words, the interactions between religious and other cultures are intrinsic to the creative re/making of Christian traditions (110-19).
20. Ibid., 151-55.
21. Ibid., 125.
22. Ibid., 151-55, 172-75.

This discursive vision of both public and Christian life, as well as their associated communicative practices and virtues of debate, may provide strong faith-based taproots for overcoming white habitus and participating in Kristof's commission. But, this "spiritual spectacle in which sins are confessed and blame taken and burdens lifted"[23] is not likely to take place. As feminist and womanist theologians of U.S. public life have argued, deliberative democracy trades on and perpetuates patriarchal ideologies of citizenship; conversation partners must conform to privileged gendered, raced, and classed social constructs of political subjectivity and agency.[24] Moreover, prior U.S. Congressional hearings—an analogue to Kristof's commission—have vividly revealed the persistent political marginality of African American communities affected, for example, by Hurricane Katrina and by FEMA's failures.

U.S. Congressional hearings about Katrina and its aftermath a decade ago underscored the theo-political significance of subaltern narratives as an important means for marginalized peoples *both* to reclaim political recognition and regain political participation in U.S. public life, *and* to interrelate personal and communal well-being, that is, to tell and weave personal stories into a collective story with potentially national impact on the common good.[25] In December 2005, a bipartisan Congressional committee listened to New Orleans' victim-survivors and community activists recount their stories of FEMA's hyper-militarized and grossly mismanaged response to Katrina, in which mainly African American citizens were displaced,

23. Charles M. Blow, "A Kaffeklatsch on Race," *The New York Times* February16, 2015: A17.

24. Carbine, "*Ekklesial* Work," 442–45.

25. Elsewhere, I have offered critical philosophical, feminist, sociological, and theological reflections on narrative, especially in feminist, womanist, and *mujerista* theologies, in an effort to construct an explicitly feminist theological interpretation of political participation and subjectivity. See Rosemary P. Carbine, "Turning to Narrative: Toward a Feminist Theological Interpretation of Political Participation and Personhood," *Journal of the American Academy of Religion* 78, no. 2 (2010): 375-412.

interned, and/or abandoned, lacking food, water, shelter, and sanitary facilities. Testimony in the Katrina hearings educated the broader U.S. public about racial vulnerability and disposability in the wake of natural and subsequent social disasters; moreover, these hearings rebuilt relationships, enabling nationwide recognition, empathy, and deeper solidarity with African American communities. These religio-political narratives functioned in an irruptive and constructive way: they broke open political space for hearing and empathizing with excluded peoples and stories from dominant U.S. politics, and thereby began to reconfigure our public discourse and our common life. Nevertheless, when the victim-survivors and activists attempted to connect FEMA's failed response to Katrina into a larger socio-historical legacy of practices associated with the slave trade in New Orleans (which laid a socio-historical foundation for the city's present-day race and class structural relations), they could not build coalition politics or political solidarity with U.S. legislators. Despite reasoned and evidenced-based arguments, Congressional leaders frankly did not believe the witnesses' narratives, thereby failing in part to face the complex realities of structural racism in pre- and post-Katrina New Orleans, and leaving little hope for Kristof's recommended commission to provide a much needed public forum to do the same in the present crisis.

Rational, evidenced-based civic discourse in conventional U.S. public forums about racism and antiracism, whether in the media (Kristof's blog) or in U.S. Congressional hearings (after Katrina), appears to have reached an impasse, yet again. Other modes of public engagement at times mediated by religious groups—which I have elsewhere elaborated from a feminist theological perspective as rhetorical, symbolic, and prophetic practices of public engagement—are surfacing in salient ways.

Walk the Talk: Other Practices of Public Engagement

The protests began in Ferguson in August 2014, calling for both reform of police tactics as well as accountability for police brutality. In August, October, and again in November, clergy from different faith traditions (in coordination with about 170 actions around the country) marched alongside and accompanied protesters, both to decry the criminalization of black men and to testify to the truth from different religious perspectives that black lives matter. Racist stereotypes of black men as criminals or in other ways aggressive threats also extend to African-Americans who serve as police officers. In a Reuters interview with 25 African American male NYPD officers, all except one recounted harsh treatment by fellow cops, ranging from unjustified stop-and-frisks to having guns pointed at them. A 2010 New York State report showed that about 14 officers nationwide were killed by fellow cops in mistaken identity shootings since 1995, and the majority of these officers were of color. Finally, recent studies by ProPublica reported that black men are shot and killed by police about 20% more often that white men.[26] Religious leaders thus proclaimed this truth about the equal dignity of black lives

> in the face of racism—that fundamental lie that runs through American history. In the Jim Crow era, the false claim that some people matter more than others was proclaimed from every drinking fountain, voting booth, and restaurant counter.... [Now] we are swimming in a sea of deception and spin. That peaceful protesters are criminals, that tanks are needed on suburban streets, that jaywalking is a capital offense. It is vital in this context to lay hold of a truth that cannot be undone by media representation, by grand jury decisions, by legislation, or by indifference.[27]

26. These interviews, reports, and studies are recounted in Nicholas Kristof, "Race, the Police, and Propaganda," *The New York Times* January 11, 2015: SR1.

27. Shannon Craigo-Snell, "What the Ferguson Protests Mean for Religious Progressive Activism,"

While different religions express this transcendent truth differently, interfaith civic engagement in Ferguson was neither founded upon conformity to American civic religion nor preceded by interreligious dialogue. Instead, as Shannon Craigo-Snell writes, "we just prayed. With our words, with our hearts, and with our feet."[28]

In the wake of the grand jury decisions that exonerated police officers, #BlackLivesMatter protests took place across the United States. During the first two weeks of Advent in 2014, churches participated in faith-based protests in response to these grand jury decisions which so sharply demonstrated pervasive racist structures in America. On November 30 in St. Louis, some churches offered Lay It on the Table services, a public forum in which congregants spoke and listened to one another about their deepest fears and hopes in these terrible times. After "'laying down their lives' on the sacramental table, the congregations celebrated the sacrament at this table."[29] The Eucharist, or the re-membering of the church as the body of Christ through the consumption of blessed ritual elements of bread and wine, paved the way for the re-membering or the revitalization of the U.S. body politic suffering from the scandal of racism: "Perhaps conversations started during [these] services … will make their way into homes, and workplaces, and educational institutions, and civic forums, until people can envision change in the structures that constitute our lives together."[30]

Religion Dispatches November 26, 2014, http://religiondispatches.org/what-the-ferguson-protests-mean-for-religious-progressive-activism/ (accessed July 20, 2015).

28. Ibid. Similarly, the late Latina *mujerista* theologian Ada María Isasi-Díaz portrayed the praxis-based struggle for justice in spiritual terms as prayer. See Isasi-Díaz, "*Luchar por la Justicia Es Rezar*—To Struggle for Justice is to Pray," in *Mujerista Theology: A Theology for the 21st Century* (Maryknoll, NY: Orbis Books, 1996), 29–34.

29. Rick Nutt, "Ferguson Congregations 'Lay It on the Table,' Taking a Step Toward Honest Dialogue," *Sightings* December 4, 2014, https://divinity.uchicago.edu/sightings/ferguson-congregations-lay-it-table-taking-step-toward-honest-dialogue-rick-nutt (accessed July 20, 2015).

30. Ibid.

On December 7, Father Michael Pfleger of Saint Sabina Catholic Church on Chicago's South Side urged and lead his parishioners in acts of nonviolent civil disobedience, marching in and thereby disrupting status quo daily traffic at the intersection of South Racine Avenue and West 79th Street. Before exiting the church, Father Pfleger, during morning services, said that "It is no coincidence to me that Michael Brown lifted his hands up because he understood what we know, when your hands are up its reaching to the strength and the power of who it is that holds us." Led by the youth group at Saint Sabina, the congregants repeatedly chanted "Black life matters" and "Hands up, don't shoot," performed a die-in in the street, and sang Amazing Grace while walking back to the church.[31] Characterizing the protests that occurred around Chicago and briefly halted ordinary daily life on the North, South, and West Side of the city, Pfleger argued that "The church, the synagogue, the mosque are supposed to be the conscience of a society.... If we do not speak out, and if we remain silent, if we do not show our outrage with this, then I think the church is going to become irrelevant."[32] In addition to this socio-ethical role of religion in U.S. public life,[33] Ruth Goring of Living Water Community Church in Chicago's Rogers Park neighborhood

---

31. Stephanie K. Baer, "Chicago Pastors Lead Protests over Deaths by Police in Ferguson, NYC," *Chicago Tribune* December 7, 2014, http://www.chicagotribune.com/news/local/breaking/ct-chicago-protests-1208-20141207-story.html (accessed July 20, 2015).

32. Mike Krauser, "Pfleger Wants Churches to Lead Protests of Ferguson, NYC Police Killing Cases," CBS Chicago, December 4, 2014, http://chicago.cbslocal.com/2014/12/04/pfleger-wants-churches-to-lead-protests-of-ferguson-nyc-police-killing-cases/ (accessed July 20, 2015).

33. Pfleger echoed Martin Luther King, Jr.'s argument for U.S. Christian churches to engage in struggles for African-American civil rights or otherwise run the theo-political risk of further scarring the body of Christ and of becoming an irrelevant social club. See Martin Luther King, Jr., "Letter from a Birmingham Jail (1963)," in *I Have A Dream: Writings and Speeches That Changed the World*, ed. James M. Washington (New York: Harper Collins, 1992), 83-100, esp. 95-98. Kristin Heyer overviews various understandings of the relationships between religion and U.S. public life from the perspectives of political theory, Christian theology, and sociology in *Prophetic and Public: The Social Witness of U.S. Catholicism* (Washington, DC: Georgetown University Press, 2006), 1-25.

articulated a theological—specifically, christological, ecclesiological, and anthropological—rationale for faith-based nonviolent civic engagement during these harsh but significant times: "Jesus calls us to stand up for each other and we learn as members of the church that when one part of our body—which is the body of Christ—suffers, then we all suffer."[34]

Within a week, nationwide marches coincided on December 13 in Washington, DC, and New York. In Washington, nearly 10,000 people occupied Pennsylvania Avenue, and in New York protesters packed Washington Square, with similar chants and cries for justice despite these grand jury decisions. Speaking at the Washington rally sponsored by the National Action Committee, the NAACP, and the Urban League, Rev. Al Sharpton called "this a march for the rights of the American people." Gwen Carr, Garner's mother, stressed the racial and religious diversity of the march, calling it "a history-making moment. We need to stand like this at all times." Sybrina Fulton, the mother of Trayvon Martin—the 17 year old black student who was shot and killed by a neighborhood watch volunteer in Florida in 2012—urged the protesters to continue this work for justice: "This is not something new that started.... Don't just come to the rally and go home.... It cannot stop here."[35]

African-American churches simultaneously staged their own in-church protests, which resonated throughout the U.S. public square. On Black Lives Matter Sunday, organized by many historically African-American churches to occur the day after U.S. nationwide nonviolent protests and demonstrations, church members wore black or T-shirts with the slogans "Black Lives Matter" and "I Can't Breathe" to services on December 14: "Men at the West Angeles

---

34. Baer, "Chicago Pastors Lead Protests."
35. Matt Hansen, "Marches Against Police Killings Draw Thousands in Washington, New York," *Los Angeles Times* December 13, 2014, http://www.latimes.com/nation/nationnow/la-na-march-police-violence-20141212-story.html (accessed July 20, 2015).

Church of God in Christ in Los Angeles stood more than four rows deep around the altar for a special blessing."[36] Mostly white churches within the Assemblies of God, a major U.S. branch of Pentecostalism, expressed solidarity with black churches in their community: "Rev. George O. Wood, head of the Assemblies of God … asked churchgoers to take part…. 'Whatever your opinion of those controversial [grand jury] decisions, can we stand with our brothers and sisters and affirm the value of black lives generally and of their lives specifically?'"[37]

On New Year's Eve 2014 in New York, protesters marched from Union Square to Times Square, carrying placards which read "we can't breathe," recalling Garner's death by a police chokehold and calling for justice amid the increased militarization of police tactics. On the same night in Boston, Massachusetts, protesters carried similar placards and staged a die-in during First Night celebrations, in which protesters laid on the ground recalling Brown's death in the street after he was shot. In both nonviolent protests, some participants, perhaps still in vigil, lit candles, not only in prolonged Advent-like anticipation of a new year but also in hope for justice for these victims and their families as well as ultimately for equal treatment by police.

Finally, protesters marked Martin Luther King Day in January 2015 with nationwide calls to action that included a sit-in on Peachtree Street in Atlanta near Ebenezer Baptist Church and die-ins in New York's Union Square, as well as in Boston Common. At a thousand-strong gathering in Harlem, a #BlackLivesMatter march broadcasted King's speeches as they walked through the Upper East Side.[38] Together with smaller protests in Chicago's Magnificent Mile

---

36. Associated Press, "Black Churches Protest Police Slayings of Michael Brown, Eric Garner with Prayer," December 14, 2014, http://www.cleveland.com/nation/index.ssf/2014/12/black_churches_protest_police.html (accessed July 20, 2015).
37. Ibid.
38. Michael Paulson, "Martin Luther King's Birthday Marked by Protests over Deaths of Black

and in front of the White House, these actions "demanded that the traditional holiday rituals of speechmaking, community service, and prayer breakfasts give way to denunciations of injustice and inequality," calling for police reforms, educational funding for high need schools, and an increased minimum wage.[39] In Atlanta, "the protesters argued that the holiday had become corrupted by corporate involvement, diluting Dr. King's ideas about economics as well as race. With signs, slogans and shouts, they inserted themselves into the annual parade.... Several times, the group sat and lay en masse in the middle of the street, raising fists toward the air."[40] Near Ebenezer Baptist Church, protesters carried a cardboard coffin to the stage during a service and chanted "black people are dying."[41]

This snapshot of the protests between August 2014 and January 2015 described above exemplifies what I have developed elsewhere as rhetorical practices of public engagement.[42] Rhetorical practices of public engagement encompass a variety of communicative genres that gain public recognition for, give voice to, and urge solidarity with minoritized and marginalized peoples too often denied political subjectivity and agency. Indeed, the protests since August 2014 embody what feminist philosopher and critical theorist Judith Butler terms "modes of address." As Butler explains, "a mode of address is quite simply a way of speaking ... [or] a general way of approaching another.... We address each other with gesture, signs, and movement, but also through media and technology."[43] As a counter-

Men," *The New York Times* January 19, 2015, http://www.nytimes.com/2015/01/20/us/king-holiday-events-include-air-of-protest-over-deaths-of-black-men.html (accessed July 20, 2015).

39. Ibid.
40. Ibid.
41. Ibid.
42. Rosemary P. Carbine, "Public Theology: A Feminist Anthropological View of Political Subjectivity and Praxis, " in *Questioning the Human: Toward a Theological Anthropology for the 21st Century*, ed. Lieven Bove, Yves de Maeseneer, and Ellen van Stichel (New York: Fordham University Press, 2014), 160.

address to the predominant racist hermeneutics which views and treats people of color as not belonging to the U.S. body politic, as a threat to the U.S. way of life, or, worse, as less than fully human and thereby lacking political subjectivity, the chants, placards, and T-shirts with slogans which said or read "black lives matter," "hands up, don't shoot," and "I/we can't breathe" signify a rhetorical practice to recognize and reclaim black humanity, and thereby reassert black political subjectivity.

As Butler queries in her book *Precarious Life*, "the question that preoccupies me in the light of recent global violence is, Who counts as human? Whose lives count as lives?"[44] Critics of the protests have asserted that all lives matter, including the lives of police officers gunned down in New York City and Ferguson in apparent retaliatory violence for police brutality. Yet, all lives matter parallels the U.S. constitutional claim that all men are created equal, a foundational part of the American mythos and ethos which has yet to be fully instantiated and which many social movements and subsequent constitutional amendments have aimed to fully realize. Akin to past movements for abolition, suffrage, and civil rights, "we have to foreground those lives that are not mattering now, to mark that exclusion, and militate against it. Achieving that universal, 'all lives matter,' is a struggle."[45] The counter-address of the protests—black lives matter—runs contrary to both historical and ongoing U.S. racist realities and their accompanying institutionalized and in other ways normalized discourses about people of color that degrade, disenfranchise, and consistently dispose of black lives,

43. George Yancy and Judith Butler, "What's Wrong with 'All Lives Matter'?," *The New York Times* January 12, 2015, http://opinionator.blogs.nytimes.com/2015/01/12/whats-wrong-with-all-lives-matter/?_r=0 (accessed July 20, 2015).
44. Ibid. See Judith Butler, *Precarious Life: The Powers of Mourning and Violence* (New York: Verso, 2004).
45. Yancy and Butler, "What's Wrong with 'All Lives Matter'?"

because they differ from dominant race, gender, class, sexual, and other norms or identity markers of citizenship and personhood.

Often converging with and reinforcing the message of rhetorical practices but in a signs-based way, symbolic practices stress, as I have argued, the sociopolitical significance and implications of central religious symbols in order to construct a transcendent normative moral framework of shared rights and responsibilities and thereby shore up as well as begin to repair our public life.[46] As sketched above, protesters in street rallies and marches re-interpreted "hands up, don't shoot" as a religious symbol of prayer. Church and street vigils gathered black men for rituals of remembrance and blessing. Demonstrators performed die-ins, for example, by inserting ritual memorials into MLK Day celebrations. Finally, eucharistic celebrations re-membered the church as the broken and restored body of Christ, offering a powerful religio-political resource to re-narrate socio-political fragmentation *and* begin, albeit in small grassroots ways, to reconcile all bodies in the U.S. body politic. In all these ways, this faith-based antiracist activism *both* challenged racism and its multiple dehumanizing as well as death-dealing forms in American life *and* recovered the role of religion in a new social justice movement rooted in part in faith-based notions of equality and solidarity. Moreover, this new antiracist movement can be characterized as religious because people of different faiths are involved, the protesters engage in prayer, liturgy, and faith-based nonviolent protest training in preparation for political action, and, most importantly, they "stak[e] a truth claim about the value of black life that transcends the rhetoric and realities of American culture."[47]

Re-membering relationality through eucharistic symbols serves as a theological starting point to confront and correct what undoes

46. Carbine, "Public Theology," 160–61.
47. Craigo-Snell, "What the Ferguson Protests Mean."

this truth: our collective blindness to the growing polarities and inequalities in U.S. society not only around race but also gender, class, sexuality, religion, and national identity. As womanist theologian M. Shawn Copeland argues, these "body marks" are framed historically by patriarchy, slavocracy, empire, and globalization in order to disrupt and devalue our relations by reducing most of humanity to parts to be cannibalized for the pleasure and profit of the few.[48] Thus, reconciling—or re-membering—our bodies from a Christian perspective takes place by ritually consuming and becoming the body of Christ, which incorporates and embraces all bodies, and thereby provides a symbolic icon of social change and transfiguration, not only of personal bodies but also of the body politic. Enacting eucharistic solidarity stands, for Copeland, as a countersign to violence against bodies, and thus demands radical Christian socio-political engagement for justice.[49]

In addition to eucharistic symbols, black theologians have identified Trinitarian theology as a religio-political symbol that can aid and abet the social repair of U.S. public life. Reframing black identity by the "God ... who calls us into relationship with the divine, reconciles us to the divine, and then helps to sustain us in that relationship"[50] provides a theological way to ensure the complexity of black identities, rather than the conformity of black identities to particular idealized standards of blackness, or whiteness for that matter. Moreover, understanding God as inherently relational through the doctrine of *perichoresis*, or the way in which the Trinitarian persons engage in a divine dance of "mak[ing] space

---

48. M. Shawn Copeland, *Enfleshing Freedom: Body, Race, and Being* (Minneapolis: Fortress Press, 2010), 29–38, 56–57, 65–66.
49. Ibid., 81–83. For a ritual re-membering of bodies with theological implications for creation and with political implications for re-creating the socio-political order, see 51–53.
50. Sims, Powe, and Hill, *Religio-Political Narratives in the United States*, 89.

for one another in community," creates a model of "a dynamic and relational community [which] will change how we dialogue publicly."[51] A God constituted by a divine dance of mutual co-equal relationship acts as an analogy to emulate, not an exact blueprint to directly imitate—*pace* Tanner's concerns noted earlier—in our own negotiated and improvised dances of public conversation. Due to our persistently broken relations, our conversations about race, when shaped by the notion of a perichoretic God, demand "calls ... to action ... going around the room and inviting those left out of the floor. It may require transporting some to the dance or moving the dance to where they are located."[52] While Tanner eschews social Trinitarian theologies for too easily mapping divine relations onto human relations, black theologians—as well as feminist and womanist theologians[53]—are keenly aware of the finite and fraught nature of human relations. Thus, they appeal to Trinitiarian theology to testify to a deep truth about human beings as made in the image of a relational God, and thereby expose how U.S. political culture and common life damage and distort that relationality from a religio-political perspective.

Finally, in keeping with scriptural studies of prophetic traditions, prophetic practices as I have elsewhere explained criticize or challenge injustices in public life and simultaneously energize or engage in practices that both imagine and live into—or, in feminist theological words, perform—hope in more just future alternative possibilities for our common life.[54] Indeed, undoing U.S. racist social structures, or undoing whiteness as the norm of being human and

51. Ibid., 90-91.
52. Ibid., 92.
53. For example, see Karen Baker-Fletcher, *Dancing with God: The Trinity from a Womanist Perspective* (St. Louis: Chalice Press, 2006); and Catherine Mowry LaCugna, *God For Us: The Trinity and Christian Life* (New York: HarperCollins, 1993).
54. Carbine, "Public Theology," 161-62.

subsequently of human rights, entails not only being socialized with a new set of civic virtues and being schooled in the effective history of black oppression and struggles, but also being willing to practice an ethical and political solidarity.[55] As Butler puts it, "On the streets, we see a complex set of solidarities ... that seek to show what a concrete and living sense of bodies that matter can be."[56] The protests since August 2014 can be portrayed as public assemblies that signify in their interracial and interreligious character the inclusive, just, and egalitarian U.S. public life that these protests seek to incarnate and create.

These racially and religiously diverse protests across the U.S. did not reach consensus and then articulate a transcendent truth claim about the dignity of human life through interreligious dialogue; rather, the socio-political implications of differing religious traditions motivated these political actors and actions, and consequently wrought a new, albeit fleeting, community. As Kathryn Tanner contends, public theology examines and evaluates the socially and politically significant conclusions of religious claims for human dignity and flourishing.[57] Focusing on the public/political conclusions of religious claims for their critical, practical, and transformative implications on public life does not altogether occlude the theological dimensions of these claims. Theology is not necessarily sidestepped or overlooked in favor of its critical and practical effects, especially if we treat these effects as faith-based contributions to a more transformative vision of public life.

For example, more than 30 African American presidents and deans of U.S. theological schools reflected on the religio-political conclusions of Christian God-talk at their annual meeting at Shaw

---

55. Yancy and Butler, "What's Wrong with 'All Lives Matter'?"
56. Ibid.
57. Kathryn Tanner, "Public Theology and the Character of Public Debate," *Annual of the Society of Christian Ethics* (1996): 79–101, esp. 87–91, 94–96.

University Divinity School. Beneath a picture of a protest marcher carrying a placard that read "God Can't Breathe," African American leaders in theological education recounted, in a breathless rhythm reminiscent of King's own sermonic and rhetorical style, the recent events which galvanized their theological call to engaged socio-political action:

> From a manger in Bethlehem, a Bantustan in Soweto, a bus in Montgomery, a freedom Summer in Mississippi, a bridge in Selma, a street in Ferguson, a doorway and shots fired in Detroit, a Moral Monday in Raleigh, an assault in an elevator in Atlantic City, an office building in Colorado Springs, a market in Paris, a wall in Palestine, a pilgrimage to the shrine of Rincon and a restoration of ties between Cuba and the United States on December 17th, the kidnapping and assault of young school-aged girls and the reported killing of 2000 women, children and men in Nigeria, a new generation of dream defenders, a transgender teen's suicide note, to our abuse of the environment—God sends a sign—a Kairos moment. The racial climate in the United States, and the respect for our common humanity everywhere, is clearly in decline.[58]

Appealing to both foundational principles in the U.S. Constitution regarding a divinely-created equal creation and a common commitment to liberty and justice and for all, these leaders called on the U.S. Congress to model civility and humanity in politics and they called on local leaders as well as ordinary citizens to reject practices which contradict these constitutional claims, instead embracing King's "beloved community" grounded in the protection of human rights. These leaders particularly counseled "churches and every house of faith to challenge their members and communities to live out an inclusive commitment to love God, self, the neighbor-enemy, and creation across any and all boundaries that would dehumanize,

---

58. "An Open Letter to Presidents and Deans of Theological Schools in the United States," January 17, 2015, http://kineticslive.com/2015/01/an-open-letter-to-presidents-and-deans-of-theological-schools-in-the-united-states/ (accessed July 20, 2015).

alienate, and separate."[59] On my reading, the protests since August 2014 embody such prophetic action across racial and many other lines that divide rather than unite us in community.

Efficacy of Antiracist Activism, Then and Now

As the lead stories in the news shift from Ferguson to the Islamic State's terror tactics, #BlackLivesMatter protesters—and critics—query the efficacy of their public engagement. #BlackLivesMatter protests, sparked by the deaths of young black men due to police brutality, parallel Civil-Rights era protests which were similarly mobilized and galvanized by the police brutality and mob attacks against Southern Christian Leadership Conference and Student Nonviolent Coordinating Committee protesters as well as their allies, black and white.

March 7, 2015, marked the 50th anniversary of Bloody Sunday, the first of three marches for black voting rights from Selma to Montgomery, Alabama, during which the police tear-gassed, trampled on, and brutally beat the marchers at the Edmund Pettus Bridge. This march was spurred by another demonstration organized in the previous month in Marion, Alabama, during which Jimmie Lee Jackson—a young black man and Army veteran—was shot and killed by police amid the state, county, and local police pushback and assault on protesters who, after a sermon at a local Methodist church, marched to the city jail where SCLC leaders were imprisoned. Jackson was shot by state police while defending his mother in a local café, but he was charged with assault on and attempted murder of a police officer.[60] After Bloody Sunday aroused the public conscience

---

59. Ibid.
60. Gary May, "Bloody Thursday: The Riot that Sparked the Selma March," *The Daily Beast* February 18, 2015, http://www.thedailybeast.com/articles/2015/02/18/the-riot-that-sparked-the-selma-march.html (accessed July 20, 2015).

and demonstrations of solidarity occurred in cities across the U.S., President Lyndon Johnson prioritized and later signed the Voting Rights Act of 1965. Yet, in his mid-March address, Johnson cited neither the death of Jackson nor the police's violent retaliation against the marchers, but instead referred to Rev. James Reeb—a white Unitarian minister who died at the hands of vigilante townsfolk in Selma in the days after the march—as the social suffering which served the pedagogical purpose of educating the nation about the illegality and immorality of U.S. racism and the state's means of enacting and enforcing it.[61]

Fifty years after Bloody Sunday, voter redistricting, identification laws, and other protocols across the U.S. find their legal footing in the U.S. Supreme Court's recent ruling to dismantle parts of the Voting Rights Acts, which effectively undermines voter equality in Alabama and elsewhere in primarily southern U.S. states.[62] Then and now, black lives, both personally and politically, are still dismissed, disregarded, and considered at best peripheral and at worst disposable in America.

Ferguson's racially, geographically, and economically segregated and thus polarized context is a lightning rod for reflecting on the situation of U.S. black voting rights particularly and black political power generally since the 1960s: "Ferguson's population is two-thirds African-American, and yet its mayor, city manager and five of its six City Council members are white. So are its police chief and all but three officers on its 53-member police force.... More than three-quarters of the [school] district's 12,000 students are black,

61. Andrew Beck Grace, "A Call from Selma," *The New York Times* Op-Docs, March 6, 2015, http://www.nytimes.com/2015/03/06/opinion/a-call-from-selma.html (accessed July 20, 2015).
62. For the U.S. Supreme Court case which scuttled parts of the Voting Rights Act, see Adam Liptak, "Supreme Court Invalidates Key Part of Voting Rights Act," *The New York Times* June 25, 2013: A1. For a recent example of the effects of this decision, see Editorial Board, "Race, Politics, and Drawing Maps: The Supreme Court Hears an Alabama Case on the Voting Rights Act," *The New York Times* November 13, 2014: A26.

but the seven-member [school] board includes only one African-American."[63] At-large voting is used to elect school board members, but this method ensures a white majority on the board which trades on a white majority voting population. An ACLU lawsuit against the Ferguson school board proposes an alternative method, in which voters elect officials from their districts and thereby enable black majority neighborhoods to gain more political leverage and stronger representation in school governance. In Ferguson's wake, President Obama created the Task Force on 21st Century Policing, which in part hosted listening sessions and roundtable discussions on equity and accountability in police practices.[64] The Department of Justice also recently issued an investigative report on the Ferguson Police Department, confirming its systemic racist practices which ranged from unlawful arrests to disproportionate traffic tickets to unnecessary use of force (such as tasers and dogs): "The Justice Department did not simply find indirect evidence of unintentionally racist practices which harm black people, but 'discriminatory intent'—that is to say willful racism.... Justice in Ferguson is not a matter of 'racism without racists,' but racism with racists so secure, so proud, [and] so brazen."[65] Although vindicated in their protests, how do #BlackLivesMatter protesters avoid skepticism and cynicism about faith-based antiracist activism in the face of the apparent police lynching of black women in July 2015, Sandra Bland in Texas and Kindra Chapman in Alabama?[66]

63. Editorial Board, "Race and Voting Rights in Ferguson," *The New York Times* January 5, 2015: A16.

64. Charles M. Blow, "Beyond 'Black Lives Matter'," *The New York Times* February 9, 2015: A17.

65. Ta-Nehisi Coates, "The Gangsters of Ferguson," *The Atlantic* March 5, 2015, http://www.theatlantic.com/politics/archive/2015/03/The-Gangsters-Of-Ferguson/386893/ (accessed July 20, 2015).

66. Charles Blow, "Sandra and Kindra: Suicides or Something Sinister?," *The New York Times* July 20, 2015, http://www.nytimes.com/2015/07/20/opinion/charles-blow-sandra-and-kindra-suicides-or-something-sinister.html (accessed August 6, 2015).

President Obama's speech at the 50th anniversary of Bloody Sunday in Selma provides fresh and meaningful ways to assess the effects and efficacy of past and present antiracist activism.[67] In this speech, Obama took account of historical progress in the U.S. with regard to race without espousing a white habitus-based gradualist approach to antiracist social change. He situated the march within America's creed which professes equality, liberty, and justice as divinely-endowed rights for ordering and transforming our national unity, without reverting to the white habitus-based conversational styles which invoke these same values to scuttle affirmative action, to ignore educational inequalities, and so on. This creed functions as "a call to action, a roadmap for citizenship, and an insistence on the capacity of free men and women to shape our own destiny."[68] Against this constitutional and religious backdrop, he framed the march within a multigenerational perspective that spanned the landscape of U.S. history, from slavery and the Civil War to legalized segregation and the Civil Rights Movement. This march for African American civil rights blazed a legal and social trail for other marginalized groups, such as women, Latin@s, Asian Americans, Americans with disabilities, and LGBT Americans, to advocate for and begin to win their equal rights in public policy, if not yet fully implemented in our political culture and everyday practices.

Amid these multiple achievements in making America's creed not only an ideational but an incarnate reality, the American experiment or project is still "not yet finished" but requires each generation to respond to the "imperative of citizenship" and practice both collective self-criticism and self-government "to remake this nation to more closely align with our highest ideals."[69] Referring to police brutality

67. "Transcript: Read Full Text of President Barack Obama's Speech in Selma," *Time* March 7, 2015, http://time.com/3736357/barack-obama-selma-speech-transcript/ (accessed July 20, 2015).
68. Ibid.

in and beyond Ferguson, Obama said, "What happened in Ferguson may not be unique, but it's no longer endemic, or sanctioned by law and custom." Racism, thus, may not be "inherent to America" but is by no means entirely eradicated from America.[70] He continued:

> To deny this progress—our progress—would be to rob us of our own agency; our responsibility to do what we can to make America better. Of course, a more common mistake is to suggest that racism is banished, that the work that drew men and women to Selma is complete, and that whatever racial tensions remain are a consequence of those seeking to play the "race card" for their own purposes.... We know the march is not yet over, the race is not yet won.... Fifty years from Bloody Sunday, our march is not yet finished. But we are getting closer. Two hundred and thirty-nine years after this nation's founding, our union is not yet perfect. But we are getting closer. Our job's easier because somebody already got us through that first mile. Somebody already got us over that bridge. When it feels the road's too hard, when the torch we've been passed feels too heavy, we will remember these early travelers, and draw strength from their example, and hold firmly the words of the prophet Isaiah: "Those who hope in the Lord will renew their strength. They will soar on wings like eagles. They will run and not grow weary. They will walk and not be faint."[71]

Antiracist activists involved in the American project will thus continue to draw lifegiving water from the wellsprings of multiple social justice movements and from multiple religious traditions in order to bolster their religio-political agency and to foster their religio-political practices of public engagement bent on further perfecting our common life.

Indeed, after a young white supremacist killed nine African-Americans, including State Senator and Pastor Clementa Pinckney, during a midweek Bible study meeting on June 17, 2015, at the historic Emanuel A.M.E Church in Charleston, South Carolina,

69. Ibid.
70. Ibid.
71. Ibid.

elected officials like Governor Nikki Haley, faith leaders like Auburn Seminary Senior Fellows Sharon Groves and Jacqui Lewis, and growing public opinion united to confront racism and other forms of institutionalized violence against marginalized communities, symbolized by the Confederate flag at the South Carolina state capitol. That flag was erected in resistance to civil rights and racial equality in the 1960s. In the past, arguments from Southern tradition and heritage kept that flag and other Confederate emblems on public display and on sale (at Walmart and Amazon among other retailers). Sweeping aside these arguments and acknowledging the flag's role in perpetuating a racist worldview which must be dismantled, these elected officials and faith leaders testify to our ability as a collective community and a nation to overcome another form of white habitus or what E. J. Dionne calls a "politics of evasion."[72]

Yet, achieving racial justice from a feminist perspective on public theology goes beyond improving public dialogue and changing public symbols of American civil religion, especially since seven Southern black churches burned in two weeks after the Charleston shootings. Prophetic action that enables mourning and motivates social change is also needed.[73] For example, faith leaders Groves and Lewis termed the prayers of solidarity and the social media pray-ins that they organized for Mother Emanuel "prophetic grief." While a politics of evasion previously dismissed these efforts as "politicizing a tragedy," faith-based antiracist activism will continue to enter into these tragedies, to deconstruct what passes for status quo discourse about our shared public or common life, and to offer new symbols,

72. E. J. Dionne, Jr., "Charleston and the Politics of Evasion," *Commonweal* June 22, 2015, https://www.commonwealmagazine.org/charleston-politics-evasion (accessed July 20, 2015).
73. Robert M. Franklin, Jr., "What Can We Learn from the Charleston Shootings? Hard Choices Yield Great Rewards," *Sightings* June 25, 2015, http://us6.campaign-archive1.com/?u=6b2c705bf61d6edb1d5e0549d&id=00f067e16f (accessed July 20, 2015).

both religious and civic, that urge ever more inclusive and just ways of being and living in community.

Afterword

Serene Jones

I first met Kathy Tanner in 1981 when she was working as a teaching assistant for Hans Frei's legendary *History of Christian Thought: 1650-1800* course at Yale University. I had just arrived in New Haven from Oklahoma, and felt awkward yet wonderfully lost in the presence of Frei's extraordinary mind. His lectures were wild flights of history and theology, filled with inscrutable turns of phrase and doctrines that operated like characters in novels, unwieldy and complex. He would twirl elf-like and pull at his tie as he whispered to the class his secret thoughts about the meaning of it all. For two months, we wandered through Pilgrim's Progress, trying to find our way towards the Enlightenment, most of us confused but delighted. In Frei's hands, theology was an enigmatic narrative, quirky and lithe and always spinning freely just beyond our reach.

Later as a teacher, Kathy invoked a different pedagogical style. Each week, she would arrive for our discussion section in black jeans and a black t-shirt, carrying a black satchel filled with yellow tablets of penciled notes and two or three dog-eared books with exotic philosophical titles. She gave the impression—and still does—that she'd been reading all night and wrestling with the fullness of pages and words.

Her classroom words, in contrast, were spare and direct. She would settle in awkwardly at the seminar table and begin the discussion by asking if there were any questions. She would then wait quietly for us to speak. If no one spoke, as was often the case, she would eventually chuckle wryly, "Come on, guys. Nothing? Nothing?" encouraging us, almost daring us, to take the lead.

The first time I got my courage up to ask about an odd passage in Bunyan, she answered: "Yeah, that is weird. Pretty weird. I'm not sure what he meant. Anyone?" It would go on like this for the full hour—no question directly answered, only conversations begun and ponderings encouraged—until the end of session. Then, in the last five minutes, without failure, she would offer us, as if it were a passing thought, her own impression of the material and our discussion. What a gift those few sentences were. They changed everything. The ideas that had seemed theologically beyond our reach were suddenly there-at-hand. Brilliant. Simple. Open. Ready to be used.

Time and again, in the years that followed, I watched Kathy do that same uncanny thing she did then, be it in the middle of a doctoral seminar on Schleiermacher, a high church conference on gay marriage, an opening book chapter on Providence, or an evening dinner party. I saw it as well when I had the chance to teach with her and to see how she interacts with many different kinds of students. First, she listens carefully and, except for an occasional laugh, says little as she absorbs what's unfolding around her. Then, second, with what appears to be effortless candor, she takes the chaos of all those ideas and texts-in-conversation and pulls them into a bustling, ordered whole. She does this by describing what she sees as a network of paths that run between them, allowing for intertextual commerce.

Third, to finish the process, she offers the teeming whole to you—the reader, the student, and the colleague—so that you can use it as you want. A gift.

In describing this process, I do not mean to imply that Kathy is simply good at summarizing things or stating the obvious. It is more than that. She is an open-minded listener and reader with a rare ability to get out of her own way when she is puzzling through something. This openness, I believe, is what allows her to see connections between things that others miss. She finds patterns in discourse that other experts have failed to discern. Anyone familiar with her work knows this. She can take hold of just about any imaginable subject matter and quickly figure out its basic structures and core tensions. Then, she can take that structure and put it into play with another and another and on it goes.

As this book's essays bear witness, the range of topics and disciplines Kathy has engaged in this manner over the last thirty-five years of writing is remarkable in both its scope and density. She has never written an easy book or crafted an essay that was merely entertaining. On the theological side, she has engaged voices ranging from Paul and Augustine to Barth and Cone, and has traced the play of doctrine from creation to the end times. Outside of theology, she has taken on disciplinary conversation partners as diverse as politics, economics, game theory, theories of culture, understandings of time and space, and philosophies of identity and embodiment. The list is still growing.

Moreover, with those theologians and doctrines in one hand and those disparate disciplines in the other, she has time and again laid out for us pathways for travel between them that have surprised and delighted both sides. Who would have imagined taking "supply-side economics" and bringing it across the street to meet "Calvinists views of sins," or taking game theory and dragging it to the other side of the tracks where grace and gift–giving define the landscape? Moreover, the exchanges she makes possible between things are never static. Her networked connections stay in motion. There is no final doctrinal truth. No interdisciplinary still-point ever appears. What we discover, instead, is a series of opened pathways and an invitation to walk them, to see if the exchanges they have enabled are useful. Again, her work is generous and labile.

When asked to contribute to this volume, I initially agreed to write about the work she has done in the area of theology and economic theory, a topic close to my own work. As I began wresting with her materials, I stumbled upon a short statement she had made in a 2009 interview at Trinity Wall Street about theology—not about economics, per se. It was a classic example of the clarity I have been describing.

> I am trying to look at very basic Christian beliefs or the general story of God's dealing with the world and to think of those basic claims…as laying out an alternative economy. The Christian story is about the production and circulation of goods- physical goods, the distribution of grace and salvation, how you get it, how you keep it. The principles underlying this story are unconditional giving, non-competitive relationships and universal inclusion. God's gift to you is not something born of your merit. This also means that you have an obligation to act as God is acting towards you.[1]

For those who are familiar with her work, this statement is not unusual. It summarizes, succinctly, her doctrinal account of the economy of God's relation to the world. She laid it out first in her earliest book, *God and Creation in Christian Theology: Tyranny or Empowerment*, and has perfected and clarified it further with each new book. God relates to the world in a manner that is best understood as

---

1. See "An Interview with Kathryn Tanner," https://www.trinitywallstreet.org/video/interview-kathryn-tanner (accessed August 5, 2015).

"economic" in its dramatic structure. Here, "economic" means much the same thing it does in common use, albeit not limited to money. An economy is the process by which goods are produced, exchanged, and distributed. What Christians can say about God is, according to her, economic in so far as it consists of claims about how God interacts with us, or better, God's commerce with us. God offers us goods (that are God's very self)—love, grace, freedom, salvation, and relationship—that God enables us to receive and which transform us. This divine-human commerce is regulated by true openness, radical inclusion, and it seeks to be useful and empowering, not utilitarian and coercive.

What this small summary sparked for me, in addition to summarizing the God-world story once again, was that it also described in short form the basic dramatic script of how Kathy's own theological mind functions. Kathy not only thinks about God economically, she actually does *theology* economically. In all that she does—as a teacher, writer, intellectual, colleague, scholarly leader—her own practices are essentially economic in character: productive, evaluative, transactional, distributive. Just as Frei had the mind of a poet and the narrative instincts of a novelist, so, too, Kathy has the mind of an economist and the transactional instincts of an exchange theorist. As an aside, I cannot help but think that had her life followed a different path, she could have made millions working for the Department of Defense or Wall Street (although I am sure she would not have had as much fun or impact as she has had as a teacher and scholar).[2]

2. My own initial work with Kathy occurred in the intellectual world of the Yale Religious Studies Department and Yale Divinity School in the 1980's and 90's. In those early days, our professors spent a good deal of time showing us that we did not need to find an all-purpose "methodological map" to guide us as we journeyed through the theological canon. We should just start walking, they told us, and see what truths would reveal themselves if we followed the curve of the land. It was an attractive model because it encouraged a kind of creative abandon that the theological academy at that time desperately needed, but it was not long

Her economic play of mind goes even deeper than this, however. Not only does she view the world of thought and theology economically, her own mode of engagement reflects the "alternative economics" of her theological vision. She does what she describes. Think about her account of the God-world relation I just cited. Recall the three traits of that divine economy that Christians are called to embrace.

Kathy's work is *non-competitive*. She is encouraging of others and has never fallen prey to the temptations of scholarly arrogance. Just as I experienced her in her early teaching assistant days, she engages students as peers. In the classroom, she waits for others' questions, not her own, to set the agenda and she is willing to tolerate silence and to listen deeply in order to hear what is being asked, what we are searching for, what we want. So, too, she is *inclusive* in her reach towards others. In Kathy's theological corpus there is no room for exclusionary judgments about the doctrinal propriety or right-minded faithfulness. She opens up paths, not closes them, and in so doing has avoided the stifling dogmatisms of many of her peers. Lastly, she is a very good *gift-giver*. Just as she used to do in those last-five-minutes-of-class summaries in 1981, so too, time and again, she gives us insights into the meaning of faith without requiring us to agree with her or for us to assign to her work a use-value that can be easily measured in terms of truth or propriety. She simply gives it to us for us to do with it what we will. She gives us the gift of her theology quite simply because she sees it so clearly. She enables freedom.

before that abandon was tamped down by the realization that our map-less teachers were holding compasses in their hands. Frei was not as interested as the others in finding a path, but the threads of meaning that language and stories and novelistic characters drew were for him a clue as to where his foot should fall. George Lindbeck was the most adept mapmaker, even when he did not intend it. History and eventually cultural anthropology provided the support he needed. David Kelsey found his way by following an existential, analytic map—closer to architecture than to economics.

Writing these things about Kathy's deep theological disposition will no doubt make her extremely uncomfortable. It's not how she sees it, I am sure. To be clear, I am not trying to make Kathy into a god-like figure of perfectly-graced proportions. No one should be made to bear that mantel. I do hope, however, that these comments illumine dimensions of Kathy's life-work that are ever-present, but often in a quiet and understated form.

When I began working on this piece, I asked Kathy if she understood herself as a public theologian or as a progressive theological activist. As to the first, it's not surprising that she answered yes. One of the greatest benefits to all of us has been Kathy's ability to open up the conversation between theology and other disciplines and, in doing so, to teach us how theology is always and inevitably public. No discipline, indeed no aspect of life, exists outside the realm of theology's commerce.

As for the activist question, she responded that no, she doesn't understand herself primarily as an activist, but intends her theological work on the deep logic of traditions and cultures to support struggles in and beyond the academy. To this I would add, her work addresses theological conflicts and in turn she draws the maps, makes the connections, and enables new economies of imagination that will help to move both theological and activist praxis forward. Activism thus takes different forms, and in God's economy these different sorts of activism matter equally to the common good.

We have never needed that alternate economy more desperately than we need it now. Our economic system is presently in a state of such profound collapse that nothing short of a total revolution, I believe, will save us from the tyranny of the wealthy. As movement seeking that revolution grows, I take great comfort in knowing the work of Kathy Tanner continues, tracing new connections of thoughts for us as they emerge, and tying them back to age-old wisdoms we still need. Coursing just below the surface of this moment in our history stand truths yet-to-be-seen, much less mapped. And chances are, she will feel their rumblings before the rest of us, because, just like in those early days, she has been up all night reading and wants to know if we have any questions.

List of Kathryn E. Tanner's Main Works

Books

Christ the Key. Current Issues in Theology. Cambridge: Cambridge University Press, 2010.

Economy of Grace. Minneapolis: Fortress Press, 2005.

Jesus, Humanity and the Trinity: A Brief Systematic Theology. Minneapolis: Fortress Press, 2001.

Theories of Culture: A New Agenda for Theology. Guides to Theological Inquiry. Minneapolis: Fortress Press, 1997.

The Politics of God: Christian Theologies and Social Justice. Minneapolis: Fortress Press, 1992.

God and Creation in Christian Theology: Tyranny or Empowerment? Oxford: Blackwell, 1988 Repr., Minneapolis: Fortress Press, 2005.

Key Articles and Essays

"Absolute Difference." In *Divine Multiplicities: Trinities, Diversities, and the Nature of Religion* (Transdisciplinary Theological Colloquia). Edited by Christopher Boesel and S. Wesley Ariarajah. New York: Fordham University Press, 2013, 217-33.

"Creation Ex Nihilo as Mixed Metaphor." *Modern Theology* 29, no. 2 (2013): 138-55.

"Why Support the Occupy Movement?" *Union Seminary Quarterly Review* 64, no. 1 (2013): 28-35.

"Globalization, Women's Transnational Migration and Religious De-Traditioning." In *The Oxford Handbook of Feminist Theology*. Edited by Sheila Briggs and Mary Fulkerson. Oxford: Oxford University Press, 2011, 544-60.

"Theological Perspectives on God as an Invisible Force." In *Invisible Forces and Powerful Beliefs: Gravity, Gods, and Minds*. Edited by The Chicago Social Brain Network. Upper Saddle River, NJ: Pearson FT Press, 2011, 157-68.

"Is Capitalism a Belief System?" *Anglican Theological Review* 92, no. 4 (2010): 617-35.

"Shifts in Theology over the Last Quarter Century." *Modern Theology* 26, no. 1 (2010): 39-44.

"Grace and Gambling." In *Gambling: Mapping the American Moral Landscape*, ed. Alan Wolfe and Erik C. Owens. Waco, TX: Baylor University Press, 2009, 227-56.

"Openness to Moral Insight: Socio-Cultural Considerations." *Journal of Law, Philosophy and Culture* 3, no. 1 (2009): 163-76.

"Theology at the Limits of Phenomenology." In *Counter Experience: Reading Jean-Luc Marion*. Edited by Kevin Hart. Notre Dame: University of Notre Dame Press, 2007, 201-31.

"Hooker and the New Puritans." In *Authorizing Marriage? Canon, Tradition, and Critique in the Blessing of Same-Sex Unions*. Edited by Mark D. Jordan, Meghan T. Sweeney, and David M. Mellott. Princeton: Princeton University Press, 2006, 121-38.

"Towards a New Theology of Confirmation." *Anglican Theological Review* 88, no. 1 (2006): 85-94.

"In Praise of Open Communion: A Rejoinder to James Farwell." *Anglican Theological Review* 86, no. 3 (2004): 473-85.

"Is God in Charge?" In *Essentials of Christian Theology* Edited by William C. Placher. Louisville: Westminster John Knox, 2003, 116-30.

"Theological Reflection and Christian Practices." In *Practicing Theology:*

Beliefs and Practices in Christian Life. Edited by Miroslav Volf and Dorothy C. Bass. Grand Rapids: Eerdmans, 2002, 228-41.

"Theology and Cultural Contest in the University." In *Religious Studies, Theology, and the University: Conflicting Maps, Changing Terrain.* Edited by Linell E. Cady and Delwin Brown. Albany: State University of New York Press, 2002, 199-211.

"The Religious Significance of Christian Engagement in the Culture Wars." *Theology Today* 58, no. 1 (2001): 28-43.

"Creation and Providence." In *The Cambridge Companion to Karl Barth.* Edited by J. B. Webster. Cambridge: Cambridge University Press, 2000, 111-26.

"Justification and Justice in a Theology of Grace." *Theology Today* 55 (1999): 510-23.

"Scripture as Popular Text." *Modern Theology* 14, no. 2 (1998): 279-98.

"Scripture as Popular Text." In *Theology and Scriptural Imagination: Directions in Modern Theology.* Edited by L. Gregory Jones and James Buckley. Oxford: Blackwell, 1998, 117-36.

"Why Are We Here?" In *Why Are We Here?: Everyday Questions and the Christian Life.* Edited by Ronald Thiemann. Harrisburg, PA: Trinity Press International, 1998, 5-16.

"Jesus Christ." In *The Cambridge Companion to Christian Doctrine.* Edited by Colin E. Gunton. Cambridge: Cambridge University Press, 1997, 245-72.

"Social Theory Concerning the 'New Social Movements' and the Practice of Feminist Theology." In *Horizons in Feminist Theology: Identity, Tradition, and Norms.* Edited by Rebecca S. Chopp and Sheila Greeve Davaney. Minneapolis: Fortress Press, 1997, 179-97.

"Public Theology and the Character of Public Debate." *Annual of the Society of Christian Ethics* 16 (1996): 79-101.

"The Care that Does Justice: Recent Writings in Feminist Ethics and Theology." *Journal of Religious Ethics* 24, no. 1 (1996): 169-191.

"Theology and Popular Culture." In *Changing Conversations: Religious*

Reflection and Cultural Analysis. Edited by Dwight N. Hopkins and Sheila Greeve Davaney. New York: Routledge, 1996, 101–22.

"Human Freedom, Human Sin, and God the Creator." In *The God Who Acts: Philosophical and Theological Explorations.* Edited by Thomas F. Tracy. University Park, PA: Penn State University Press, 1994, 111–35.

"The Difference Theological Anthropology Makes." *Theology Today* 50 (1994): 567–79.

"A Theological Case for Human Responsibility in Moral Choice." In *Realism and Responsibility in Contemporary Ethics.* Edited by Franklin Gamwell and William Schweiker. *Journal of Religion* 73, no. 4 (October 1993): 592–612.

"Creation, Environmental Crisis, and Ecological Justice." In *Reconstructing Christian Theology.* Edited by Rebecca S. Chopp and Mark Lewis Taylor. Minneapolis: Fortress Press, 1993, 99–123.

"Respect for Other Religions: A Christian Antidote to Colonialist Discourse." *Modern Theology* 9, no. 1 (1993): 1–18.

"Theology and the Plain Sense." In *Scriptural Authority and Narrative Interpretation.* Edited by Garrett Green. Minneapolis: Fortress Press, 1987, 59–78.

Index